lonely planet

Athens

David Willett
Kim Wildman

LONELY PLANET PUBLICATIONS
Melbourne • Oakland • London • Paris

Athens
1st edition – August 2001

Published by
Lonely Planet Publications Pty Ltd ABN 36 005 607 983
90 Maribyrnong St, Footscray, Victoria 3011, Australia

Lonely Planet Offices
Australia Locked Bag 1, Footscray, Victoria 3011
USA 150 Linden St, Oakland, CA 94607
UK 10a Spring Place, London NW5 3BH
France 1 rue du Dahomey, 75011 Paris

Photographs
Many of the images in this guide are available for licensing from
Lonely Planet Images.
email: lpi@lonelyplanet.com.au

Front cover photograph
Ceremonial Guard, Parliament (Neil Setchfield; image digitally modified
by Lonely Planet)

Title page of map section
View of Athens (Juliet Coombe)

ISBN 1 86450 295 9

Printed by SNP SPrint (M) Sdn Bhd
Printed in Malaysia

Although the authors
and Lonely Planet try
to make the informa-
tion as accurate as
possible, we accept
no responsibility for
any loss, injury or
inconvenience sus-
tained by anyone
using this book.

Contents – Text

2 Contents – Text

Contents – Maps

The Authors

David Willett
David is a freelance journalist based near Bellingen on the mid-north coast of New South Wales, Australia. He grew up in Hampshire, England, and wound up in Australia in 1980 after stints working on newspapers in Iran (1975-78) and Bahrain. He spent two years working as a sub-editor on the Melbourne Sun before trading a steady job for a warmer climate. Between jobs, David has travelled extensively in Europe, the Middle East and Asia.

He is a regular visitor to Athens as coordinator of Lonely Planet's guide to *Greece*, and has contributed to various other guides, including *Africa, Australia, Indonesia, South-East Asia, Mediterranean Europe* and *Western Europe*.

Kim Wildman
Kim grew up in Toowoomba, Queensland, with parents who unwittingly instilled in her the desire to travel at a very young age by extending the immediate family to include 11 exchange students. After graduating from Queensland College of Art, having studied photography, Kim packed her backpack and headed to the USA and Bermuda. Her next adventure was Southern Africa. It was there she decided to combine her three loves: photography, writing and travelling. Kim has a BA in journalism and has worked on Lonely Planet's *Romania & Moldova 2* and has contributed to the Romanian chapters of *Eastern Europe* and *Europe on a Shoestring*.

FROM THE AUTHOR

David Willett I'd like to thank all the friends who have contributed so much to my understanding of Athens over the years, especially Maria Economou from the Greek National Tourism Office; the Kanakis family; Ana Kamais; Matt Barrett; Tolis Houtzoumis; and Alex and Pavlo.

Thanks also to my partner, Rowan, and our son Tom for holding the fort at home during my frequent trips away.

Kim Wildman My biggest thanks must go to David Willett for all his help and advice. In Athens I wish to thank Yiannis and Katerina, and their two beautiful daughters Irini and Lilla; Tolis; Alexis Valassidis and Pavlos Georgiadis; Sophia Tsagaraki; Maria Economou from the Greek National Tourism Office; and Ourania Vrondou and Panayiotis Douvitsas from Athens 2004 Olympic Committee.

Back home I'd like to thank my two dear friends Chris Diamond and Donnita White for their endless patience and proof reading.

This Book

This is the first edition of *Athens*. Coordinating author David Willett wrote the introductory chapters as well as compiling the Things to See & Do and Places to Stay chapters. Kim Wildman was responsible for the Places to Eat, Entertainment, Shopping and Excursions chapters.

FROM THE PUBLISHER

This book was produced at Lonely Planet's Melbourne office by Darren O'Connell (editorial) and Joelene Kowalski (maps). Editorial assistance was provided by Janine Eberle and Kalya Ryan. Lonely Planet's Knowledge Bank team provided invaluable assistance, with a special mention to Nadine Fogale, Simon Tillema and Piotr Czajkowski. Valuable mapping assistance was also provided by Louise Klep. Adrian Persoglia laid out the book. Maria Vallianos designed the cover. Thanks to Barbara Dombrowski and LPI for the images. Andrew Tudor and Mark Germanchis provided technical support, and David Kemp sweated over the book's design. Thanks to Quentin Frayne for laying out the language section. Special thanks also to Rachel Imeson, Kieran Grogan and Tony Davidson for the many hours spent developing this title.

ACKNOWLEDGMENTS

Maps

Portions of the maps in this book include intellectual property of EPSILON and are used by permission. Copyright © 2000 Epsilon International SA. All Rights Reserved.

Foreword

ABOUT LONELY PLANET GUIDEBOOKS

The story begins with a classic travel adventure: Tony and Maureen Wheeler's 1972 journey across Europe and Asia to Australia. Useful information about the overland trail did not exist at that time, so Tony and Maureen published the first Lonely Planet guidebook to meet a growing need.

From a kitchen table, then from a tiny office in Melbourne (Australia), Lonely Planet has become the largest independent travel publisher in the world, an international company with offices in Melbourne, Oakland (USA), London (UK) and Paris (France).

Today Lonely Planet guidebooks cover the globe. There is an ever-growing list of books and there's information in a variety of forms and media. Some things haven't changed. The main aim is still to help make it possible for adventurous travellers to get out there – to explore and better understand the world.

At Lonely Planet we believe travellers can make a positive contribution to the countries they visit – if they respect their host communities and spend their money wisely. Since 1986 a percentage of the income from each book has been donated to aid projects and human rights campaigns.

Updates Lonely Planet thoroughly updates each guidebook as often as possible. This usually means there are around two years between editions, although for more unusual or more stable destinations the gap can be longer. Check the imprint page (following the colour map at the beginning of the book) for publication dates.

Between editions up-to-date information is available in two free newsletters – the paper *Planet Talk* and email *Comet* (to subscribe, contact any Lonely Planet office) – and on our Web site at www.lonelyplanet.com. The *Upgrades* section of the Web site covers a number of important and volatile destinations and is regularly updated by Lonely Planet authors. *Scoop* covers news and current affairs relevant to travellers. And, lastly, the *Thorn Tree* bulletin board and *Postcards* section of the site carry unverified, but fascinating, reports from travellers.

Correspondence The process of creating new editions begins with the letters, postcards and emails received from travellers. This correspondence often includes suggestions, criticisms and comments about the current editions. Interesting excerpts are immediately passed on via newsletters and the Web site, and everything goes to our authors to be verified when they're researching on the road. We're keen to get more feedback from organisations or individuals who represent communities visited by travellers.

Lonely Planet gathers information for everyone who's curious about the planet – and especially for those who explore it first-hand. Through guidebooks, phrasebooks, activity guides, maps, literature, newsletters, image library, TV series and Web site we act as an information exchange for a worldwide community of travellers.

Research Authors aim to gather sufficient practical information to enable travellers to make informed choices and to make the mechanics of a journey run smoothly. They also research historical and cultural background to help enrich the travel experience and allow travellers to understand and respond appropriately to cultural and environmental issues.

Authors don't stay in every hotel because that would mean spending a couple of months in each medium-sized city and, no, they don't eat at every restaurant because that would mean stretching belts beyond capacity. They do visit hotels and restaurants to check standards and prices, but feedback based on readers' direct experiences can be very helpful.

Many of our authors work undercover, others aren't so secretive. None of them accept freebies in exchange for positive write-ups. And none of our guidebooks contain any advertising.

Production Authors submit their raw manuscripts and maps to offices in Australia, USA, UK or France. Editors and cartographers – all experienced travellers themselves – then begin the process of assembling the pieces. When the book finally hits the shops, some things are already out of date, we start getting feedback from readers and the process begins again …

WARNING & REQUEST

Things change – prices go up, schedules change, good places go bad and bad places go bankrupt – nothing stays the same. So, if you find things better or worse, recently opened or long since closed, please tell us and help make the next edition even more accurate and useful. We genuinely value all the feedback we receive. A well travelled team reads and acknowledges every letter, postcard and email and ensures that every morsel of information finds its way to the appropriate authors, editors and cartographers for verification.

Everyone who writes to us will find their name in the next edition of the appropriate guidebook. They will also receive the latest issue of *Planet Talk*, our quarterly printed newsletter, or *Comet*, our monthly email newsletter. Subscriptions to both newsletters are free. The very best contributions will be rewarded with a free guidebook.

Excerpts from your correspondence may appear in new editions of Lonely Planet guidebooks, the Lonely Planet Web site, *Planet Talk* or *Comet*, so please let us know if you *don't* want your letter published or your name acknowledged.

Send all correspondence to the Lonely Planet office closest to you:

Australia: Locked Bag 1, Footscray, Victoria 3011
USA: 150 Linden St, Oakland, CA 94607
UK: 10A Spring Place, London NW5 3BH
France: 1 rue du Dahomey, 75011 Paris

Or email us at: talk2us@lonelyplanet.com.au

For news, views and updates see our Web site: www.lonelyplanet.com

HOW TO USE A LONELY PLANET GUIDEBOOK

The best way to use a Lonely Planet guidebook is any way you choose. At Lonely Planet we believe the most memorable travel experiences are often those that are unexpected, and the finest discoveries are those you make yourself. Guidebooks are not intended to be used as if they provide a detailed set of infallible instructions!

Contents All Lonely Planet guidebooks follow roughly the same format. The Facts about the Destination chapters or sections give background information ranging from history to weather. Facts for the Visitor gives practical information on issues like visas and health. Getting There & Away gives a brief starting point for researching travel to and from the destination. Getting Around gives an overview of the transport options when you arrive.

The peculiar demands of each destination determine how subsequent chapters are broken up, but some things remain constant. We always start with background, then proceed to sights, places to stay, places to eat, entertainment, getting there and away, and getting around information – in that order.

Heading Hierarchy Lonely Planet headings are used in a strict hierarchical structure that can be visualised as a set of Russian dolls. Each heading (and its following text) is encompassed by any preceding heading that is higher on the hierarchical ladder.

Entry Points We do not assume guidebooks will be read from beginning to end, but that people will dip into them. The traditional entry points are the list of contents and the index. In addition, however, some books have a complete list of maps and an index map illustrating map coverage.

There may also be a colour map that shows highlights. These highlights are dealt with in greater detail in the Facts for the Visitor chapter, along with planning questions and suggested itineraries. Each chapter covering a geographical region usually begins with a locator map and another list of highlights. Once you find something of interest in a list of highlights, turn to the index.

Maps Maps play a crucial role in Lonely Planet guidebooks and include a huge amount of information. A legend is printed on the back page. We seek to have complete consistency between maps and text, and to have every important place in the text captured on a map. Map key numbers usually start in the top left corner.

KEY TO SYMBOLS

- ☎ telephone number
- [e] email address
- [w] Web site
- 🕘 opening hours
- $ prices (high/low season in places to stay information unless otherwise designated)
- [c] credit cards
- AE American Express
- DC Diner's Club
- JCB Japan Credit Bureau
- MC MasterCard
- V Visa Card
- Ⓜ metro station
- 🚎 trolleybus
- 🚌 bus stop
- 🚆 train station
- ⛴ ferry
- [V] restaurant has many vegetarian options

Although inclusion in a guidebook usually implies a recommendation we cannot list every good place. Exclusion does not necessarily imply criticism. In fact there are a number of reasons why we might exclude a place – sometimes it is simply inappropriate to encourage an influx of travellers.

Introduction

There can be few moments more inspiring than the first sight of the Parthenon, ancient symbol of the city of Athens, standing proudly on the skyline atop the Acropolis. By night, it seems to hover above the city, its floodlit columns of white Pentelic marble gleaming majestically against the night sky.

It was the crowning glory of the city's Golden Age, when Athens was at the height of its powers following the defeat of the Persians at the Battle of Salamis in 480 BC. It was a period of unprecedented architectural, artistic and intellectual achievement that continues to have a profound effect on Western thinking. Most of the buildings of the Acropolis were constructed at this time; Socrates taught in the agora and the plays of Aeschylus, Euripedes and Sophocles were performed at the Theatre of Great Dionysios. This is the city that most visitors come to see: the city named in honour of Athena, the Greek goddess of wisdom.

Few are prepared for the modern city that awaits them, a teeming traffic-clogged metropolis that is home to more than 3.5 million people – a third of the country's total population. Most beat a hasty retreat to the calm of their hotel room after the obligatory visit to the Acropolis and the National Archaeological Museum.

To appreciate Athens, it's important to be aware of the traumatic side of the city's long history. Unlike most major European cities, the story of Athens is not one of continuous expansion. The glory days were followed by centuries of gradual decline until its rebirth as the capital of independent Greece in 1834. By then it comprised no more than a collection of red-tiled Turkish houses on the northern slope of the Acropolis, the area now known as Plaka.

After a promising start, the 20th century proved as traumatic as any in its long history, with a succession of governments unable to cope with the problems created by massive population growth and poor town planning. The city's stocks hit a new low in the 1980s when scientists warned that the city's notoriously polluted air was destroying the Parthenon. Worse was to come. The decision to award the 1996 Olympics to Atlanta ahead of Athens stunned the nation.

The turnaround in the city's fortunes since then has been remarkable, culminating in the successful bid to stage the Games of the 28th Olympiad in 2004. Money has been pouring into the city and signs of urban revival are everywhere. Run-down inner city suburbs have metamorphosed into chic districts of trendy cafes and bars; the gloom of the '90s has given way to a spirit of buoyant optimism that the city has at last found the way forward. The traffic hasn't disappeared, but you can bypass it using the magnificent new metro system. Athenians are eagerly awaiting the opening of their new airport, the most modern in Europe.

Modern Athens is a vibrant city with a sophisticated nightlife and plenty of surprises for those who explore beyond the standard tourist haunts. To experience the best of what Athens has to offer, you'll need to adjust to the rhythm of Athens life. It's a city that stays up late. Few Athenians consider eating their evening meal until after 9pm, and most forms of entertainment don't begin until midnight – so come prepared for some long nights!

Culturally, Athens is a fascinating blend of East and West – a lingering legacy of centuries of Ottoman rule. Evidence of the Orient is everywhere: the sounds, the street hawkers, the colourful street markets, the (Turkish) coffee and the kebabs wrapped in pitta bread.

Athens is also great value. Prices, especially for food and accommodation, remain some of the cheapest in Europe.

Facts About Athens

EARLY HISTORY

The early history of Athens is inextricably interwoven with mythology, making it impossible to disentangle fact from fiction.

According to mythology, the city was founded by a Phoenician called Cecrops, who came to Attica and established a city on a huge rock near the sea. The gods of Olympus proclaimed that the city should be named after the deity who could produce the most valuable legacy for mortals. Athena (goddess of wisdom) and Poseidon (god of the sea) were the contenders. Athena produced an olive tree, symbol of peace and prosperity. Poseidon struck a rock with his trident and a horse sprang forth, which symbolised all the qualities of strength and fortitude for which he was renowned. Athena was the victor, for the gods proclaimed that her gift would better serve the citizens of Athens than the arts of war personified by Poseidon's gift.

Whatever its origins, it is known that the Acropolis, endowed with two bounteous springs, drew some of Greece's earliest Neolithic settlers. When a peaceful agricultural

Athena and Poseidon fight for naming rights.

existence gave way to the war-oriented city-states, the Acropolis provided an ideal defensive position: its steep slopes formed natural defences on three sides and it was an excellent vantage point from which to spot danger approaching from land or sea.

By 1400 BC, the settlement on the Acropolis had become a powerful Mycenaean city whose territory covered most of Attica. This was the age of the mythical Theseus, whose feats included the slaying of the Minotaur at the court of King Minos at Knossos on Crete. The city was reported to have contributed 50 ships to the Greek fleet that set sail for Troy.

Unlike the cities of Mycenae, Pylos and Tiryns, it survived the Dorian assault on Greece in 1200 BC. Very little is known about life in Athens in Dorian times, the so-called Dark Age of Greek history that continued for the next 400 years.

Athens emerged from the Dark Ages in better shape than most, thanks to economic benefits deriving from the development of the geometric style of pottery. It had, however, lost control of Attica, which had split into a number of minor kingdoms such as Eleusis (Elefsina), Brauron (Vravrona), Marathon and Ramnous.

Archaeological evidence suggests that Athens regained control of Attica by the end of the 7th century BC. It became the artistic centre of Greece, excelling in ceramics. Geometric designs evolved into the narrative Proto-Attic style, depicting scenes from everyday life and mythology.

ARISTOCRATS AND TYRANTS

Until the start of the 6th century BC, Athens was ruled by aristocrats, generals and the *arhon* (chief magistrate). A person's position in the hierarchy depended on their wealth, which was gained either from commerce or agriculture. Labourers and peasants had no say at all in the functioning of the city until the reform-oriented Solon became arhon in 594 BC.

Solon was appointed with a far-reaching mandate to defuse the mounting tensions between the haves and the have-nots. He cancelled all debts and freed those who had become enslaved because of their debts. Declaring all free Athenians equal by law, he implemented trial by jury and abolished inherited privileges. He restructured political power by creating four classes based on wealth. Although only the first two classes were eligible for office, all four were allowed to elect magistrates and vote on legislation in the general assembly, known as the *ecclesia*. These reforms have led him to be hailed as the harbinger of democracy.

The reforms weren't to everyone's liking, and continuing unrest created the pretext for the tyrant Peisistratos, formerly head of the military, to seize power in 560 BC. Peisistratos built up a formidable navy, much to the consternation of other city-states, and extended the boundaries of Athenian influence on land. He was a patron of the arts as well as a general, inaugurating the Festival of the Great Dionysia, which was the precursor of Attic drama, and commissioning many splendid sacred and secular buildings – most of which were destroyed by the Persians on the eve of the Battle of Salamis in 480 BC.

Peisistratos was succeeded by his son Hippias, who was very much a tyrant in the modern sense of the word. Athens managed to rid itself of this oppressor in 510 BC only by swallowing its pride and accepting the help of Sparta. Hippias wasn't finished, however, heading off to Persia to stir up trouble. He returned with Darius 20 years later to be defeated at the Battle of Marathon.

THE PERSIAN WARS

The Persian drive to destroy Athens was sparked by the city's support for a rebellion in the Persian colonies on the coast of Asia Minor. Emperor Darius spent five years suppressing the revolt, and emerged hellbent on revenge. He appealed to Sparta to attack Athens from behind, but the Spartans threw his envoy in a well and Darius was left to do the job alone.

A 25,000-strong Persian army reached Attica in 490 BC, but suffered a humiliating defeat when outmanoeuvred by an Athenian force of 10,000 at the Battle of Marathon.

Darius died in 485 BC before he could mount another assault, so it was left to his son Xerxes to fulfil his father's ambition of conquering Greece. In 480 BC Xerxes gathered men from every nation of his far-flung empire and launched a coordinated invasion by army and navy, the size of which the world had never seen. The historian Herodotus estimated that there were five million Persian soldiers. No doubt this was a gross exaggeration, but it was obvious Xerxes intended to give the Greeks more than a bloody nose.

Some 30 city-states of central and southern Greece met in Corinth to devise a common defence (others, including Delphi, sided with the Persians). They agreed on a combined army and navy under Spartan command, with the Athenian leader Themistocles providing the strategy. The Spartan king, Leonidas, led the army to the pass at Thermopylae, near present-day Lamia, the main passage into central Greece from the north. This bottleneck was easy to defend, and although the Greeks were greatly outnumbered they held the pass until a traitor showed the Persians a way over the mountains. The Greeks were forced to retreat, but Leonidas, along with 300 of his elite Spartan troops, fought to the death. The fleet, which held off the Persian navy north of Euboea (Evia), had no choice but to retreat as well.

The Spartans and their Peloponnesian allies fell back on their second line of defence (an earthen wall across the Isthmus of Corinth), while the Persians advanced upon Athens. Themistocles ordered his people to flee the city: the women and children to Salamis, and the men to sea with the Athenian fleet. The Persians razed Attica and burned Athens to the ground.

Things did not go so well for the Persian navy. By skilful manoeuvring, the Greek navy trapped the larger Persian ships in the narrow waters off Salamis, where they became easy pickings for the more mobile Greek vessels. Xerxes, who watched the defeat of his mighty fleet from the shore, returned to Persia in disgust, leaving his general Mardonius and the army to subdue

Greece. The result was quite the reverse. A year later the Greeks, under the Spartan general Pausanias, obliterated the Persian army at the Battle of Plataea. The Athenian navy then sailed to Asia Minor and destroyed what was left of the Persian fleet at Mykale, freeing the Ionian city-states there from Persian rule.

CLASSICAL AGE

After defeating the Persians, the disciplined Spartans once again retreated to their Peloponnesian 'fortress', while Athens basked in its role as liberator and embarked on a policy of blatant imperialism. In 477 BC it founded the Delian League, so called because the treasury was kept on the sacred island of Delos. The league consisted of almost every state with a navy, no matter how small, including many of the Aegean islands and some of the Ionian city-states in Asia Minor.

Ostensibly its purpose was twofold: to create a naval force to liberate the city-states that were still occupied by Persia, and to protect against another Persian attack. The swearing of allegiance to Athens and an annual contribution of ships (later just money) were mandatory. The league, in effect, became an Athenian empire.

Indeed, when Pericles became leader of Athens in 461 BC, he moved the treasury from Delos to the Acropolis and used its contents to begin a building program in which no expense was spared. His first objectives were to rebuild the temple complex of the Acropolis, which had been destroyed by the Persians, and to link Athens to its lifeline, the port of Piraeus, with fortified walls designed to withstand any future siege.

Under Pericles' leadership (r. 461–429 BC), Athens experienced a golden age of unprecedented cultural, artistic and scientific achievement. Most of the monuments on the Acropolis today date from this time. Drama and literature flourished in the form of the tragedies written by Aeschylus, Sophocles and Euripides. The sculptors Pheidias and Myron and the historians Herodotus, Thucydides and Xenophon also lived at this time.

FIRST PELOPONNESIAN WAR

With the Aegean Sea safely under its control, Athens began to look westward for further expansion, bringing it into conflict with the city-states of the mainland. It started off by threatening Corinth, which belonged to the Sparta-dominated Peloponnesian League. A series of skirmishes and provocations led to the Peloponnesian Wars.

The First Peloponnesian War (431–421 BC) was triggered by Athenian support for Corcyra (present-day Kerkyra or Corfu) in a row with Corinth. Sparta, whose power depended to a large extent on Corinth's wealth, entered the fray.

Athens knew it couldn't defeat Sparta on land, so it abandoned Attica to the Spartans and withdrew behind its mighty walls, opting to rely on its navy to put pressure on Sparta by blockading the Peloponnese. Athens suffered badly during the siege. Plague broke out in the overcrowded city, killing a third of the population – including Pericles – but the defences held firm. The blockade of the Peloponnese eventually began to hurt, and the first phase of the war ended in an uneasy truce.

Imperialistic ambitions now switched to Sicily. Throughout the war, the island had kept Athens supplied with grain, which the soil in Attica was too poor to produce. The Greek colonies there mirrored the city-states in Greece, the most powerful being Syracuse, which had remained neutral during the war.

The opportunity to act presented itself in 416 BC when the Sicilian city of Segesta asked Athens to intervene in a squabble it was having with Selinus, an ally of Syracuse. A hot-headed second cousin of Pericles, Alcibiades, convinced the Athenian assembly to send a flotilla to Sicily; it would go on the pretext of helping Segesta, and then attack Syracuse.

The flotilla, under the joint leadership of Alcibiades, Nicïas and Lamachos, was ill-fated from the outset. Nicias' health suffered and Lamachos, the most adept of the three, was killed. After laying siege to Syracuse for over three years, Alcibiades was called back to Athens on blasphemy charges arising from a drinking binge in which he knocked the heads off a few sacred statues. Enraged, he travelled not to Athens but to Sparta and persuaded the surprised Spartans to go to the aid of Syracuse. Sparta followed Alcibiades' advice and broke the siege in 413 BC, destroying the Athenian fleet and army and starting the Second Peloponnesian War.

Athens was in a bad way. Depleted of troops, money and ships, its subject states were ripe for revolt. The Spartans quickly occupied Decelea in northern Attica, and used it as a base to harass the region's farmers. Athens, deprived of its Sicilian grain supplies, soon began to feel the pinch. Its prospects grew even bleaker when Darius II of Persia, who had been keeping a close eye on events in Sicily and Greece, offered Sparta money to build a navy in return for a promise to return the Ionian cities of Asia Minor to Persia.

Athens went on the attack and even gained the upper hand for a while under the leadership of the reinstated Alcibiades, but its days were numbered once Persia entered the fray in Asia Minor, and Sparta regained its composure under the outstanding general Lysander. Athens surrendered to Sparta in 404 BC.

Corinth urged the total destruction of Athens but Lysander felt honour-bound to spare the city that had saved Greece from the Persians. Instead he crippled it by confiscating its fleet, abolishing the Delian League and tearing down the walls between the city and Piraeus.

SPARTAN RULE

The Peloponnesian Wars had exhausted the city-states, leaving only Sparta in a position of any strength. During the wars, Sparta had promised to restore liberty to the city-states who had turned against Athens, but Lysander now changed his mind and installed oligarchies (governments run by the super-rich) supervised by Spartan garrisons. Soon there was widespread dissatisfaction.

Sparta found it had bitten off more than it could chew when it began a campaign to reclaim the cities of Asia Minor from Persian rule. This brought the Persians back

Spartan warrior

into Greek affairs, where they found willing clients in Athens and increasingly powerful Thebes. Thebes, which had freed itself from Spartan control and revived the Boeotian League, soon became the main threat to Sparta. Meanwhile, Athens regained some of its former swagger as the head of a new league of Aegean states known as the Second Confederacy – this time aimed against Sparta rather than Persia.

The rivalry culminated in the decisive Battle of Leuctra in 371 BC, where Thebes, under the leadership of Epaminondas, inflicted Sparta's first defeat in a pitched battle. Spartan influence collapsed, and Thebes filled the vacuum.

In a surprise about-turn Athens now allied itself with Sparta, and their combined forces met the Theban army at Mantinea in the Peloponnese in 362 BC. The battle was won by Thebes, but Epaminondas was killed. Without him, Theban power soon crumbled.

Three Pillars of Western Philosophy

MARTIN HARRIS

Socrates
'Know thyself'

Little is certain about Socrates because he committed nothing to paper. Historians and philosophers have constructed a picture of Socrates through the writings of Plato, a one-time pupil.

Socrates was born in Athens in about 470 BC and fought in the First Peloponnesian War. Thereafter he gave his life over to teaching in the streets and, particularly, the gymnasia – a mission bestowed on him by his god, the daimon.

He was deeply religious but regarded mythology with disdain. The daimon's existence was demonstrated by the perfect order of nature, the universality of people's belief in the divine and the revelations that come in dreams.

Socrates' method was dialectic: he sought to illuminate truth by question and answer, responding to a pupil's question with another question, and then another, until the pupil came to answer their own inquiry.

He believed that bodily desires corrupted people's souls, and a person's soul was directly responsible for their happiness. The soul was neither good nor bad, but well or poorly realised. Accordingly, unethical actions were in some sense involuntary – people committed bad actions only because they had poor conceptions of themselves. However, those who knew good would always act in accordance with it.

Believing that a profound understanding of goodness was a prerequisite for those who governed society, Socrates held that democracy was flawed because it left the state in the hands of the unenlightened and valued all opinion as equal.

In 399 BC, at the age of 70, Socrates was indicted for 'impiety'. He was convicted with 'corruption of the young' and 'the practice of religious novelties', and sentenced to death by the drinking of hemlock. The story of Socrates' day of execution is told in Plato's Phaedo.

Plato
'Until philosophers are kings ... cities will never cease from ill, nor the human race'

Plato was born in about 428 BC in Athens, or perhaps Aegina, and studied under Socrates, who had a great influence upon him.

In about 387 BC, Plato founded his famous Academy in Athens as an institute of philosophical and scientific studies.

MARTIN HARRIS

The Second Confederacy also collapsed amid infighting fomented by the Persians, and with it went Athenian hopes of a return to the glory days. The 4th century BC did, however, produce three of the West's greatest orators and philosophers: Socrates, Plato and Aristotle. The degeneracy into which Athens had now slipped was perhaps epitomised by the ignominious death sentence passed on Socrates for the crime of corrupting the young with his speeches.

THE MACEDONIAN CONQUEST

Athens and the other city-states were now spent forces, and a new power was rising in the north: the kingdom of Macedon.

Three Pillars of Western Philosophy

Plato's prolific writings take the form of dialogues and read like scripts. He never introduced himself as a character in his dialogues, but he did use real people as speakers, including Socrates.

Politically, Plato was an authoritarian. The Republic is, in part, given over to his view of the ideal state. He divided people into commoners, soldiers and rulers. Plato declared that all people should live simply and modestly; that women and men should be equal, and given the same education and prospects; that marriages should be arranged by the state and children be removed from their parents at birth. This would minimise personal, possessive emotions, so that public spirit would be the prime emotion that individuals felt.

Plato held that knowledge cannot be derived from the senses. He argued that we perceive through our senses, not with them. We have knowledge of concepts that are not derived from experience: perfect symmetry has no manifestation in the material world. Plato believed that knowledge was inside everybody, and claimed that all knowledge is recollection – that it comes as revelation to the intellect.

Aristotle
'He who exercises his reason and cultivates it seems to be both in the best state of mind and most dear to the gods'

Aristotle was born in 384 BC in Stagira, Macedonia. He travelled to Athens in 367 BC to study at Plato's Academy. He remained for nearly 20 years, until Plato's death.

Aristotle then quit Athens following a disagreement with the Academy. He spent 10 years travelling before he returning to found a rival institution, the Lyceum, working there for another 12 years and writing prolifically.

After the death of Alexander the Great in 323 BC, the strong anti-Macedonian sentiment that ensued led to Aristotle being indicted for 'impiety'. He fled Athens and died a year later.

Central to Aristotle's beliefs is his distinction between 'form' and 'matter'. The sculptor of a statue confers shape, the form, onto marble, the matter. A thing's form is that which is unified about it – its essence. Matter without form is just potentiality, but by acquiring form its actuality increases. God has no matter, but is pure form and absolute actuality. Thus humans, by increasing form in the world, by building houses and bridges, make it more divine.

MARTIN HARRIS

Aristotle was the first thinker to look at structures of deductive arguments, or syllogisms, and for 2000 years was unsurpassed in the study of logic, until Gottlob Frege and Bertrand Russell, the 20th century's great symbolic logicians, picked up his thread.

The Macedonians, previously looked on as barbarians, had been forged into a formidable army by Phillip II following his accession to the throne in 359 BC. This development had not gone unnoticed, and the inspirational Athenian orator Demosthenes urged the city-states to prepare to defend themselves. Only Thebes took heed of his warnings and the two cities formed an alliance.

In 339 BC, Philip marched south into Greece and defeated a combined army of Athenians and Thebans at the Battle of Khaironeia in Boeotia (338 BC). The following year, Philip called together all the city-states (except Sparta, which remained

MARTIN HARRIS

Alexander the Great

aloof) at Corinth and persuaded them to form the League of Corinth and swear allegiance to Macedonia by promising to lead a campaign against Persia, thereby assuming the mantle of leader of the Greeks.

Philip's ambition to tackle Persia never materialised. In 336 BC he was assassinated by a Macedonian noble. His son, the 20-year-old Alexander, became king. Alexander, who had been tutored by Aristotle, was highly educated, fearless and ambitious. He was also an astute politician and intent upon finishing what his father had begun. Philip II's death had been the signal for rebellions throughout the budding empire, which Alexander wasted no time in crushing. He made an example of Thebes by razing it to the ground, but spared Athens after the Athenians abandoned their rebellion at the last minute. Alexander then set off to conquer the Persians, carving out a vast empire in the course of 12 years of campaigning.

Athens and the other Greek city-states reclaimed their independence after Alexander's death in 323 BC, and the subsequent division of his empire among his generals. Athens became part of the Delphi-based Aetolian League, while the cities of the Peloponnese banded together to form the Achaean League. Although no longer a political force, Athens continued to flourish as an educational centre. Its schools of philosophy made it the ancient equivalent of a university town.

ROMAN & BYZANTINE RULE

By the end of the 3rd century BC, a new threat had emerged to the west. Rome had finally emerged victorious from its epic struggle against Carthage, and was undisputed master of the Western Mediterranean. Now it was ready to turn its attentions east. Their first target was the Macedonians, who had incurred the wrath of Rome by collaborating with the Carthaginian general Hannibal during the Second Punic War (218–202 BC). The Macedonians fought hard before suffering a decisive defeat at the Battle of Pydnaa in 168 BC.

Meanwhile, Athens and its Aetolian League partners, who had previously declared for Rome, got sucked into a sideshow in Asia Minor involving the mini state of Pergamum, which was a key Roman ally, and the Seleucid empire, which controlled the bulk of Asian Minor. The Aetolian League backed the Seleucids, and were defeated by the combined forces of Rome and Pergamum in a three-year campaign that ended in 189 BC.

Athens escaped very lightly. The Romans had great respect for Athenian scholarship, and the Athenians were left largely to their own devices. Unwisely, as it happened, because in 86 BC Athens joined an ill-fated rebellion against the Romans staged by the Mithridates VI, the King of Pontus, a small kingdom on the Black Sea coast of Asia Minor. Mithridates had succeeded in pushing the Romans out of Asia Minor and had advanced as far as Boeotia (central Greece), where the Pontians and their Athenian allies were defeated by the Roman general Sulla. This time Athens didn't escape so lightly: the city walls were destroyed, and many of its finest statues were carted off to Rome.

Athens showed it was good at picking losers, siding first with Pompey against Caesar, and then with Anthony against Octavian during the Roman Civil Wars (49–30 BC).

For the next 300 years Athens, as part of the Roman province of Achaea, experienced an unprecedented period of peace – the Pax Romana. The Romans had always venerated Greek art, literature and philosophy, and anybody who was anybody in Rome at the time spoke Greek. Aristocratic Roman families sent their offspring to the many schools in Athens. Indeed, the Romans adopted most aspects of Hellenistic culture, spreading its unifying traditions throughout their empire. The Roman emperors, particularly Hadrian, graced Athens with many grand buildings.

CHRISTIANITY & THE BYZANTINE EMPIRE

The Pax Romana began to crumble in AD 250 when the Goths invaded Greece, the first of a succession of invaders spurred on by the 'great migrations' affecting eastern and northern Europe.

Christianity, meantime, was emerging as the empire's new religion. St Paul had made several visits to Greece in the 1st century AD and made converts in many places, but the clincher came with the conversion of the Roman emperors and the rise of the Byzantine Empire, which blended Hellenistic culture with Christianity.

In 324 Emperor Constantine I (also known as Constantine the Great), a Christian convert, transferred the capital of the empire from Rome to Byzantium, which was renamed Constantinople (present-day İstanbul). This was as much due to insecurity in Italy itself as to the growing importance of the wealthy eastern regions of the empire. By the end of the 4th century, the Roman Empire was formally divided into a western and eastern half. While Rome went into terminal decline, the eastern capital grew in wealth and strength, long outliving its western counterpart (the Byzantine Empire lasted until the capture of Constantinople by the Turks in 1453). Emperor Theodosius I made Christianity the official religion in Greece in 394 and outlawed the worship of Greek and Roman gods, now branded as pagan.

Athens remained an important cultural centre until 529, when Emperor Justinian forbade the teaching of classical philosophy in favour of Christian theology, then seen as the supreme form of intellectual endeavour. The ruling was a devastating blow to Athens, which soon declined to little more than a rural backwater.

Between 1200 and 1450, Athens was occupied by a succession of invaders – Franks, Catalans, Florentines and Venetians, all opportunists preoccupied only with grabbing for themselves principalities from the crumbling Byzantine Empire.

OTTOMAN RULE & INDEPENDENCE

Athens was finally captured by the Turks in 1456, and nearly 400 years of Ottoman rule followed. The Acropolis became the home of the Turkish governor, the Parthenon was converted into a mosque and the Erechtheion was used as a harem.

Turkish control of the city was interrupted briefly in 1687 when the Venetian general swept up from the Peloponnese and laid siege to the Acropolis for two months before retreating in the face of Turkish reinforcements. It was during this campaign that the Parthenon was blown up when Venetian artillery struck gunpowder stored inside the temple.

The War of Independence was launched on 25 March 1821. Fighting broke out almost simultaneously across most of Greece and the occupied islands, with the Greeks making big early gains. Within a year the Greeks had captured the fortresses of Monemvasia, Navarino (modern Pylos) and Nafplio in the Peloponnese, as well as Athens, Messolongi, and Thiva (Thebes). Greek independence was proclaimed at Epidaurus on 13 January 1822.

The independence cause then foundered. Internal disagreements twice escalated into civil war, allowing the Ottomans time to call in Egyptian reinforcements, who arrived in 1825. Athens was soon recaptured, and by 1827 virtually all the early Greek gains had been reversed. The western powers, who had resisted earlier calls to intervene, now decided that it was time to step in. A combined Russian, French and British fleet destroyed the Turkish-Egyptian fleet in the

Bay of Navarino in October 1827. Sultan Mahmud II defied the odds and proclaimed a holy war, prompting Russia to send troops into the Balkans to engage the Ottoman army. Fighting continued until 1829 when, with Russian troops at the gates of Constantinople, the sultan accepted Greek independence by the Treaty of Adrianople.

BIRTH OF THE GREEK NATION

The Greeks, meanwhile, had been busy organising the independent state they had proclaimed several years earlier. In April 1827 they elected as their first president a Corfiot who had been the foreign minister of Tsar Alexander I, Ioannis Kapodistrias. Nafplio, in the Peloponnese, was chosen as the capital.

Kapodistrias was assassinated in 1831. Amid the ensuing anarchy, Britain, France and Russia again intervened. They declared that Greece should become a monarchy and that the throne be given to a non-Greek to avoid favouring any one faction. Eventually, 17-year-old Prince Otto of Bavaria was chosen, arriving in Nafplio in January 1833. His new kingdom (established by the London Convention of 1832) consisted of the Peloponnese, Sterea Ellada, the Cyclades and the Sporades.

King Otho (as his name became) soon decided to transfer his court to Athens, which became the capital of independent Greece in 1834. At the time he arrived, Athens was little more than a village nestled on the north slope of the Acropolis: the old Turkish district of Plaka. Otho set about transforming the sparsely populated, war-scarred town into something worthy of a capital. Bavarian architects created a city of imposing neoclassical buildings, tree-lined boulevards, flower gardens and squares. Sadly, many of these buildings have been demolished. The best surviving examples are on Vasilissis Sofias.

THE 20TH CENTURY

Athens continued to grow steadily throughout the latter half of the 19th and early 20th centuries, and enjoyed a brief heyday as the 'Paris of the Eastern Mediterranean' in the days before WWI.

All that ended with the Treaty of Lausanne in July 1923, which brought to a humiliating end a Greek attempt to seize former Greek territories in southern Turkey from a war-weary and depleted Turkish army. The treaty called for a population exchange between the two countries to avoid future disputes. Many of the more than one million Greeks forced out of Turkey headed for Athens, virtually doubling the city's population overnight and necessitating the hasty erection of apartment blocks to house the newcomers: the start of the much maligned concrete sprawl.

Along with the rest of the country, Athens suffered appallingly during the German occupation of WWII. During this time more Athenians were killed by starvation than by the enemy. The Germans were pushed out of Greece in October 1944, but communist and monarchist resistance groups continued to fight one another.

On 3 December 1944, the police fired on a communist demonstration in Plateia Syntagmatos. The ensuing six weeks of fighting between the left and the right were known as the Dekemvriana (Events of December); it was the first round of the civil war, and only the intervention of British troops prevented a communist victory. An election held in March 1946 and boycotted by the communists was won by the royalists, and a rigged plebiscite put George II back on the throne.

In October, the left-wing Democratic Army of Greece (DAG) was formed to resume the fight against the monarchy and its British supporters. Under the leadership of Markos Vafiadis, the Soviet-backed DAG swiftly occupied a large swathe of land along Greece's northern border with Albania and Yugoslavia.

The fighting continued until October 1949, when Yugoslavia fell out with the Soviet Union and cut the DAG's supply lines. Vafiades was assassinated and the remnants of his army capitulated.

The war left the country in an almighty mess, both politically and economically. More Greeks had been killed in the three years of bitter civil war than in WWII; a quarter of a million people were homeless and many thousands more had been taken prisoner or exiled. The resulting sense of despair became the trigger for a mass exodus. Almost a million Greeks headed off in search of a better life elsewhere, primarily to Australia, Canada and the USA.

Athens, like the rest of the country, was left in shock. Recovery came in the form of a massive industrialisation program, launched with the help of US aid. Industrialisation brought another population boom as people from the islands and mainland villages headed to Athens in search of work.

The '60s brought further trauma in the form of a military coup by a group of right-wing army colonels. The junta (1967–74) instituted something approaching a reign of terror, banning all political parties and trade unions and jailing or exiling their opponents. The critical moment of the junta's rule came in November 1973, when students began a protest sit-in at Athens' Polytehnio. On 17 November, tanks stormed the building, injuring many and killing at least 20.

The junta members also proved to be cultural vandals. With characteristic insensitivity, they tore down many of the crumbling old Turkish houses of Plaka and the imposing neoclassical buildings of King Otho's time. The junta failed, however, to take any action on the chronic infrastructural problems resulting from the city's rapid and unplanned growth.

The elected governments that followed in the late '70s and '80s didn't do much better, and by the end of the 80s the city had developed a sorry reputation as one of the most traffic-clogged and polluted in Europe.

The 1990s appear to have been a turning point in the city's development, with politicians finally accepting the need for radical solutions. Inspired initially by the failed bid to stage the 1996 Olympics, authorities embarked on an ambitious program to prepare the city for the 21st century. Two key elements in this program have been a major expansion of the metro network, and a new international airport at Spata, east of Athens.

Urban Guerilla Terror

Security concerns in the lead-up to the 2004 Olympics are centred on the threat of action by Greece's deadly November 17 urban guerilla group.

The group takes its name from the date in 1973 on which the military junta used tanks to crush a student protest at Athens Polytehnio, killing at least 20 students.

Despite an absence of clear objectives, it has proved the most durable of the many left-wing guerilla groups that emerged in Europe in the 1970s. Its philosophy remains staunchly anti-American, anti-NATO and anti-capitalist. To the acute embarrassment of the police, not one member of the gang has been caught in more than 25 years of activity.

The group claimed the first of its victims on Christmas Eve 1975 when CIA bureau chief Richard Welsh was gunned down in the driveway of his Athens home. It has continued to strike at regular intervals ever since. The 22 who have died since then include Dimitrios Angelopoulos, assassinated in 1986. The elderly industrialist was a close relative of Greek Olympic organiser Gianna Angelopoulos-Daskalaki.

Rocket attacks have become the group's trademark, following a raid on a military depot at Larisa in 1987 that netted a haul of antitank missiles. They have been used in a string of attacks over the years, including an assault on the US embassy in Athens in 1998.

The group was busy during the NATO air war against Yugoslavia, firing missiles at the offices of the ruling PASOK party, several banks and at the German ambassador's house.

These projects played an important role in the city's successful bid to stage the 2004 Olympics. The Olympics have now created a momentum of their own; confidence is riding high and billions are being poured into city centre redevelopment.

GEOGRAPHY

Greece lies at the southern tip of the rugged Balkan Peninsula. It is the only EU country without a land frontier with another member, sharing land borders with Albania, the Former Yugoslav Republic of Macedonia and Bulgaria to the north, and with Turkey to the east.

Greece is a very mountainous country where flat land is at a premium, either for building or for agriculture. The city of Athens occupies the Attic Basin, a broad expanse of plain that divides the mountains of Central Greece from the hills of the Attic Peninsula to the south. The city is surrounded by hills: Mt Aigali to the west, Mt Parnitha to the north, Mt Pendelis to the north-east and Mt Hymettos to the east. Several other hills dot the plain: the most famous of these is, of course, the Acropolis. The high point of the city is Lykavittos Hill (277m), which lies north of the Acropolis and is linked by a saddle to Strefi Hill.

To the south, Athens is bounded by the waters of the Saronic Gulf. In ancient times, much of the area between the Acropolis and the sea was covered by coastal swamp.

GEOLOGY

The earthquake which struck Athens on 7 September, 1998, leaving 139 dead and 100,000 homeless, served as a savage reminder that Greece lies in one of most seismically active regions in the world.

Registering 5.9 on the Richter Scale, the quake's epicentre was about 20km north of Athens near Mt Parnitha. Most of the fatalities occurred in the northern suburbs of Menidi, Metamorfosi and Nea Eritrea, but the effects were felt throughout the city. It dislodged fragments of marble from the pillars of the Parthenon, and smashed pottery in the National Archaeological Museum.

The quake was just one of more than 20,000 quakes recorded in Greece in the last 40 years. Fortunately, most of them are very minor – detectable only by sensitive seismic monitoring equipment. The reason for all this activity is that the Eastern Mediterranean lies at the meeting point of three continental plates: the Eurasian, African and Arabian. The three grind away at each other constantly, generating countless earthquakes

as the land surface reacts to the intense activity beneath the earth's crust.

The system has two main fault lines. The most active is the North Aegean Fault, which starts as a volcano-dotted rift between Greece and Turkey, snakes under Greece and then runs north up the Ionian and Adriatic coasts. Less active but more dramatic is the North Anatolian fault that runs across Turkey, which is renowned for major tremors like the 7.4 monster that struck western Turkey on 17 August, 1998, leaving more than 40,000 dead. Seismologists maintain that activity along the two fault lines is not related.

CLIMATE

The Athens climate is typically Mediterranean climate with hot, dry summers followed by mild winters.

July and August are the hottest months, when the mercury can soar above 40°C (over 100°F) for days on end. July and August are also the months of the *meltemi*, a strong northerly wind caused by air pressure differences between North Africa and the Balkans. The wind is a mixed blessing: it reduces humidity, but plays havoc with ferry schedules and sends everything flying – from washing to beach umbrellas.

Temperatures start to drop in September, but it's normally warm enough for swimming until mid- to late October. October can also be wet: the bulk of the city's annual rainfall of just over 350mm falls between October and January. Snow is quite common on the hills north of Athens, but very rare in the city centre.

It stays quite cool, especially at night, until the middle of March. April and May are warm and sunny: the perfect time to visit.

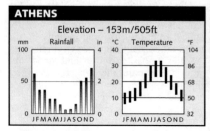

ATHENS
Elevation – 153m/505ft

ECOLOGY & ENVIRONMENT

Greece is belatedly becoming environmentally conscious; regrettably, it is often a case of closing the gate long after the horse has bolted.

General environmental awareness remains at a very low level, especially where litter is concerned. Athens City Council employs an army of road-sweepers to keep on top of the problem, but most rural areas are a disgrace. Environmental education has begun in schools, but it will be some time before community attitudes change.

Athens has a whole host of environmental problems of its own. The most obvious prblems are vehicle pollution and unplanned development.

Forest fires are major problem throughout Greece, with an estimated 25,000 hectares destroyed every year, and Athens is no exception. In 1998, a forest fire destroyed dozens of homes in the hills just north of Athens, and left pine-covered Mt Pendeli so devastated that ecologists fear it may never recover.

NATIONAL PARKS

Visitors who expect Greek national parks to provide facilities on a par with those in countries like Australia and the US will be very disappointed. Although all have refuges and some have marked hiking trails, Greek national parks have little else by way of facilities.

The closest national park to Athens is Mt Parnitha, about 20km north of Athens. It has walking trails, but is best known as the home of Athens' only casino, the Hotel Mt Parnes Casino.

GOVERNMENT & POLITICS

Since 1975, democratic Greece has been a parliamentary republic with a president as head of state. The president and parliament, which has 300 deputies, have joint legislative power. The PASOK party of Prime Minister Simitis holds 163 seats in the current parliament. Greek governments traditionally name very large cabinets – Simitis fronts a team of 41, with 19 ministries. Papandreou had 52 in his last cabinet!

Greece is divided into regions and island groups. The mainland regions are the Peloponnese, central Greece (officially called Sterea Ellada), Epiros, Thessaly, Macedonia and Thrace. The island groups are the Cyclades, Dodecanese, North-Eastern Aegean, Sporades and Saronic Gulf, all in the Aegean Sea, and the Ionian, which is in the Ionian Sea. The large islands of Evia and Crete do not belong to any group. For administrative purposes these regions and groups are divided into prefectures (nomoi in Greek). Athens is part of *nomos Attikis*, Attica.

ECONOMY

Greece is an agricultural country, but the importance of agriculture to the economy has declined rapidly since WWII. Some 50% of the workforce is now employed in services (contributing 59% of GDP), 22% in agriculture (contributing 15%), and 27% in industry and construction (contributing 26%). Tourism is by far the biggest industry; shipping comes next.

Although Greece remains one of the poorest countries in the European Union, its economic prospects have never looked brighter. Following years of tough austerity measures imposed by successive governments, Greece has achieved all the targets set by the EU for monetary union, and will introduce the euro along with the original 11 member states.

This was achieved despite a bad year in 1999 when the tourist industry was hit hard by the fallout from the Kosovo conflict and the NATO bombing of Yugoslavia, combined with reports of anti-NATO sentiments in Greece. The 2000 season was the best ever, with more than 9.5 million visitors.

The population of Athens is estimated at 3.5 million. More precise figures will be available after the 2001 census. The last census, held in 1991, revealed a population of 3.1 million. These figures are for Greater Athens, which includes Piraeus, Glyfada and Kifissia.

PEOPLE

Athens was little more than a village when it became the capital of Greece in 1834, and it remained a small town until the beginning of the 20th century. Most residents are relative newcomers, who migrated to Athens from other parts of Greece or from Greek communities in other countries.

Many are descended from families forced out of the Smyrna (now Izmir) region of south-western Turkey by the Treaty of Lausanne in 1923 (see the History section earlier in this chapter). They settled in new suburbs like Nea Smyrni, south of the city centre, and formed their own soccer club, Panionios – a name that harks back to classical times, when south-western Turkey was called Ionia.

Greece's belated entry into the industrial era in the 1950s brought migrants from all parts of Greece in search of work. These new arrivals also tended to stick together, forming new communities within the city.

Athens continues to attract large number of migrants, both legal and illegal. The collapse of the communist regimes in Albania and Romania in the early 1990s brought a wave of economic refugees across Greece's poorly guarded northern borders, with an estimated 300,000 arriving from Albania alone. These refugees have been a source of cheap labour. Albanians also have a reputation as fine stonemasons, and their skills are much in evidence around Athens.

Greece, with its long coastline and many islands, has now become a prime destination for people-smugglers bringing in illegal migrants from countries like Bangladesh, Iran and Iraq. Most of these illegal migrants wind up in Athens, which now has a substantial Bangladeshi community north of Plateia Koumoundourou.

The city's small Jewish community is comprised mainly of descendants of German Jews who arrived with King Otho in the 1830s.

EDUCATION

Education in Greece is free at all levels of the state system, from kindergarten to tertiary. Primary schooling begins at the age of six, but most children attend a state-run kindergarten from the age of five. Private kindergartens are popular with those who can afford them. Primary school classes tend to be larger than those in most European countries – usually 30 to 35 children. Primary school hours are short (8am to 1pm), but children get a lot of homework.

At 12, children enter the *gymnasio* (high school), and at 15 they may leave school, or enter the *lykeio* (senior high school), from where they take university-entrance examinations. Although there is a high percentage of literacy, many parents and pupils are dissatisfied with the education system, especially beyond primary level. The private sector therefore flourishes, and even relatively poor parents struggle to send their children to one of the country's 5000 *frontistiria* (intensive coaching colleges) to prepare them for the very competitive university-entrance exams. Parents complain that the education system is badly underfunded, and that there is a lack of modern teaching aids in both gymnasio and lykeio.

Grievances reached a peak in 1991, when lykeio students staged a series of sit-ins in schools throughout the country, and organised protest marches. In 1992, gymnasio pupils followed suit, and the government responded by making proposals that called for stricter discipline and a more demanding curriculum. More sit-ins followed, and in the end the government changed its plans and is still reassessing the situation.

ARTS

Walk around any capital city in Europe, America or Australasia and the influence of ancient Greek art and architecture is plain to see. It's there in the civic buildings, in the monumental public sculptures, in the plan of the city streets themselves. The product of a truly extraordinary civilisation, the humanism and purity of form of Greek art has inspired artists and architects throughout history. Be it in the paintings and sculptures of the Italian Renaissance or in the playful postmodernist buildings of the late 20th century, the influence of the ancient Greeks cannot be overemphasised.

Ironically, the influence of Greek art has spread throughout the world due to a reality that many travellers (and indeed the Greeks themselves) find unpalatable. This is the fact that many of the greatest works of ancient Greek art haven't had a home in Greece itself for hundreds, sometimes thousands, of years. From the Parthenon frieze taken by Lord Elgin and now displayed in the British Museum to the famous *Nike* (Winged Victory of Samothrace) in Paris' Louvre museum, the work of the Greek masters is held in the collections of the great museums of the world. Many of the great ancient Greek buildings, too, are found in countries other than Greece as they date from the time of the expansive ancient Greek world, which encompassed parts or all of countries such as Italy, Iran, Turkey, Syria and Libya.

Travellers to Greece itself shouldn't despair, however. There's plenty left to see! The buildings, paintings, pots, sculptures and decorative arts of the ancient and Byzantine worlds can be found in the country's streets, cities and islands, as well as in its wonderful museums. They may not be in their original form (it takes a stretch of the imagination to envisage the *Hermes of Praxiteles* with arms, and the magnificent and austere forms of buildings such as the Parthenon overlaid with gaudily coloured paintings and sculptures), but they manage to evoke the history of the Greek nation more powerfully than a library of history books ever could.

ARCHITECTURE

Of all the ancient Greek arts, architecture has perhaps had the greatest influence. Greek temples, seen throughout history as symbols of democracy, have been the inspiration for architectural movements such as the Italian Renaissance and the British Greek Revival.

One of the earliest known architectural sites of ancient Greece is the huge palace and residential complex at Knossos on Crete, built in the Minoan period. The Minoan period was followed by the Mycenaean. Instead of the open, labyrinthine palaces of the Minoans, the Mycenaeans used their advanced skills in engineering to build citadels on a compact, orderly plan, fortified by strong walls. Visitors to Greece today can appreciate Mycenaean sites such as those of the ancient city states of Mycenae and Tiryns, in The Peloponnese, excavated by the German archaeologist Heinrich Schliemann in the 1870s. The famous Lion Gate at the palace at Mycenae and the stupendous galleries of the palace at Tiryns both illustrate the engineering expertise of the Mycenaeans.

The next great advance in ancient Greek architecture came with the building of the first monumental stone temples in the Archaic and classical periods. From this time, temples were characterised by the famous orders of columns, particularly the Doric, Ionic and Corinthian. These orders were applied to the exteriors of temples, which retained their traditional simple plan of porch and hall but were now regularly surrounded by a colonnade or at least a columnar facade.

Doric columns feature cushion capitals, fluted shafts and no bases. Doric temples still part extant include the Temple of Apollo at Corinth and the Temple of Hephaestus in Athens. The most famous Doric temple in Greece is, of course, the Parthenon.

The shaft of the Ionic column has a base in several tiers and has more flutes. Unlike the austere Doric style, its capital has an ornamented necking. In all, the Ionic order is less massive than the Doric, and is generally more graceful. The little Temple of Athena Nike by the entrance to the Athenian Acropolis, and the Erechtheion, opposite the Parthenon, are two famous Ionic temples.

The distinct and ornate Corinthian column features a single or double row of leafy scrolls (usually acanthus). This order was introduced at the end of the classical period and was subsequently used by the Romans in many of their buildings. The Temple of Olympian Zeus in Athens, completed in Hadrian's time, is a good example of a Corinthian temple.

Theatre design was also a hallmark of the classical period. The tragedies of Aeschylus, Sophocles and Euripides and the comedies of Aristophanes were written and first performed in the Theatre of Dionysos, built into the slope of Athens' Acropolis in the 5th century BC. Other theatres dating from this period can be found at Dodoni, Megalopolis, Epidaurus and Argos (the latter seats about 20,000). They all feature excellent acoustics and most are still used for summer festivals.

During the Hellenistic period, private houses and palaces, rather than temples and public buildings, were the main focus of building. The houses at Delos, built around peristyled (surrounded by columns) courtyards and featuring striking mosaics, are perhaps the best examples in existence.

The Roman period saw Corinth become an important Roman city, with recent excavations revealing fountains, baths and gymnasia. Athens obtained a new commercial *agora* (now known as the Roman Agora) in the time of Augustus and a century and a half later the emperor Hadrian endowed the city with Hadrian's Library and built an elegant arch, the Arch of Hadrian, that still stands between the old and new parts of the city.

During the Byzantine period the Parthenon in Athens was converted into a church and other churches were built throughout Greece. These usually featured a central dome supported by four arches on piers and flanked by vaults, with smaller domes at the four corners and three apses to the east. The external brickwork, which alternated with stone, was sometimes set in patterns.

After the temporary fall of Constantinople to a crusading army in 1204, much of Greece became the fiefdoms of western aristocrats. The most notable of these was the Villehardouin family, who built castles in the Peloponnese at Hlemoutsi, Nafplio, Kalamata and Mystras.

After the War of Independence, Greece continued the neoclassical style that had been dominant in western European architecture and sculpture from 1760 to 1820, thus providing a sense of continuity with its ancient past. This neoclassical style is apparent in Nafplio, initially the capital, and in Athens, notably in the Doric and Ionic ensemble of the National Library and the Athens University building on Panepistimiou. Noteworthy, too, are the old royal palace, the Polytehnio, and the mansions which are now the Byzantine, Benaki and Kanellopoulos Museums.

DANCE

Music and dancing have played an important role in Greek social life since the dawn of Hellenism. You may even think at times that Greeks live solely for the chance to sing and dance. You wouldn't be far wrong.

The folk dances of today derive from the ritual dances performed in ancient Greek temples. Many dances are performed in a circular formation; in ancient times, dancers formed a circle in order to seal themselves off from evil influences.

Every region has its own special dances, and the style often reflects the climate or disposition of the participants. In Epiros, the stately *tsamiko* is slow and highly emotive, reflecting the often cold and insular nature of mountain life. The Pontian Greeks, on the contrary, have a highly visual, vigorous and warlike form of dancing, reflecting years of altercations with their Turkish neighbours. The *kotsari* is one of the best examples of this unique dance form.

The islands, with their bright and cheery atmosphere, give rise to lilting music and matching dances such as the *ballos* or the *syrtos*, while the graceful *kalamatianos* circle dance, where dancers stand in a row with their hands on one another's shoulders, reflects years of proud Peloponnese tradition. Originally from Kalamata in the Peloponnese, this dance can be seen everywhere, most commonly on festive occasions.

The so-called 'Zorba's dance' or *syrtaki* is a stylised dance for two or three men or women with linked arms on shoulders, while the often spectacular solo male *zeïmbekikos* with its whirling improvisations has its roots in the Greek blues of the hashish dens and prisons of prewar times. The women counterpoint this self-indulgent and showy male display with their own sensuous *tsifteteli*, a svelte, sinewy show of femininity evolved from the Middle Eastern belly dance.

MUSIC

Singing and the playing of musical instruments have also been an integral part of life in Greece since ancient times, and are as widely divergent as Greek dancing. Cycladic figurines holding musical instruments

'Get your fresh fish here...' – Central Market

Fans and worry beads

A quick snack on the run, Plaka

Trinket seller with 'unique' religious icons

Nuts galore at Central Market

Outdoor dining experience at a Plaka taverna

GEORGE TSAFOS

The National Gardens provide a well-needed respite from the hustle and bustle of central Athens.

STELLA HELLANDER

Karagiozis figures provide some local colour.

JOHN ELK III

'I'm telling you, those socks clash with that shirt.'

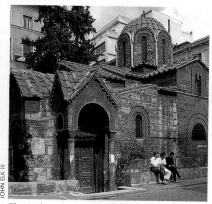

JOHN ELK III

The 11th-century Church of Kapnikarea

resembling harps and flutes date back to 2000 BC. Musical instruments of ancient Greece included the lyre, lute, *piktis* (pipes), *kroupeza* (a percussion instrument), *kithara* (a stringed instrument), *aulos* (a wind instrument), *barbitos* (similar to a cello) and the *magadio* (similar to a harp).

If ancient Greeks did not have a musical instrument to accompany their songs, they imitated the sound of one. It is believed that unaccompanied Byzantine choral singing derived from this custom.

The ubiquitous stringed *bouzouki*, which you will hear everywhere in Greece, is a relative newcomer to the game. It is a mandolin-like instrument similar to the Turkish *saz* and *baglama*.

The plucked strings of the bulbous *outi* (oud), the strident sound of the Cretan *lyra* (lyre) and the staccato rap of the *toumberleki* (lap drum) bear witness to a rich range of musical instruments that share many common characteristics with instruments all over the Middle East.

The bouzouki is one of the main instruments of *rembetika* music, the Greek equivalent of the American blues (see the boxed text 'Rembetika – the Greek Blues' in the Entertainment chapter). There are now a number of rembetika clubs in Athens.

Other musical forms in Greece include *dimotika* – poetry sung and more often than not accompanied by the *klarino* (clarinet) and *defi* (tambourine) – and the widely popular middle-of-the-road *elafrolaïka*, best exemplified by the songs of Giannis Parios. The unaccompanied, polyphonic *pogonisia* songs of northern Epiros and southern Albania are spine-chilling examples of a musical genre that owes its origins to Byzantium. At the lesser end of the scale, the curiously popular *skyladika* or 'dog songs' – presumably because they resemble a whining dog – are hugely popular in night clubs known as *bouzouxidika* where the bouzouki reigns supreme, but where musical taste sometimes takes a back seat.

Since independence, Greece has followed mainstream developments in classical music. The Athens Concert Hall has performances by national and international musicians.

You'll also find all the main forms of Western popular music. Rock, particularly heavy metal, seems to have struck a chord with young urban Greeks, and Athens has a lively local scene and plays host to big international names.

Few Greek performers have made it big on the international scene. The best known are Demis Roussos, the larger than life singer who spent the 1980s strutting the world stage clad in his caftan, and the US-based techno wizard Yanni.

SCULPTURE

Taking pride of place in the collections of the great museums of the world, the sculptures of ancient Greece have extraordinary visual power and beauty.

The prehistoric art of Greece has been discovered only recently, notably in the Cyclades and on Crete. The pared-down sculptures of this period, with their smooth and flattish appearance, were carved from the high-quality marble of Paros and Naxos in the middle of the 3rd millennium BC. Their primitive and powerful forms have inspired many artists since, particularly those of the 20th century.

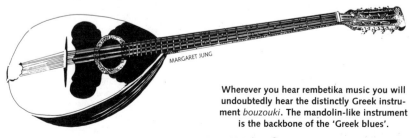

MARGARET JUNG

Wherever you hear rembetika music you will undoubtedly hear the distinctly Greek instrument *bouzouki*. The mandolin-like instrument is the backbone of the 'Greek blues'.

In the Mycenaean period, small terracottas of women with a circular body or with arms upraised were widely produced. These are known to modern scholars as phi (φ) psi (ψ) figurines from their resemblance to these letters of the Greek alphabet.

Displaying an obvious debt to Egyptian sculpture, the marble sculptures of the Archaic period are the true precursors of the famed Greek sculpture of the classical period. The artists of this period moved away from the examples of their Oriental predecessors and began to represent figures that were true to nature, rather than flat and stylised. For the first time in history a sculptured shape was made to reproduce the complex mechanism of the human body. Seeking to master the depiction of both the naked body and of drapery, sculptors of the period focused on figures of naked youths *(kouroi)*, with their set symmetrical stance and enigmatic smiles. Many great kouros sculptures and draped female kore can be admired at the National Archaeological Museum in Athens.

The sculpture of the classical period shows an obsession with the human figure and with drapery. At first the classical style was rather severe, as can be seen in the bronze charioteer at Delphi and the sculpture from the temple at Olympia. Later, as sculptors sought ideal proportions for the human figure, it became more animated. New poses were explored and the figures became increasingly sinuous, with smaller heads in relation to the body.

Unfortunately, little original work of the classical period survives. Most freestanding classical sculpture described by ancient writers was made of bronze and survives only as marble copies made by the Romans. Looking at these copies is a bittersweet experience. On the one hand, they are marvellous works of art in their own right. On the other, copies of works such as *Diskobolos* (The Discus Thrower) by Myron, *Apoxyomenos* (Scraper) by Lysippos and the various Aphrodites by Praxiteles have made us aware of what an extraordinary body of work has been lost. Fortunately, a few classical bronzes, lost when they were being shipped abroad in antiquity, were recovered from the sea in the 20th century. These include the statue of a youth (c. 350–330 BC) found in the sea off Antikythira, now in the collection of the National Archaeological Museum. Also on show here is the wonderful *Poseidon of Artemision*, thought to date from 470–450 BC.

The sculpture of the Hellenistic period continued the Greeks' quest to attain total naturalism in their work. Works of this period were animated, almost theatrical, in contrast to their serene Archaic and classical predecessors. The focus was on realism. Just how successful the artists of this period were is shown in the way later artists, such as Michelangelo, revered them. Michelangelo, in fact, was at the forefront of the rediscovery and appreciation of Greek works in the Renaissance. He is said to have been at the site in Rome in 1506 when the famous Roman copy of the *Laocoön group*, one of the iconic sculptural works of the Hellenistic period, was unearthed.

The end of the Hellenistic age signalled the decline of Greek sculpture's pre-eminent position in the history of the artform. The torch was handed to the Romans, who proved worthy successors. Sculpture in Greece itself never again attained any degree of true innovation.

POTTERY

Say the words 'Greek art' and many people immediately visualise a painted terracotta pot. Represented in museums and art galleries throughout the world, the pots of ancient Greece have such a high profile for a number of reasons, chief among these being that there are lots of them around! The excavation of these pots, buried throughout Greece over millennia, has enabled us to appreciate in small measure the tradition of ancient pictorial art. Quite simply, in the absence of significant examples of Greek painting, pots are all we've got!

Practised from the Stone Age on, pottery is one of the most ancient arts. At first, vases were built with coils and wads of clay but the art of throwing on the wheel was introduced in about 2000 BC and was practised with great skill by Minoan and Mycenaean artists.

Minoan pottery is often characterised by a high centre of gravity and beak-like spouts. Painted decoration was applied as a white clay slip (a thin paste of clay and water) or one which fired to a greyish black or dull red. Flowing designs with spiral or marine and plant motifs were used.

Mycenaean pottery shapes include a long-stemmed goblet and a globular vase with handles resembling a pair of stirrups. Decorative motifs are similar to those on Minoan pottery but are less fluid.

The 10th century BC saw the introduction of the Protogeometric style, with its substantial pots decorated with blackish-brown horizontal lines around the circumference, hatched triangles, and compass-drawn concentric circles. This was followed by the new vase shape and more crowded decoration of the pots of the Geometric period. The decorations on these pots are painted in a lustrous brown glaze on the light surface of the clay, and the same dark glaze is used as a wash to cover the undecorated areas. Occasionally a touch of white is added. By the early 8th century, figures were introduced, marking the introduction of the most fundamental element in the later tradition of classical art – the representation of gods, men and animals.

By the 7th century BC, Corinth was producing pottery with added white and purple-red clay slip. These pots often featured friezes of lions, goats and swans and a background fill of rosettes. In 6th-century Athens, artists used red clay with a high iron content. A thick colloidal slip made from this clay produced a glossy black surface that contrasted with the red and was enlivened with added white and purple-red. Attic pots, famed for their high quality, were exported throughout the Greek Empire during this time. Many of these exports are the pots that grace the collections of international museums today.

PAINTING

The lack of any comprehensive archaeological record of ancient Greek painting has forced art historians to largely rely on the painted decoration of terracotta pots as ev-idence of the development of this Greek art-form. There are a few exceptions, such as the Cycladic frescoes in houses on Santorini, excavated in the mid- to late 20th century. Some of these frescoes are now in the collection of the National Archaeological Museum in Athens. These works were painted in fresco technique using yellow, blue, red and black pigments, with some details added after the plaster had dried. Plants and animals are depicted, as well as men and women. Figures are usually shown in profile or in a combination of profile and frontal views. Stylistically, the frescoes are similar to the paintings of Minoan Crete, which are less well preserved.

Greek painting came into its own during the Byzantine period. Byzantine churches were usually decorated with frescoes on a dark blue background with a bust of Christ in the dome, the four Gospel writers in the pendentives supporting the dome and the Virgin and Child in the apse.

They also featured scenes from the life of Christ (Annunciation, Nativity, Baptism, Entry into Jerusalem, Crucifixion and Transfiguration) and figures of the saints. In the later centuries of the period, the scenes involved more detailed narratives, including cycles of the life of the Virgin and the miracles of Christ.

Painting after the Byzantine period became more secular in nature, with 19th-century Greek painters specialising in portraits, nautical themes and pictorial representation of the War of Independence. Major 19th-century painters included Dionysios Tsokos, Andreas Kriezis, Theodoros Vryzakis, Nikiphoros Lytras, Konstantinos Volanakis and Nicholas Gyzis. Gyzis' historical paintings, which were painted at the time of the fascination with the 'Great Idea' of a new Greek Empire, feature particularly interesting subject matter.

From the first decades of the 20th century, artists such as Konstantinos Parthenis, Konstantinos Kaleas and, later, George Bouzianis were able to use the heritage of the past and at the same time assimilate various developments in modern art. These paintings are best studied in the National Art Gallery in Athens.

LITERATURE

The first, and greatest, ancient Greek writer was Homer, author of the *Iliad* and *Odyssey*. Nothing is known of Homer's life; where or when he lived, or whether, as it is alleged, he was blind. The historian Herodotus thought Homer lived in the 9th century BC, and no scholar since has proved or disproved this.

Herodotus (5th century BC) was the author of the first historical work about Western civilisation. His highly subjective account of the Persian Wars has, however, led him to be regarded as the 'father of lies' as well as the 'father of history'. The historian Thucydides (5th century BC) was more objective in his approach, but took a high moral stance. He wrote an account of the Peloponnesian Wars, and also the famous *Melian Dialogue*, which chronicles the talks between the Athenians and Melians prior to the Athenian siege of Melos.

Pindar (c. 518–438 BC) is regarded as the pre-eminent lyric poet of ancient Greece. He was commissioned to recite his odes at the Olympic Games. The greatest writers of love poetry were Sappho (6th century BC) and Alcaeus (5th century BC), both of whom lived on Lesvos. Sappho's poetic descriptions of her affections for other women gave rise to the term 'lesbian'.

In Byzantine times, poetry, like all of the arts, was of a religious nature. During Ottoman rule, poetry was inextricably linked with folk songs, which were not written down but passed on by word of mouth. Many of these songs were composed by the *klephts* (independence fighters), and told of the harshness of life in the mountains and of their uprisings against the Turks.

Dionysios Solomos (1798–1857) and Andreas Kalvos (1796–1869), who were both born on Zakynthos, are regarded as the first modern Greek poets. Solomos' work was heavily nationalistic and his *Hymn to Freedom* became the Greek national anthem. At this time there were heated debates among writers, politicians and educators about whether the official language should be Demotiki or Katharevousa. Demotiki was the spoken language of the people and Katharevousa was an artificial language loosely based on Ancient Greek. Almost all writers favoured Demotic, and from the time of Solomos, most wrote only in that language.

The highly acclaimed poet Constantine Cavafy (1863–1933) was less concerned with nationalism, being a resident of Alexandria in Egypt; his themes ranged from the erotic to the philosophical.

The best known 20th-century Greek poets are George Seferis (1900–71), who won the Nobel Prize for literature in 1963, and Odysseus Elytis (1911–96), who won the same prize in 1979. Seferis drew his inspiration from the Greek myths, whereas Elytis' work is surreal. Angelos Sikelianos (1884–1951) was another poet who drew inspiration from ancient Greece, particularly Delphi. His poetry is highly evocative, and includes incantatory verses emulating the Delphic oracle. Yiannis Ritsos is another highly acclaimed Greek poet; his work draws on many aspects of Greece – its landscape, mythology and social issues. The most celebrated 20th-century Greek novelist is Nikos Kazantzakis (see Books in the Facts for the Visitor chapter).

DRAMA

Drama in Greece can be dated back to the contests staged at the Theatre of Dionysos in Athens during the 6th century BC for the annual Dionysia festival. During one of these competitions, Thespis left the ensemble and took centre stage for a solo performance regarded as the first true dramatic performance. The term 'thespian' for actor derives from this event.

Aeschylus (525–456 BC) is the so-called 'father of tragedy'; his best-known work is the *Oresteia* trilogy. Sophocles (c.496–406 BC) is regarded as the greatest tragedian. He is thought to have written over 100 plays, of which only seven major works survive. These include *Ajax*, *Antigone*, *Electra*, *Trachiniae* and his most famous play, *Oedipus Rex*. His plays dealt mainly with tales from mythology and had complex plots. Sophocles won first prize 18 times at the Dionysia festival, beating Aeschylus in 468 BC, whereupon Aeschylus went off to Sicily in a huff.

Euripides (c.485–406 BC) was another famous tragedian, more popular than either Aeschylus or Sophocles because his plots were considered more exciting. He wrote 80 plays of which 19 are extant (although one, *Rhesus*, is disputed). His most famous works are *Medea*, *Andromache*, *Orestias* and *Bacchae*. Aristophanes (c.427–387 BC) wrote comedies – often ribald – which dealt with topical issues. His play *The Wasp* ridicules Athenians who resorted to litigation over trivialities; *The Birds* pokes fun at Athenian gullibility; and *Plutus* deals with the unfair distribution of wealth.

You can see plays by the ancient Greek playwrights at the Athens and Epidaurus festivals (see Athens Festival in the Entertainment chapter for details).

FILM

Athenians are avid cinema-goers, although most of the films they watch are North American or British. The Greek film industry has long been in the doldrums, largely due to inadequate funding. The problem is compounded by the type of films the Greeks produce, which are famously slow moving, loaded with symbolism and generally too avant-garde to have mass appeal.

The leader of this school is Theodoros Angelopoulos, winner of the Palmes d'Or award at the 1998 Cannes Film Festival for *An Eternity and One Day*. It tells the story of a terminally ill writer who spends his last day revisiting his youth in the company of a 10-year-old boy. His other films include *The Beekeeper*, *Alexander the Great* and *The Hesitant Step of the Stork*.

SOCIETY & CONDUCT

TRADITIONAL CULTURE

Greece is steeped in traditional customs. Name days (which celebrate the saint after whom a person is named), weddings and funerals all have great significance. On someone's name day an open-house policy is adopted and refreshments are served to well-wishers who stop by to give gifts. Weddings are highly festive occasions, with dancing, feasting and drinking sometimes continuing for days.

Greeks tend to be more superstitious than other Europeans. Tuesday is considered an unlucky day because on that day the Byzantine Empire fell to the Ottomans. Many Greeks will not sign an important transaction, get married or begin a trip on a Tuesday. Greeks also believe in the 'evil eye', a superstition prevalent in many Middle Eastern countries. If someone is the victim of the evil eye, then bad luck will befall them. The bad luck is the result of someone's envy, so one should avoid being too complimentary about things of beauty, especially newborn babies. To ward off the evil eye, Greeks often wear a piece of blue glass, resembling an eye, on a chain around their necks.

DOS & DON'TS

If you are lucky enough to be invited to a Greek home, you will find that the Greeks' reputation for hospitality is not a myth – just a bit harder to find these days in a big city like Athens.

Greeks are very generous hosts, and guests are expected to contribute nothing to a meal or social gathering (although flowers for the hostess never go astray). A similar situation arises if you are invited out for a meal; the bill is not shared as in northern European countries, but paid by the host.

When drinking wine it is the custom to only half fill the glass. It is bad manners to empty the glass, so it must be constantly replenished. When visiting someone you will be offered coffee; again, it is bad manners to refuse. You will also be given a glass of water and perhaps a small serve of preserves. It is the custom to drink the water, then eat the preserves and then drink the coffee.

Personal questions are not considered rude in Greece, and if you react as if they are you will be the one causing offence. You will be inundated with queries about your age, salary, marital status etc.

If you go into a *kafeneio*, taverna or shop, it is the custom to greet the waiters or assistant with *'kalimera'* (good day) or *'kalispera'* (good evening) – likewise if you meet someone in the street.

Ancient Greek Mythology

Mythology was an integral part of life in ancient times. The myths of ancient Greece are the most familiar to us, for they are deeply entrenched in the consciousness of Western civilisation. They are accounts of the lives of the deities whom the Greeks worshipped and of the heroes they idolised.

The myths are all things to all people – a ripping good yarn, expressions of deep psychological insights, words of spine-tingling poetic beauty and food for the imagination. They have inspired great literature, art and music – as well as the odd TV show.

The myths we know are thought to be a blend of Dorian and Mycenaean mythology. Most accounts derive from the works of the poets Hesiod and Homer, produced in about 900 BC. The original myths have been chopped and changed countless times – dramatised, moralised and even adapted for ancient political propaganda, so numerous versions exist.

The Greek Myths by Robert Graves is regarded as being the ultimate book on the subject. It can be heavy going, though. *An Iconoclast's Guide to the Greek Gods* by Maureen O'Sullivan makes more entertaining reading.

The Twelve Deities

The main characters of the myths are the 12 deities, who lived on Mt Olympus.

The supreme deity was **Zeus**, who was also god of the heavens. His job was to make laws and keep his unruly family in order by brandishing his thunderbolt. He was also the possessor of an astonishing libido and vented his lust on just about everyone he came across, including his own mother. Mythology is littered with his offspring.

Zeus was married to his sister **Hera**, the protector of women and the family. Hera was able to renew her virginity each year by bathing in a spring. She was the mother of Ares and Hephaestus.

Ares, god of war, was the embodiment of everything warlike. Strong and brave, he was definitely someone to have on your side in a fight – but he was also hot-tempered and violent, liking nothing better than a good massacre. Athenians, who fought only for such noble ideals as liberty, thought that Ares must be a Thracian – whom they regarded as bloodthirsty barbarians.

Hephaestus was worshipped for his matchless skills as a craftsman. When Zeus decided to punish man, he asked Hephaestus to make a woman. So Hephaestus created Pandora from clay and water and, as everyone knows, she opened a box which unleashed all the evils afflicting humankind.

Athena, the powerful goddess of wisdom and guardian of Athens, is said to have been born (complete with helmet, armour and spear) from Zeus' head, with Hephaestus acting as midwife. Unlike Ares, she derived no pleasure from fighting, preferring to settle disputes peacefully. If need be, however, she went valiantly into battle.

Poseidon, the brother of Zeus, was god of the sea and preferred his sumptuous palace in the depths of the Aegean to Mt Olympus. When he was angry (which was often) he would use his trident to create massive waves and floods. His moods could also trigger earthquakes and volcanic eruptions. He was always on the lookout for some real estate on dry land and challenged Athena for Athens, Dionysos for Naxos and Hera for Argos at various times.

Coin depicting Dionysos

Apollo, god of light, was the son of Zeus by the nymph Leto. He was the sort of person everybody wanted to have around. The ancient Greeks associated sunshine with spiritual and intellectual illumination. Apollo was also worshipped as the god of music and song, which the ancients believed were heard only where there was light and security.

Apollo's twin sister, **Artemis**, seems to have been a bit confused by her portfolio. She was worshipped as the goddess of

Ancient Greek Mythology

childbirth, yet she asked Zeus to grant her eternal virginity; she was also the protector of suckling animals, but loved hunting!

The next time you have a bowl of corn flakes, give thanks to **Demeter**, the goddess of earth and fertility. The English word 'cereal', for products of corn or edible grain, derives from the goddess' Roman name, Ceres. The Greek word for such products is demetriaka.

The goddess of love (and lust) was the beautiful **Aphrodite**. Her tour de force was her magic girdle which made everyone fall in love with its wearer. The girdle meant she was constantly pursued by both gods and goddesses – the gods because they wanted to make love to her, the goddesses because they wanted to borrow the girdle. Zeus became so fed up with her promiscuity that he married her off to Hephaestus, the ugliest of the gods.

Hermes, messenger of the gods, was another son of Zeus – this time by Maia, daughter of Atlas. He was a colourful character who smooth-talked his way into the top ranks of the Greek pantheon. Convicted of rustling Apollo's cattle while still in his cradle, he emerged from the case as the guardian of all divine property. Zeus then made Hermes his messenger, and fitted him out with a pair of winged golden sandals to speed him on his way. His job included responsibility for commerce, treaties and the safety of travellers. He remained, however, the patron of thieves.

Hermes completes the first XI – the gods whose position in the pantheon is agreed by everyone. The final berth is normally reserved for **Hestia**, goddess of the hearth. She was as pure as driven snow, a symbol of security, happiness and hospitality. She spurned disputes and wars and swore to be a virgin forever.

She was a bit too virtuous for some, who relegated her to the ranks of the Lesser Gods and promoted the fun-loving **Dionysos**, god of wine, in her place. Dionysos was a son of Zeus by another of the supreme deity's dalliances. He had the job of touring the world with an entourage of fellow revellers spreading the word about the vine and wine.

Lesser Gods

After his brothers Zeus and Poseidon had taken the heavens and seas, **Hades** was left with the underworld (the earth was common ground). This vast and mysterious region was thought by the Greeks to be as far beneath the earth as the sky was above it. The underworld was divided into three regions: the Elysian Fields for the virtuous, Tartarus for sinners and the Asphodel Meadows for those who fitted neither category. Hades was also the god of wealth, in the form of the precious stones and metals found deep in the earth. Other gods included **Asclepius**, the god of healing; **Eros**, the god of love; **Hypnos**, the god of sleep; **Helios**, god of the sun; and **Selene**, goddess of the moon.

Mythical Heroes

Heroes such as **Heracles** and **Theseus** were elevated almost to the ranks of the gods. Heracles, yet another of Zeus' offspring, was performing astonishing feats of strength before he had left the cradle. His 12 labours were performed to atone for the murder of his wife and children in a bout of madness. The deeds of Theseus included the slaying of the Minotaur at Knossos.

Other heroes include **Odysseus**, whose wanderings after the fall of Troy are recorded in Homer's Odyssey, and **Jason**, who led his Argonauts to recover the golden fleece from Colchis (in modern Georgia). Xena, regrettably, does not feature anywhere. The strapping 'warrior princess' of TV fame is a scriptwriter's invention – not a myth!

TAMSIN WILSON

Theseus killing the Minotaur

Transliteration & Variant Spellings: An Explanation

The issue of correctly transliterating Greek into the Latin alphabet is a vexed one, fraught with inconsistencies and pitfalls. The Greeks themselves are not very consistent in this respect, though things are gradually improving. The word 'Piraeus', for example, has been variously represented by the following transliterations: Pireas, Piraievs and Pireefs; and when appearing as a street name (eg, Piraeus Street) you will also find Pireos!

This has been compounded by the linguistic minefield of diglossy, or the two forms of the Greek language. The purist form is called Katharevousa and the popular form is Dimotiki (Demotic). The Katharevousa form was never more than an artificiality and Dimotiki has always been spoken as the mainstream language, but this linguistic schizophrenia means there are often two Greek words for each English word. Thus, the word for 'baker' in everyday language is *fournos*, but the shop sign will more often than not say *artopoieion*. The baker's product will be known in the street as *psomi*, but in church as *artos*.

A further complication is the issue of anglicised vs hellenised forms of place names: Athina vs Athens, Patra vs Patras, Thiva vs Thebes, Evia vs Euboia – the list goes on and on! Toponymic diglossy (the existence of both an official and everyday name for a place) is responsible for Kerkyra/Corfu, Zante/Zakynthos, and Santorini/Thira.

In this guide we usually provide modern Greek equivalents for town names, with one or two well known exceptions, eg Athens and Patras. For ancient sites, settlements or people from antiquity, we have tried to stick to the more familiar classical names; so we have Thucydides instead of Thoukididis, Mycenae instead of Mykines.

You may have come to Greece for sun, sand and sea, but if you want to bare all, other than on a designated nude beach, remember that Greece is a traditional country, so take care not to offend the locals.

If you wish to look around a church, you should always dress appropriately. Women should wear skirts that reach below the knees, and men should wear long trousers and have their arms covered. Regrettably, many churches are kept locked nowadays, but it's usually easy enough to locate caretakers, who will be happy to open them up for you.

TREATMENT OF ANIMALS

The Greek attitude to animals depends on whether the animal is a cat or not. It's definitely cool to be a cat. Even the mangiest-looking stray can be assured of a warm welcome and a choice titbit on approaching the restaurant table of a Greek. Most other domestic animals are greeted with a certain indifference. You don't see many pet dogs, or pets of any sort for that matter. The various societies for animal protection in Greece are listed in *Atlantis* magazine.

RELIGION

About 98% of the Greek population belongs to the Greek Orthodox Church. Most of the remainder are Roman Catholic, Jewish or Muslim.

The Greek Orthodox Church is closely related to the Russian Orthodox Church; together they form the third-largest branch of Christianity. Orthodox, meaning 'right belief', was founded in the 4th century by Constantine the Great, who was converted to Christianity by a vision of the Cross.

By the 8th century, there were a number of differences of opinion, as well as increasing rivalry, between the pope in Rome and the patriarch of Constantinople. One dispute was over the wording of the Creed. The original Creed stated that the Holy Spirit proceeds 'from the Father', which the Orthodox Church adhered to, whereas Rome added 'and the Son'. Another bone of contention concerned the celibacy of the clergy. Rome decreed priests had to be celibate; in the Orthodox Church, a priest could marry before becoming ordained. There were also differences in fasting: in the

Transliteration & Variant Spellings: An Explanation

Problems in transliteration have particular implications for vowels, especially given that Greek has six ways of rendering the vowel sound *ee*, two ways of rendering the *o* sound and two ways of rendering the *e* sound. In most instances in this book, *y* has been used for the *ee* sound when a Greek upsilon (υ, Y) has been used, and *i* for Greek ita (η, H) and iota (ι, I). In the case of the Greek vowel combinations that make the *ee* sound, that is οι, ει and υι, an *i* has been used. For the two Greek *e* sounds, αι and ε, an *e* has been employed. As far as consonants are concerned, the Greek letter *gamma* (γ, Γ) appears as *g* rather than *y* throughout this book. This means that *agios* (Greek for male saint) is used rather than *ayios*, and *agia* (female saint) rather than *ayia*. The letter *delta* (δ, Δ) appears as *d* rather than *dh* throughout this book, so *domatia* (rooms), rather than *dhomatia*, is used. The letter *fi* (φ, Φ) can be transliterated as either *f* or *ph*. Here, a general rule of thumb is that classical names are spelt with a *ph* and modern names with an *f*. So Phaistos is used rather than Festos, and Folegandros is used rather than Pholegandros. The Greek *chi* (ξ, Ξ) has usually been represented as *h* in order to approximate the Greek pronunciation as closely as possible. Thus, we have 'Haralambos' instead of 'Charalambos' and 'Polytehniou' instead of 'Polytechniou'. Bear in mind that the *h* is to be pronounced as an aspirated *h*, much like the *ch* in loch. The letter *kapa* (κ, K) has been used to represent that sound, except where well-known names from antiquity have adopted by convention the letter *c*, eg Polycrates, Acropolis.

Wherever reference to a street name is made, we have omitted the Greek word *'odos'*, but words for avenue *(leoforos)* and square *(plateia)* have been included.

For useful words and phrases, see the language guide at the back of this book. For a more detailed guide to the language, check out Lonely Planet's Greek phrasebook.

Orthodox Church, not only was meat forbidden during Lent, but wine and oil also.

By the 11th century these differences had become irreconcilable, and in 1054 the pope and the patriarch excommunicated one another. Ever since, the two have gone their own ways as the (Greek/Russian) Orthodox Church and the Roman Catholic Church.

During Ottoman times membership of the Orthodox Church was one of the most important criteria in defining a Greek, regardless of where he or she lived. The church was the principal upholder of Greek culture and traditions.

Religion is still integral to life in Greece, and the Greek year is centred on the festivals of the church calendar. Most Greeks, when they have a problem, will go into a church and light a candle to the saint they feel is most likely to help them. On the islands you will see hundreds of tiny churches dotted around the countryside. Most have been built by individual families in the name of their selected patron saint as thanksgiving for God's protection.

LANGUAGE

See the Language chapter at the back of this book for pronunciation details and useful phrases. The boxed text 'Transliteration & Variant Spellings: An Explanation' takes a look at the vagaries of turning Greek into English. The Glossary chapter, also at the back of the book, contains some common Greek words.

Αθήνα

OLYMPICS 2004

After more than a century, 108 years to be precise, the Olympic Games are finally returning to the country of their birth. Amid cries of jubilation it was announced on 5 September, 1997, in Lausanne, Switzerland, that Athens would be the host city of the Games of the XXVIII Olympiad. Having suffered incredulous disappointment at losing the 100 year celebration to Atlanta, the collective breath of a nation was held as the announcement was made.

History

The origin of the Olympic Games dates back to Mycenaean times. The Great Goddess, identified with Rea, was worshipped in Greece during the first millennium BC. By the classical era, Rea had been surpassed by her son Zeus. A small regional festival, which probably included athletic events, was begun in the 11th century BC.

The first record of the official quadrennial Olympic Games is in 776 BC. By 676 BC, they were open to all male Greeks, reaching the height of their prestige in 576 BC. The Games were held in honour of Zeus, popularly acclaimed as their founder. They took place at the time of the first full moon in August.

The athletic festival lasted five days and included wrestling, chariot and horse racing, the pentathlon (wrestling, long jump, running, discus and javelin throwing) and the pancratium (a vicious form of fisticuffs).

Originally only Greek-born males were allowed to participate, but later Romans were permitted. Slaves and women were not allowed to enter the sanctuary as participants or spectators. Women trying to sneak in were thrown from a nearby cliff.

The event served purposes besides athletic competition. Writers, poets and historians read their works to a large audience, and the citizens of various city-states came together. Traders clinched business deals and city-state leaders talked in an atmosphere of festivity that was conducive to resolving differences through discussion, rather than battle.

Left: A classical running style.

MARTIN HARRIS

The Games continued during the first years of Roman rule. By this time, however, their importance had declined and, thanks to Nero, they had become less edifying. In AD 67 Nero entered the chariot race with 10 horses, ordering that other competitors could have no more than four. Despite this advantage, he fell and abandoned the race. He was still declared the winner by the judges.

The Games were held for the last time in AD 394, before they were banned by Emperor Theodosius I as part of a purge of pagan festivals. In AD 426, Theodosius II decreed that the temples of Olympia be destroyed.

Ancient Olympic Trivia
- The word *stadium* comes from the word *stade*, a 200-yard foot race raced on a track that ran the length of the Olympic complex.
- The first recorded Olympian was Corobeus, a cook from Elis, in 776 BC.
- To prevent cheating and in the interest of safety, from 720 BC onwards athletes competed naked.
- Prizes awarded to athletes during ancient times ranged from shields and woollen cloaks to crowns of wild olives.
- Athletes who made false starts in foot races were whipped as punishment.
- Foot racing, wrestling, discus and javelin are the only ancient sports to still be included in the modern Games.

Modern Olympics

The reinstitution of the Olympic Games may never have been realised if not for the persistence and tenacity of Frenchman Pierre de Coubertin (1863–1937). Disillusioned by the effect of the Franco-Prussian War on his countrymen, Coubertin sought to instil in them renewed faith and hope for their futures. Through his observations of team sports in England and the United States, Coubertin came to believe that sport possessed the power to inspire the human spirit and encourage peace amongst the world's nations. He believed this could be achieved through the revival of the Olympic Games.

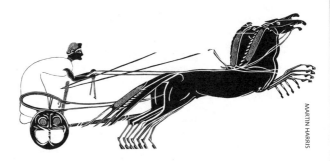

MARTIN HARRIS

Right: Chariot racing.

Coubertin first publicly voiced his idea of the modern Olympic Games at a meeting of the Athletic Sports Union at the Sorbonne in Paris in 1892. However, his passionate plea drew no support.

Undeterred, Coubertin's next opportunity presented itself in 1894 at an International Congress convened to study athletic amateurism. In attendance were delegates from Belgium, England, France, Greece, Italy, Russia, Spain, Sweden and the United States. On the agenda for discussion there were initially only seven items, to which Coubertin added an eighth, 'Regarding the possibility of the revival of the Olympic Games'. This time his enthusiasm was infectious and on June 23 1894 the revival of the Olympic Games was unanimously agreed upon and the International Olympic Committee (IOC) was founded.

Two years later his dream was realised and the modern Olympic Games were inaugurated in Athens, with 14 nations sending 311 athletes to compete in 42 events across 10 sports. Of the 311 athletes – all of whom were male – 230 were Greek.

Coubertin, who was president of the IOC for 29 years, described the concept of the 1896 Games as:

> ...competitions at regular periodical intervals at which representatives of all countries and all sports would be invited under the aegis of the same authority, which would impart to them a halo of grandeur and glory, that is the patronage of classical antiquity. To do this was to revive the Olympic Games – the name imposed itself – it was not possible to find another.

Other than during WWI and WWII, the modern Olympic Games have been held every four years in different cities around the world ever since.

The Olympic Flag

The Olympic Flag as we know it today – the five coloured interlocking rings on a white background – was the inspiration of Pierre de Coubertin, the founder of the modern Olympic Games. Coubertin, eager to capture the idealism of the Olympics, created the flag as a celebration for the 20th anniversary of the Games' revival.

In 1913 his design was first presented to the world in the pages of the Paris magazine *Le Bon Marche*. Almost a century later Coubertin's flag and its design have come to represent the Olympic ideals of peace and humanity.

The flag's five interlocking rings represent the union of athletes from the five continents and the six colours (blue, black, red, yellow, green and white) were chosen because they featured prominently in the national flags of the world.

Over the years a closer association has been drawn between the colours of the rings and the five continents, with each continent being linked to a colour – blue for Europe, black for Africa, red for the Americas, yellow for Asia and green for Oceania. It is important to note that Pierre de Coubertin never stipulated nor endorsed such associations.

The Rocky Road to 2004

Greece's initial jubilation at having won the honour of staging the 2004 Olympic Games soon subsided and disillusionment set in. Despite having over 70% of the facilities for the Games already built when they won the bid in 1997 there has been little progress since. Chronic delays, bureaucratic red tape and constant infighting have plagued the 2004 Olympic Committee from the start.

With three years already lost and concern mounting that Athens would not be ready in time, in April 2000 IOC president, Juan Antonio Samaranch, stepped in and his report called for 'drastic measures' to be taken. Not since the Melbourne Games of 1956 has a country been so publicly criticised by the IOC or been threatened with the removal of the Games.

With the clock ticking and a crisis looming, Gianna Angelopous-Daskaki, the woman who led Athens' successful bid for the Games, was called back in to take over the helm of the ailing 2004 Olympic Committee. Faced with growing public condemnation, Greece's premier, Costas Simitis, has also stepped into the ring vowing to take a more active role in the organisation of the Games by assuming full government responsibility.

Since that scathing report substantial progress has been made. In early November 2000, groundbreaking finally began on the Olympic Village, the largest of the Games projects and one of the IOC's greatest concerns. The Olympic Village, located some 10km from Athens' centre in the Lekanes district at Acharnai, will be home to some 17,000 athletes and trainers.

The construction of the rowing and canoeing centre in Shinias, south-east of Marathon, is also underway. The centre, though, has not been without controversy. Environmentalists, concerned with the impact on the wetlands, strongly opposed the centre's construction and unsuccessfully lobbied the government for an alternative location to be found.

In an announcement in late November 2000 Jacques Rogge, IOC Coordination Commission chairperson, stated he was 'very pleased' by the efforts of

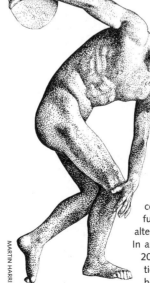

MARTIN HARRIS

Right: The *Discus Thrower*.

the Organising Committee over the previous months. However, Rogge still expressed concern as to the tight scheduling dates for the construction of the remaining facilities, and urged that the deadline for their completion be brought forward from May 2004 to the end of 2003 so that adequate testing can take place.

Athens' Olympic Wreath

On 30 September 1999, the Athens Olympic Committee unveiled the new 2004 Olympic emblem. The emblem – a white olive wreath set on an aquamarine background – while simplistic in design, is rich in symbolism.

The olive wreath, a symbol commonly identified with the ancient Greek Olympic spirit, exemplifies the ideals of peace, unity and democracy; the blue background is a reflection of the blue sky and the Greek sea. The colours, drawn from the Greek flag, epitomise the tradition of the Greek people and the Olympic dreams of their nation.

2004 Olympic Venues

The eyes of the world will be upon Athens for 17 days in August 2004, as athletes from some 200 countries descend upon the city. The centrepiece of Athens 2004 is the 80,000-seat Olympic Stadium, in the northern suburb of Maroussi, which will stage the athletics events as well as the opening and closing ceremonies. The stadium has doubled as the city's number one soccer venue since it was completed in 1996.

The stadium is part of the Athens Olympic Sports complex, next to Irini metro station, which also includes an indoor sports hall for gymnastics, a swimming complex, diving pool, a velodrome and a tennis centre. The rhythmic gymnastics, table tennis and water polo will take place 4km south of the stadium at the Galatsi Olympic Indoor Hall.

The other main area of Olympic activity is in the coastal suburb of Faliro. Karaïskaki Stadium, home ground for the Olympiakos soccer club, will host the preliminary rounds of – what else – soccer (the semifinals and finals will take place at the Nea Philadelphia Stadium, 3km west of the Olympic Stadium), while the nearby Peace and Friendship Stadium will be used for handball and basketball. On the beach, close by, the volleyball will take place and farther back around the bay at the Faliro Ippodromo, Athens' premier horse-racing track, the judo, boxing and taekwondo events will be staged. The yachting will be held in Faliro Bay.

Fittingly, the 2004 marathon will start from the ancient site of Marathon, from which the race derived its name. Over 100 years of Olympic tradition will then be honoured as the marathon runners, following in the footsteps of the 1896 Greek victor Spiridon Loues, race to the finish line in the Panathenaic Stadium – the home of the first modern Olympic Games. This stadium will also host the archery.

Other venues include the Markopoulo Olympic Shooting and Equestrian Centre, 10km south of Peania; the Ano Liossia Olympic Indoor Hall, in northern Athens, which will stage the wrestling; the Nikea Olympic Hall, in western Athens, where the weightlifting will take place; the new Olympic Centre at Ellinikon, the old international airport, which will hold the baseball, softball, hockey and badminton events; the Vouliagmeni Olympic Triathlon Centre, 8km south of Glyfada; and the Goudi Olympic Modern Pentathlon Centre, west of central Athens. The cycling road race will be raced through Athens' historical centre and the mountain biking event will be staged at Mt Parnitha.

For updated details on Olympic venues and other news log on to the official Athens 2004 Web site at www.athens.olympic.org.

A Cloud Over Athens

While the debate over the Olympic facilities continues, another ominous cloud is threatening to cover Athens during the 2004 Olympic Games. Environmental watchdog, Greenpeace, has expressed grave concerns over the effect the city's high level of air pollution will have on the visiting athletes.

During summer, Athens, ranked by Greenpeace as the most polluted city in the European Union, is covered by smog so thick that it is referred to locally as *nefos* (cloud). The organisation's concerns were given weight by Costas Bakouris, the managing director of the Athens' 2004 Olympic Bid Committee, who admitted that on heavy smog days, the athletes may have difficulty breathing.

A major contributor to Athens' pollution woes is the city's hectic and often congested traffic. But whilst the city has taken action to reduce the levels of pollution emitted through the initiation of programs such as alternative driving days and staggered peak driving hours, the number of cars on Athens' roads have tripled since their introduction.

Greenpeace has stated that unless drastic action is taken the city may find itself 'unfit' to host the 2004 Olympic Games.

Facts for the Visitor

WHEN TO GO

Spring and late autumn are the best times to visit Athens. The weather is pleasantly warm, making it ideal for walking around and exploring. Tourists are relatively thin on the ground, so the sites and museums are less crowded, and hotel rooms easier to find – and cheaper.

Winter is not a bad time to visit, providing you don't mind the occasional rainy day. Winter visitors will discover a different city as Athenians retreat indoors. Accommodation is at its cheapest, with some excellent deals for long-term visitors.

Summer is probably the worst time to visit, particularly in July and August. The temperatures can hover around 40°C for days on end and it's too hot to do anything after 10am. It's also high season on the tourist front as Athens becomes a transit point for thousands of tourists heading for the islands. Hotel rooms are expensive and hard to find. Athenians know what to do: they abandon the city en masse in August.

ORIENTATION

CITY CENTRE

Although Greater Athens is a huge, sprawling city, most things of interest to visitors are to be found within a compact central area surrounding Plateia Syntagmatos (Syntagma Square), the heart of the modern city.

This area includes the city's two major landmarks, the Acropolis and Lykavittos Hill, which can be seen from just about everywhere and are useful for finding one's bearings. The streets are clearly signposted in Greek and English.

Here's a brief introduction to the main suburbs:

Syntagma

Plateia Syntagmatos is flanked by luxury hotels, banks, airline offices and fast-food outlets. The square is overlooked by the old royal palace. It was from the palace balcony that the constitution (syntagma) was declared on 3 September 1843. The building has housed the Greek parliament since 1935.

Syntagma is where you will be deposited if arriving by bus. It's a pleasant introduction to the city, despite the manic speed at which the traffic zooms around it. At its centre is a large, paved square, planted with orange, oleander and cypress trees.

Amalias is the main street heading south from the eastern side of Plateia Syntagmatos. Next to it are the National Gardens, with subtropical trees and ornamental ponds, and the more formal Zappeio Gardens. Amalias skirts the Arch of Hadrian and the Temple of Olympian Zeus and leads into Syngrou, which runs all the way to the coast at Faliro.

Panepistimiou and Stadiou, which run north-west to Plateia Omonias, are the main streets of the city centre, lined with fine neoclassical buildings. Confusingly, the signs on Panepistimiou are for Eleftherias Venizelou, although everyone knows it as Panepistimiou (University) after the Athens University building halfway to Omonia.

Mitropoleos and Ermou run west from Syntagma to Monastiraki. Ermou deteriorates farther west, but the stretch just west of Syntagma is home to the most expensive retail space in Athens.

Syntagma is also the hub of the new metro system.

South of Syntagma

The first suburb south of Syntagma is **Plaka**, the old Turkish quarter of Athens and virtually all that existed when Athens was declared the capital of independent Greece.

Its narrow, labyrinthine streets nestle into the north-eastern slope of the Acropolis, and most of the city's ancient sites are close by. Plaka is touristy in the extreme. Its main streets, Kydathineon and Adrianou, are packed solid with restaurants and souvenir shops. It is also the most attractive and interesting part of Athens and most visitors make it their base.

South of Plaka is the trendy residential suburb of **Makrigianni**, which occupies the southern slope of the Acropolis between Filopappos Hill and Syngrou. Although just a few minutes' walk from the hurly burly of Plaka, it's like a different world, with none of the souvenir shops and tourist restaurants. Makrigianni has some good upmarket hotels and restaurants. It is also home to the city's main gay area – on Lembessi between Makrigianni and Kallirois.

Athens authorities are in the process of establishing a special museum area just south of the Acropolis between Dionysos Areopagitou and Hatzihristou, just west of the new Akropoli metro station.

The quiet residential districts of **Veikou** and **Koukaki** stretch south-east from Makrigianni, on the southern slopes of Filopappos Hill. There are a few small hotels, but the area retains something akin to village atmosphere.

West of Syntagma

The first stop west of Syntagma is **Monastiraki**. Centred on busy Plateia Monastirakiou, 700m west of Syntagma, this is the city's market district. The famous Athens flea market is south-west of the square on Ifestou, while the central meat and fish markets, **Kentriki Agora**, are to the north on Athinas, opposite the fruit and vegetable market. Shops along the streets bordering the markets sell cheeses, nuts, herbs, honey, dried fruits and cold meats. On Eolou most shops sell cut-price clothing and street vendors offer items such as sheets, towels, tablecloths and underwear.

The suburbs west of Monastiraki have undergone a remarkable transformation during the 1990s. **Thisio**, to the south-west, led the way in the early 90s when young professionals started buying up the run-down area's cheap housing. It's now a thriving area full of music bars and cafes, particularly around the junction of Apostolou Pavlou and Iraklidon. Places like Stavlos, at Iraklidon 8, were pioneers of the Athens retro style of renovation – ripping out modern finishings to expose and highlight old stonework and chunky timber beams.

This style is now being taken a step further in nearby **Psiri**, north-west of Monastiraki. As recently as 1997, Psiri rated as 'Athens at its most clapped-out'; it still looks that way from the outside, but the maze of narrow streets within are now brimming with dozens of stylish restaurants and bars.

A new Asian quarter has emerged just north of Psiri, in the blocks north-east of Plateia Koumoundourou. There are several Bangladeshi shops as well as cheap Asian restaurants.

North of Syntagma

The main streets leading north-west from Syntagma, Panepistimiou and Stadiou, terminate at Plateia Omonias at the centre of the **Omonia** district. Once one of the city's smarter areas with some excellent examples of neoclassical architecture, Omonia slipped into decline during the 1970s and '80s, developing a sorry reputation as one of the sleaziest areas of the city – better known for its pickpockets and prostitutes than its architecture. This trend is slowly being reversed, and big investors have been pouring money into the area. More high-profile projects are scheduled in the lead-up to the 2004 Olympics, and police have been making an effort to clean up the area.

On a practical level, Plateia Omonias is an important transport hub. All the major streets of central Athens meet here: Panepistimiou and Stadiou run south-east to Syntagma; Athinas heads south from Omonia to Plateia Monastirakiou; Pireos runs south-west to Piraeus; Agiou Konstantinou goes west towards the Larisis and Peloponnese train stations; and 3 Septemvriou heads north – although the major street heading north is 28 Oktovriou-Patission, which starts 50m south-east along Panepistimiou from the square.

The area north of Plateia Omonias, particularly the streets around Plateia Vathis, remain notorious for the many hotels that double as bordellos. The city's main red-light area is actually farther north on Filis, near Plateia Viktorias.

Generally, though, the seediness gradually recedes as you head north from Plateia

Vathis, giving way to a respectable, if characterless, neighbourhood. Athens' two train stations are at the western edge of this area, on Deligianni. The National Archaeological Museum is on the eastern side, on 28 Oktovriou-Patission.

Just south of the National Archaeological Museum is the Athens Polytehnio. This establishment has university status, with faculties of fine arts and engineering. It also has a long tradition of radical thinking and alternative culture, and led the student sit-in of 1973 in opposition to the junta.

Squashed between the Polytehnio and Strefi Hill is the student residential area of **Exarhia**. It's a lively area with graffiti-covered walls and lots of cheap restaurants catering for Bohemian-looking professors and crowds of rebellious-looking students.

East of Syntagma

Vasilissis Sofias, which runs east from Syntagma along the northern edge of the Botanical Gardens, is one of Athens' most imposing streets. It was laid out by the Bavarian architects brought in by King Otho in the 1830s. Its neoclassical buildings now house various museums, embassies and government offices.

Vasilissis Sofias forms the southern boundary of the smart residential district of **Kolonaki**, home of Athens chic. Tucked beneath Lykavittos Hill, it has long been the favoured address of Athenian socialites; its streets are full of trendy boutiques and private art galleries, as well as dozens of smart cafes and international restaurants.

Farther east are the districts of **Ambelokipi** and **Ilissia**, two more smart residential districts. The streets are dotted with embassies and consulates, as well as smart hotels catering for foreign businessmen. South of here are the quieter residential districts of Mets and Pangrati. Between them, nestled into the north-eastern slope of Ardettos Hill, is the city's old Roman Stadium.

COASTAL SUBURBS

With so much emphasis on the Acropolis and the city centre, it's easy to forget that Athens is a coastal city. The most attractive section of the coast is to the south-east, starting at Glyfada and continuing south-east through Voula, Vouliagmeni and Varkiza.

Glyfada, 10km south-east of the city centre, is Attica's premier resort, with dozens of hotels, bars, clubs and restaurants. The best beaches are at Vouliagmeni and Varkiza. See the Glyfada section of the Excursions chapter for more information.

KIFISSIA

Athens also stretches a long way inland, incorporating many smaller settlements that once lay well beyond the city boundaries.

Kifissia, 18km north-east of the city centre, comes as quite a shock to first time visitors. Nestled below Mt Pentelikon, its leafy streets are a cool retreat from the urban sprawl. Not surprisingly, Kifissia is home to the city's wealthy elite, who pay for the privilege of living here with depressingly long commuting times – up to 1½ hours to the city centre by car. The trip takes only 20 minutes by metro from Omonia. See the Kifissia section of the Excursions chapter for more information.

MAPS

The free Athens map handed out by the tourist office has good coverage of the city centre and Piraeus, as well as maps of Greater Athens and Attica.

If you want to get serious about exploring Athens beyond the city centre, you'll need to buy yourself a copy of the Athens-Piraeus *Proasteia* (street directory). Unfortunately, it's published only in Greek.

Local company Road Editions' 1:50,000 map of Attica has the best coverage of the Attica region.

RESPONSIBLE TOURISM

Ideally, being a responsible tourist entails an effort to minimise the detrimental effects of tourism – and maximise the benefits. This starts with such fundamental things as being polite and respectful.

The most irresponsible thing that a tourist can do is to "souvenir" stones or small pieces of pottery from ancient sites. If every visitor picked up a stone from the Acropolis, there would soon be nothing left.

An easy way to be a responsible tourist is to economise on water use. Greece is a dry country and fresh water is a precious commodity, so turn the tap off while you're brushing your teeth and don't spend hours in the shower.

See the Society & Conduct section of the Facts about Athens chapter for tips about dress and avoiding causing offence.

TOURIST OFFICES

LOCAL TOURIST OFFICES
EOT main tourist office Map 5, A7
Amerikis 2, Syntagma ☎ **331 0561/2**
fax 325 2895 ℮ **info@gnto.gr** ⓦ **www.gnto.gr**
☉ **9am-5pm Mon-Fri, 9.30am-2pm Sat**
Ⓜ **Syntagma**
Athens' main EOT tourist office has information sheets and brochures on just about every topic you care to mention, including a very useful time-table of the week's ferry departures from Piraeus and information about public transport prices and schedules from Athens. It also has a useful free map of Athens, which has most of the places of interest, and the main trolleybus routes, clearly marked.

TOURIST POLICE
Map 7, D2
Dimitrakopoulou 77, Koukaki ☎ **924 2700,**
toll-free 24-hour information service 171
☉ **24 hours daily** 🚊 **1,5,22**
The tourist police's head office is open 24 hours a day, but it's quite a trek from the city centre. The tourist police also have a 24-hour information service, for general tourist information or for emergency help – someone who speaks English is always available. They will also act as interpreters for any dealings you might have with the crime police or the traffic police.

TOURIST OFFICES ABROAD
GNTO offices abroad include:

Australia
(☎ 02-9241 1663/4/5) 51 Pitt St,
Sydney NSW 2000
Austria
(☎ 1-512 5317/8) Opernring 8, Vienna
A-10105
Belgium
(☎ 2-647 5770) 172 Ave Louise Louizalaan,
B1050 Brussels
Canada
(☎ 416-968 2220) 1300 Bay St, Toronto,
Ontario M5R 3K8

Denmark
(☎ 3-325 332) Vester Farimagsgade 1, 1606
Copenhagen
France
(☎ 01-42 60 65 75) 3 Ave de l'Opéra, Paris
75001
Germany
Frankfurt: (☎ 69-237 735) Neue Mainzer-
strasse 22, 60311 Frankfurt
Munich: (☎ 89-222 035/6) Pacellistrasse 5,
W 80333 Munich 2
Hamburg: (☎ 40-454 498) Abteistrasse 33,
20149 Hamburg 13
Berlin: (☎ 30-217 6262) Wittenbergplatz 3A,
10789 Berlin 30
Israel
(☎ 23-517 0501) 5 Shalom Aleichem St,
Tel Aviv 61262
Italy
Rome: (☎ 06-474 4249) Via L Bissolati 78-80,
Rome 00187
Milan: (☎ 02-860 470) Piazza Diaz 1, 20123
Milan
Japan
(☎ 03-350 55 911) Fukuda Building West,
5F 2-11-3 Akasaka, Minato-Ku, Tokyo 107
Netherlands
(☎ 020-625 4212/3/4) Leidsestraat 13,
Amsterdam NS 1017
Norway
(☎ 2-426 501) Ovre Slottsgate 15B, 0157 Oslo 1
Sweden
(☎ 8-679 6480) Birger Jarlsgatan 30,
Box 5298 S, 10246 Stockholm
Switzerland
(☎ 01-221 0105) Loewenstrasse 25, CH 8001
Zürich
UK
(☎ 020-7499 4976) 4 Conduit St, London
W1R ODJ
USA
New York: (☎ 212-421 5777) Olympic Tower,
645 5th Ave, New York, NY 10022
Chicago: (☎ 312-782 1084) Suite 600, 168
North Michigan Ave, Chicago, Illinois 60601
Los Angeles: (☎ 213-626 6696) Suite 2198,
611 West 6th St, Los Angeles,
California 92668

TRAVEL AGENCIES

The bulk of the city's travel agencies are around Plateia Syntagmatos, particularly just south of it on Filellinon, Nikis and Voulis. Many of these agencies employ touts to roam the area looking for custom. Give them a miss – these places are responsible for most of the rip-offs described under Travel Agents in the 'Dangers and Annoyances' boxed text later in this chapter.

STA Travel Map 5, D5
Voulis 43, Plaka ☎ 321 1188 fax 321 1194
ⓔ statravel@robissa.gr ⊘ 9.30am-5pm Mon-Fri, 10am-2pm Sat ⓜ Syntagma

USIT-ETOS Travel Map 5, D6
Filellinon 7, Syntagma ☎ 323 0483 fax 322 8447 ⓔ usit@usitetos.gr ⓦ www.usitetos.gr
⊘ 9am-5pm Mon-Fri, 10am-2pm Sat
ⓜ Syntagma

USIT-ETOS Travel Map 3, C7
Patission 53A, Mouseio ☎ 522 2228
ⓔ etosath@usitetos.gr ⓦ www.usitetos.gr
⊘ 9am-5pm Mon-Fri, 10am-2pm Sat
ⓜ Syntagma

Magic Bus Travel Services Map 4, F9
Filellinon 20, Plaka ☎ 323 7471 fax 322 0219
ⓔ magic25@attglobal.net ⓦ www.magic.gr
⊘ 9am-6.30pm Mon-Fri, 10am-2pm Sat
ⓜ Syntagma

DOCUMENTS

PASSPORT

To enter Greece you need a valid passport or, for EU nationals, travel documents (ID cards). You must produce your passport or EU travel documents when you register in a hotel or pension in Greece. You will find that many accommodation proprietors will want to keep your passport during your stay. This is not a compulsory requirement; they need it only long enough to take down the details.

VISAS

The list of countries whose nationals can stay in Greece for up to three months without a visa includes Australia, Canada, all EU countries, Iceland, Israel, Japan, New Zealand, Norway, Switzerland and the USA. Other countries included are Cyprus, Malta, the European principalities of Monaco and San Marino and most South American countries. The list changes – contact Greek embassies for the full list. Those not included can expect to pay about US$20 for a three month visa.

North Cyprus

Greece will refuse entry to people whose passport indicates that, since November 1983, they have visited Turkish-occupied North Cyprus. This can be overcome if, upon entering North Cyprus, you ask the immigration officials to stamp a piece of paper (loose-leaf visa) rather than your passport. If you enter North Cyprus from the Greek Republic of Cyprus (only possible for a day visit), an exit stamp is not put into your passport.

Visa Extensions

If you wish to stay in Greece for longer than three months, apply at a consulate abroad or at least 20 days in advance to the Aliens Bureau at the Athens Central Police Station. Take your passport and four passport photographs along. You may be asked for proof that you can support yourself financially, so keep all your bank exchange slips (or the equivalent from a post office). These slips are not always automatically given – you may have to ask for them.

Elsewhere in Greece apply to the local police authority. You will be given a permit which will authorise you to stay in the country for a period of up to six months.

Most travellers get around this by visiting Bulgaria or Turkey briefly and then re-entering Greece.

Aliens Bureau Map 8, A3
Leoforos Alexandras 173 ☎ 770 5711
⊘ 8am-1pm Mon-Fri

TRAVEL INSURANCE

A travel insurance policy to cover theft, loss and medical problems is essential. The policies handled by STA Travel and other student travel organisations are usually good value. There is a wide variety of policies available; check the small print.

Some policies specifically exclude 'dangerous activities' which can include scuba diving, motorcycling, even trekking. A locally acquired motorcycle licence is not valid under some policies.

You may prefer a policy that pays doctors or hospitals direct rather than you having to pay on the spot and claim later. If you have to claim later make sure you keep all documentation. Some policies ask you to call back (reverse charges) to a centre in your home country where an immediate assessment of your problem is made.

Check that the policy covers ambulances or an emergency flight home.

DRIVING LICENCE & PERMITS

Greece recognises all national driving licences, provided the licence has been held for at least one year. It also recognises an International Driving Permit, which should be obtained before you leave home.

HOSTEL CARDS

A Hostelling International (HI) card is of limited use. The only place you will be able to use it is at the Athens International Youth Hostel.

STUDENT & YOUTH CARDS

The most widely recognised form of student ID is the International Student Identity Card (ISIC), a plastic ID-style card displaying your photograph. These cards are widely available from budget travel agencies. In Athens these are issued by STA Travel and USIT-ETOS Travel (see the Travel Agencies section earlier in this chapter). You'll need to take along proof that you are a student, a passport photo and 3000 dr.

The card qualifies the holder for half-price admission to museums and ancient sites, substantial discounts on tickets for the Athens Festival and discounts at some budget hotels and hostels. Cardholders will find some good deals on international airfares, but there are no student discounts on domestic flights (unless linked to an international flight), and none to be had on buses, ferries or trains.

SENIORS CARDS

See the Senior Travellers section later in this chapter.

COPIES

The hassles created by losing your passport, travellers cheques and other important documents can be reduced considerably if you take the precaution of taking photocopies. It is a good idea to have photocopies of the passport pages that cover personal details, issue and expiry date and the current entry stamp or visa. Other items worth photocopying are airline tickets, credit cards, driving licence and insurance details. You should also keep a record of the serial numbers of your travellers cheques, and cross them off as you cash them.

This emergency material should be kept separate from the originals, so that hopefully they won't both get lost (or stolen) at the same time. Leave an extra copy with someone at home just in case.

There is another option for storing details of your vital travel documents before you leave – Lonely Planet's online Travel Vault.

Lonely Planet online Travel Vault
W www.ekno.lonelyplanet.com
Storing details of your important documents in the vault is safer than carrying photocopies. Your password-protected travel vault is accessible at any time, and is a free service. It's the best option if you travel in a country with easy Internet access.

EMBASSIES & CONSULATES

GREEK EMBASSIES & CONSULATES

The following is a selection of Greek diplomatic missions abroad:

Albania
(☎ 42-34 290/1) Rruga Frederik Shiroka, Tiranë
Australia
(☎ 02-6273 3011) 9 Turrana St, Yarralumla, Canberra ACT 2600
Bulgaria
(☎ 92-946 1027) San Stefano 33, Sofia 1504
Canada
(☎ 613-238 6271) 76-80 Maclaren St, Ottawa, Ontario K2P OK6
Cyprus
(☎ 02-441 880/1) Byron Boulevard 8-10, Lefkosia
Denmark
(☎ 33-11 4533) Borgergade 16, 1300 Copenhagen K
Egypt
(☎ 02-355 1074) 18 Aisha el Taymouria, Garden City, Cairo
France
(☎ 01-47 23 72 28) 17 Rue Auguste Vacquerie, 75116 Paris
Germany
(☎ 228-83010) An Der Marienkapelleb 10, 53 179 Bonn
Ireland
(☎ 01-676 7254) 1 Upper Pembroke St, Dublin 2
Israel
(☎ 03-605 5461) 47 Bodenheimer St, Tel Aviv 62008
Italy
(☎ 06-854 9630) Via S Mercadante 36, Rome 00198

Japan
(☎ 03-340 0871/2) 3-16-30 Nishi Azabu, Minato-ku, Tokyo 106
Netherlands
(☎ 070-363 87 00) Koninginnegracht 37, 2514 AD, The Hague
New Zealand
(☎ 04-473 7775) 5-7 Willeston St, Wellington
Norway
(☎ 22-44 2728) Nobels Gate 45, 0244 Oslo 2
South Africa
(☎ 12-437 351/2) 995, Pretorius Street, Arcadia, Pretoria 0083
Spain
(☎ 01-564 4653) Avenida Doctor Arce 24, Madrid 28002
Sweden
(☎ 08-663 7577) Riddargatan 60, 11457 Stockholm
Switzerland
(☎ 31-951 0814) Postfach, 3000 Berne 6, Kirchenfeld
Turkey
(☎ 312-436 8860) Ziya-ul-Rahman Caddesi 911, Gaziosmanpasa 06700, Ankara
UK
(☎ 020-7229 3850) 1A Holland Park, London W11 3TP
USA
(☎ 202-939 5818) 2221 Massachusetts Ave NW, Washington DC 20008

EMBASSIES & CONSULATES IN GREECE

The following is a selection of foreign diplomatic missions in Athens:

Albania
(☎ 723 4412) Karahristou 1, Ambelokipi
Australia
(Map 8, B4; ☎ 645 0404) Dimitrou Soutsou 37, Ambelokipi
Bulgaria
(☎ 647 8105) Stratigou Kalari 33A, Psyhiko
Canada
(Map 8, F1; ☎ 727 3400) Genadiou 4, Evangelismos
Cyprus
(☎ 723 7883) Irodotou 16, Kolonaki
Czech Republic
(☎ 671 3755, 672 5332) Seferi 6, Psyhiko
Egypt
(Map 4, D10; ☎ 361 8612/3) Vasilissis Sofias 3, Syntagma
France
(Map 6, D1; ☎ 729 7700, 339 1000) Vasilissis Sofias 7, Kolonaki
Germany
(Map 6, D4; ☎ 728 5111) Dimitriou 3, Kolonaki

Hungary
(☎ 672 5337) Kalvou 16, Psyhiko
Ireland
(☎ 723 2771/2/3) Leoforos Vasileos Konstantinou 7, Zappeio
Israel
(☎ 671 9530/1, 672 2183) Marathonodromou 1, Psyhiko
Italy
(Map 6, D2; ☎ 361 7260/3) Sekeri 2
Japan
(☎ 775 8101/2, 723 3732) Leoforos Messogion 2-4, Ambelokipi
Netherlands
(☎ 723 9701/2/3/4, 723 5159) Vasileos Konstantinou 5-7, Zappeio
New Zealand
(☎ 687 4701) Kifissias 268, Halandri
Norway
(☎ 724 6173/4) Vassilissis Sofias 23, Kolonaki
Romania
(☎ 672 8875/6) Emmanuel Benaki 7, Psyhiko
Slovak Republic
(☎ 677 6757) Seferi , Psyhiko
South Africa
(☎ 680 665/6/7) Kifissias 60, Maroussi
Spain
(☎ 921 3123) Dionysiou Aeropagitou 21, Makrigianni
Sweden
(☎ 729 0421) Vasileos Konstantinou 7, Zappeio
Turkey
(☎ 724 5915/6, 721 3659) Vasilissis Georgiou 8, Zappeio
UK
(☎ 727 2600) Ploutarhou 1, Kolonaki
USA
(Map 8, D3; ☎ 721 2951) Vasilissis Sofias 91, Ambelokopi
Yugoslavia
(☎ 777 4355/44) Vasilissis Sofias 106, Ambelokopi

Generally speaking, your own country's embassy won't be much help in emergencies if the trouble you're in is remotely your own fault. Remember that you are bound by Greek laws. Your embassy will not be sympathetic if you end up in jail after committing a crime locally, even if such actions are legal in your own country.

In genuine emergencies you might get some assistance, but only if other channels have been exhausted. For example, if you need to get home urgently, a free ticket home is exceedingly unlikely – the embassy would expect you to have insurance. If you have all your money and documents stolen, it might assist with getting a new passport, but a loan for onward travel is out of the question.

CUSTOMS

There are no longer duty-free restrictions within the EU. This does not mean, however, that customs checks have been dispensed with: random searches are still made for drugs.

Upon entering the country from outside the EU, customs inspection is usually cursory for foreign tourists. There may be spot checks, but you probably won't have to open your bags. A verbal declaration is usually all that is required.

You may bring the following into Greece duty-free from outside the EU: 200 cigarettes or 50 cigars; 1L of spirits or 2L of wine; 50g of perfume; 250mL of eau de Cologne; one camera (still or video) and film; a pair of binoculars; a portable musical instrument; a portable radio or tape recorder; a typewriter; sports equipment; and dogs and cats (with a veterinary certificate).

Importation of works of art and antiquities is free, but they must be declared on entry, so that they can be re-exported. Import regulations for medicines are strict; if you are taking medication, make sure you get a statement from your doctor before you leave home. It is illegal, for instance, to take codeine into Greece without an accompanying doctor's certificate.

An unlimited amount of foreign currency and travellers cheques may be brought into Greece. If, however, you intend to leave the country with foreign banknotes in excess of US$1000, you must declare the sum upon entry.

It is strictly forbidden to export antiquities (anything over 100 years old) without an export permit. This crime is second only to drug smuggling in the penalties imposed. It is an offence to remove even the smallest article from an archaeological site.

The place to apply for an export permit for antiques is the Antique Dealers & Private Collections Section, Archaeological Service, Polygnotou 13, Athens.

VEHICLES

Cars can be brought into Greece for four months without a carnet; only a green card (international third party insurance) is required. Your vehicle will be registered in your passport when you enter Greece in order to prevent you leaving the country without it.

MONEY

CURRENCY

At the time of research, the unit of currency in Greece was still the drachma (dr), although it was due to disappear at the beginning of 2002 when Greece is scheduled to adopt the euro (see the boxed text 'Introduction of the euro'). Until then, the drachma remains in circulation. Coins come in denominations of five, 10, 20, 50 and 100 dr. Banknotes come in 100, 200, 500, 1000, 5000 and 10,000 dr.

EXCHANGE RATES (DRACHMA)

country	unit		drachma (dr)
Albania	100 lekë	=	267.37
Australia	A$1	=	194.51
Bulgaria	1 leva	=	175.40
Canada	C$1	=	247.32
euro	€1	=	340.75
France	1FF	=	51.94
Germany	DM1	=	174.23
Italy	L1000	=	175.99
Japan	¥100	=	313.27
New Zealand	NZ$1	=	155.85
United Kingdom	£1	=	552.80
United States	US$1	=	386.35

EXCHANGE RATES (EURO)

country	unit		euro (€)
Albania	1000 lekë	=	7.84
Australia	A$10	=	5.71
Bulgaria	10 leva	=	5.14
Canada	C$10	=	7.25
France	10FF	=	1.52
Germany	DM10	=	5.11
Greece	1000 dr	=	2.93
Italy	L10,000	=	5.16
Japan	¥1000	=	9.19
New Zealand	NZ$10	=	4.57
United Kingdom	£10	=	16.22
United States	US$10	=	11.34

FACTS FOR THE VISITOR

Warning

It's all but impossible to exchange Turkish lira in Greece.

The only place you can change them is at the head office of the National Bank of Greece, Panepistimiou 36, Athens – and it'll give only about 75% of the going international rate.

EXCHANGING MONEY

Banks will exchange all major currencies in either cash, travellers cheques or Eurocheques. The best-known travellers cheques in Greece are Thomas Cook and American Express. A passport is required to change travellers cheques, but not cash.

Commission charged on the exchange of banknotes and travellers cheques varies not only from bank to bank but from branch to branch. It's less for cash than for travellers cheques. For travellers cheques the commission is 350 dr for up to 20,000 dr; 450 dr for amounts between 20,000 dr and 30,000 dr; and a flat rate of 1.5% on amounts over 30,000 dr.

Post offices can exchange banknotes – but not travellers cheques – and charge less commission than banks. Many travel agencies and hotels will also change money and travellers cheques at bank rates, but their commission charges are higher.

If there is a chance that you may apply for a visa extension, make sure you receive, and keep hold of, a bank exchange slip after each transaction.

Cash

Nothing beats cash for convenience – or for risk. If you lose cash, it's gone for good and very few travel insurers will come to your rescue. Those that will, normally limit the amount to about US$300. It's best to carry no more cash than you need for the next few days, which means working out your likely needs whenever you change travellers cheques or withdraw cash from an ATM.

It's also a good idea to set aside a small amount of cash, say US$50, as an emergency stash.

Introduction of the Euro

Europe will enter a new era in the first two months of 2002. Euro banknotes and coins will be introduced on 1 January, 2002 and will completely replace the local currency of participating countries – Austria, Belgium, Finland, France, Germany, Greece, Ireland, Italy, Luxembourg, the Netherlands, Portugal and Spain – by the end of February, 2002. During the first two months of 2002, participating countries will, on different dates, withdraw the use of their local currency as legal tender.

Travellers need not worry about any unused banknotes or coins as they will be able to be exchanged at central banks for at least two years after the dual currency period (and they could be worth a bit as collectors items in years to come). The European Union has a dedicated euro Web site at europa.eu.int/euro/html/entry.html which will be able to provide you with specific withdrawal dates and any updated information. Greece plans to withdraw the drachma's status as legal tender on 28 February, 2002 but it may pay to check the government's Web site on the euro at www.euro-hellas.gr for updated information.

The euro will have the same value in all member countries of the EU; the €5 note in Finland will be the same €5 note you will use in Germany or France. The official exchange rates for the 12 currencies were set on 1 January 1999; the value of the euro against the dollar and all other currencies – including the four EU members remaining outside the euro zone – will fluctuate according to market conditions.

The banknotes come in denominations ranging from €5 to €500. All bills feature a generic 'European' bridge on one side and a vaguely familiar but unidentifiable 'European' arch on the reverse. Each country will be permitted to design coins with one side bearing a national emblem (the other side will be standard for all euro coins).

Travellers Cheques

The main reason to carry travellers cheques rather than cash is the protection they offer against theft. They are, however, losing popularity as more and more travellers opt

euro currency converter €1 = 340.75 dr

to put their money in a bank at home and withdraw it at ATMs as they go along.

American Express, Visa and Thomas Cook cheques are all widely accepted and have efficient replacement policies. Maintaining a record of the cheque numbers and recording when you use them is vital when it comes to replacing lost cheques – keep this separate from the cheques themselves. US dollars are a good currency to use.

ATMs
ATMs (automatic teller machines) are everywhere in Athens – and certainly in all the tourist areas. If you've got MasterCard or Visa/Access, there are plenty of places to withdraw money. Cirrus and Maestro users can make withdrawals all over town.

Some of the banks around Syntagma also have AFEMs (Automatic Foreign Exchange Machines). They take all the major European currencies, Australian and US dollars and Japanese yen, and are useful in an emergency. Note that they charge a hefty commission, though.

Credit Cards
The great advantage of credit cards is that they allow you to pay for major items without carrying around great wads of cash. Credit cards are now an accepted part of the commercial scene in Greece just about everywhere. They can be used to pay for a wide range of goods and services such as upmarket meals and accommodation, car hire and souvenir shopping.

If you are not familiar with the card options, ask your bank to explain the workings and relative merits of the various schemes: cash cards, charge cards and credit cards. Ask whether the card can be replaced in Greece if it is lost or stolen.

The main credit cards are MasterCard, Visa (Access in the UK) and Eurocard, all of which are widely accepted in Greece. They can also be used as cash cards to draw drachma from the ATMs of affiliated Greek banks in the same way as at home. Daily withdrawal limits are set by the issuing bank. Cash advances are given in local currency only. Credit cards can be used to pay

for accommodation in all the smarter hotels. Some C-class hotels will accept credit cards, but D- and E-class hotels rarely do. Most up-market shops and restaurants accept credit cards.

The main charge cards are American Express and Diners Club Card, which are both widely accepted.

International Transfers
If you run out of money or need more for whatever reason, you can instruct your bank back home to send you a draft. Specify the city and the bank as well as the branch that you want the money sent to. If you have the choice, select a large bank and ask for the international division. Money sent by electronic transfer should reach you within 48 hours.

National Bank of Greece Map 5, B6
Karageorgi Servias 2, Syntagma ☎ 334 0015 ☺ 8am-2pm & 3.30pm-6.30pm Mon-Thur, 8am-1.30pm & 3pm-6.30pm Fri, 9am-3pm & 9am-1pm Sun Ⓜ Syntagma
The Syntagma branch of the National Bank of Greece is open extended hours for foreign exchange.

American Express Map 5, C5
Ermou 7, Syntagma ☎ 322 3380, 324 4979 ☺ 8.30am-5pm Mon-Fri May-Sep, 8.30am-6pm Sat May-Sep, 8.30am-1.30pm Sun May-Sep, 8.30am-4pm Mon-Fri Oct-Apr, 8.30am-1.30pm Sat Oct-Apr Ⓜ Syntagma

Eurochange Map 5, B6
Karageorgi Servias 4, Syntagma ☎ 322 0155 fax 322 8998 ☺ 8am-8pm Mon-Fri, 10am-6pm Sat, Sun Ⓜ Syntagma
Eurochange changes Thomas Cook travellers cheques without commission.

Eurochange Map 4, F9
Filellinon 22, Plaka ☎/fax 324 3997 ☺ 8am-8pm Mon-Fri, 9am-5pm Sat, 10am-5pm Sun Ⓜ Syntagma

Acropole Foreign Exchange Map 4, F8
Kydathineon 23, Plaka ☎ 331 2765 fax 331 2764 ☺ 9am-11pm daily Ⓜ Akropoli
Acropole Foreign Exchange charges a hefty 2.5% commission on travellers cheque exchanges.

SECURITY
The safest way of carrying cash and valuables (passport, travellers cheques, credit cards etc) is a favourite topic of travel conversation. The simple answer is that there is no foolproof method. The general principle

is to keep things out of sight. The front pouch belt, for example, presents an obvious target for a would-be thief – only marginally less inviting than a fat wallet bulging from your back pocket.

The best place is under your clothes in contact with your skin where, hopefully, you will be aware of an alien hand before it's too late. Most people opt for a money belt, while others prefer a leather pouch hung around the neck. Another possibility is to sew a secret stash pocket into the inside of your clothes. Whichever method you choose, put your valuables in a plastic bag first – otherwise they will get soaked in sweat as you wander around in the heat. After a few soakings, they will end up looking like they've been through the washing machine.

COSTS

Athens is a cheap city by northern European standards, and it's possible to get by for as little as 6000 dr a day. This would mean using dormitory accommodation at hostels, staying away from bars and a lot of self-catering. Life would be more of a survival exercise than a holiday.

You'll need to allow at least 15,000 dr per day if you want your own room, albeit at the bottom end of the budget scale, and plan to eat out occasionally as well as seeing the sights. You will still need to do a fair bit of self-catering. If you really want a holiday – comfortable rooms and restaurants all the way – you will need closer to 30,000 dr per day. These budgets are for individuals in high season. Couples sharing a double room can get by on less, much less in low season.

Business visitors will find hotel prices more on a par with world prices. If facilities like business centres and fitness rooms are required, allow close to 200,000 dr per day.

TIPPING & BARGAINING

In restaurants the service charge is included in the bill but it is the custom to leave a small tip. The practice is often just to round off the bill. Likewise for taxis – a small amount is appreciated.

Bargaining is not as widespread in Greece as it is farther east. Prices in most shops are clearly marked and non-negotiable. The same applies to restaurants and public transport. It is always worth bargaining over the price of hotel rooms or *domatia* (the Greek equivalent of the British bed and breakfast, minus the breakfast), especially if you are intending to stay a few days. You may get short shrift in peak season, but prices can drop dramatically in the off season. Souvenir shops and market stalls are other places where your negotiating skills will come in handy. If you feel uncomfortable about haggling, walking away can be just as effective – you can always go back.

POST & COMMUNICATIONS

Post offices *(tahydromio)* are easily identifiable by the yellow signs outside. There are lots of post offices around town. Most are open 7.30am to 2pm Monday to Friday. Regular post boxes are also yellow. The red boxes are for express mail only.

POSTAL RATES

The postal rate for postcards and airmail letters to destinations within the EU is 180 dr for up to 20g and 280 dr for up to 50g. To other destinations the rate is 200 dr up to 20g and 300 dr for up to 50g. Post within Europe takes five to eight days and to the USA, Australia and New Zealand, nine to 11 days. Some tourist shops also sell stamps, but with a 10% surcharge.

Express mail costs an extra 400 dr and should ensure delivery in three days within the EU – use the special red post boxes. Valuables should be sent registered post, which costs an extra 350 dr.

SENDING MAIL

Do not wrap a parcel until it has been inspected at a post office. In Athens, take your parcel to the Parcel Post Office.

Parcel Post Office Map 5, A7
Stadiou 4, Syntagma ☎ 322 8940 ☉ 7.30am-2pm Mon-Fri Ⓜ Syntagma

RECEIVING MAIL

You can receive mail poste restante (general delivery) at any main post office. The service is free of charge, but you are required to show your passport. Ask senders to write your family name in capital letters and underline it, and to mark the envelope 'poste restante'. It is a good idea to ask the post office clerk to check under your first name as well if letters you are expecting cannot be located. After one month, uncollected mail is returned to the sender. If you are about to leave a town and expected mail hasn't arrived, ask at the post office to have it forwarded to your next destination, c/o poste restante.

Parcels are not delivered in Greece; they must be collected from the parcel counter of a post office – or, in Athens, from the Parcel Post Office.

Athens Central Post Office Map 3, G6
Eolou 100, Omonia ☎ 321 6023 ☉ 7.30am-8pm Mon-Fri, 7.30am-2pm Sat, 9am-1pm Sun Ⓜ Omonia
Unless specified otherwise, poste restante will be sent to the Athens Central Post Office, near Plateia Omonias.

Syntagma Post Office Map 5, D6
Plateia Syntagmatos 2, Plaka ☎ 321 5645 ☉ 7.30am-8pm Mon-Fri, 7.30am-2pm Sat, 9am-1pm Sun Ⓜ Syntagma
If you're staying in Plaka, it's far more convenient to get your mail sent poste restante to the large post office nearby.

Mail Boxes Etc Map 5, B5
Leka 14, Syntagma ☎ 324 5060 fax 324 5070 ⓔ mbeathens@interfranchise.gr ☉ 8am-6pm Mon & Wed, 8am-8pm Tues, Thur & Fri, 8am-6pm Wed, 9am-3pm Sat Ⓜ Syntagma
Business communications specialist Mail Boxes Etc hires out private mail boxes (three months 14,000 dr; six months 24,000 dr; one year 40,000 dr).

TELEPHONE

The Greek telephone service is maintained by the public corporation known as Organismos Tilepikoinonion Ellados, which is always referred to by the acronym OTE (pronounced O-tay). The system is modern and efficient. Public telephones all use phonecards, which cost 1000 dr for 100 units, 1900 dr for 200 units, 4200 dr for 500 units, and 8200 dr for 1000 units. The 100-unit cards are widely available at *periptera* (street kiosks), corner shops and tourist shops; the others can be bought at OTE offices.

The phones are easy to operate and can be used for local, long distance and international calls. The 'I' at the top left of the push-button dialling panel brings up the operating instructions in English. Don't remove your card before you are told to do so

FACTS FOR THE VISITOR

Warning: Phone Number Changes

As this book was going to press it was announced that Greece is implementing a new national numbering plan to alleviate a shortage of numbers in the telephone system and to allow users to better understand the call charges. As a result dialling numbers in Greece could be a little problematic during 2001/2002.

The new plan will mean that all numbers will have 10 digits from September 2001. The key features of the scheme are:

- From 20 September 2001, you need to dial the area code for every number, even when calling from within the same geographical area. So, for instance, to call an Athens number from within Athens, you will need to include the area code 01.
- Also from 20 September 2001, all numbers will have a 0 added at the start of the local number (and following the area code). For example, if you were dialling the old Athens number 01-123 4567 after 20 September 2001, you would have to dial 01 0123 4567. The Rhodes number 0241-12 345 will change to 0241 012 345.
- From 20 October 2002, the area code's leading 0 will be replaced with a 2 for fixed phones and with a 6 for mobile phones. So the Athens number 01 0123 4567 will change to 21 0123 4567. The Rhodes number 0241 012 345 changes to 2241 012 345.

The old numbers will work until 20 January 2002; from then until 20 October 2002 callers to old numbers will get a recorded message.

---

or you will wipe out the remaining credit. Local calls cost one unit per minute.

It is possible to use various national card schemes, such as Telstra Australia's Telecard, to make international calls. You will still need a phonecard to dial the scheme's access number, which will cost you one unit, and the time you spend on the phone is also charged at local call rates.

International calls can also be made from OTE offices. A counter clerk directs you to a cubicle equipped with a metered phone, and payment is made afterwards. Reverse charge (collect) calls can be made from an OTE office. The time you have to wait for a connection can vary considerably, from a few minutes to two hours. If you are using a private phone to make a reverse charge call, dial the operator (domestic ☎ 151, international ☎ 161).

To call overseas direct from Greece, dial the Greek overseas access code (☎ 00), followed by the country code for the country you are calling, then the local area code (dropping the leading zero if there is one) and then the number.

Off-peak rates are 25% cheaper. They are available to Africa, Europe, the Middle East and India between 10pm and 6am; to the Americas between 11pm and 8am; and to Asia and Oceania between 8pm and 5am.

To call Greece, the international access code is ☎ 30.

OTE Mouseio branch Map 3, A7
28 Oktovriou-Patission 85, Mouseio
☉ 24 hours daily ⓜ Plateia Viktorias

The table below lists some country codes and per-minute charges:

country	☎ code	cost per minute (dr)
Australia	61	98
France	33	98
Germany	49	98
Ireland	353	98
Italy	39	98
Japan	81	140
Netherlands	31	98
New Zealand	64	230
Turkey	90	120
UK	44	98
USA & Canada	1	98

Some useful telephone numbers include:

general telephone information	☎ 134
numbers in Athens and Attica	☎ 131
numbers elsewhere in Greece	☎ 132
international telephone	☎ 161/2
international telegrams	☎ 165
domestic operator	☎ 151 or 152
domestic telegrams	☎ 155
wake-up service	☎ 182
weather	☎ 149
Attica Weather	☎ 148

eKno Communication Service

Lonely Planet's eKno global communication service provides low-cost international calls – for local calls you're usually better off with a local phonecard. eKno also offers free messaging services, email, travel information and an online travel vault, where you can securely store all your important documents.

You can join online at www.ekno.lonelyplanet.com, where you will find the local-access numbers for the 24-hour customer-service centre. Once you have joined, always check the eKno Web site for the latest access numbers for each country and updates on new features.

MOBILE PHONES

Few countries in the world have embraced the mobile phone with as much enthusiasm as Greece. The mobile phone has become the essential Greek accessory: everyone seems to have one.

Unfortunately for foreigners coming to Greece, obtaining a mobile phone is lengthy process strewn with bureaucratic obstacles. You can't just go to one of the many shops that sell mobile phones, buy one and start making calls. In order to buy a phone, you will need to show a Greek ID card as proof of residency status.

You will then need to reprogram the phone from Greek into English, and to obtain a phone number you will need to quote a Greek tax file number.

You can get around these problems by renting a mobile phone for the duration of your trip. Greek Travel Phones (☎ 322 4932, fax 324 9104, blakjohn@athena.compulink.gr),

Voulis 31-33, Plaka, operates a buy-back scheme. It charges 57,000 dr, and your phone will be handed over fully charged, programmed in English and ready to use. You can sell the phone back (for 19,000 dr) at the end of your stay, or just hang on to it until your next trip. Greek Travel Phones operates from the same shop as Acropolis Rugs.

FAX & TELEGRAPH

Most post offices have fax machines; telegrams can be sent from any OTE office. Mail Boxes Etc (see under 'Receiving Mail' earlier in this chapter for contact details) offers better prices and service for sending faxes than do the post offices.

EMAIL & INTERNET ACCESS

Travelling with a portable computer is a great way to stay in touch with life back home, but unless you know what you're doing it's fraught with potential problems.

If you plan to carry your notebook or palmtop computer with you, it's a good idea to invest in a universal AC adaptor, which will enable you to plug it in anywhere without fear of frying the innards. You'll also need a two-pin plug adaptor – best bought before you leave home.

Also, your PC-card modem may or may not work once you leave your home country – and you won't know for sure until you try. The safest option is to buy a reputable 'global' modem before you leave home, or to buy a local PC-card modem if you're spending an extended time in Athens.

It also pays to have a US RJ-11 telephone adaptor that works with your modem. You can almost always find an adaptor that will convert from RJ-11 to the local variety. For more information on travelling with a portable computer, see www.teleadapt.com or www.warrior.com.

If you intend to rely on cybercafes to access your mail, a good option is to open a free eKno Web-based email account online at www.ekno.lonelyplanet.com. You can then access your mail from anywhere in the world from any net-connected machine running a standard Web browser.

Internet cafes are popping up like mushrooms all over Athens. Most charge from 1000 dr to 1500 dr per hour of computer time, whether you're on the Net or not.

Astor Internet Café Map 3, E6
28 Oktovriou-Patission 27, Omonia
☎ mobile 093-283 6298 ⓦ www.astorcafe.gr
⊙ 10am-10pm daily ⓜ Omonia ▨ 7

Bits and Bytes Internet Café Map 3, F8
Akadimias 78, Exarhia ☎ 382 2545/6
ⓦ www.b-and-b.gr ⊙ 9am-midnight daily
ⓜ Omonia

Cafe4U Map 3, G10
Ippokratous 44, Exarhia ☎/fax 361 1981
ⓔ cafe4U@mail.com ⊙ 24 hours daily
ⓜ Panepistimiou

Enydreion Net Café Map 7, B5
Syngrou 13, Makrigianni ☎ 921 2396
⊙ 7am-midnight Mon-Sat ⓜ Akropoli

Ivis Internet Services Map 5, D6
Mitropoleos 3, Syntagma ☎ 324 3365 fax 322 4205 ⓔ ivis@travelling.gr ⊙ 9am-midnight daily
ⓜ Syntagma

Museum Internet Café Map 3, C7
28 Oktovriou-Patission 46, Mouseio ☎ 883 3418 ⓔ musem_netcafe@yahoo.com
ⓦ www.museumcafe.gr ⊙ 9am-3am daily ▨ 5

Plaka Internet World Map 5, C1
Pandrosou 29, Plaka ☎ 331 6056 ⓔ plakaworld @internet.gr ⊙ 11am-11pm daily ⓜ Monastiraki

Skynet Internet Centre Map 5, D5
Apollonos 10, Syntagma ☎ 322 7551 fax 960 5228 ⓔ info@skynet.gr ⓦ www.skynet.gr
⊙ 9am-11pm Mon-Sat ⓜ Syntagma

Sofokleous.com Internet Café Map 5, B6
Stadiou 5, Syntagma ☎/fax 324 8105
ⓔ sofos1@ath.forthnet.gr, sofos1@telehouse.gr
ⓦ www.sofokleous.com ⊙ 10am-10pm Mon-Sat, 1pm-9pm Sun ⓜ Syntagma

The Web Café Map 3, E7
George 10, Omonia ☎ 330 3063 ⓦ www .web-cafe.gr ⊙ 10am-2am daily ⓜ Omonia

INTERNET RESOURCES

The World Wide Web is a rich resource for travellers. You can research your trip, hunt down bargain air fares, book hotels, check on weather conditions or chat with locals and other travellers about the best places to visit (or avoid!).

Lonely Planet Web site
ⓦ www.lonelyplanet.com
There's no better place to start your Web explorations than the Lonely Planet Web site.

Here you'll find succinct summaries on travelling to most places on earth, postcards from other travellers and the Thorn Tree bulletin board, where you can ask questions before you go or dispense advice when you get back. You can also find travel news and updates to many of our most popular guidebooks, and the subWWWay section links you to the most useful travel resources elsewhere on the Web.

500 Links to Greece Web site
W www.viking1.com/corfu/link.htm
Predictably enough, there has recently been a huge increase in the number of Web sites providing information about Greece. A good place to start is the 500 Links to Greece site. It has links to a huge range of sites on everything from accommodation to Zeus.

Greek Ministry of Culture
W www.culture.gr
The Greek Ministry of Culture has put together an excellent site with loads of information about museums and ancient sites.

BOOKS

Most books are published in different editions by different publishers in different countries. As a result, a book might be a hardcover rarity in one country while it's readily available in paperback in another. Fortunately, bookshops and libraries search by title or author, so your local bookshop or library is best placed to advise you on the availability of the following recommendations.

LONELY PLANET
The Lonely Planet guides to *Mediterranean Europe* and *Western Europe* also include coverage of Greece, as does *Europe on a shoestring*. The country guide *Greece* and regional titles *Greek Islands, Corfu & the Ionian Islands, Crete, Rhodes & the Dodecanese* and *Crete Condensed* will help you with further travels around Greece. The handy *Greek phrasebook* will help enrich your visit.

These titles are available at all the major English-language bookshops in Athens. See the Bookshop entries in the Shopping chapter.

GUIDEBOOKS
The ancient Greek traveller Pausanias is acclaimed as the world's first travel writer. *The Guide to Greece* was written in the 2nd century AD. Umpteen editions later, it is now available in English in paperback. Athens is covered in some detail in *Volume 1: Central Greece*. For archaeology buffs, the *Blue Guides* are hard to beat. They go into tremendous detail about all the major sites, and many of the lesser-known ones.

TRAVEL
Many famous people have written about their experiences in Greece. Unfortunately few of them spent much time in Athens, and very few books about Greece feature Athens.

One writer who did opt to spend time in Athens was Henry Miller, who visited in 1938 with war clouds gathering over Europe. He recounts his adventures in *The Colossus of Maroussi*, starting with a rip-off taxi ride from Piraeus. Miller waxed lyrical about the extraordinary quality of the city's light and rhythm, and spent his time getting 'blasted' on retsina with an assortment of interesting characters.

Lawrence Durrell, who spent an idyllic childhood on Corfu, is the best known of the 20th-century philhellenes. His evocative books *Prospero's Cell* and *Reflections on a Marine Venus* are about Corfu and Rhodes respectively. His coffee-table book *The Greek Islands* is one of the most popular books of its kind.

PEOPLE & SOCIETY
Of the numerous festivals held in Greece, one of the most bizarre and overtly pagan is the carnival held on the island of Skyros, described in *The Goat Dancers of Skyros* by Joy Coulentianou.

The Cyclades, or Life Amongst the Insular Greeks by James Theodore Bent (first published 1885) is still the greatest English-language book about the Greek Islands. It relates the experiences of the author and his wife while travelling around the Cyclades in the late 19th century. The book is now out of print, but the Hellenic Book Service may have a second-hand copy.

Time, Religion & Social Experience in Rural Greece by Laurie Kain Hart is a fascinating account of village traditions –

many of which are alive and well beneath the tourist veneer.

Portrait of a Greek Mountain Village by Juliet du Boulay is in a similar vein, based on her experiences in an isolated village.

A Traveller's Journey is Done and *An Affair of the Heart* by Dilys Powell, wife of archaeologist Humfry Payne, are very readable, affectionate insights into Peloponnese village life during the 1920s and 1930s.

Road to Rembetica: Music of a Greek Subculture – Songs of Love, Sorrow and Hashish by Gail Holst explores the intriguing subculture which emerged from the poverty and suffering of the refugees from Asia Minor.

Another book which will whet your appetite for a holiday in Greece is *Hellas: A Portrait of Greece* by Nicholas Gage.

HISTORY & MYTHOLOGY

A Traveller's History of Greece by Timothy Boatswain & Colin Nicholson is a good one-volume guide to the country's historical background from Neolithic times to the present day. *Modern Greece: A Short History* by CM Woodhouse is in a similar vein, although it has a right-wing bent. It covers the period from Constantine the Great to 1990.

Mythology was an intrinsic part of life in ancient Greece, and some knowledge of it will enhance your visit. One of the best publications on the subject is *The Greek Myths* by Robert Graves (two volumes) which relates and interprets the adventures of the main gods and heroes worshipped by the ancient Greeks. Maureen O'Sullivan's *An Iconoclast's Guide to the Greek Gods* presents entertaining and accessible versions of the myths.

There are many translations around of Homer's *Iliad* and *Odyssey*, which tell the story of the Trojan War and the subsequent adventures of Odysseus (known as Ulysses in Latin). The translations by EV Rien are among the best.

Women in Athenian Law and Life by Roger Just is the first in-depth study of the role of women in ancient Greece.

The Jaguar by Alexander Kotzias is a moving story about the leftist resistance to the Nazi occupation of Greece. Although a novel, it is packed with historical facts. *Greek Women in Resistance* by Eleni Fountouri is a compilation of journals, poems and personal accounts of women in the resistance movement from the 1940s to the 1950s. The book also contains poignant photographs and drawings.

Eleni by Nicholas Gage is an account by the author of his family's struggle to survive the horrors of WWII, the civil war, and his mother's death at the hands of the communists. It was made into a film in 1985.

The third volume of Olivia Manning's Balkan trilogy, *Friends & Heroes*, has Greece as its setting. It is a riveting account of the chaos and confusion among the emigre community fleeing the Nazi invasion of Europe. In another classic, *The Flight of Ikaros*, Kevin Andrews relates his travels in Greece during the 1940s civil war. *Greece in the Dark* by the same author tells of his life in Greece during the junta years.

POETRY

Sappho: A New Translation by Mary Bernard is the best translation of this great ancient poet's works.

Collected Poems by George Seferis, *Selected Poems* by Odysseus Elytis and *Collected Poems* by Constantine Cavafy are all excellent translations of Greece's greatest modern poets.

NOVELS

The most well-known and widely read Greek author is the Cretan writer Nikos Kazantzakis, whose novels are full of drama and larger-than-life characters. His most famous works are *The Last Temptation*, *Zorba the Greek*, *Christ Recrucified* and *Freedom or Death*. The first two have been made into films.

Athenian writer Apostolis Doxiadis has charmed critics the world over with his latest novel, *Uncle Petros and Goldbach's Conjecture*. It's an unlikely blend of family drama and mathematical theory, woven together to create a compelling read. You don't need to be a mathematical genius to enjoy the book, but if you are and you can prove the conjecture – that every even number greater than two is the product of two prime numbers – you could be in line to collect a prize of US$1 million offered by the publishers. It won't be easy. The problem of proof has defied the world's finest mathematical minds for more than 250 years, so there's every chance you'll pick up a bonus Nobel Prize as well!

English writer Louis de Berniéres has become almost a cult figure following the success of *Captain Corelli's Mandolin*, which tells the emotional story of a young Italian army officer sent to the island of Kefallonia during WWII.

The Australian journalists George Johnston and Charmian Clift wrote several books with Greek themes during their 19 years as expatriates, including Johnston's novel *The Sponge Divers*, set on Kalymnos, and Clift's autobiographical *A Mermaid Singing*, which is about their experiences on Hydra.

Australian writer Gillian Bouras writes of living in Greece in *A Foreign Wife* and *Aphrodite and the Others*. Fellow Australian Beverley Farmer has two collections of beautifully written short stories, *Home Time* and *Milk*, many of which are about foreigners endeavouring to make their home in Greece.

Dinner with Persephone by Patricia Storace has been well-reviewed and is of particular interest to women.

MUSEUM GUIDES

Museums and Galleries of Greece and Cyprus by Maria Kontou, of the Greek Ministry of Culture, lists 165 museums in Greek and English with about 1000 photographs to illustrate exhibits that relate to visual arts, natural history, navigation, science, technology and the theatre.

CHILDREN'S BOOKS

The Greek publisher Malliaris-Paedia puts out a good series of books on the myths, retold in English for young readers by Aristides Kesopoulos. The titles are *The Gods of Olympus and the Lesser Gods*, *The Labours of Hercules*, *Theseus and the Voyage of the Argonauts*, *The Trojan War and the Wanderings of Odysseus* and *Heroes and Mythical Creatures*. Robin Lister's retelling of *The Odyssey* is aimed at slightly older readers (ages 10 to 12), but makes compelling listening for younger ones when read aloud.

FILMS

Greece is nothing if not photogenic, and countless films have made the most of the country's range of superb locations. The islands do, of course, figure prominently. Mykonos was the setting for the smash hit *Shirley Valentine*, featuring Pauline Collins in the title role and Tom Conti as her Greek toy boy. *Mediterraneo* (1991) is an Italian movie that achieved cult status worldwide. It was set on Kastellorizo.

James Bond came to Greece too, and *For Your Eyes Only* features some dramatic shots of Roger Moore doing his 007 impersonation around the monasteries of Meteora. Moni Agias Triados features prominently.

NEWSPAPERS & MAGAZINES

Greeks are great newspaper readers. There are 15 daily newspapers, of which the most widely read are *Ta Nea*, *Kathimerini* and *Eleftheros Typos*.

The main English-language newspapers are the daily (except Monday) *Athens News* (250 dr) which carries Greek and international news, and the weekly *Hellenic Times* (300 dr), with predominantly Greek news. In addition to these, the Athens edition of the *International Herald Tribune* (350 dr) includes an eight page English-language edition of the Greek daily *Kathimerini*. All are widely available in Athens and at major resorts. You'll find the *Athens News* electronic edition, archived from 1995 onwards, on the Web at athensnews.dolnet.gr.

Atlantis (1000 dr) is a glossy monthly magazine with articles on politics, travel and the arts.

Foreign newspapers are also widely available, although only between April and October in smaller resort areas. You'll find all the British and other major European dailies, as well as international magazines such as *Time*, *Newsweek* and the *Economist*.

Athens' transport future acknowledges the past at Syntagma's metro station.

The fever has begun. The Olympics are on their way home to Athens.

Now if we can only work out why there's so much damn pollution – Plateia Syntagmatos.

Cats rule the roost in Plaka.

Athena looks over Socrates' shoulder outside the Athens Academy.

For all of your sponging needs head straight for Plaka.

Men gathered around a periptera reading the headlines

Old Metropolitan Church

The papers reach Athens (Syntagma) at 3pm on the day of publication on weekdays, and at 7pm on weekends. They are not available until the following day in other areas.

RADIO & TV

Greece has two state-owned radio channels, ET 1 and ET 2. ET 1 runs three programs; two are devoted to popular music and news, while the third plays mostly classical music. It has a news update in English at 7.30am from Monday to Saturday, and at 9pm from Monday to Friday. It can be heard on 91.6 MHz and 105.8 MHz on the FM band, and 729 KHz on the AM band. ET 2 broadcasts mainly popular music. Local radio stations are proliferating at such a rate that the mountains around Athens have begun to look like pincushions. Western music can be heard on Radio Gold (105 FM), which plays mainly '60s music, Kiss FM (90.9 FM), which plays a mix of rock and techno, and Nitro (108.2 FM), which plays alternative rock.

The best short-wave frequencies for picking up the BBC World Service are:

GMT	frequency
3am-7.30am	9.41 MHz (31m band)
	6.18 MHz (49m band)
	15.07 MHz (19m band)
7.30am-6pm	12.09 MHz (25m band)
	15.07 MHz (19m band)
6.30pm-11.15pm	12.09 MHz (25m band)
	9.41 MHz (31m band)
	6.18 MHz (49m band)

As far as Greek TV is concerned, quantity rather than quality is the operative word. There are nine TV channels and various pay-TV channels. All the channels show English and US films and soapies with Greek subtitles. A bit of channel-swapping will normally turn up something in English.

VIDEO SYSTEMS

If you want to record or buy video tapes to play back home, you won't get a picture unless the image registration systems are the same. Greece uses PAL, which is incompatible with the North American and Japanese NTSC system. Australia and most of Europe uses PAL.

PHOTOGRAPHY & VIDEO

FILM & EQUIPMENT

Major brands of film are widely available in Athens, expect to pay about 1500 dr for a 36-exposure roll of Kodak Gold ASA 100; less for other brands.

As elsewhere in the world, developing film is a competitive business. Most places charge around 2500 dr to develop and print a roll of 36 colour prints.

Fuji Film Photo Express Map 5, D6
Nikis 18, Syntagma ☎ 323 7445 ⏱ 8am-8pm Mon-Fri, 8am-4pm Sat Ⓜ Syntagma
This outlet stocks and processes all major brands of film (Kodak Gold ASA 100 36 for 1300 dr, 8mm video cassettes 2000 dr for one hour, digital cassettes 5000 dr for one hour), and sells accessories.

TECHNICAL TIPS

Because of the brilliant sunlight in summer, you'll get better results using a polarising lens filter.

VIDEO

Properly used, a video camera can give a fascinating record of your holiday. As well as videoing the obvious things – sunsets, spectacular views – remember to record some of the ordinary everyday details of life in the country. Often the most interesting things occur when you're actually intent on filming something else. Remember too that, unlike still photography, video 'flows' so, for example, you can shoot scenes of countryside rolling past the train window, to give an overall impression that isn't possible with ordinary photos.

Video cameras these days have amazingly sensitive microphones, and you might be surprised how much sound will be picked up. This can also be a problem if there is a lot of ambient noise – filming by the side of a busy road might seem OK when you do it, but viewing it back home might simply give you a deafening cacophony of traffic noise. One good rule to follow for beginners is to try to film in long takes, and don't move the camera around too much. Otherwise, your video could well make your viewers seasick! If your camera has a stabiliser, you can use it to obtain good footage while travelling on various means of transport, even on bumpy roads. And remember, you're on holiday – don't let the video take over your life, and turn your trip into a Cecil B de Mille production.

Make sure you keep the camera's batteries charged, and have the necessary charger, plugs and transformer.

RESTRICTIONS & ETIQUETTE
Never photograph a military installation or anything else that has a sign forbidding photography. Flash photography is not allowed inside churches, and it's considered taboo to photograph the main altar.

Greeks usually love having their photos taken but you should always ask permission first. The same goes for video cameras, probably even more annoying and offensive for locals than a still camera.

TIME
Greece is two hours ahead of GMT/UTC and three hours ahead on daylight-saving time, which begins on the last Sunday in March, when clocks are put forward one hour. Daylight saving ends on the last Sunday in September.

So, when it is noon in Athens it is also noon in İstanbul, 10am in London, 11am in Rome, 2am in San Francisco, 5am in New York and Toronto, 8pm in Sydney and 10pm in Auckland.

ELECTRICITY
Electricity is 220V, 50 Hz. Plugs are the standard continental type with two round pins. All hotel rooms have power points and most camping grounds have supply points.

WEIGHTS & MEASURES
Greece uses the metric system. Liquids – especially barrel wine – are often sold by weight rather than volume: 959g of wine, for example, is equivalent to 1000mL.

Remember that, like other continental Europeans, Greeks indicate decimals with commas and thousands with points.

LAUNDRY
Laundrettes are something of a rarity in Athens, with just three in the city centre. Both call themselves self-service laundrettes, which is strange because both employ attendants who do all the work – washing, drying and folding. You just hand over your washing, and return a couple of hours later to collect it. You can insist on doing it yourself, but you'll pay the same. A typical charge would be 2500 dr for wash and dry of 5kg of clothing.

Dry-cleaning shops are much more common. Your hotel reception will be able to direct you to the local shop. Typical charges are 2000 dr for a jacket and 1500 dr for a pair of trousers or skirt.

The bigger hotels have house laundry and dry-cleaning services.

Plaka Laundrette Map 4, G8
Angelou Geronta 10, Plaka ☉ 8am-5pm
Mon-Sat, 9am-2pm Sun ⓜ Akropoli

Laundry Self Service Map 3, E3
Psaron 9, Omonia ☎ 522 2856 ☉ 8am-8pm
Mon-Fri, 10am-5pm Sat, 8am-2pm Sun
ⓜ Metaxourghio

Sun Laundry Map 3, G2
Kolokinthous 41, Omonia ☎ 522 6233
☉ 8am- 8pm Mon-Fri, 10am-5pm Sat,
8am-2pm Sun ⓜ Metaxourghio

TOILETS
Most places in Greece have Western-style toilets, especially hotels and restaurants which cater for tourists. You'll occasionally come across Asian-style squat toilets in older houses, kafeneia and public toilets.

Public toilets are a rarity in Athens – except at airports, and bus and train stations. Those that do exist are so primitive that they are best avoided except in an absolute emergency. Fortunately there are fast-food outlets everywhere in Central Athens: very handy in an emergency. Failing that, head to a cafe, although you'll be expected to buy something for the privilege of using the facilities.

WARNING
A peculiarity of the Greek plumbing system is that it can't handle toilet paper; apparently the pipes are too narrow. Whatever

the reason, anything larger than a postage stamp seems to cause a problem; flushing away tampons and sanitary napkins is guaranteed to block the system. Toilet paper and other items should be placed in the small bin provided in every toilet.

LEFT LUGGAGE

Many of Athens' hotels will store luggage free for guests, although a lot of them do no more than pile the bags in a hallway. There are also left luggage facilities at the airport and Larisis train station.

HEALTH

PREDEPARTURE PLANNING

Travel health depends on your predeparture preparations, your day-to-day health care while travelling and how you handle any medical problem or emergency that does develop. While the list of potential dangers can seem quite frightening, few travellers experience more than upset stomachs.

Health Insurance

See Travel Insurance under Documents earlier in this chapter for information.

Warning

Codeine, which is commonly found in headache preparations, is banned in Greece;

> ### Everyday Health
>
> Normal body temperature is up to 37°C (98.6°F); more than 2°C (4°F) higher indicates a high fever. The normal adult pulse rate is 60 to 100 per minute (children 80 to 100, babies 100 to 140). As a general rule the pulse increases about 20 beats per minute for each 1°C (2°F) rise in fever.
>
> Respiration (breathing) rate is also an indicator of illness. Count the number of breaths per minute: Between 12 and 20 is normal for adults and older children (up to 30 for younger children, 40 for babies). People with a high fever or serious respiratory illness breathe more quickly than normal. More than 40 shallow breaths a minute may indicate pneumonia.

---

check labels carefully, or risk prosecution. There are strict regulations applying to the importation of medicines into Greece, so obtain a certificate from your doctor which outlines any medication you may have to carry into the country with you.

Health Preparations

Make sure you're healthy before you start travelling. If you are embarking on a long trip make sure your teeth are OK.

If you wear glasses, take a spare pair and your prescription.

If you require a particular medication take an adequate supply, as it may not be available locally. Take the prescription or, better still, part of the packaging showing the generic rather than the brand name (which may not be locally available), as it will make getting replacements easier.

Immunisations

No jabs are required for travel to Greece but a yellow fever vaccination certificate is required if you are coming from an infected area. There are, however, a few routine vaccinations that are recommended. These should be recorded on an international health certificate, available from your doctor or government health department. Don't leave your vaccinations until the last minute as some require more than one injection. Recommended vaccinations include:

Tetanus & Diphtheria Boosters are needed every 10 years and protection is highly recommended.
Polio A booster of either the oral or injected vaccine is required every 10 years to maintain immunity after childhood vaccination. Polio is still prevalent in many developing countries.
Hepatitis A The most common travel-acquired illness that can be prevented by vaccination. Protection can be provided in two ways – either with the antibody gamma globulin or with the vaccine Havrix 1440. Havrix 1440 provides long-term immunity (possibly more than 10 years) after an initial injection and a booster at six to 12 months. Gamma globulin is a ready-made antibody, which should be given as close as possible to departure because it is at its most effective in the first few weeks after administration; the effectiveness tapers off gradually between three and six months.

BASIC RULES

Care in what you eat and drink is the most important health rule; stomach upsets are the

Medical Kit Check List

Following is a list of items you should consider including in your medical kit – consult your pharmacist for brands available in your country.

- ☐ **Aspirin or paracetamol (acetaminophen in the USA)** – for pain or fever
- ☐ **Antihistamine** – for allergies, eg, hay fever; to ease the itch from insect bites or stings; and to prevent motion sickness
- ☐ **Cold and flu tablets, throat lozenges and nasal decongestant**
- ☐ **Multivitamins** – consider for long trips, when dietary vitamin intake may be inadequate
- ☐ **Antibiotics** – consider including these if you're travelling well off the beaten track; see your doctor, as they must be prescribed, and carry the prescription with you
- ☐ **Loperamide or diphenoxylate** –'blockers' for diarrhoea
- ☐ **Prochlorperazine or metaclopramide** – for nausea and vomiting
- ☐ **Rehydration mixture** – to prevent dehydration, which may occur, for example, during bouts of diarrhoea; particularly important when travelling with children
- ☐ **Insect repellent, sunscreen, lip balm and eye drops**
- ☐ **Calamine lotion, sting relief spray or aloe vera** – to ease irritation from sunburn and insect bites or stings
- ☐ **Antifungal cream or powder** – for fungal skin infections and thrush
- ☐ **Antiseptic (such as povidone-iodine)** – for cuts and grazes
- ☐ **Bandages, Band-Aids (plasters) and other wound dressings**
- ☐ **Water purification tablets or iodine**
- ☐ **Scissors, tweezers and a thermometer** – note that mercury thermometers are prohibited by airlines

most likely travel health problem (between 30% and 50% of travellers in a two-week stay experience this) but the majority of these upsets will be relatively minor. Don't become paranoid; trying the local food is part of the experience of travel, after all.

Avoid climatic extremes: keep out of the sun when it's hot, dress warmly when it's cold. You can avoid insect bites by covering bare skin when insects are around, by screening windows or beds and by using insect repellents.

Food & Water

The tap water is safe to drink in Athens, although it doesn't taste fantastic. Mineral water is widely available if you prefer it. You might experience mild intestinal problems if you're not used to copious amounts of olive oil; however, you'll get used to it and current research says it's good for you.

If you don't vary your diet, are travelling hard and fast and missing meals, or simply lose your appetite, you can soon start to lose weight and place your health at risk. Fruit and vegetables are good sources of vitamins and these than almost any other European country. Eat plenty of grains (including rice) and bread. If your diet isn't well-balanced or if your food intake is insufficient, it's a good idea to take vitamin and iron pills.

In hot weather make sure you drink enough – don't rely on feeling thirsty to indicate when you should drink. Not needing to urinate or very dark yellow urine is a danger sign. Always carry a water bottle with you on long trips. Excessive sweating can lead to loss of salt and therefore muscle cramping. Salt tablets are not a good idea as a preventative, but in places where salt is not used much adding salt to food can help.

ENVIRONMENTAL HAZARDS
Sunburn

By far the biggest health risk in Greece comes from the intensity of the sun. You can get sunburnt surprisingly quickly, even through cloud. Use a sunscreen and take extra care to cover areas which don't normally see sun. A hat helps, as does zinc cream or some other barrier cream for your nose and lips. Calamine lotion is good for mild sunburn. Greeks claim that yogurt applied to sunburn is soothing. Protect your eyes with good-quality sunglasses.

Nutrition

If your diet is poor or limited in variety, if you're travelling hard and fast and therefore missing meals or if you simply lose your appetite, you can soon start to lose weight and place your health at risk.

Make sure your diet is well balanced. Cooked eggs, tofu, beans, lentils (dhal in India) and nuts are all safe ways to get protein. Fruit you can peel (bananas, oranges or mandarins, for example) is usually safe and a good source of vitamins. Melons can harbour bacteria in their flesh and are best avoided. Try to eat plenty of grains (including rice) and bread. Remember that although food is generally safer if it is cooked well, overcooked food loses much of its nutritional value. If your diet isn't well balanced or if your food intake is insufficient, it's a good idea to take vitamin and iron pills.

In hot climates make sure you drink enough – don't rely on feeling thirsty to indicate when you should drink. Not needing to urinate or voiding small amounts of very dark yellow urine is a danger sign. Always carry a water bottle with you on long trips. Excessive sweating can lead to loss of salt and therefore muscle cramping. Salt tablets are not a good idea as a preventative, but in places where salt is not used much, adding salt to food can help.

Prickly Heat

Prickly Heat is an itchy rash caused by excessive perspiration trapped under the skin. Keeping cool, bathing often, drying the skin and using a mild talcum powder, or resorting to air-conditioning even, may help until you acclimatise.

Heat Exhaustion

Dehydration or salt deficiency can cause heat exhaustion. Take time to acclimatise to high temperatures, and drink sufficient liquids. Wear loose clothing and a broad-brimmed hat. Avoid activities that are too physically demanding.

Salt deficiency is characterised by fatigue, lethargy, headaches, giddiness and muscle cramps and in this case salt tablets may help. Vomiting or diarrhoea can deplete your liquid and salt levels.

Heat Stroke

This serious, sometimes fatal, condition can occur if the body's heat-regulating mechanism breaks down and the body temperature rises to dangerous levels. Long, continuous periods of exposure to high temperatures can leave you vulnerable to heat stroke. You should avoid excessive alcohol consumption or strenuous activity when you first arrive in a hot climate.

The symptoms are feeling unwell, not sweating very much or at all and a high body temperature (39 to 41°C or 102 to 106°F). Where sweating has ceased the skin becomes flushed and red.

Severe, throbbing headaches and lack of coordination will also occur, and the sufferer may be confused or aggressive. Eventually the victim will become delirious or convulse.

Hospitalisation is essential, but in the interim get victims out of the sun, remove their clothing, cover them with a wet sheet or towel and then fan continually. Give fluids, if they are conscious.

Fungal Infections

Fungal infections, which are more frequent in hot weather, are most likely to occur on the scalp, between the toes (athlete's foot) or fingers, in the groin and on the body (ringworm).

You can get ringworm (a fungal infection, not a worm) from infected animals or by walking on damp areas like shower floors.

To prevent fungal infections wear loose, comfortable clothes, avoid artificial fibres, wash frequently and dry carefully. If you do get an infection, wash the infected area daily with a disinfectant or medicated soap and water, and dry well.

Apply an antifungal cream or powder (tolnaftate). Expose the infected area to air or sunlight as much as possible and wash all

Dangers & Annoyances

Athens is a big city, and it has its fair share of the problems found in all major cities. Fortunately, violent street crime remains very rare, but travellers should be alert to the following traps:

Pickpockets

Pickpockets have become a major problem in Athens. Their favourite hunting grounds are the metro system and the crowded streets around Omonia, particularly Athinas. The Sunday market on Ermou is another place where it pays to take extra care of your valuables. There have been numerous reports of thefts from day-packs and bags.

Taxi Drivers

Many Athens residents will tell you that their taxi drivers are the biggest bunch of bastards in the world. It seems that they have as much trouble getting a fair deal as tourists do.

Most (but not all) rip-off stories involve cabs picked up late at night from the taxi ranks at the city's main arrival and departure points: the airport, the train stations, the two bus terminals – particularly Terminal A at Kifissou, and the port of Piraeus.

The trouble is that the cabbies who work these ranks don't like to bother with the meter, especially after midnight when most public transport stops. They prefer to demand whatever they think they can get away with. If you insist on using the meter, many will simply refuse to take you. You can either negotiate a set fare, or attempt to find a taxi elsewhere.

Every now and again, the police conduct well publicised clamp-downs. One such purge turned up an airport cabby who was well prepared for tourists who want to see the meter working – he was equipped with a handy remote-controlled device that could make the meter spin round at 2000 dr per minute!

A more common trick is to set the meter on night rate (tariff 2) during the day. Between 6am and midnight the day rate (tariff 1) should be charged. If there is a dispute over the fare, take the driver's number and report them to the tourist police.

towels and underwear in hot water as well as changing them often.

Motion Sickness

Sea sickness can be a problem. The Aegean is very unpredictable and gets very rough when the *meltemi* wind blows. If you are prone to motion sickness, eat lightly before and during a trip, and try to find a place that minimises disturbance – near the wing on aircraft, close to midships on boats, near the centre on buses.

Fresh air usually helps; reading and cigarette smoke don't. Commercial motion-

Dangers & Annoyances

Taxi Touts

Taxi drivers working in league with some of the overpriced C-class hotels around Omonia are another problem. The scam involves taxi drivers picking up late night arrivals, particularly at the airport and Bus Terminal A, and persuading them that the hotel they want to go to is full – even if they have a booking. The taxi driver will pretend to phone the hotel of your choice, announce that it's full and suggest an alternative. You can ask to speak to your chosen hotel yourself, or simply insist on going where you want.

Taxi drivers frequently attempt to claim commissions from hotel owners even if they have just gone where they were told. If the taxi driver comes into the hotel, make it clear to hotel staff that there is no reason to pay a commission.

Bar Scams

Lonely Planet continues to hear from readers who have been taken in by one of the various bar scams that operate around central Athens, particularly around Syntagma.

The basic scam runs something like this: friendly Greek approaches solo male traveller and discovers that the traveller knows little about Athens; friendly Greek then reveals that he, too, is from out of town. Why don't they go to this great little bar that he's just discovered and have a beer? They order a drink, and the equally friendly owner then offers another drink. Women appear, more drinks are provided and the visitor relaxes as he realises that the women are not prostitutes, just friendly Greeks. The crunch comes at the end of the evening when the traveller is presented with an exorbitant bill and the smiles disappear. The con men who cruise the streets playing the role of the friendly Greek can be very convincing: some people have been taken in more than once.

Other bars (see under Bars in the Entertainment section) don't bother with the acting. They target intoxicated males with talk of sex and present them with outrageous bills.

Travel Agents

Several travel agents in the Plaka/Syntagma area employ touts to patrol the streets promoting 'cheap' packages to the islands. These touts like to hang out at the bus stops on Amalias, hoping to find naive new arrivals who have no idea of prices in Greece. Potential customers are then taken back to the agency, where slick salespeople pressure them into buying outrageously overpriced packages. Lonely Planet regularly hears complaints from victims of this scam.

There is no need to buy a package; you will always be able to negotiate a better deal yourself when you get to the island of your choice. If you are worried that everywhere will be full, select a place from the pages of this guide and make a booking.

Slippery Surfaces

Many of Athens' pavements and other surfaces underfoot are made of marble and become incredibly slippery when wet, so if you are caught in the rain, be very careful how you tread.

---

sickness preparations, which can cause drowsiness, have to be taken before the trip commences; when you're feeling sick it's too late.

Two natural preventatives are ginger (available in capsule form) and peppermint (including mint-flavoured sweets).

INFECTIOUS DISEASES
Diarrhoea

Simple things like a change of water, food or climate can all cause a mild bout of diarrhoea, but a few rushed toilet trips with no other symptoms is not indicative of a major problem.

euro currency converter 1000 dr = €2.93

Dehydration is the main danger with any diarrhoea, particularly in children or the elderly as dehydration can occur quite quickly. Under all circumstances *fluid replacement* (at least equal to the volume being lost) is the most important thing to remember. Weak black tea with a little sugar, soda water, or soft drinks allowed to go flat and diluted 50% with clean water are all good.

Hepatitis

Hepatitis is a general term for inflammation of the liver. It is a common disease worldwide. The symptoms are fever, chills, headache, fatigue, feelings of weakness and aches and pains, followed by loss of appetite, nausea, vomiting, abdominal pain, dark urine, light-coloured faeces, jaundiced (yellow) skin and the whites of the eyes may turn yellow. **Hepatitis A** is transmitted by contaminated food and drinking water. The disease poses a real threat to the Western traveller. You should seek medical advice, but there is not much you can do apart from resting, drinking lots of fluids, eating lightly and avoiding fatty foods. People who have had hepatitis should avoid alcohol for some time after the illness, as the liver needs time to recover.

Hepatitis E is transmitted in the same way, and can be very serious in pregnant women.

There are almost 300 million chronic carriers of **Hepatitis B** in the world. It is spread through contact with infected blood, blood products or body fluids; for example, through sexual contact, unsterilised needles and blood transfusions, or contact with blood via small breaks in the skin. Other risk situations include having a shave, tattoo, or having your body pierced with contaminated equipment. The symptoms of type B may be more severe and may lead to long-term problems. **Hepatitis D** is spread in the same way, but the risk is mainly in shared needles.

Hepatitis C

Can lead to chronic liver disease. The virus is spread by contact with blood – usually via contaminated transfusions or shared needles.

Tetanus

This potentially fatal disease is found worldwide. It is difficult to treat but is preventable with immunisation.

Sexually Transmitted Diseases

Sexual contact with an infected sexual partner spreads these diseases. While abstinence is the only 100% preventative, using condoms is also effective. Gonorrhoea, herpes and syphilis are among these diseases; sores, blisters or rashes around the genitals, discharges or pain when urinating are common symptoms. In some STDs, such as wart virus or chlamydia, symptoms may be less marked or not observed at all in women. Syphilis symptoms eventually disappear completely but the disease continues and can cause severe problems in later years. The treatment of gonorrhoea and syphilis is with antibiotics.

There are numerous other sexually transmitted diseases, for most of which effective treatment is available. There is currently no cure for herpes.

HIV/AIDS

Infection with the human immunodeficiency virus (HIV) may lead to acquired immune deficiency syndrome (AIDS), which is a fatal disease. Any exposure to blood, blood products or body fluids may put the individual at risk. The disease is often transmitted through sexual contact or dirty needles – vaccinations, acupuncture, tattooing and body piercing can be potentially as dangerous as intravenous drug use.

If you do need an injection, ask to see the syringe unwrapped in front of you, or take a needle and syringe pack with you.

The fear of HIV infection should never preclude treatment for serious medical conditions.

CUTS, BITES & STINGS

Skin punctures can easily become infected in hot climates and may be difficult to heal. Treat any cut with an antiseptic such as povidone-iodine. Where possible avoid bandages and Band-Aids, which can keep wounds wet.

Although there are a lot of bees and wasps in Greece, their stings are usually painful rather than dangerous. Calamine lotion or sting relief spray will give relief and ice packs will reduce the pain and swelling.

Jelly Fish, Sea Urchins & Weever Fish

Watch out for sea urchins around rocky beaches; if you get some of their needles embedded in your skin, olive oil will help to loosen them. If they are not removed they will become infected.

Be wary also of jelly fish, particularly during the months of September and October. Although they are not lethal in Greece, their stings can be painful. Dousing in vinegar will deactivate any stingers which have not 'fired'. Calamine lotion, antihistamines and analgesics may reduce the reaction and relieve the pain.

Much more painful than either of these, but thankfully much rarer, is an encounter with the weever fish. It buries itself in the sand of the tidal zone with only its spines protruding, and injects a painful and powerful toxin if trodden on. Soaking your foot in very hot water (which breaks down the poison) should solve the problem. It can cause permanent local paralysis in the worst instance.

Bedbugs & Lice

Bedbugs live in various places, but particularly in dirty mattresses and bedding. Spots of blood on bedclothes or on the wall around the bed can be read as a suggestion to find another hotel. Bedbugs leave itchy bites in neat rows. Calamine lotion or sting relief spray may help.

All lice cause itching and discomfort. They make themselves at home in your hair, your clothing or in your pubic hair. You catch lice through direct contact with infected people or by sharing combs, clothing and the like. Powder or shampoo treatment will kill the lice and infected clothing should then be washed in very hot water.

WOMEN'S HEALTH

Antibiotic use, synthetic underwear, sweating and contraceptive pills can lead to fungal vaginal infections, especially when travelling in hot climates. Fungal infections are characterised by a rash, itch and discharge and can be treated with a vinegar or lemon-juice douche, or with yogurt. Nystatin, miconazole or clotrimazole pessaries or vaginal cream are the usual treatment. Maintaining good personal hygiene and wearing loose-fitting clothes and cotton underwear may help prevent these infections.

Sexually transmitted diseases are a major cause of vaginal problems. Symptoms include a smelly discharge, painful intercourse and sometimes a burning sensation when urinating. Medical attention should be sought and male sexual partners must also be treated. For more details see the earlier section on Sexually Transmitted Diseases. Besides abstinence, the best thing is to practise safe sex using condoms.

HOSPITAL TREATMENT

Citizens of EU countries are covered for free treatment in public hospitals within Greece on presentation of an E111 form. Inquire at your national health service or travel agent in advance. Emergency treatment is free to all nationalities in public hospitals. In an emergency, dial ☎ 166 Ambulance (Athens) elsewhere. There is at least one doctor on every island in Greece and larger islands have hospitals. Pharmacies can dispense medicines which are available only on prescription in most European countries, so you can consult a pharmacist for minor ailments.

All this sounds fine, but although medical training is of a high standard in Greece, the health service is badly underfunded and one of the worst in Europe. Hospitals are overcrowded, hygiene is not always what it should be and relatives are expected to bring in food for the patient – which could be a problem for a tourist. Conditions and treatment are better in private hospitals, which are expensive. All this means that a good health-insurance policy is essential.

WOMEN TRAVELLERS

Many women travel alone in Greece. The crime rate remains relatively low, and solo travel is probably safer than in most European countries. This does not mean that you should be lulled into complacency; bag snatching and rapes do occur, although violent offences are rare.

The biggest nuisance to foreign women travelling alone are the guys the Greeks have nicknamed *kamaki*. The word means 'fishing trident' and refers to the kamaki's favourite pastime, 'fishing' for foreign women. You'll find them everywhere there are lots of tourists; young (for the most part), smooth-talking guys who aren't in the least bashful about sidling up to foreign women in the street. They can be very persistent, but they are a hassle rather than a threat.

The majority of Greek men treat foreign women with respect, and are genuinely helpful.

GAY & LESBIAN TRAVELLERS

In a country where the church still plays a prominent role in shaping society's views on issues such as sexuality, it should come as no surprise that homosexuality is generally frowned upon – especially outside the major cities. While there is no legislation against homosexual activity, it pays to be discreet and to avoid open displays of togetherness.

This has not prevented Greece from becoming an extremely popular destination for gay travellers. Most gay travellers head for the islands, Mykonos in particular, but Athens also has a busy gay scene. See the Entertainment chapter for details.

INFORMATION

The *Spartacus International Gay Guide*, published by Bruno Gmünder (Berlin), is widely regarded as the leading authority on the gay travel scene. There's also stacks of information on the Internet:

Roz Mov
W www.geocities.com/WestHollywood/2225 /index.html
Roz Mov is a good place to start looking for gay info on the Internet. It has pages on travel info,

gay health, the gay press, organisations, events and legal issues – and links to lots more sites.

Gayscape
W www.jwpublishing.com/gayscape /menugreece.html
Gayscape is a useful site with lots of links.

ORGANISATIONS

Many Internet sites still list the Elladas Omofilofilon Kommunitas (EOK) as being the main gay rights organisation in Greece. Unfortunately this volunteer organisation folded a couple of years ago, and no new organisation has emerged to take its place.

DISABLED TRAVELLERS

Athens is a difficult city for people with mobility problems. The hard fact is that most museums and ancient sites are not wheelchair accessible. In fact, the uneven terrain and slippery surfaces at some sites are challenging even for able-bodied people.

If you are determined, then take heart in the knowledge that disabled people do come to Athens for holidays. But the trip needs careful planning, so get as much information as you can before you leave home.

Royal Association for Disability and Rehabilitation
12 City Forum, 250 City Road, London EC1V 8AF ☎ 7250 3222 fax 7250 0212
e radar@radar.org.uk
The British-based Royal Association for Disability and Rehabilitation (RADAR) publishes a useful guide called *Holidays & Travel Abroad: A Guide for Disabled People*, which gives a good overview of facilities available to disabled travellers in Europe.

SENIOR TRAVELLERS

Card-carrying EU pensioners can claim a range of benefits such as reduced admission charges at museums and ancient sites and discounts on trains.

ATHENS FOR CHILDREN

Greece is a safe and relatively easy place to travel with children.

Hotels and restaurants are very accommodating when it comes to meeting the needs of children, although highchairs are a rarity. Service in restaurants is normally very quick, which is great when you've got hungry children on your hands.

Fresh milk is readily available from shops and kiosks. Formula is also available everywhere, as is condensed and heat-treated milk.

Mobility is an issue for parents with very small children. Strollers (pushchairs) aren't much use in Greece unless you're going to spend all your time in one of the few flat spots. They are hopeless on rough stone paths and up steps, and a curse when getting on and off buses and ferries. Backpacks or front pouches are best.

Travel on ferries and buses is free for children under four. They pay half fare up to the age of 10 (ferries) and 12 (buses). Full fares apply otherwise. On domestic flights, you'll pay 10% of the fare to have a child under two sitting on your knee. Kids aged two to 12 pay half fare.

USEFUL ORGANISATIONS

AUTOMOBILE ASSOCIATIONS
ELPA Map 8, C5
Ground Floor, Athens Tower, Messogion 2-4
☎ 779 1615, toll-free 24-hour emergency number 104
ELPA, the Greek automobile club, offers reciprocal services to members of national automobile associations on production of a valid membership card. If your vehicle breaks down, dial ☎ 104.

LIBRARIES

National Library of Greece Map 4, A9
Panepistimiou 32, Syntagma ☎ 360 8185 fax 338 2502 ☼ 9am-8pm Mon-Thur, 9am-2pm Fri, Sat Ⓜ Panepistimiou

Hellenic-American Union Map 6, A1
Massalias 22, Kolonaki ☎ 362 9886 fax 363 3174 ⓔ vioannou@hau ⓦ www.hau.gr
☼ 9am-5pm daily Ⓜ Panepistimiou

UNIVERSITIES

Athens University Map 4, A9
Panepistimiou 30, Syntagma ☎ 362 0020 fax 360 2145 Ⓜ Panepistimiou

Athens School of Economics Map 3, A8
Patission 76, Mouseio ☎ 820 3911 fax 822 6204 ⓔ sakel@aueb.gr Ⓜ Plateia Viktorias

Athens University of Agriculture
Iera 75, Gazi ☎ 529 4901 fax 346 0885

Athens College of Fine Arts Map 3, D7
(at Athens Polytehnio)
Patission 42, Mouseio ☎ 381 6930
fax 381 6926

Athens College of Social and Political Studies
Syngrou 136, Kallithea ☎ 923 9559
fax 922 3690

CULTURAL CENTRES

These cultural centres hold concerts, film shows and exhibitions from time to time. Major events are listed in various English-language newspapers and magazines.

British Council Map 6, C2
Plateia Kolonakiou 17, Kolonaki ☎ 369 2314/33 fax 360 9164, 363 4769
ⓔ library@britishcouncil.gr
ⓦ www.britishcouncil.gr ☼ 7.45am-3pm Mon-Fri Ⓜ Evangelismos

French Institute of Athens Map 3, G10
Sina 31, Kolonaki ☎ 362 4301/5 fax 364 6873
ⓔ ifa@ifa.gr ⓦ www.ifa.gr ☼ library 10am-5pm Tues, Wed, Thur, Fri, 2pm-5pm Mon
Ⓜ Panepistimiou

Goethe Institute Map 4, B10
Omirou 14-16, Kolonaki ☎ 360 8114 fax 364 3518 ⓔ gi@athen.goethe.org
ⓦ www.goethe.de/athen ☼ 9am-5pm daily Ⓜ Panepistimiou

Hellenic-American Union Map 6, A1
Massalias 22, Kolonaki ☎ 362 9886 fax 363 3174 ⓔ vioannou@hau ⓦ www.hau.gr
☼ 9am-5pm daily Ⓜ Panepistimiou

EMERGENCIES

Athens Central Police Station Map 8, A3
Leoforos Alexandras 173 ☎ 770 5711/7

Traffic Police Map 3, D2
Deligianni 24-26, Exarhia ☎ 528 4000

Toll-free 24-hour emergency numbers:

Police	☎ 100
Tourist Police	☎ 171
Ambulance (Athens)	☎ 166
Fire Brigade	☎ 199
Roadside Assistance (ELPA)	☎ 104
Duty Hospitals	☎ 106
Pharmacies	☎ 107
Coast Guard	☎ 108
Doctors on Call	☎ 105
Emergency medical aid for US citizens	☎ 721 2951

LEGAL MATTERS

CONSUMER ADVICE
Tourist Assistance Programme
Valtetsiou 43-45 ☎ 330 0673 fax 330 0591
⏱ 10am-2pm Mon-Fri Jul-Sep
The Tourist Assistance Programme exists to help
people who are having trouble with any tourism-
related service. Free legal advice is available in
English, French and German.

DRUGS
Greek drug laws are the strictest in Europe.
Greek courts make no distinction between
possession and pushing. Possession of even
a small amount of marijuana is likely to
land you in jail.

BUSINESS HOURS

Banks are open 8am to 2pm Monday to
Thursday, and 8am to 1.30pm Friday.

In summer, the usual opening hours for
shops are 8am to 1.30pm and 5.30pm to
8.30pm on Tuesday, Thursday and Friday,
and 8am to 2.30pm on Monday, Wednesday
and Saturday. Shops open 30 minutes later
in winter. These times are not always
strictly adhered to. Many shops in tourist
resorts are open seven days a week.

Department stores and supermarkets are
open 8am to 8pm Monday to Friday, 8am to
at least 3pm on Saturday and closed Sunday.

Periptera are open from early morning
until late at night. They sell everything from
bus tickets and cigarettes to hard-core
pornography.

PUBLIC HOLIDAYS

All banks and shops and most museums and
ancient sites close on public holidays.
National public holidays in Greece are:

New Year's Day	1 January
Epiphany	6 January
First Sunday in Lent	February
Greek Independence Day	25 March
Good Friday	March/April
(Orthodox) Easter Sunday	March/April
Spring Festival/Labour Day	1 May
Feast of the Assumption	15 August
Ohi Day	28 October
Christmas Day	25 December
St Stephen's Day	26 December

SPECIAL EVENTS

The Greek year is a succession of festivals
and events, some of which are religious,
some cultural, others an excuse for a good
knees-up, and some a combination of all
three. The following is by no means an ex-
haustive list, but it covers the most important events, both national and regional. If
you're in the right place at the right time,
you'll certainly be invited to join the revelry.

JANUARY
Feast of Agios Vasilios (St Basil)
The year kicks off with this festival on 1
January. A church ceremony is followed by
the exchanging of gifts, singing, dancing
and feasting; the New Year pie *(vasilopitta)*
is sliced and the person who gets the slice
containing a coin will supposedly have a
lucky year.

Epiphany (the Blessing of the Waters)
Christ's baptism by St John is celebrated on
6 January, when seas, lakes and rivers are
blessed and crosses immersed in them. The
largest ceremony is at Piraeus.

FEBRUARY-MARCH
Carnival
The three weeks before the beginning of
Lent (the 40 day period before Easter,
which is traditionally a period of fasting)
are carnival time throughout Greece. These
carnivals are ostensibly Christian pre-
Lenten celebrations, but many derive from
pagan festivals. There are many regional
variations, but fancy dress, feasting, traditional dancing and general merrymaking
prevail.

Shrove Monday (Clean Monday)
On the Monday before Ash Wednesday (the
first day of Lent), people take to the hills
throughout Greece to have picnics and fly
kites.

MARCH
Independence Day
The anniversary of the hoisting of the Greek
flag by Bishop Germanos at Moni Agias

Lavras is celebrated on 25 March with parades and dancing. Germanos' act of revolt marked the start of the War of Independence. Independence Day coincides with the **Feast of the Annunciation**, so it is also a religious festival.

MARCH-APRIL
Easter

Easter is the most important festival in the Greek Orthodox religion. Emphasis is placed on the Resurrection rather than on the Crucifixion, so it is a joyous, rather than sombre, occasion. The festival commences on the evening of Good Friday with the *perifora epitavios*, when a shrouded bier (representing Christ's funeral bier) is carried through the streets to the local church. This moving candlelit procession can be seen in towns and villages throughout the country. From a spectator's viewpoint, the most impressive of these processions climbs Lykavittos Hill in Athens to the Chapel of Agios Georgos.

The Resurrection Mass starts at 11pm on Easter Saturday night. At midnight, packed churches throughout Greece are plunged into darkness to symbolise Christ's passing through the underworld.

The ceremony of the lighting of candles which follows is the most significant moment in the Orthodox year, for it symbolises the Resurrection. Its poignancy and beauty are spellbinding. If you are in Greece at Easter you should endeavour to attend this ceremony, which ends with the setting off of fireworks and candlelit processions through the streets. The Lenten fast ends on Easter Sunday with the cracking of red-dyed Easter eggs and an outdoor feast of roast lamb followed by Greek dancing. The day's greeting is *Hristos anesti* (Christ is risen), to which the reply is *Alithos anesti* (Truly He is risen).

MAY
May Day

On the first day of May there is a mass exodus to the country. People picnic and gather wild flowers, which are made into wreaths to decorate houses.

JUNE
Feast of St John the Baptist

This feast day on 24 June is widely celebrated around Greece. Wreaths made on May Day are kept until this day, when they are burned on bonfires.

AUGUST
Assumption

Greeks celebrate Assumption Day (15 August) with family reunions. The whole population seems to be on the move either side of the big day, so it's a good time to avoid public transport. The island of Tinos gets particularly busy because of its miracle-working icon of Panagia Evangelistria. It becomes a place of pilgrimage for thousands, who come to be blessed, healed or baptised, or just for the excitement of being there. Many are unable to find hotels and sleep out on the streets.

SEPTEMBER
Genesis tis Panagias (the Virgin's Birthday)

This day is celebrated on 8 September throughout Greece with religious services and feasting.

Exaltation of the Cross

This is celebrated on 14 September throughout Greece with processions and hymns.

OCTOBER
Ohi (No) Day

Metaxas' refusal to allow Mussolini's troops free passage through Greece in WWII is commemorated on 28 October with remembrance services, military parades, folk dancing and feasting.

DECEMBER
Christmas Day

Although not as important as Easter, Christmas is still celebrated with religious services and feasting. Nowadays much 'Western' influence is apparent, including Christmas trees, decorations and presents.

DOING BUSINESS

Doing business in Greece can be a frustrating business. The biggest single problem is

FACTS FOR THE VISITOR

inertia, especially when dealing with bureaucracy. Some people like to trace this inertia back to the days of Turkish rule, when no patriotic civil servant wanted to be seen doing anything. Whatever the story, the tradition continues. Things do happen, but not at the pace at which most foreign business people would like it to happen. Expect long-promised documents, vital to the success of your trip, to be delivered to your hotel just as you climbing into your taxi to the airport – no sooner.

Image is very important. Greek businessmen and women dress very stylishly, and expect their foreign counterparts to do likewise.

The investment climate remains healthy, despite the bursting of the stock market bubble in 2000 after several years. Many Greeks lost a fortune in the crash after a buying frenzy had pushed the stock index to an insupportable high of almost 11,000 points. At the time of research, it was hovering around a more realistic 6000.

USEFUL ORGANISATIONS

Athens Chamber of Commerce and Industry Map 6, C1
Akadimias 7, Syntagma ☎ 362 7337, 362 5342, 338 2258 fax 360 7897, 361 8810
e info@acci.gr w www.acci.gr, www.ebeh.gr
◷ 8.30am-3pm Mon-Fri Ⓜ Syntagma
The Athens Chamber of Commerce & Industry has answers to most of the questions posed by people wanting to do business in Athens. The helpful public relations department is the best place to start. It can send out a copy of its CD, *Investment Opportunities in Greece* or the annual *Greek Export Directory* with comprehensive listings of Greek producers. It covers everything from abrasives to zucchinis.

Mail Boxes Etc Map 5, B5
Leka 14, Syntagma ☎ 324 5060 fax 324 5070
e mbeathens@interfranchise.gr ◷ 8am-6pm Mon & Wed, 8am-8pm Tues, Thur & Fri, 9am-3pm Sat Ⓜ Syntagma
Business communications specialist Mail Boxes Etc offers a host of services of interest to visiting business people. As well as renting out mail boxes (three months 14,000 dr; six months 24,000 dr; one year 40,000 dr), it also hires computer equipment, handles photocopying, send faxes and organises parcels and courier services. It can also organise translation services: 4000 dr for 400 words for technical/business documents.

Other useful business organisations include the following:

Athens Customs Office
(☎ 513 1591) Larisis train station, 100 00
Athens Stock Exchange
(☎ 321 1301) Sofokleous 10, Omonia 105 59
Bank of Greece
(☎ 320 1111) Panepistimiou 21, Syntagma 105 64
Federation of Greek Industries
(☎ 323 7325, fax 322 2929) Xenofontos 5, Plaka 105 57
Ministry of Commerce
(☎ 361 62 41) Plateia Kaningos, Omonia 106 77
Ministry of Finance (taxation)
(☎ 322 4071) Karageorgi Servias 10, Syntagma 101 84
Ministry of Foreign Affairs
(☎ 361 0581) Akadimias 1, Syntagma 106 71
Ministry of Industry, Energy and Technology
(☎ 770 8615) Mihalakopoulou 80, Ambelokipi 115 28
Ministry of Justice
(☎ 777 1871) Messogion 96, Ambelokipi 115 26
Ministry of Labour
(☎ 523 3111) Pireos 40, Omonia 101 82

TRANSLATION & INTERPRETING SERVICES

Executive Services
☎ 778 3698 fax 779 5509
e info@executiveservices.gr
Handles all EU and Balkan languages.

Panhellenic Association of Translators
☎ 821 6789, 823 5778 fax 822 1945

SETTING UP A BANK ACCOUNT

Opening a bank account in Athens is easy. All you need is your passport and a minimum opening deposit of 50,000 dr.

USEFUL PUBLICATIONS

Doing Business in Greece, part of US publisher Ernst & Young's international business series, provides a comprehensive overview of the business climate in Greece. It includes sections on investment, taxation, business organisation and accounting practices as well as listings of useful telephone numbers and addresses.

The Athens Chamber of Commerce and Industry publishes an annual *Greek Export Directory* (see Useful Organisations earlier in this section.)

euro currency converter €1 = 340.75 dr

WORK

PERMITS

EU nationals don't need a work permit, but they need a residency permit if they intend to stay longer than three months. Nationals of other countries are supposed to have a work permit.

ENGLISH TUTORING

If you're looking for a permanent job, the most widely available option is to teach English. A TEFL (Teaching English as a Foreign Language) certificate or a university degree is an advantage but not essential. In the UK, look through the *Times Educational Supplement* or Tuesday's edition of the *Guardian* newspaper for opportunities – in other countries, contact the Greek embassy.

Another possibility is to find a job teaching English once you are in Greece. You will see language schools everywhere. Strictly speaking, you need a licence to teach in these schools, but many will employ teachers without one. The best time to look around for such a job is late summer.

People who are looking for private English lessons sometimes place advertisements on the notice board at the Compendium bookshop.

BAR & HOSTEL WORK

There's a limited amount of hotel work available at some of the travellers' hotels, but no bar work to speak of. If you're after bar work, head for the islands. The islands could not survive without foreign workers and there are thousands of summer jobs up for grabs every year. April/May is the time to go looking.

STREET PERFORMERS

Buskers reckon that the richest pickings are to be found on the islands, particularly Mykonos, Paros and Santorini, but there are also some good spots in Athens.

The area outside the Church of Metamorphosis on Kydathineon can be very rewarding in summer when the summer tourist crowds are around. The pedestrian precinct section of Ermou, west of Plateia Syntagmatos, is good all year, as is the centre of Plateia Syntagmatos outside the metro entrance.

OTHER WORK

There are often jobs advertised in the classifieds of the English-language newspapers, or you can place an advertisement yourself. EU nationals can also make use of the OAED (Organismos Apasholiseos Ergatikou Dynamikou), the Greek National Employment Service, in their search for a job. The OAED has offices throughout Athens.

Αθήνα

Getting There & Away

Most visitors to Athens arrive by air. Athens handles the vast majority of Greece's international air traffic, including all intercontinental flights. The city's new international airport at Spata, 21km east of Athens, began operation in March 2001.

Facilities at the new airport, called Eleftherios Venizelos International, in honour of the country's leading 20th-century politician, are immeasurably better than at the city's former airport at Ellnikon. Where Ellnikon was shabby and outdated, the new airport gleams. Built by a German consortium, everything is absolutely state-of-the-art. In addition to standard facilities like cafes, restaurants, shops and banks, the new airport also has a hotel for transit passengers.

Ellnikon, which occupies a prime expanse of coastal real estate 9km south-east of the city centre, will be redeveloped – initially to host Olympic events.

DEPARTURE TAX

The airport tax is 3400 dr for domestic flights and 6800 dr for international flights. Both taxes are paid as part of the ticket. The fares from Athens quoted in this section include tax.

OTHER PARTS OF GREECE

The majority of flights are handled by the country's much-maligned national carrier, Olympic Airways. Aegean Air, Air Greece and Cronus Airlines offer a cheaper and more traveller friendly alternative to popular destinations like Corfu, Iraklio, Rhodes and Thessaloniki.

Cronus Airlines also offers discounts for students and for travellers aged over 60, and special rates for advance purchase, while Aegean Air and Air Greece offer youth discounts (under 26). Olympic offers a 25% student discount on domestic flights, but only if the flight is part of an international journey.

Thessaloniki

Athens-Thessaloniki is the busiest route in the country with at least a dozen flights a day. The bulk of them are operated by Olympic (one hour, 22,000 dr one way), which also offers business class (27,400 dr).

Cronus (45 minutes, 19,400 dr) is the main competitor with at least four flights a day. Air Greece and Aegean Air also fly this route.

Other Mainland Cities

Olympic Airlines operates two flights a day to Alexandroupolis (65 minutes, 18,600 dr), Ioannina (70 minutes, 18,400 dr) and Kavala (one hour, 18,300 dr). It also has five flights a week to Preveza (one hour, 13,900 dr), four to Kalamata (50 minutes, 13,400 dr) and Kastoria (75 minutes, 19,200 dr), and three a week to Kozani (70 minutes, 17,400 dr).

Greek Islands

Athens has flights to 22 islands, with services to all the island groups as well as to three destinations on Crete – Hania, Iraklio and Sitia.

Once again, most of the flights are operated by Olympic (see the table of summer flights for details). In spite of the number of flights, it can be hard to find a seat during July and August. Early bookings are recommended. Flight schedules are greatly reduced in winter, especially to Mykonos, Paros, Skiathos and Santorini.

THE USA

Discount travel agents in the USA are known as consolidators (although you won't see a sign on the door saying Consolidator). San Francisco is the ticket consolidator capital of America, although some good deals can be found in Los Angeles, New York and other big cities. Consolidators can be found through the Yellow Pages or the major daily newspapers. The *New York Times*, the *Los Angeles Times*, the *Chicago Tribune* and the *San Francisco*

Examiner all produce weekly travel sections in which you will find a number of travel agency ads.

New York has the widest range of options to Athens. The route to Europe is very competitive and there are new deals almost every day. At the time of research, Virgin Atlantic led the way, offering a flight to Athens for US$944 return in high season via London, falling to US$740 at other times. Olympic Airways flies direct at least once a day, and Delta Airlines flies direct three times a week. Apex fares with Olympic range from US$730 to US$1015, depending on the season. These fares don't include taxes.

Boston is the only other east coast city with direct flights to Athens – on Saturday with Olympic Airways. Fares are the same as for flights from New York.

There are no direct flights to Athens from the west coast. There are, however, connecting flights to Athens from many US cities, either linking with Olympic Airways in New York or flying with one of the European national airlines to their home country, and then on to Athens. At the time of research, Virgin Atlantic was offering Los Angeles–Athens for US$982 return in high season, falling to US$879 at other times.

If you're travelling from Athens to the USA, the travel agents around Syntagma offer the following one-way fares (prices do not include airport tax): Atlanta 110,000 dr, Chicago 110,000 dr, Los Angeles 125,000 dr and New York 85,000 dr.

Council Travel
205 E 42 St, New York ☎ 800-226 8624
W www.ciee.org.
America's largest student travel organisation has around 60 offices in the USA. Call for the office nearest you or visit its Web site.

STA Travel
☎ 800-777 0112 W www.statravel.com
STA has offices in Boston, Chicago, Miami, New York, Philadelphia, San Francisco and other major cities. Call the toll-free 800 number for office locations or visit its Web site.

US courier flights
Courier flights to Athens are occasionally advertised in the newspapers, or you could contact air freight companies listed in the phone book. You may have to go to the air freight company to get an answer – the companies aren't always keen to give out information over the phone.

International Association of Air Travel Couriers
☎ 561-582 8320 W www.courier.org
Members (US residents only) of IAATC get a bi-monthly update of air courier offerings, access to a fax-on-demand service with daily updates of last minute specials and the bimonthly newsletter the *Shoestring Traveler*. However, be aware that joining this organisation does not guarantee that you'll get a courier flight.

Travel Unlimited
PO Box 1058, Allston, MA 02134, USA
Travel Unlimited publish a monthly travel newsletter from the USA with many courier flight deals from destinations worldwide.
    A 12-month subscription costs $US25 for US residents and $US35 for residents outside the US.

CANADA
Canadian discount air ticket sellers are also known as consolidators and their air fares tend to be about 10% higher than those sold in the USA. *The Globe & Mail*, the *Toronto Star*, the *Montreal Gazette* and the *Vancouver Sun* carry travel agents ads and are a good place to look for cheap fares.

Olympic Airways has two flights weekly from Toronto to Athens via Montreal. There are no direct flights from Vancouver, but there are connecting flights via Toronto, Amsterdam, Frankfurt and London on Canadian Airlines, KLM, Lufthansa and British Airways. You should be able to get to Athens from Toronto and Montreal for about C$1150/950 in high/low season or from Vancouver for C$1500/1300.

At the time of writing, budget travel agencies in Athens were advertising flights to Toronto for 105,000 dr and to Montreal for 100,000 dr, plus airport tax.

Travel CUTS
☎ 1800-667 2887 W www.travelcuts.com
Canada's national student travel agency has offices in all major cities.

FB On Board Courier Services
☎ 514-631 7929
FB can get you on board to London for C$760 return.

euro currency converter 1000 dr = €2.93

Air Travel Glossary

Alliances Many of the world's leading airlines are now intimately involved with each other, sharing everything from reservations systems and check-in to aircraft and frequent-flyer schemes. Opponents say that alliances restrict competition. Whatever the arguments, there is no doubt that big alliances are the way of the future.

Courier Fares Businesses often need to send urgent documents or freight securely and quickly. Courier companies hire people to accompany the package through customs and, in return, offer a discount ticket which is sometimes a bargain. However, you may have to surrender all your baggage allowance and take only carry-on luggage.

Fares Airlines traditionally offer 1st class (coded F), business class (coded J) and economy class (coded Y) tickets. These days there are so many promotional and discounted fares available that few passengers pay full fare.

Lost Tickets If you lose your airline ticket, an airline will usually treat it like a travellers cheque and, after inquiries, issue you with another one. Legally, however, an airline is entitled to treat it like cash and if you lose it then it's gone forever. Take very good care of your tickets.

Onward Tickets An entry requirement for many countries is that you have a ticket out of the country. If you're unsure of your next move, the easiest solution is to buy the cheapest onward ticket to a neighbouring country or a ticket from a reliable airline which can later be refunded if you do not use it.

Open-Jaw Tickets These are return tickets where you fly out to one place but return from another. If available, this can save you backtracking to your arrival point.

Overbooking Since every flight has some passengers who fail to show up, airlines often book more passengers than they have seats. Usually excess passengers make up for the no-shows, but occasionally somebody gets 'bumped' onto the next available flight. Guess who it is most likely to be? The passengers who check in late. If you do get 'bumped', you are normally offered some form of compensation.

Reconfirmation Some airlines require you to reconfirm your flight at least 72 hours prior to departure. Check your travel documents to see if this is the case.

Restrictions Discounted tickets often have various restrictions on them – such as needing to be paid for in advance and incurring a penalty to be altered or cancelled. Others are restrictions on the minimum and maximum period you must be away.

Round-the-World Tickets RTW tickets give you a limited period (usually a year) in which to circumnavigate the globe. You can go anywhere the carrying airlines go, as long as you don't backtrack. The number of stopovers or total number of separate flights is decided before you set off and they usually cost a bit more than a basic return flight.

Ticketless Travel Airlines are gradually waking up to the realisation that paper tickets are unnecessary encumbrances. On simple one-way or return trips, reservations details can be held on computer and the passenger merely shows ID to claim their seat.

Transferred Tickets Airline tickets cannot be transferred from one person to another. Travellers sometimes try to sell the return half of their ticket, but officials can ask you to prove that you are the person named on the ticket. On an international flight, tickets are compared with passports.

AUSTRALIA

Olympic Airways has two flights weekly from Sydney and Melbourne to Athens. Return fares normally cost from about A$1799 in low season to A$2199 in high season.

Thai International and Singapore Airlines also have convenient connections to Athens, as well as a reputation for good service. If you're planning on doing a bit of flying around Europe, it's worth checking around for special deals from the major European airlines. Alitalia, KLM and Lufthansa are three likely candidates with good European networks.

If you're travelling from Athens to Australia, a one-way ticket to Sydney or Melbourne costs about 180,000 dr, plus airport tax.

Two well-known agents for cheap fares are STA Travel and Flight Centre.

Flight Centre
82 Elizabeth St, Sydney ☎ toll-free 131 600
W www.flightcentre.com.au
Flight Centre's head office is in Sydney, with dozens of offices throughout Australia.

STA Travel
224 Faraday St, Carlton ☎ 03-9349 2411,
toll-free 131 776 W www.statravel.com.au
STA has offices in all major cities and on many university campuses. Call the Australia-wide number for the location of your nearest branch or visit its Web site.

NEW ZEALAND

Round-the-World (RTW) and Circle Pacific fares are usually the best value, often cheaper than a return ticket. Depending on which airline you choose, you may fly across Asia, with possible stopovers in India, Bangkok or Singapore, or across the USA, with possible stopovers in Honolulu, Australia or one of the Pacific Islands.

The *New Zealand Herald* has a travel section in which travel agents advertise fares.

Flight Centre
cnr Queen & Darby Sts, Auckland
☎ 09-309 6171
Flight Centre has many branches throughout New Zealand

STA Travel
10 High St, Auckland ☎ 09-309 0458
W www.sta.travel.com.au
STA has a number of other offices in Auckland as

well as in Hamilton, Palmerston North, Wellington, Christchurch and Dunedin.

THE UK

Airline ticket discounters are known as bucket shops in the UK. Despite the somewhat disreputable name, there is nothing under-the-counter about them. Discount air travel is big business in London. Advertisements for many travel agents appear in the travel pages of the weekend broadsheets, such as the *Independent* on Saturday and the *Sunday Times*. Look out for the free magazines, such as *TNT*, which are widely available in London – start by looking outside the main railway and underground stations.

British Airways, Olympic Airways and Virgin Atlantic operate daily flights between London and Athens. Pricing is very competitive, with all three offering return tickets for around UK£220 in high season, plus tax. At other times, prices fall as low at UK£104, plus tax. British Airways has flights from Edinburgh, Glasgow and Manchester.

Charter flights can work out as a cheaper alternative to scheduled flights, especially if you do not qualify for the under-26 and student discounts.

Cronus Airlines
☎ 020-7580 3500 W www.cronus.gr
Cronus flies the London-Athens route five times weekly for UK£210, and offers connections to Thessaloniki on the same fare. Most scheduled flights from London leave from Heathrow.

EasyJet
☎ 0870-6 000 000 W www.easyjet.com
The cheapest scheduled flights are with EasyJet, the no-frills specialist, which has two Luton-Athens flights daily. One-way fares range from UK£89 to UK£139 in high season, and from a bargain UK£39 to UK£69 at other times.

There are numerous charter flights between the UK and Greece. Typical London-Athens charter fares are UK£79/129 one way/return in the low season and UK£99/189 in the high season. These prices are for advance bookings, but even in high season it's possible to pick up last-minute deals for as little as UK£59/99. There are also charter flights from

Birmingham, Cardiff, Glasgow, Luton, Manchester and Newcastle.

If you're flying from Athens to the UK, budget fares start at 25,000 dr to London or 30,000 dr to Manchester, plus airport tax.

Bridge the World
4 Regent Place, London ☎ 020-7734 7447

Flightbookers
177-178 Tottenham Court Rd, London
☎ 020-7757 2000

STA Travel
86 Old Brompton Rd, London
☎ 020-7361 6161 W www.statravel.co.uk
With other offices in London and Manchester, STA sells tickets to all travellers but cater especially to travellers under 26 and students.

Trailfinders
194 Kensington High St, London
☎ 020-7937 1234

USIT Campus Travel
52 Grosvenor Gardens, London
☎ 020-7730 3402 W www.usitcampus.com
USIT has branches throughout the UK and sells tickets to all travellers but caters especially to young people and students.

CONTINENTAL EUROPE

Athens is linked to every major city in Europe by either Olympic Airways or the flag carrier of each country.

London is the discount capital of Europe, but Amsterdam, Frankfurt, Berlin and Paris are also major centres for cheap airfares. Belgium, Switzerland, the Netherlands and Greece are also good places for buying discount air tickets.

Across Europe many travel agencies have ties with STA Travel, where cheap tickets can be purchased and STA-issued tickets can be altered (usually for a US$25 fee).

Acceuil des Jeunes en France
119 rue Saint Martin (4e),
Paris ☎ 01 42 77 87 80
Acceuil des Jeunes en France is one of the most popular discount travel agencies in Paris.

Acotra Student Travel Agency
rue de la Madeline, Brussels ☎ 02-512 86 07

Malibu Travel
Prinsengracht 230, Amsterdam
☎ 020-626 32 30

NBBS Reizen
Rokin 66, Amsterdam ☎ 020-624 09 89
You can find the official student travel agency in

Amsterdam with several other agencies around the city.

Nouvelles Frontières
5 Ave de l'Opéra (1er), Paris
☎ 08 03 33 33 33 (only within France)
W www.nouvelles-frontieres.com

OTU Voyages
39 Ave Georges Bernanos (5e), Paris
☎ 01 44 41 38 50 W www.otu.fr
OTU has another 42 offices around the country.

Passaggi
Stazione Termini FS, Galleria Di Tesla, Rome
☎ 06-474 0923 fax 482 7436

SSR Voyages
Leonhardstrasse 10, Zurich ☎ 01-297 11 11
W www.ssr.ch
SSR Voyages specialises in student, youth and budget fares with branches in most major cities.

STA Travel
Goethestrasse 73, Berlin ☎ 311 0950
fax 313 0948

Voyages Wasteels
11 rue Dupuytren, Paris ☎ 08 03 88 70 04
(only within France) fax 01 43 25 46 25

Voyageurs du Monde
55 rue Sainte Anne (2e),
Paris ☎ 01 42 86 16 00

WATS Reizen
de Keyserlei 44, Antwerp ☎ 03-226 16 26

If you're travelling from Athens to Europe, budget fares to a host of European cities are widely advertised by the travel agents around Syntagma. Following are some typical one-way fares (not including airport tax):

destination	one-way fare (dr)
Amsterdam	57,500
Copenhagen	59,500
Frankfurt	55,000
Geneva	54,000
Hamburg	52,000
Madrid	73,000
Milan	48,000
Munich	55,000
Paris	55,500
Rome	42,000
Zürich	53,500

TURKEY

Olympic Airways and Turkish Airlines share the İstanbul-Athens route, with at least one flight a day each. The full fare is

GETTING THERE & AWAY

US$250 one way. Students qualify for a 50% discount on both routes.

There are no direct flights from Ankara to Athens; all flights go via İstanbul.

CYPRUS

Olympic Airways and Cyprus Airways share the Cyprus-Greece routes. Both airlines have three flights daily from Larnaca to Athens, and there are five flights weekly to Thessaloniki. Cyprus Airways also flies from Paphos to Athens once a week in winter, and twice a week in summer.

Travel agents in Athens charge 50,000 dr one way to Larnaca and Paphos, or 83,000 dr return.

AIRLINE OFFICES

Domestic airline offices in Athens include:

Olympic Airways
headquarters (Map 7, D3; ☎ 966 6666)
Syngrou 96, Koukaki
(☎ 775 9562) Messoghion 2, Ambelokipi
(☎ 894 4220) Athinon 13, Glyfada
(☎ 801 6119) Kifissias 267, Kifissia
(☎ 926 7216) Kotopouli 2, Omonia
(☎ 926 7445) Vassilis Sofias 46, Ilissia
(Map 9, C4; ☎ 452 0968) Akti Miaouli 27, Piraeus

Aegean Air
(☎ 998 8300) Vouliagmenis 572, Ellnikon

Cronus Airlines
(Map 5, D7; ☎ 331 5515) Othonos 10, Syntagma

International airline offices in Athens include:

Aeroflot	☎ 322 0986
Aerolineas Argentinas	☎ 324 0233
Air Canada	☎ 617 5321
Air France	☎ 960 1100
Air India	☎ 360 2001
Air New Zealand	☎ 323 9503
Alitalia	☎ 998 8888
American Airlines	☎ 331 1045
Bangladesh Biman	☎ 322 8089
British Airways	☎ 890 6666
Cathay Pacific	☎ 324 0233
Continental Airlines	☎ 324 9300
CSA-Czech Airlines	☎ 965 2957
Cyprus Airways	☎ 322 6413/4
Delta Airlines	☎ 331 1660
EasyJet	☎ 967 0000
Egypt Air	☎ 921 2818/9
El Al	☎ 677 4029
Emirates Airlines	☎ 933 3400
Garuda Indonesia	☎ 679 5600
Gulf Air	☎ 322 9544
Iberia	☎ 323 4523/6
Japan Airlines	☎ 324 8211
KLM	☎ 960 5000
Lufthansa	☎ 617 5200
Malaysian Airlines	☎ 921 2470
Monarch	☎ 679 5555
Northwest Airlines	☎ 960 5000
Royal Jordanian	☎ 924 2600
Sabena	☎ 337 0520
SAS	☎ 361 3910
Singapore Airlines	☎ 324 4113
South African Airways	☎ 361 6305
Swissair	☎ 337 0520
Thai Airways	☎ 969 2022
Turkish Airlines	☎ 324 6024
TWA	☎ 921 3400
United Airlines	☎ 924 2645
Virgin Atlantic	☎ 690 5300

BUS

OTHER PARTS OF GREECE

Athens has two main intercity bus stations. Terminal A is about 7km north-west of Plateia Omonias at Kifissou 100 and has departures to the Peloponnese, the Ionian Islands and western Greece. Terminal B is about 5km north of Omonia off Liossion and has departures to central and northern Greece as well as to Evia. The EOT gives out an intercity bus schedule.

Terminal A

Terminal A is not a good introduction to Athens – particularly if you arrive between midnight and 5am when there is no public transport.

See the Getting Around chapter for details of fares, and the boxed text 'Dangers & Annoyances' earlier in the Facts for Visitor chapter for information on avoiding rip-offs.

The only public transport to the city centre is bus No 051, which runs between the terminal and the junction of Zinonos and Menandrou, near Omonia. Don't bother visiting the Tourist Information office at the terminal. It's a booking agency.

Buses leave Bus Terminal A for the following destinations:

destination	duration (hours)	price (dr)	frequency
Argos	2	2500	hourly
Corinth	1½	1850	half-hourly
Epidaurus	2½	2650	2 daily
Igoumenitsa	8½	9250	4 daily
Nafplio	2½	2800	hourly
Olympia	5½	6200	4 daily
Patras	3	4000	half-hourly
Thessaloniki	7½	9000	8 daily

Terminal B

Terminal B, on Agiou Dimitriou Oplon, is much easier to handle than Terminal A, although again there is no public transport from midnight to 5am. The EOT information sheet misleadingly lists the address of the terminal as being Liossion 260, which turns out to be a small car repair workshop. A taxi from the terminal to Syntagma should cost no more than 1500 dr at any time.

Buses leave Bus Terminal B for the folowing destinations:

destination	duration (hours)	price (dr)	frequency
Delphi	3	3300	6 daily
Larisa	4½	6600	6 daily
Trikala	5½	6000	8 daily
Volos	5	5800	9 daily

Mavromateon Terminal Map 3, B7

Buses for nearly all destinations in Attica leave from the Mavromateon terminal, at the junction of Alexandras and 28 Oktovriou-Patission. Buses for southern Attica leave from this terminal, while buses to Rafina and Marathon leave from the bus stops 150m north on Mavromateon.

Buses leave Mavromateon terminal for the folowing destinations:

destination	duration (hours)	price (dr)	frequency
Cape Sounion (via coast road)	1½	1350	hourly
Cape Sounion (via Lavrio)	1½	1250	hourly
Lavrio	1¼	1050	half-hourly
Marathon	1	800	hourly

ALBANIA

There is a daily Organismos Sidirodromon Ellados (OSE; Greek Railways Organisation) bus between Athens and Tirana (21 hours, 12,600 dr), leaving from Peloponnese train station at 8.30am every day except Sunday.

BULGARIA

OSE operates two Athens-Sofia buses (15 hours, 13,400 dr) daily except Monday, leaving at 7am and 5pm.

TURKEY

OSE operates a daily service from Athens to İstanbul (22 hours, 23,000 dr), leaving the Peloponnese train station in Athens at 11pm. Students qualify for a 15% discount and children under 12 travel for half price.

Buses from İstanbul to Athens leave the Anadolu Terminal (Anatolia Terminal) at the Topkapı (bus station) at 10am.

TRAIN

Trains are operated by the Greek Railways Organisation which offers two very different levels of service. There are slow, stopping-all-stations services that crawl around the countryside, and the faster, modern intercity trains that link most major cities.

The slow trains represent the country's cheapest form of public transport. The fares haven't changed for years; 2nd-class fares are absurdly cheap, and even 1st class is cheaper than bus travel. The downside is that the trains are painfully slow, uncomfortable and unreliable. There seems to be no effort to upgrade the dilapidated rolling stock on these services. Unless you are travelling on a very tight budget, they are best left alone – except on shorter runs.

OTHER PARTS OF GREECE

Athens has two train stations, conveniently located right next to each other about 1km north-east of Plateia Omonias.

GETTING THERE & AWAY

Larisis station Map 3, B2

Larisis station, on Deligianni, is for trains to Evia, northern Greece and all international services. Services include nine trains a day to Thessaloniki. Five of these are Intercity services, which take six hours and cost 9400 dr in 2nd class and 12,700 dr in 1st class. Couchettes are available on overnight services, priced from 1750 dr in 2nd class and 5800 dr in 1st class.

Peloponnese station Map 3, C1

The Peloponnese station, on Sidirodromon, is only for trains to the Peloponnese. Useful services include eight trains a day to Patras. Four of these are Intercity services, which take 3½ hours and cost 3400 dr in 2nd class, 4700 dr in 1st class. These trains travel via Corinth (1½ hours, 1800/2400 dr in 2nd/1st class).

It's also possible to travel to Nafplio by train. The trains that work this route are real old rattlers that take 3½ hours to do the trip. The only reason to catch these services is the magnificent countryside between Corinth and Nafplio. Fares from Athens to Nafplio are 1600/2400 dr in 2nd/1st class.

The easiest way to get to the stations is to catch the metro to the Larisa stop on Line 2, which is right outside Larisis station. To get to the Peloponnese train station, cross over the metal bridge at the southern end of Larisis train station. You can also get to the stations on trolleybus No 1.

There is baggage storage at Larisis station, open from 6.30am to 9.30pm, and the cost is 400 dr per piece.

More information on services is available from the OSE offices which also handle advance bookings. They accept Mastercard and Visa.

OSE Omonia branch, Map 3, E3
Karolou 1, Omonia ☎ 524 0647 ☉ Mon-Fri 8am-3.30pm, Sat 8am-3pm

OSE Syntagma branch Map 4, B10
Sina 6, Syntagma ☎ 362 4402 ☉ Mon-Fri 8am-6pm, Sat 8am-3pm

TURKEY

There is a daily train from Athens to İstanbul (20,000 dr) via Thessaloniki and Alexandroupolis. There are often delays at the border and the journey can take much longer than the supposed 22 hours. You'd be well advised to take the bus.

BULGARIA

There is a daily train from Athens to Sofia (18 hours, 10,330 dr), travelling via Thessaloniki.

FORMER YUGOSLAV REPUBLIC OF MACEDONIA (FYROM)

There are Thessaloniki-Skopje trains (three hours, 4200 dr, two daily), which cross the border between Idomeni and Gevgelija. The trains leave Thessaloniki at 6am and 5.30pm. Both trains continue to the Serbian capital of Belgrade (12 hours, 11,500 dr). The 5.30pm service goes all the way to Budapest (21 hours, 20,000 dr).

There are no trains between Florina and FYROM, although there may be trains to Skopje from the FYROM side of the border.

NORTHERN EUROPE

Unless you have a Eurail pass or are aged under 26 and eligible for a discounted fare, travelling to Greece by train is prohibitively expensive. For example, the full one-way/return fare from London to Athens is UK£265/521, including the Eurostar service from London to Paris.

Greece is part of the Eurail network. Eurail passes can only be bought by residents of non-European countries and are supposed to be purchased before arriving in Europe. They can, however, be bought in Europe as long as your passport proves that you've been there for less than six months. In London, head for the Rail Europe Travel Centre (☎ 08705 848 848), 179 Piccadilly, W1. Sample fares include UK£461 for an adult Eurail Flexipass, which permits 10 days 1st-class travel in two months, and UK£323 for the equivalent youth pass.

If you are starting your European travels in Greece, you can buy your Eurail pass from the OSE office at Karolou 1 in Omonia.

CAR & MOTORCYCLE

National Road 1 is the main route north from Athens. It starts at Nea Kifissia. To get there from central Athens, take Vasilissis Sofias from Syntagma. National Road 8, which begins beyond Dafni, is the road to the Peloponnese. Take Agiou Konstantinou from Omonia.

GETTING THERE & AWAY

RENTAL

Rental cars are widely available, but are more expensive than in most other European countries. All the big multinational car hire companies are represented in Athens.

The multinationals are, however, the most expensive places to hire a car. High season weekly rates with unlimited mileage start at about 126,000 dr for the smallest models, such as a 900cc Fiat Panda. The rate drops to about 100,000 dr per week in winter. To these prices must be added VAT of 18%, as well as a string of the optional extras, such as a collision damage waiver of 3300 dr per day (more for larger models), without which you will be liable for the first 1,500,000 dr of the repair bill (much more for larger models). Other costs include a theft waiver of at least 1000 dr per day and personal accident insurance. It all adds up to an expensive exercise. The major companies offer much cheaper prebooked and prepaid rates.

Local companies offer some good deals for those prepared to shop around. They are normally more open to negotiation, especially if business is slow. Their advertised rates are about 25% cheaper than those offered by the multinationals.

If you want to take a hire car to another country or onto a ferry, you will need advance written authorisation from the hire company. Unless you pay with a credit card, most hire companies will require a minimum deposit of 20,000 dr per day.

The minimum driving age in Greece is 18 years, but most car hire firms require you to be at least 23, although a few will rent vehicles to 21-year-olds.

The northern reaches of Syngrou, just south of the Temple of Olympian Zeus, are packed with car rental firms. They include:

Avis (Map 4, G8; ☎ 322 4951) Amalias 48
Budget (Map 7, A6; ☎ 921 4771) Syngrou 8
Europcar (Map 7, A6; ☎ 924 8810) Syngrou 36-8
Hertz (Map 7, A6; ☎ 922 0102) Syngrou 12
Sixt (Map 7, B5; ☎ 922 0171) Syngrou 23

It's also possible to rent mopeds and motorcycles.

Motorent (Map 7, B4; ☎ 923 4939) Rovertou Galli 1, Makrigianni ⓦ www.motorent.com
Has a choice ranging from 50 to 250cc

ALBANIA

The main crossing is at Kakavia, 60km north-west of Ioannina. There is a second crossing at Krystallopigi, 14km west of Kotas on the Florina-Kastoria road. Kapshtica is the closest town on the Albanian side. It is possible to take a private vehicle into Albania, although it's not a great idea, because of security concerns and problems with obtaining spare parts. Always carry your passport in areas near the Albanian border.

FORMER YUGOSLAV REPUBLIC OF MACEDONIA

The main crossing is at Evzoni, 68km north of Thessaloniki. This is the main highway to Skopje which continues to Belgrade. There is another crossing is at Niki, 16km north of Florina. This road leads to Bitola, and continues to Ohrid, once a popular tourist resort on the shores of Lake Ohrid.

TURKEY

The main crossing points are at Kipi, 43km north-east of Alexandroupolis, and at Kastanies, 139km north-east of Alexandroupolis. Kipi is more convenient if you're heading for İstanbul, but the route through Kastanies goes via the fascinating towns of Soufli and Didymotiho, in Greece, and Edirne (ancient Adrianople) in Turkey.

BULGARIA

The crossing is at Promahonas, 145km north-east of Thessaloniki and 50km from Serres.

NORTHERN EUROPE

Before the troubles in the former Yugoslavia began, most motorists driving from the UK to Greece opted for the direct route: Ostend, Brussels, Salzburg and then down the Yugoslav highway through Zagreb, Belgrade and Skopje and crossing the border to Evzoni.

These days most people drive to an Italian port and catch a ferry across to Greece. Coming from the UK, this means driving through France, where petrol costs and road tolls are exorbitant.

BICYCLE

Cycling is a wonderful way to visit many parts of Greece, but not Athens. Manic traffic and serious air pollution make the capital city a nightmarish place for the cyclist.

Most people prefer to get a safe distance from the capital before considering getting the wheels out. Slow trains, but not intercity trains, will carry bicycles, so the best bet is to catch a train as far as Corinth (for the Peloponnese) or Thebes (for central and northern Greece).

HITCHING

Athens is the most difficult place in Greece to hitchhike from. For the Peloponnese, take bus No 860 or 880 from Panepistimiou to Dafni, where National Road 8 begins. For northern Greece, take the metro to Kifissia, then a bus to Nea Kifissia and walk to National Road 1.

BOAT

DEPARTURE TAX

Port taxes are included in the price of tickets for travel within Greece. International departure taxes vary according to the destination: 2000 dr to Italy, 3000 dr to Turkey and 5000 dr to Cyprus and Israel.

OTHER PARTS OF GREECE
Ferry

Piraeus is the busiest port in Greece with a bewildering array of departures and destinations, including daily services to all the island groups except the Ionians and the Sporades.

The following table lists all the destinations that can be reached by ferry. The information is for the high season – from mid-June to September.

For the latest departure information, pick up a weekly ferry schedule from a tourist office in Athens.

The departure points for the various ferry destinations are shown on the map of Piraeus. Note that there are two departure points for Crete. Ferries for Iraklio leave from the western end of Akti Kondyli, but ferries for other Cretan ports occasionally dock there as well. It's a long way to the

other departure point for Crete on Akti Miaouli, so check where to find your boat when you buy your ticket.

Ferry prices are fixed by the government. All ferries charge the same for any given route, although the facilities on board differ – quite radically at times. The small differences in prices charged by agents are the result of them sacrificing part of their allotted commission to increase sales (allowing them to call themselves 'discount' agencies). These discounts seldom amount to more than 50 dr. Agents cannot charge more than the fixed price.

If you want to book a cabin or take a car on board a ferry, it is advisable to buy a ticket in advance in Athens. Otherwise, you should wait until you get to Piraeus; agents selling ferry tickets are thick on the ground around Plateia Karaïskaki. If you're running short of time, you can buy your ticket at the quay from the tables set up next to each ferry. It costs no more to buy your ticket at the boat, contrary to what some agents might tell you.

Ferries leave from Piraeus for the following destinations:

destination	duration (hours)	price (dr)	frequency
Cyclades			
Amorgos	10	4800	6 weekly
Anafi	11	6400	4 weekly
Folegandros	9	4700	daily
Ios	7½	5390	4 daily
Kimolos	6	4300	daily
Kythnos	2½	2900	daily
Milos	7	4800	daily
Mykonos	5½	4800	daily
Naxos	6	4700	8 daily
Paros	5	4700	6 daily
Santorini	9	5600	5 daily
Serifos	4½	3700	daily
Sifnos	5½	4200	daily
Sikinos	8-10	5700	daily
Syros	4	4200	3 daily
Tinos	4½	4500	2 daily
Crete			
Agios Nikolaos	12	5900	3 weekly
Hania	10	5370	daily
Iraklio	14	4500	2 daily

Kastelli-Kissamou	22	10,620	8 daily
Rethymno	10-12	6450	daily
Sitia	14	7130	3 weekly
Dodecanese			
Astpalea	12	6500	2 weekly
Halki	24	9060	weekly
Kalymnos	12	6720	2 daily
Karpathos	19	7620	3 weekly
Kassos	17½	7500	3 weekly
Kos	11-18	7210	2 daily
Leros	11	6130	daily
Lipsi	11	7000	weekly
Nissiros	16	7170	weekly
Patmos	10	6500	daily
Rhodes	14-18	8560	daily
Symi	14-18	8300	weekly
Tilos	16	7160	weekly
North-Eastern Aegean Sea			
Chios	8	5500	daily
Fournoi	11	5500	weekly
Ikaria	8	5100	daily
Lesvoa (Mytilini)	12	6680	daily
Limnos	20	6720	2 weekly
Samos	12	6400	daily
Saronic Gulf Islands			
Aegina	1	1400	hourly
Hydra	3½	2230	2 daily
Poros	2½	2000	3 daily
Spetses	3½	3100	daily

Hydrofoil

Minoan Lines operates its Flying Dolphin hydrofoil services from Piraeus to the Saronic Gulf Islands, the Peloponnese and a growing range of destinations in the Cyclades. Services to the Cyclades leave from Great Harbour, while other departures are split between Great Harbour and Zea Marina – check when you buy your ticket.

The information in the hydrofoil timetable is for the high season, from mid-June to September.

Although it is often possible to buy tickets at Minoan's quayside offices at both Great Harbour and Zea Marina, reservations are strongly recommended – especially at weekends. You can book seats, and pay by credit card, by phoning Minoan's bookings centre on ☎ 428 0001.

Ferries leave from Piraeus for the following destinations:

destination	duration (hours)	price (dr)	frequency
Cyclades			
Kythnos	1½	4700	daily
Milos	4½	7700	daily
Mykonos	3	7800	daily
Naxos	3½	7600	daily
Paros	3	7600	daily
Serifos	2½	5900	daily
Sifnos	3	6700	daily
Syros	2¼	6800	daily
Peloponnese (*from Zea Marina)			
Ermioni*	1½	4200	3 daily
Gerakas *	3¾	6500	daily
Kyparissi*	3¼	6100	daily
Leonidio *	2¾	5700	daily
Methana*	1	2800	3 daily
Monemvasia*	2½	7200	daily
Porto Heli*	2	4600	3 daily
Saronic Gulf Islands			
Aegina	40 mins	1700	hourly
Hydra*	1¼	3600	9 daily
Poros *	1	3300	9 daily
Spetses*	2	5000	9 daily

Flying Dolphin Office Map 9, A2
cnr Akti Kondyli & Etolikou, Piraeus
☎ 419 9000 fax 413 1111 ⓔ booking@mfd.gr
🕓 8am-8pm Mon-Fri, 8am-4pm Sat & Sun

ITALY

There are no ferries to Italy from Piraeus. The main ports for services to Italy are Patras, in the Peloponnese, and Igoumenitsa, in north-western Greece. Patras, 3½ hours west of Athens by train, is far more convenient.

The most popular crossing is between Patras and Brindisi. There are up to five ferries a day in summer, falling to three or four a week in winter. Deck-class fares start at 7600 dr in low season and 12,000 dr in high season. The trip takes 18 hours. Most ferries stop at Igoumenitsa and Corfu on the way. There are also regular ferries from Patras to Ancona, Bari, Trieste and Venice.

CYPRUS & ISRAEL

Poseidon Lines and Salamis Lines operate weekly services between Piraeus and the

Israeli port of Haifa, via Lemesos (Limassol) on Cyprus. These boats also stop at Rhodes and various other Greek islands. Deck-class fares from Piraeus are 16,000/20,000 dr to Lemessos and 26,000/29,000 dr to Haifa in low/high season. High season fares apply only during July and August. Cabins are priced from 30,000/36,000 dr to Lemessos, and 43,000/49,000 dr to Haifa.

TURKEY

There are no scheduled ferry services from Piraeus to Turkey, but there are regular boats from the Greek Islands: Chios-Çeşme, Kos-Bodrum, Lesvos-Ayvalık, Rhodes-Marmaris and Samos-Kuşadası. Tickets for all ferries to Turkey must be bought a day in advance. Port tax for departures to Turkey is 3000 dr.

Αθήνα

Getting Around

There was a time, in the not so distant past, when getting around – or getting anywhere – in Athens was almost impossibly time-consuming and exasperating. So traffic-clogged were the streets of the city centre that travel by public transport was a waste of time: it was invariably quicker to walk than to catch a bus.

These days, the streets are still clogged with traffic, but they can be avoided by using the magnificent new metro network. The network is far from complete, but already it's had an enormous impact. Travel around central Athens is now a breeze.

THE AIRPORT

Eleftherios Venizelos international airport is 21km east of Athens, outside the small village of Spata.

BUS

There are two special express bus services operating between the airport and the city as well as a service between the airport and Piraeus.

Tickets for all these services cost 1000 dr. The tickets are valid for 24 hours, and can be used on all forms of public transport in Athens - buses, trolleybuses and the metro.

Express Line E94 – Ethniki Amina-Airport

Service E94 operates between the airport and the eastern terminus of Metro line 3 at Ethniki Amyna. The journey takes about 25 minutes.

from Ethniki Amina	frequency
6am-8.30pm	every 16 min
8.30pm-midnight	every 25-30 min

from the airport	
6.40am-9.05pm	every 16 min
9.05pm-11.20pm	every 25-30 min

Express Line E95 – Syntagma-Airport

Service E95 operates between the airport and Plateia Syntagmatos. This line operates

24 hours with services approximately every 30 minutes. The bus stop is on the eastern side of Plateia Syntagmatos on Amalias outside the National Gardens. The journey takes between an hour and 90 minutes, depending on traffic conditions.

from Syntagma	frequency
6am-7.50pm	every 25 min
7.50pm-6am	every 25 min

from the airport	
6.30am-9.20pm	every 25 min
9.20pm-11.35pm	every 25-30 min
11.35pm-1.30am	every 15-20 min
1.30am-6.30am	every 30-35 min

Express Line E96 – Piraeus-Airport

Service E96 operates between the airport and Plateia Karaiskaki in Piraeus. This line also operates 24 hours, with services approximately every 40 minutes.

from Piraeus	frequency
5am-7pm	every 20 min
7pm-8.30pm	every 30 min
8.30pm-5am	every 40 min

from the airport	
7pm-8.45pm	every 20 min
8.45pm-10.05pm	every 25 min
10.05pm-6am	every 40 min
6am-7am	every 30 min

AIRPORT TAXIS

The move from Ellnikon to Spata has done nothing to mend the ways of the notorious airport cabbies. It seems to be virtually impossible to catch a cab from the airport without getting involved in an argument about the fare. See the boxed text 'Dangers & Annoyances' in the Facts for the Visitor chapter for the full run-down on the scams operated by the city's notorious cabbies.

Whatever happens, make sure that the meter is set to the correct tariff (see the Taxi section later in this chapter for details). You will also have to pay a 300 dr airport sur-charge. Fares vary according to the time of day and level of traffic, but you should ex-pect to pay 5000-7000 dr from the airport to the city centre, and 6000-8000 dr to Piraeus, depending on traffic conditions. Both trips should take no longer than an hour. If you have any problems, do not hesitate to threaten to involve the tourist police.

BUS & TROLLEYBUS

Since most of Athens' ancient sites are within easy walking distance of Syntagma, and many of the museums are close by on Vasilissis Sofias, the chances are that you won't have much need for public transport.

The blue-and-white buses that serve Athens and the suburbs operate every 15 minutes from 5am until midnight. There are two types of service. Regular services, which stop every few hundred metres, are indicated by a three figure number – such as bus No 224 from Akadimias to Moni Kaissarianis. Express buses are indicated by a letter followed by a one or two figure number – such as bus A2 from Panepis-timiou to Glyfada, and the E91 between the airport and Syntagma.

There are also special buses operating 24 hours a day between the city centre and Piraeus – every 20 minutes from 6am until midnight and then hourly. Bus No 040 runs from Filellinon, near Plateia Syntagmatos, to Akti Xaveriou in Piraeus, and No 049 runs from the northern end of Athinas, near Plateia Omonias, to Plateia Themistokleous in Piraeus.

Trolleybuses also operate from 5am until midnight. The free map handed out by EOT shows most of the routes.

There is a flat fare of 150 dr throughout the city on both buses and trolleybuses. Tickets must be purchased before you board, either at a transport kiosk or at most *periptera*. They can be bought in blocks of 10, but there is no discount for bulk buying. The same tickets can be used on either buses or trolleybuses and must be validated using the red ticket machine as soon as you board. Plain-clothed inspectors make spot checks, and the penalty for travelling with-out a validated ticket is 4800 dr.

METRO

The opening of the first phase of the long-awaited new metro system has transformed travel around central Athens. Athenians can hardly believe their luck. Journeys that once took more than an hour above ground can now be completed in a matter of minutes. Some people have even turned up on time for meetings, quite accidentally.

Coverage is still largely confined to the city centre, but that's good enough for most visitors. The following is a brief outline of the three lines that make up the network:

LINE 1

Line 1 is the old Kifissia-Piraeus line. Until the opening of lines 2 and 3, this was the metro system. It is indicated in green on maps and signs.

Useful stops include Piraeus (for the port), Monastiraki and Omonia (city centre), Plateia Viktorias (National Archaeological Museum) and Irini (Olym-pic Stadium). Omonia and Attiki are transfer stations with connections to Line 2; Monastiraki will eventually become a transfer station with connections to Line 3.

LINE 2

Line 2 runs from Sepolia in the north-west to Dafni in the south-east. It is indicated in red on maps and signs. Useful stops include Larisa (for the train stations), Omonia, Panepistimiou and Syntagma (city centre) and Akropoli (Makrigianni). Attiki and Omonia are transfer stations for Line 1, while Syntagma is the transfer station for Line 3.

LINE 3

Line 3 runs north-east from Syntagma to Ethniki Amyna. It is indicated in blue on maps and signs. Useful stops are Evangel-ismos (for the museums on Vasilissis Sofias) and Megaro Musikis (Athens Con-cert Hall). Syntagma is the transfer station for Line 2. This line is scheduled to be ex-tended south-west to Monastiraki, and

GETTING AROUND

Traffic Chaos

Athens suffers from a sorry reputation as one of the most traffic-clogged cities in the world.

From a mere 39,000 private vehicles in 1961, there are now almost 1.7 million cars in circulation – and a further 500,000 motorcycles. The number of vehicles continues to grow at an alarming rate. Car dealers reported record sales in 2000, adding 170,000 cars to the pool.

As well as producing something approaching traffic gridlock across the city, the exhaust emissions from all these vehicles are the major contributor to the grey *nefos* (toxic cloud) that envelops the city. The city's once famous sunsets disappeared long ago, and archaeologists have warned that the fumes are destroying the Parthenon and other famous monuments.

The problem has been taxing the ingenuity of cash-strapped city authorities for a long time. The first attempt at controlling vehicle numbers came way back in 1980 with the introduction of the famous odds and evens number-plate legislation. The system, which continues to this day, bars odd and even plates from the city centre on alternate days. This, it was calculated, would halve the number of vehicles in the city centre. Instead it resulted in many families buying a second car with the requisite number-plate.

The next attempt, at the beginning of 1993, was more sophisticated – but equally ill-fated. It was decreed that all cars circulating in central Athens must be fitted with catalytic converters. This was promoted by a regulation reducing import duties on cars fitted with the devices, as long as the owner scrapped a vehicle at least 15 years old. Many low income families then became car owners for the first time by buying an old banger and trading it in for a new clean car.

Since then, hopes have been pinned on the new metro system to reverse the trend. The first indications have not been particularly encouraging. Passenger statistics for the metro look impressive, but it appears that the majority of users have been lured from other forms of public transport. The roads remain as clogged as ever, and Athenian drivers still prefer to spend an hour in a car rather than 10 minutes in a train. The situation may improve as the metro is extended into new population centres.

The metro is just part of a major overhaul of the city's road and public transport systems. Another major project is the construction of a ring road, known as Leoforos Attikis, which will connect the city's south-eastern suburbs with the national roads north to Thessaloniki and west to the Peloponnese. The first section was completed in March 2001 and provides access to the airport and Spata. The remainder is expected to be completed towards the end of 2002.

A third project, yet to be started but supposed to be completed before the Olympics in 2004, will be the construction of a tram line from the city centre to the coast. It will run from the Temple of Olympian Zeus along Syngrou to the coast, where one branch will run south-east along the seafront to Glyfada and a second will run west to the Peace and Friendship Stadium at Faliro.

---

north-east to Stavros. Eventually, according to the master plan, Stavros will have rail service to the airport.

The ticket pricing is unnecessarily complicated. Travel on lines 2 and 3 costs 250 dr, while Line 1 is split into three sections: Piraeus-Monastiraki, Monastiraki-Attiki and Attiki-Kifissia. Travel within one section costs 200 dr, and a journey covering two or more sections costs 250 dr. The same conditions apply everywhere though: tickets must be validated at the machines at platform entrances before travelling. The penalty for travelling without a validated ticket is 8000 dr.

The trains operate between 5am and midnight. They run every three minutes during peak periods, dropping to every 10 minutes at other times.

CAR & MOTORCYCLE

Appalling traffic, confusing signposting as well as the one-way system that operates on most streets in the city centre combine to make Athens a nightmarish place to drive in. The traffic jams do at least offer an opportunity to work out where you're going!

Athenian drivers have a cavalier attitude towards driving laws. Contrary to what you will see, parking *is* illegal alongside kerbs marked with yellow lines, where street signs prohibit parking and on pavements and in pedestrian malls.

Athens has numerous small car parks, but these are totally insufficient for the number of cars in the city.

For details of car and motorcycle rental agencies in Athens, see the Getting There & Away chapter.

TAXI

Athens' taxis are yellow. If you see an Athenian standing in the road bellowing and waving their arms frantically, the chances are they will be trying to get a taxi at rush hour. Despite the large number of taxis careering around the streets of Athens, it can be incredibly difficult to get one.

To hail a taxi, stand on a pavement and shout your destination as they pass. If a taxi is going your way the driver may stop even if there are already passengers inside. This does not mean the fare will be shared: each person will be charged the fare shown on the meter. If you get in one that does not have other passengers, make sure the meter is switched on.

The flag fall is 250 dr, with a 160 dr surcharge from ports and railway and bus stations, and a 300 dr surcharge from the airport. After that, the day rate (tariff 1 on the meter) is 76 dr/km. The rate doubles between midnight and 5am (tariff 2 on the meter). Baggage is charged at the rate of 55 dr per item over 10kg. The minimum fare is 500 dr, which covers most journeys in central Athens. It sometimes helps if you can point out your destination on a map – many taxi drivers in Athens are extremely ignorant of their city.

If it is absolutely imperative that you get somewhere on time (eg, to the airport), and you want to go by taxi, it is advisable to book a radio taxi – you will be charged 600 dr extra, but it's worth it. The radio taxis operating out of central Athens include:

name	telephone
Athina 1	☎ 921 7942
Enotita	☎ 645 9000
Ermis	☎ 411 5200
Ikaros	☎ 515 2800
Kosmos	☎ 1300
Parthenon	☎ 532 3300

For more information about Athens' taxi drivers, see the boxed text 'Dangers & Annoyances' in the Facts for the Visitor chapter.

ORGANISED TOURS

There are four main companies running organised tours around Athens.

The list starts with an Athens city tour, which involves sitting back in an air-con bus while a guide provides a commentary on the major sites. Most tours include a visit to the Acropolis, but check.

Evening tours usually involve a visit to the sound and light show, followed by dinner and folk dancing at a supposedly traditional taverna.

The third possibility is a half-day tour to visit the Temple of Poseidon at Cape Sounio.

You will find brochures for the tour companies everywhere; all the hotels listed in the following Places to Stay chapter act as a booking agent for at least one tour company. The hotels often offer substantial discounts on the official tour prices as a service to their customers - discounts that aren't available if you book directly.

CHAT tours begin from the company's terminal at the Amalias Hotel, Amalias 10; GO Tours leave from outside the *periptero* (kiosk) at the junction of Amalias and Souri; and Key Tours begin from the the combined office and terminal at Kalirois 4. If you are staying nearby, you can walk to the terminal of the respective company. If not, when you make your booking, you will be informed of the time and location of a pick-up point close to your hotel; a company bus will then collect you and transport you to its terminal.

Hop-In Tours works differently. For city tours, its buses work a set route with a number of specified pick-up points. You can get on, or off, wherever you choose – and go around as many times as you like. For tours outside Athens, Hop-In will inform you of the time and location of your pick-up point and then keep going with the tour.

Hop In Sightseeing

Zanni 29, Piraeus ☎ 428 5500
Ⓦ www.hopin.com Ⓢ 9000/10,500/15,500 dr city tour/city tour with guided Acropolis tour/city tour with Acropolis tour and lunch; 14,000 dr Athens by night, with sound and light show and dinner; 8500/15,500 dr evening tour to Cape Sounion/evening tour to Cape Sounion with seafood dinner; 21,500 dr full day tour to Delphi with lunch; 21,500 dr full day tour to Corinth Canal, Epidaurus, Nafplio, Mycenae & Ancient Corinth with lunch

CHAT Map 5, E7

Xenofontos 9, Plaka ☎ 322 3137 Ⓢ 10,500 dr half-day sightseeing tour of Athens; 10,600 dr Athens by night; 8000 dr half-day tour to Cape Sounion; 13,500 dr half day tour to Ancient Corinth; 18,500/21,500 dr full day tour to Delphi/Delphi with lunch; 18,500 dr full day tour to the Corinth Canal, Mycenae, Nafplio & Epidaurus; 21,500 dr Corinth Canal, Mycenae, Nafplio

and Epidaurus with lunch; 20,500 dr one-day cruises to Aegina, Poros and Hydra with lunch

GO Tours Map 4, F9

Athanassiou Diakou 20, Makrigianni
☎ 921 9555 Ⓢ 10,500 dr half-day sightseeing tour of Athens; 14,000 dr Athens by night; 8200 dr one-day tours to Cape Sounion; 18,500/21,500 dr Delphi/Delphi with lunch; 21,500 dr the Corinth Canal, Mycenae, Nafplio & Epidaurus (same prices); 20,500 dr one-day cruises to Aegina, Poros & Hydra including lunch

Key Tours Map 7, B6

Kaliroïs 4, Makrigianni ☎ 923 3166, 923 3266
Ⓦ www.keytours.gr Ⓢ 10,800/15,100 dr half-day sightseeing tour of Athens/half-day sight-seeing tour of Athens including the Acropolis and National Archaeological Museum; 8400 dr Athens by night; 8400 dr half-day tour to Cape Sounion; 18,800/21,800 dr full day tour to Delphi/Delphi with lunch; 18,800 dr full day tour to the Corinth Canal, Mycenae, Nafplio and Epidaurus; 21,800 dr Corinth Canal, Mycenae, Nafplio & Epidaurus with lunch; 20,500 dr one-day cruise to Aegina, Poros & Hydra with lunch; 50% discount on all tours for children aged 4-12

The Acropolis

JOHN ELK III

TREVOR CREIGHTON

TREVOR CREIGHTON

JOHN ELK III

Title page: Section of the Acropolis (Photo: Chris Christo)

Top: The Acropolis from Filopappos Hill

Middle left: The ruins of the Propylaea

Middle right: The ruins of the Erechtheion

Bottom: The graceful Caryatids look out over Athens from the Erechtheion's southern portico.

THE ACROPOLIS

Map 4, F5
Plaka ☎ 321 0219 🕒 8.30am-4.30pm Mon-Fri & 8am-3pm Sat & Sun winter, 8am-6.30pm daily summer, autumn, spring
$ adult/student 2000/1000 dr
[M] Akropoli

Athens exists because of the Acropolis, the most important ancient monument in the Western world. Crowned by the Parthenon, it stands sentinel over Athens, visible from almost everywhere within the city. Its monuments of Pentelic marble gleam white in the midday sun and gradually take on a honey hue as the sun sinks. At night they are floodlit and seem to hover above the city. No matter how harassed you may become in Athens, a sudden unexpected glimpse of this magnificent sight cannot fail to lift your spirits.

Inspiring as these monuments are, they are but faded remnants of Pericles' city, and it takes a great leap of the imagination to begin to comprehend the splendour of his creations. Pericles spared no expense – only the best materials, architects, sculptors and artists were good enough for a city dedicated to the cult of Athena, tutelary goddess of Athens. The city was a showcase of colossal buildings, lavishly coloured and gilded, and of gargantuan statues, some of bronze, others of marble plated with gold and encrusted with precious stones.

There is only one entrance to the Acropolis, which is on the western side. There are two approaches to this entrance. The approach from the north is along the path that is a continuation of Dioskouron in the southwestern corner of Plaka. From the south, there is a path leading up to the entrance from the junction of Dionysiou Areopagitou and Rovertou Galli.

The crowds that swarm over the Acropolis need to be seen to be believed. It's best to get there as early in the day as possible. You need to wear shoes with good soles because the paths around the site are uneven and very slippery.

History

The Acropolis (High City) was first inhabited in Neolithic times. The first temples were built during the Mycenaean era in homage to the goddess Athena. People lived on the Acropolis until the late 6th century BC, but in 510 BC the Delphic oracle declared that it should be the province of the gods.

After all the buildings on the Acropolis were reduced to ashes by the Persians on the eve of the Battle of Salamis (480 BC), Pericles set about his ambitious rebuilding program. He transformed the Acropolis into a city of temples which has come to be regarded as the zenith of classical Greek achievement.

All four of the surviving monuments of the Acropolis have received their fair share of battering through the ages. Ravages inflicted upon them during the years of foreign occupation, pilfering by foreign archaeologists, visitors' footsteps and earthquakes have all taken their toll. The year 1687 was a particularly bad one. The Venetians attacked the Turks and opened fire on the Acropolis, causing an explosion in the Parthenon, where the Turks were storing gunpowder. The resulting fire blazed for two days, damaging all the buildings.

However, the most recent menace, acid rain, caused by industrial pollution and traffic fumes, is proving to be the most irreversibly destructive. It is dissolving the very marble of which the monuments are built. Major renovation work is taking place in an effort to save the monuments for future generations, and the site now boasts a World Heritage Site listing.

Beulé Gate & Monument of Agrippa

Once you've bought your ticket for the Acropolis and have walked a little way along the path, you will see on your left the Beulé Gate, named after the French archaeologist Ernest Beulé, who uncovered it in 1852. The 8m-high pedestal on the left, halfway up the zigzag ramp leading to the

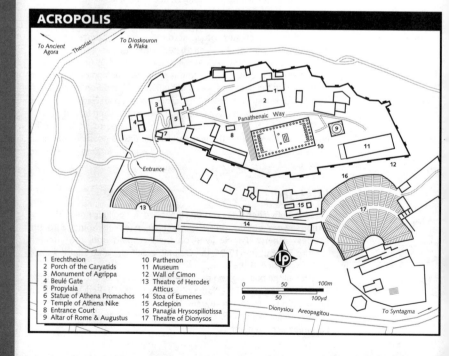

ACROPOLIS

To Ancient Agora
Theorias
To Dioskouron & Plaka
Panathenaic Way
Entrance
Dionysiou Areopagitou
To Syntagma

1 Erechtheion
2 Porch of the Caryatids
3 Monument of Agrippa
4 Beulé Gate
5 Propylaia
6 Statue of Athena Promachos
7 Temple of Athena Nike
8 Entrance Court
9 Altar of Rome & Augustus
10 Parthenon
11 Museum
12 Wall of Cimon
13 Theatre of Herodes Atticus
14 Stoa of Eumenes
15 Asclepion
16 Panagia Hrysospiliotissa
17 Theatre of Dionysos

0   50   100m
0   50   100yd

Propylaia, was once topped by the Monument of Agrippa, a bronze statue of the Roman general riding a chariot. It was erected in 27 BC to commemorate victory in a chariot race at the Panathenaic games.

Propylaia

The Propylaia formed the towering entrance to the Acropolis in ancient times. Built by Mnesicles in 437–432 BC, its architectural brilliance ranks with that of the Parthenon. It consists of a central hall, with two wings on either side. Each section had a gate, and in ancient times these five gates were the only entrances to the 'upper city'. The middle gate (which was the largest) opened onto the Panathenaic Way. The western portico of the Propylaia must indeed have been imposing, consisting of six double columns, Doric on the outside and Ionic on the inside. The fourth column along has been restored. The ceiling of the central hall was painted with gold stars on a dark blue background. The northern wing was used as a picture gallery *(pinakotheke)* and the south wing was the antechamber to the Temple of Athena Nike.

The Propylaia is aligned with the Parthenon – the earliest example of a building designed in relation to another. It remained intact until the 13th century when various occupiers started adding to it. It was badly damaged in the 17th century when a lightning strike set off an explosion in a Turkish gunpowder store. Heinrich Schliemann paid for the removal of one of its appendages – a Frankish tower – in the 19th century. Reconstruction took place between 1909 and 1917 and there was further restoration after WWII. Once you're through the Propylaia, there is a stunning view of the Parthenon ahead.

DOUG MCKINLAY

Panathenaic Way

Right: Travellers entering between the Doric columns of the Parthenon

The Panathenaic Way, which cuts across the middle of the Acropolis, was the route taken by the Panathenaic procession. The procession was the climax of the Panathenaia, the festival held to venerate the goddess Athena. The origins of the Panathenaia are uncertain. According to some accounts it was initiated by Erichthonius; according to others, by Theseus. There were two festivals: the Lesser Panathenaic Festival took place annually on Athena's birthday, and the Great Panathenaic Festival was held every fourth anniversary of the goddess' birth.

The Great Panathenaic Festival began with dancing and was followed by athletic, dramatic and musical contests. The Panathenaic procession, which took place on the final day of the festival, began at the Keramikos and ended at the Erechtheion. Men carrying animals sacrificed to Athena headed the procession, followed by maidens carrying *rhytons* (horn-shaped drinking vessels). Behind them were musicians playing a fanfare for the girls of noble birth who followed, proudly holding aloft the sacred *peplos* (a glorious saffron-coloured shawl). Bringing up the rear were old men bearing olive branches. The grand finale of the procession was the placing of the peplos on the statue of Athena Polias in the Erechtheion.

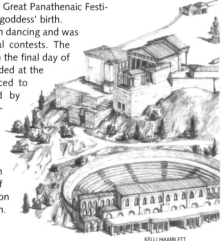

KELLI HAMBLETT

Temple of Athena Nike

On the right after leaving the Propylaia, there is a good view back to the exquisitely proportioned little Temple of Athena Nike (closed to visitors). It stands on a platform perched atop the steep south-west edge of the Acropolis, overlooking the Saronic Gulf. The temple, designed by Callicrates, was built of Pentelic marble in 427–424 BC.

The building is almost square, with four graceful Ionic columns at either end. Its frieze, of which only fragments remain, consisted of scenes from mythology on the east and south sides, and scenes from the Battle of Plataea (479 BC) and Athenians fighting Boeotians and Persians on the other sides. Parts of the frieze are in the Acropolis Museum. The platform was surrounded by a marble parapet of relief sculptures; some of these are also in the museum, including the beautiful sculpture of Athena Nike fastening her sandal.

The temple housed a statue of the goddess Athena. In her right hand was a pomegranate (symbol of fertility) and in her left, a helmet (symbol of war). The temple was dismantled in 1686 by the Turks, who positioned a huge cannon on the platform. It was carefully reconstructed between 1836 and 1842, but was taken to pieces again in 1936 because the platform was crumbling. The platform was reinforced and the temple rebuilt.

Statue of Athena Promachos

In ancient times, only the pediment of the Parthenon was visible from the Propylaia; the rest was obscured by numerous statues and two sacred buildings.

Parthenon 93

THE ACROPOLIS

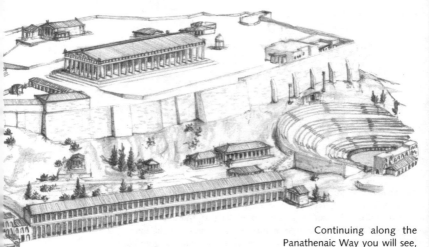

Continuing along the Panathenaic Way you will see, to your left, the foundations of pedestals for the statues which once lined the path. One of them, about 15m beyond the Propylaia, is the foundation of the gigantic statue of Athena Promachos (*promachos* means champion). The 9m-high statue was the work of Pheidias, and symbolised Athenian invincibility against the Persians. The helmeted goddess held a shield in her left hand and a spear in her right. The statue was carted off to Constantinople by Emperor Theodosius in AD 426. By 1204 it had lost its spear, so the hand appeared to be gesturing. This led the inhabitants to believe that the statue had beckoned the crusaders to the city, so they smashed it to pieces.

Parthenon

You have now reached the Parthenon, the monument which, more than any other, epitomises the glory of ancient Greece. The name Parthenon means 'virgin's apartment'. It is the largest Doric temple ever completed in Greece, and the only one to be built completely (apart from its wooden roof) of Pentelic marble. It is built on the highest part of the Acropolis, halfway between the eastern and western boundaries.

The Parthenon had a dual purpose – to house the great statue of Athena commissioned by Pericles, and to serve as a treasury for the tribute money which had been moved from Delos. It was built on the site of at least four earlier temples, all dedicated to the worship of Athena. It was designed by Ictinus and Callicrates, under the surveillance of Pheidias, to be the pre-eminent monument of the Acropolis. Building began in 447 BC and was completed in time for the Great Panathenaic Festival of 438 BC.

The temple consisted of eight fluted Doric columns at either end and 17 on each side. To achieve perfect form, its lines were ingeniously

Top: The Acropolis today is but a faded remnant of the ancient city. It takes a great leap of imagination to picture how the city would have looked in Pericles' time.

KELLI HAMBLETT

curved in order to counteract inharmonious optical illusions. As a result the foundations are slightly concave and the columns slightly convex, to make both look straight. Supervised by Pheidias, the sculptors Agoracritos and Alcamenes worked on the pediments and the sculpted sections of the frieze *(metopes)*. All of the sculptures they created were brightly coloured and gilded. There were 92 metopes, 44 statues and a frieze which went all the way around.

The metopes on the eastern side depicted Athenians fighting giants *(gigantions)*, and on the western side Theseus leading the Athenians into battle against the Amazons. Those on the southern side represented the contest of the Lapiths and Centaurs at the marriage feast of Pierithoös. An Ionic frieze 159.5m long ran all around the Parthenon. Much of it was damaged in the explosion of 1687, but the greatest existing part (over 75m) consists of the much-publicised Parthenon Marbles (known in England as the Elgin Marbles), now in the British Museum in London. The British Government continues to scorn Greek requests for their return.

The ceiling of the Parthenon, like that of the Propylaia, was painted blue and gilded with stars. At the eastern end was the *cella* (inner room of a temple), the holy of holies, into which only a few privileged initiates could enter.

Here stood the statue for which the temple was built – the **Athena Polias** (Athena of the City), which was considered one of the wonders of the ancient world. The statue was designed by Pheidias and completed in 432 BC. It was made of gold plate over an inner wooden frame, and stood almost 12m high on its pedestal. The face, hands and feet were made of ivory, and the eyes were fashioned from jewels. The goddess was clad in a long dress of gold with the head of Medusa carved in ivory on the breast. In her right hand, she held a statuette of Nike – the goddess of victory – and in her left a spear; at the base of the spear was a serpent. On her head she wore a helmet, on top of which was a sphinx with griffins in relief at either side.

In 426 BC the statue was taken to Constantinople, where it disappeared. There is a Roman copy (the Athena Varvakeion) in the National Archaeological Museum.

Top: The Parthenon was more of a showpiece than a sanctuary.

Erechtheion

Although the Parthenon was
the most impressive monument of
the Acropolis, it was more of a
showpiece than a sanctuary. That
role fell to the Erechtheion, built on
the part of the Acropolis that was
held most sacred. It was here that
Poseidon struck the ground with his
trident and that Athena produced
the olive tree. The temple is named
after Erichthonius, a mythical king of
Athens. It housed the cults of Athena,
Poseidon and Erichthonius.

KELLI HAMBLETT

If you follow the Panathenaic Way
around the northern portico of the
Parthenon, you will see the Erechtheion to your left. It is immediately
recognisable by the six larger-than-life maidens who take the place of
columns to support its southern portico, its much-photographed **Caryatids**. They are so called because the models for them were women
from Karyai (modern-day Karyes) in Lakonia.

The Erechtheion was part of Pericles' plan for the Acropolis, but the
project was postponed after the outbreak of the Peloponnesian Wars,
and work did not start until 421 BC, eight years after his death. It is
thought to have been completed in 406 BC.

Top: The upper part of a
Doric column showing
fluted column, Doric
capital and entablature.

Right: The Caryatids
hold aloft the southern
portico of the
Erechtheion.

KELLI HAMBLETT

The Erechtheion is architecturally the most unusual monument of the Acropolis. Whereas the Parthenon is considered the supreme example of Doric architecture, the Erechtheion is considered the supreme example of Ionic. Ingeniously built on several levels to counteract the unevenness of the ground, it consists of three basic parts – the main temple, northern porch and southern porch – all with different dimensions.

The main temple is of the Ionic order and is divided into two cellae, one dedicated to Athena, the other to Poseidon. Thus the temple represents a reconciliation of the two deities after their contest. In Athena's cella stood an olive-wood statue of Athena Polias holding a shield on which was a gorgon's head. The statue was illuminated by a golden lantern placed at its feet. It was this statue on which the sacred peplos was placed at the culmination of the Panathenaic Festival.

The northern porch consists of six graceful Ionic columns; on the floor are the fissures supposedly cleft by Poseidon's trident. This porch leads into the **Temenos of Pandrossos**, where, according to mythology, the sacred olive brought forth by Athena grew. To the south of here was the **Cecropion** – King Cecrops' burial place.

The southern porch is that of the Caryatids, which prop up a heavy roof of Pentelic marble. The ones you see are plaster casts – the originals (except for one removed by Lord Elgin) are in the site's museum.

Acropolis Museum

The museum at the south-east corner of the Acropolis houses a collection of sculptures and reliefs from the site. The rooms are organised in chronological order, starting with finds from the temples that predated the Parthenon and were destroyed by the Persians. They include the pedimental sculptures of Heracles slaying the Lernaian Hydra and of a lioness devouring a bull, both in Room I.

The Kora (maiden) statues in Room IV are regarded as the museum's prize exhibits. Most date from the 6th century BC and were uncovered from a pit on the Acropolis, where the Athenians buried them after the Battle of Salamis. The statues were votives dedicated to Athena, each once holding an offering to the goddess. The earliest of these Kora statues are quite stiff and formal in comparison with the later ones, which have flowing robes and elaborate headdresses.

Room VIII contains the few pieces of the Parthenon's frieze that escaped the clutches of Lord Elgin. They depict the Olympians at the Panathenaic procession. It also holds the relief of Athena Nike adjusting her sandal. Room IX is home to four of the five surviving Caryatids, safe behind a perspex screen. The fifth is in the British Museum.

DOUG MCKINLAY

JULIET COOMBE

Top: The massive Doric columns of the Parthenon, which was built to house the statue Athena Polias

Bottom: Ruin of the Erechtheion and the city of Athens in background

The reconstructed Stoa of Attalos in the Ancient Agora now houses the Agora Museum.

Tower of the Winds, Roman Agora

Temple of Olympian Zeus' Corinthian columns

Show goes on at the Theatre of Herodes Atticus

Things to See & Do

All government-run museums and sites are free on Sunday from the beginning of November to the end of March, as well as on 6 March, 18 April, 18 May, 5 June and the last weekend in September. This covers all the museums mentioned in this chapter except the Goulandris Museum of Cycladic & Ancient Greek Art and the Ilias Lalaounis Jewellery Museum, which are privately run.

Admission to government-run sites and museums is free all year for anyone under 18, card-carrying EU students and teachers, and journalists. Students from outside the EU qualify for a 50% discount with an International Student Identification Card (ISIC), while pensioners (over 65) from EU countries also pay half price.

You'll find all the latest information about Athens' museums, monuments and ancient sites on the Internet at the Ministry of Culture's official site at www.culture.gr.

HIGHLIGHTS

The Acropolis takes pride of place among the city's attractions and should be the first stop for any first-time visitor. Not far behind is the National Archaeological Museum, which houses the world's finest collection of Greek antiquities.

People with a bit more time on their hands will enjoy discovering some of the lesser sites, like the Ancient Agora and the Keramaikos. A favourite is the Tower of the Winds, part of the Roman Agora. The Benaki Museum and the Goulandris Museum of Cycladic & Ancient Greek Art are two other museums to seek out.

The best views of the city are to be had from Lykavittos Hill. The views are even more spectacular after dark, looking across to the floodlit Acropolis.

WALKING TOUR

This walk takes in most of the main sites of Plaka and Syntagma. It involves about 45 minutes' walking, but can take up to four hours if you linger and allow yourself to be lured into detours. The route is marked on Map 4.

The walk begins outside the **parliament building** on Plateia Syntagmatos. It was originally the royal palace, designed by the Bavarian architect Von Gartner, and built in 1836–42. The building remained the royal palace until 1935, when it became the seat of the Greek parliament. (The royal family moved to a new palace on the corner of Vasileos Konstantinou and Herod Atticus, which became the presidential palace upon the abolition of the monarchy in 1974.)

The building is guarded by the much-photographed *evzones* (guards traditionally from the village of Evzoni in Macedonia). Their somewhat incongruous uniform of short kilts and pom-pom shoes is the butt of

DAN HERRICK

The Parliament building, originally the royal palace is now the seat of the Greek parliament.

much mickey-taking by sightseers. Their uniform is based on the attire worn by the *klephts*, the mountain fighters who battled so ferociously in the War of Independence. Every Sunday at 11am the evzones perform a full changing-of-the-guard ceremony.

Standing with your back to the parliament building you will see ahead of you, to the right, the **Hotel Grande Bretagne**. This, the grandest of Athens' hotels, was built in 1862 as a 60-room mansion to accommodate visiting dignitaries. In 1872 it was converted into a hotel and became the place where the crowned heads of Europe and eminent politicians stayed. The Nazis made it their headquarters during WWII. The hotel was the scene of an attempt to blow up the British prime minister Winston Churchill on Christmas Eve 1944 while he was in Athens to discuss the Dekembriana fighting. A bomb was discovered in the hotel sewer. **Plateia Syntagmatos** itself is a pleasant tree-lined square, the heart of modern Athens.

Use the metro underpass to cross from the parliament building to the centre of Plateia Syntagmatos. The route takes you through the upper hall of Syntagma metro station, showpiece of the city's swish new metro system. Glass cases at the southern end of this huge marble hall display finds uncovered during construction, while the western wall has been preserved like a trench at an archaeological dig. It provides a fascinating look back through the ages.

The central square would be a pleasant place to sit and contemplate were it not for the roar of passing traffic. Head for the south-western corner of the square and cross Filellinon at the junction with Othonos, then continue west along Mitropoleos and take the first turn left into Nikis. Walk south up Nikis for about 300m to the crossroads with Kydathineon, a pedestrian walkway and one of Plaka's main thoroughfares.

Turn right and a little way along you will come to the **Church of Metamorphosis** on Plateia Satiros; opposite is the **Museum of Greek Folk Art**. Continue along here, and after Plateia Filomousou Eterias, the square with the outdoor tavernas, turn left into Adrianou, another of Plaka's main thoroughfares. At the end, turn right, and this will bring you to the square with the **Choregic Monument of Lysicrates**. (The name *choregos* was given to the wealthy citizens who financed choral and dramatic performances.) This monument was built in 334 BC to commemorate a win in a choral festival. An inscription on the architrave states:

...of Kykyna, son of Lysitheides, was choregos; the tribe of Akamantis won the victory with a chorus of boys; Theon played the flute; Lysiades of Athens trained the chorus; Euainetos was arhon.

The reliefs on the monument depict the battle between Dionysos and the Tyrrhenian pirates, whom the god had transformed into dolphins. It is the earliest known monument using Corinthian capitals externally. It stands in a cordoned-off archaeological site which is part of the **Street of Tripods**. It was here that winners of ancient dramatic and choral contests dedicated their tripod trophies to Dionysos.

In the 19th century, the monument was incorporated into the library of a French Capuchin convent, in which Lord Byron stayed in 1810–11 and wrote *Childe Harold*. The convent was destroyed by fire in 1890. Recent excavations around the monument have revealed the foundations of other choragic monuments.

Facing the monument, turn left and then right into Epimenidou. At the top of the steps, turn right into Stratonos, which skirts the Acropolis. A left fork after 150m leads to the highest part of Plaka, an area called

---

KEY TO SYMBOLS

☎	telephone number	⑤	prices	🚌	bus stop
ⓔ	email address	Ⓜ	metro station	🚊	train station
ⓦ	Web site	🚋	trolleybus	⚓	ferry
⏲	opening hours				

Anafiotika. The little whitewashed cube houses are the legacy of the people from the small Cycladic island of Anafi who were used as cheap labour in the building of Athens after Independence. It's a beautiful spot, with brightly painted olive-oil cans brimming with flowers bedecking the walls of the tiny gardens in summer.

The path winds between the houses and comes to some steps on the right, at the bottom of which is a curving pathway leading downhill to Pratiniou. Turn left at Pratiniou and veer right after 50m into Tholou. The yellow-ochre building with brown shutters at No 5 is the old university, built by the Venetians. The Turks used it as public offices and it was Athens University from 1837 to 1841. At the end of Tholou, turn left into Panos.

The restored 19th-century mansion at the top of the steps on the left houses the **Paul & Alexandra Kanellopoulos Museum**, recently reopened after lengthy renovations. The museum houses the Kanellopoulos family's extensive private collection, donated to the state in 1976.

Retracing your steps, go down Panos to the ruins of the **Roman Agora**, then turn left into Polygnotou and walk to the crossroads. Straight ahead, the road continues to the **Ancient Agora.** (Further details of these agora, or markets, are given later in this chapter.) However, turn right and then left into Peikilis, then immediately right into Areos. The giant columns on the right belong to **Library of Hadrian**. The site was being excavated at the time of research. Areos continues downhill to Plateia Monastiraki, soon to emerge from years of hiding behind metro construction hoardings. The square is named after the small church, the Church of Kimissis, on its northern side.

The white-domed building on the right, at the corner of Areos and Pandrosou, was once the Mosque of Tzistarakis, built by the Turks in 1759. After Independence it lost its minaret and was used as a prison. Now known as the Tzami, it houses the **Museum of Traditional Greek Ceramics**.

Turn right just beyond the mosque into Pandrosou. This street is a relic of the old Turkish bazaar. Today it is full of souvenir shops, selling everything from cheap kitsch to high-class jewellery and clothes. The street is named after King Cecrops' daughter, Pandrosos, who was the first priestess of Athens. At No 89 is Stavros Melissinos, the 'poet sandal-maker' of Athens who names the Beatles, Rudolph Nureyev and Jackie Onassis among his past customers. Fame and fortune have not gone to his head, however – he still makes the best-value sandals in Athens. See the Shopping chapter for more information.

Pandrosou leads to **Plateia Mitropoleos** and the **Athens Cathedral**. The cathedral has little architectural merit, which isn't surprising considering that it was constructed from the masonry of over 50 razed churches and from the designs of several architects. Next to it stands the much smaller, and far more appealing, **Church of Agios Eleftherios**, which was once the cathedral. Turn left after the cathedral, and then right into Mitropoleos and follow it back to Syntagma.

THE ACROPOLIS

See the special section 'The Acropolis' preceding this chapter.

THEATRE OF DIONYSOS

Map 4, G6
Dionysiou Areopagitou, Makrigianni
☎ 322 4625 🕒 8.30am-2.30pm daily
$ adult/student 500/300 dr [M] Akropoli

The importance of theatre in the life of the Athenian city-state can be gauged from the dimensions of the enormous Theatre of Dionysos on the south-eastern slope of the Acropolis.

The first theatre on this site was a timber structure erected sometime during the 6th century BC, after the tyrant Peisistratos had introduced the Festival of the Great Dionysia to Athens. This festival, which took place in March or April, consisted of contests where men clad in goatskins sang and performed dances. Everyone attended, and the watching of performances was punctuated by feasting, revelry and generally letting rip.

During the golden age in the 5th century BC, the annual festival had become one of

ANCIENT ATHENS

1 Acharnian Gate	17 Pantheon	33 Hippades Gate
2 North-East Gate	18 Diochares Gate	34 Northern Long Wall to Piraeus
3 Eriai Gate	19 Lyceum	35 Dipylon above Gate
4 Dipylon Gate	20 Demian Gate	36 Temple of Olympian Zeus
5 Keramikos	21 Melitides Gate	37 Diomeian Gate
6 Sacred Gate	22 Pnyx	38 Southern Long Wall
7 Pompeion	23 Parthenon	39 Monument of Filopappos
8 Stoa Poikile	24 Gymnasium	40 South Gate
9 Garden of Theophrastos	25 Baths	41 Halade Gate
10 Peiraic Gate	26 Theatre of Herodes Atticus	42 Itonian Gate
11 Temple of Hephaestus	27 Stoa of Eumenes	43 Kallirhoë Fountain
12 Metroön	28 Asclepion	44 Agrai Metroön
13 Stoa of Attalos	29 Theatre of Dionysos	45 Artemis Agrotera
14 Library of Hadrian	30 Odeon of Pericles	46 Ardettos Hill
15 Roman Agora	31 Monument of Lysicrates	47 Poseidon Heliconios
16 Tower of the Winds	32 Arch of Hadrian	48 Hadrian's Gymnasium

the major events on the calendar. Politicians would sponsor the production of dramas by writers such as Aeschylus, Sophocles and Euripides, with some light relief provided by the bawdy comedies of Aristophanes. People came from all over Attica, their expenses met by the state – if only present-day governments were as generous to the arts!

The theatre was reconstructed in stone and marble by Lycurgus between 342 and 326 BC. The auditorium had a seating capacity of 17,000, spread over 64 tiers of seats, of which about 20 survive. Apart from the front row, the seats were built of Piraeus limestone and were occupied by ordinary citizens, although women were confined to the back rows. The front row consisted of 67 thrones built of Pentelic marble, which were reserved for festival officials and important priests. The grandest was in the centre and reserved for the Priest of Dionysos, who sat shaded from the sun under a canopy. The seat can be identified by well-preserved lion-claw feet at either side. In Roman times, the theatre was also used for state events and ceremonies as well as for performances.

The reliefs at the rear of the stage, mostly of headless figures, depict the exploits of Dionysos and date from the 2nd century BC. The two hefty, hunched-up guys who have managed to keep their heads are *selini*. Selini were worshippers of the mythical Selinos, the debauched father of the satyrs, whose chief attribute seems to have been an outsized phallus. His favourite pastime was charging up mountains in lecherous pursuit of nymphs. He was also Dionysos' mentor.

ASCLEPION

Directly above the Theatre of Dionysos, wooden steps lead up to a pathway. On the left at the top of the steps is the Asclepion, which was built around a sacred spring. The worship of Asclepius, the physician son of Apollo, began in Epidaurus and was introduced to Athens in 429 BC at a time when plague was sweeping the city.

STOA OF EUMENES

Beneath the Asclepion is the Stoa of Eumenes, a long colonnade built by Eumenes II, King of Pergamum (197–159 BC), as a shelter and promenade for theatre audiences. It runs west to the Theatre of Herodes Atticus.

PANAGIA HRYSOSPILIOTISSA

The tiny Panagia Hrysospiliotissa (Chapel of our Lady of the Cavern) occupies a small grotto in the cliff face behind the Theatre of Dionysos. It is a poignant little place with old pictures and icons on the walls.

The grotto was once the site of a temple dedicated to Dionysos, built by Thrasyllos in 320 BC. The two Ionic columns above the chapel are the remains of Thrasyllos' temple. The site is reached by a rough rock-strewn path leading up from the high point of the Theatre of Dionysos.

THEATRE OF HERODES ATTICUS

Map 4, G5
Dionysiou Areopagitou, Makrigianni
☎ **323 2771, 323 5582 Ⓜ Akropoli**
The Theatre of Herodes Atticus was added to the line-up of fine buildings gracing the southern slope of the Acropolis in AD 161. Herodes Atticus was a wealthy Roman who built the theatre in memory of his wife

Regilla. The theatre, or odeion as it is more correctly called, was excavated in 1857–58 and completely restored in 1950–61. It is used for performances of drama, music and dance during the annual Athens Festival (see the Athens Festival section in the Entertainment chapter for details). The theatre is open to the public only during performances.

ANCIENT AGORA

Map 4, E4
Adrianou, Monastiraki ☎ **321 0185**
⊘ **8.30am-3pm Tues-Sun** Ⓢ **adult/student 1200/600 dr** Ⓜ **Monastiraki,Thision**
The Agora (market) was Athens' meeting place in ancient times. It was the focal point of administrative, commercial and political life, not to mention social activity. All roads led to the Agora, and it was a lively, crowded place. Socrates spent a lot of time here expounding his philosophy, and in AD 49 St Paul disputed daily in the Agora, intent upon winning converts to Christianity.

The site was first developed in the 6th century BC. It was devastated by the Persians in 480 BC, but a new agora was built in its place almost immediately. It was flourishing by Pericles' time and continued to do so until AD 267, when it was destroyed by the Herulians, a Gothic tribe from Scandinavia. The Turks built a residential quarter on the site, but this was demolished by archaeologists after Independence. If they'd had their way the archaeologists would have also knocked down the whole of Plaka, which was also Turkish. The area has been excavated to classical and, in parts, Neolithic levels.

The main monuments are the Temple of Hephaestus, the Stoa of Attalos and the Church of the Holy Apostles.

The site is bounded by Areopagus Hill in the south, the Athens-Piraeus metro line to the north, Plaka to the east and Leoforos Apostolou Pavlou to the west. There are several entrances, but the most convenient is the southern entrance at the western end of Polygnotou (see the Walking Tour section earlier).

STOA OF ATTALOS

The Agora Museum in the reconstructed Stoa of Attalos is a good place to start if you

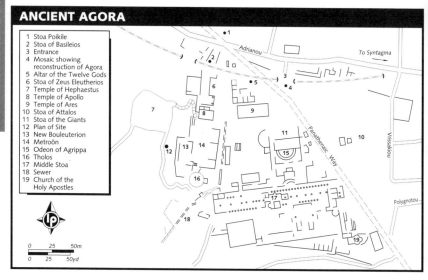

ANCIENT AGORA

1 Stoa Poikile
2 Stoa of Basileios
3 Entrance
4 Mosaic showing
   reconstruction of Agora
5 Altar of the Twelve Gods
6 Stoa of Zeus Eleutherios
7 Temple of Hephaestus
8 Temple of Apollo
9 Temple of Ares
10 Stoa of Attalos
11 Stoa of the Giants
12 Plan of Site
13 New Bouleuterion
14 Metroön
15 Odeon of Agrippa
16 Tholos
17 Middle Stoa
18 Sewer
19 Church of the
   Holy Apostles

want to make any sense of the site. The museum has a model of the Agora as well as a collection of finds from the site.

The original stoa was built by King Attalos II of Pergamum (159–138 BC). It was two storeys high with two aisles, and housed expensive shops. A popular stamping ground for wealthy Athenians, people also gathered here to watch the Panathenaic procession, which crossed in front of the stoa.

It was authentically reconstructed in 1953–56 by the American School of Archaeology. The reconstruction deviates from the original in only one detail: the facade has been left in natural Pentelic marble, but it was originally painted red and blue. The stoa has a series of 45 columns which are Doric on the ground floor and Ionic on the upper gallery.

TEMPLE OF HEPHAESTUS

This temple on the western edge of the Agora was surrounded by foundries and metalwork shops, and was dedicated to Hephaestus, god of the forge. It was one of the first buildings of Pericles' rebuilding program and is the best-preserved Doric temple in Greece. Built in 449 BC by Ictinus, one of the architects of the Parthenon, it has 34 columns and a frieze on the eastern side depicting nine of the Twelve Labours of Heracles. In AD 1300 it was converted into the **Church of Agios Georgios**. The last service held here was on 13 December 1834 in honour of King Otho's arrival in Athens.

Unlike the Parthenon, the monument does not evoke a sense of wonder, but it's nevertheless a pleasant place to wander around. The garden that surrounds the temple has been reconstructed to resemble the Roman garden that existed there in antiquity.

To the north-east of the temple are the foundations of the **Stoa of Zeus Eleutherios**, one of the places where Socrates expounded his philosophy. Farther north are the foundations of the **Stoa of Basileios** and the **Stoa Poikile** (Painted Stoa), both currently inaccessible to the public. The Stoa Poikile was so called because of its murals, painted by the leading artists of the day and depicting mythological and historical battles. At the end of the 4th century BC, Zeno taught his Stoic philosophy here.

To the south-east of the Temple of Hephaestus was the **New Bouleuterion**, or council house, where the Senate (originally created by Solon) met. To the south of here was the circular **Tholos** where the heads of government met.

CHURCH OF THE HOLY APOSTLES

This charming little church, which stands near the southern entrance, was built in the early 11th century to commemorate St Paul's teaching in the Agora. In 1954–57 it was stripped of its 19th-century additions and restored to its original form. It contains some fine Byzantine frescoes.

KERAMIKOS

Map 4, C1
Ermou 148, Keramikos ☎ 346 3552
◷ 8am-2.30pm Tues-Sun ⑨ adult/student 500/300 dr ⑩ Thision

The Keramikos was the city's cemetery from the 12th century BC to Roman times. It was discovered in 1861 during the construction of Pireos, the street which leads to Piraeus. Despite its location on the seedier part of Ermou, beyond Monastiraki, it is one of the most green and tranquil of Athens' ancient sites. Entrance to the site is at the western end of Ermou, near the junction with Pireos.

SACRED & DIPYLON GATES

Once you have entered the site, head for the small knoll ahead and to the right, to find a plan of the site. A path leads down to the right from the knoll to the remains of the city wall, which was built by Themistocles in 479 BC, and rebuilt by Konon in 394 BC. The wall is broken by the foundations of two gates.

The first, the Sacred Gate, spanned the Sacred Way and was the one by which pilgrims from Eleusis entered the city during the annual Eleusian procession. The second, the Dipylon Gate, to the north-east of the Sacred Gate, was the city's main entrance and was where the Panathenaic procession began. It was also the stamping ground of the city's prostitutes, who gathered there to offer their services to jaded travellers.

From a platform outside the Dipylon Gate, Pericles gave his famous speech extolling the virtues of Athens and honouring those who died in the first year of the Peloponnesian Wars. The speech stirred many more to battle – and to their deaths.

Between the Sacred and the Dipylon Gates are the foundations of the **Pompeion**. This building was once used as a dressing room for participants in the Panathenaic procession.

STREET OF TOMBS

The Street of Tombs leads off the Sacred Way to the left as you head away from the city. This avenue was reserved for the tombs of Athens' most prominent citizens. The surviving stelae are now in the National Archaeological Museum, and what you see are replicas. They consist of an astonishing array of funerary monuments, and their bas-reliefs warrant more than a cursory examination.

Ordinary citizens were buried in the areas bordering the Street of Tombs. One very well-preserved stele shows a little girl with her pet dog. You will find it by going up the stone steps on the northern side of the Street of Tombs. The site's largest stele, that of sisters Demetria and Pamphile, is on the path running from the south-east corner of the Street of Tombs. Pamphile is seated beside a standing Demetria.

OBERLAENDER MUSEUM

The site's Oberlaender Museum is named after its benefactor, Gustav Oberlaender, a German-American stocking manufacturer. It contains stelae and sculpture from the site, as well as an impressive collection of vases and terracotta figurines. The museum is to the left of the site entrance.

ROMAN ATHENS

ROMAN AGORA & TOWER OF THE WINDS

Map 5, E1
Monastiraki ☎ 324 5220 ◷ 8.30am-3pm Tues-Sun ⑨ adult/student 500/300 dr ⑩ Monastiraki

The site may be known as the Roman Agora, but the star attraction here is the wonderful Tower of the Winds. Built in the 1st century BC by a Syrian astronomer named Andronicus, this octagonal monument of Pentelic marble is an ingenious construction which functioned as a sundial, weather vane, water clock and compass. Each side represents a point of the compass, and has a relief of a figure floating through the air, which depicts the wind associated with that particular point. Beneath each of the reliefs are the faint markings of sundials. The weather vane, which disappeared long ago, was a bronze Triton that revolved on top of the tower. The Turks, not ones to let a good building go to waste, allowed dervishes to use the tower.

The tower stands just inside the site, but outside the Roman Agora – which lies to the south-west of the site. Only part of the agora has been excavated. The main surviving feature is the well-preserved **Gate of Athena Archegetis**, which is flanked by four Doric columns. It was erected sometime in the 1st century AD and financed by Julius Caesar.

Other features of the site include the foundations of a 1st-century public latrine, just to the right of the entrance, and the foundations of a propylon and a row of shops in the south-eastern corner.

ARCH OF HADRIAN

Map 4, G8
Amalias, Zappei $ free [M] Akropoli

The Roman emperor Hadrian had a great affection for Athens. Although, like all Roman emperors, he did his fair share of spiriting its classical artwork to Rome, he also embellished the city with many monuments influenced by classical architecture.

MARK HONAN

Massive columns in the Temple of Olympian Zeus

Grandiose as these monuments are, they lack the refinement and artistic flair of their classical predecessors.

The Arch of Hadrian is a lofty monument of Pentelic marble, now blackened by the effluent of exhausts, which stands where traffic-clogged Vasilissis Olgas and Amalias meet. It was erected by Hadrian in AD 132, probably to commemorate the consecration of the Temple of Olympian Zeus. The inscriptions show that it was also intended as a dividing point between the ancient city and the Roman city. The north-west frieze bears the inscription 'This is Athens, the Ancient city of Theseus'; while the south-east frieze states 'This is the city of Hadrian, and not of Theseus'.

TEMPLE OF OLYMPIAN ZEUS

Map 7, A7
Vassilisis Olgas, Zappeio ☎ 922 6330
🕐 8.30am-2.30pm Tues-Sun $ adult/student 500/300 dr [M] Akropoli

This is the largest temple in Greece and took over 700 years to build. It was begun in the 6th century BC by Peisistratos, but was abandoned for lack of funds. Various other leaders had stabs at completing the temple, but it was left to Hadrian to complete the work in AD 131.

The temple is impressive for the sheer size of its 104 Corinthian columns (17m high with a base diameter of 1.7m), of which 15 remain – the fallen column was blown down in a gale in 1852. Hadrian put a colossal statue of Zeus in the cella and, in typically immodest fashion, placed an equally large one of himself next to it.

LIBRARY OF HADRIAN

Map 4, D5
Areos, Monastiraki ☎ 322 9740
[M] Monastiraki

This library is to the north of the Roman Agora. The building, which was of vast dimensions, was erected in the 2nd century AD and included a cloistered courtyard bordered by 100 columns. As well as books, the building housed music and lecture rooms and a theatre. Archaeologists were excavating the site at the time of research and it was closed to the public.

DOUG MCKINLAY

Statue of Emperor Hadrian in the Roman Agora

ROMAN STADIUM

Map 7, A10
Vasileos Konstantinou, Mets ☎ 325 1724
$ free [M] Evangelismos

The last Athenian monument with Roman connections is the Roman Stadium, which lies in a fold between two pine-covered hills between the neighbourhoods of Mets and Pangrati. The stadium was originally built in the 4th century BC as a venue for the Panathenaic athletic contests. A thousand wild animals are said to have been slaughtered in the arena at Hadrian's inauguration in AD 120. Shortly after this, the seats were rebuilt in Pentelic marble by Herodes Atticus.

After hundreds of years of disuse the stadium was completely restored in 1895 by wealthy Greek benefactor Georgios Averof. The following year the first Olympic Games of modern times were held here. It is a faithful replica of the Roman Stadium, comprising seats of Pentelic marble for 70,000 spectators, a running track and a central area for field events.

BYZANTINE ATHENS

Byzantine architecture in Athens is fairly thin on the ground. By the time of the split in the Roman Empire, Athens had shrunk to little more than a provincial town and Thessaloniki had become the major city. The most important Byzantine building is the **monastery** at Dafni, 10km west of the city, which is covered in the Excursions chapter.

Church of Agios Eleftherios Map 5, D3
Plateia Mitropoleos, Plaka [M] Monastiraki

The 11th-century Church of Agios Eleftherios is considered the finest of the Byzantine churches around central Athens. It is built partly of Pentelic marble and decorated with an external frieze of symbolic beasts in bas-relief. It was once the city's cathedral, but now stands in the shadows of the much larger new cathedral.

Church of Kapnikarea Map 5, B2
Ermou, Monastiraki [M] Monastiraki

The Church of Kapnikarea was built at the beginning of the 11th century on the ruins of an earlier temple. Its dome is supported by four large Roman columns. Many of the icons inside are the work of celebrated modern artist Fotis Kontoglou.

Church of Agii Theodori Map 4, B7
Aristidou, Syntagma [M] Panepistimiou

The tiny Church of Agii Theodori, tucked away west of Plateia Klafthmonos, is possibly the oldest of the city's Byzantine relics. Its construction date is unknown, but it was renovated in 1065 – according to a plaque above the entrance in the western wall. It was badly damaged in 1821 during the opening phase of the War of Independence, and restored in 1840. It's a delightful building with a tiled dome and walls decorated with a terracotta frieze of animals and plants.

NATIONAL ARCHAEOLOGICAL MUSEUM

Map 3, C8
28 Oktovriou-Patission 44, Moussio
☎ 821 7717 [e] protcol@eam.culture.gr
🕘 12.30pm-7pm Mon, 8am-7pm Tues-Fri & 8.30am-3pm Sat & Sun Apr-Oct, 12.30pm-5pm Mon, 8am-5pm Tues-Fri & 8.30am-3pm Sat & Sun Nov-Mar $ adult/student 2000/1000 dr
🚎 5 [M] Viktorias

NATIONAL ARCHAEOLOGICAL MUSEUM

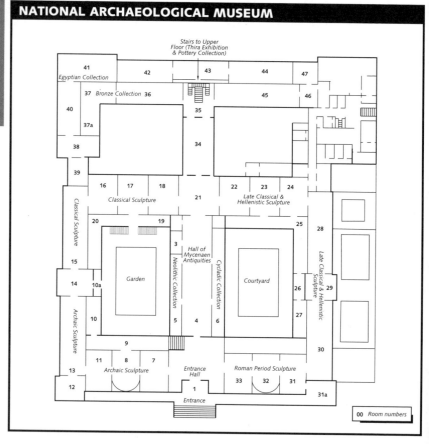

This museum, opened in 1874, stands supreme among the nation's finest. Despite all the pilfering by foreign archaeologists in the 19th century, it still has the world's finest collection of Greek antiquities – in particular, the magnificent Hall of Mycenaean Antiquities and the Thira Exhibition, which contains the celebrated collection of Minoan frescoes unearthed at Akrotiri on the island of Santorini (Thira).

The museum highlights are described here, and there are comprehensive explanations in English in each room. Guidebooks on sale (2000-2500 dr) in the foyer give more information. The museum is quite extensive so make sure you have plenty of time at your disposal. To reach the museum from Plaka, catch trolleybus No 5 from outside the National Gardens on Amalias (the walk takes about 30 minutes) or catch the metro from Monastiraki to Viktorias.

At the time of writing the museum's first floor was closed for renovation and it was not known when it would reopen. Some of the displays from this floor have been relocated to the Temporary Exhibitions room on the ground floor.

euro currency converter €1 = 340.75 dr

MYCENEAN ANTIQUITIES: ROOMS 3 & 4

The museum's *tour de force* is the Hall of Mycenaean Antiquities, straight ahead from the entrance foyer. Gold gleams at you from everywhere. The chief exhibits are finds from the six shaft graves of Grave Circle A at Mycenae. Graves one to five were excavated by Heinrich Schliemann in 1874–76 and the sixth by Panagiotes Stamatakis in 1877–78. The star attraction is the golden **Mask of Agamemnon**, housed in case 3. (It has subsequently been proven to belong to a king who died three centuries before Agamemnon.)

In the centre of the hall, cases 28 and 29 contain gold sheets that covered the bodies of two royal babies. On the left, cases 5 and 6 contain finds from Grave Circle B (from 16th century BC), which was outside the citadel at Mycenae. Case 5 has an unusual rock-crystal vase in the shape of a duck: its head and neck are gracefully turned back to form a handle. Case 30, also in the centre, contains miscellaneous finds from Mycenae, including a delightful ivory carving of two voluptuous women and a child, who may represent Demeter, Persephone and Iacchus.

On the right, just beyond here, is the famous **Warrior Vase** which, along with the Mask of Agamemnon, Schliemann rated as one of his greatest finds. It depicts men leaving for war and a woman waving them goodbye.

The rest of the hall is devoted to other Mycenaean sites. Case 9 features tablets with inscriptions in Cretan Linear B script, while case 15 contains objects from Tiryns, including the famous **Tiryns Treasure**. The treasure is believed to have been looted by a tomb robber, who then reburied it and failed to retrieve it. Back in the centre, case 32 contains the famous **gold cups** from the beehive-shaped tomb at Vaphio, which depict the taming of wild bulls. These magnificent cups are regarded as among the finest examples of Mycenaean art.

Room 3 contains Mycenaean finds from Central Greece, Thessaly and the island of Skopelos.

NEOLITHIC COLLECTION: ROOM 5

To the left of the Hall of Mycenaean Antiquities, Room 5 contains Neolithic finds – mainly from Thessaly. There is also a case of pottery, figurines and jewellery from Troy, including a beautiful necklace of delicate gold beads. These finds were presented to the museum by Sophie Schliemann, wife of Heinrich.

CYCLADIC COLLECTION: ROOM 6

The collection includes the largest Cycladic figurine ever found. It is almost life-size and was discovered on the island of Amorgos.

Cases 56, 57 and 58 contain ceramic 'frying pans' from early Cycladic cemeteries on Syros. They are black with intricate inlaid patterns in white. In case you're wondering why on earth these people took frying pans to the grave with them, they are so called merely because of their shape.

ARCHAIC SCULPTURE: ROOMS 7 TO 14

The huge sepulchral amphora (a jar with two handles and a narrow neck) in room 7 is considered the best example of the geometric style of pottery. It dates from 760 BC and found in the Kerameikos.

The chief exhibit in room 8 is the huge *kouros* dating from 600 BC. This was a votive offering found in the Temple of Poseidon at Cape Sounion.

Room 10 contains gravestones from the 6th century. Room 11 features the torso of

Linear B tablet unearthed at Knossos, Crete

another colossal kouros (540 BC), found at Megara in Attica.

Room 13 is dominated by the sepulchral kouros named Aristodikos. To the left of this sculpture is the base of a kouros found in the Kerameikos. It has reliefs on three sides: one shows four clothed youths provoking a fight between a cat and dog; another shows naked youths wrestling; and the third shows youths playing a ball game.

Room 14 is devoted to provincial stele monuments. The gravestone by Alxenor is one of the finest in the room and bears an endearing, if egocentric, inscription by the artist: 'Alxenor the Naxian made me. Admire me'.

CLASSICAL SCULPTURE: ROOMS 15 TO 20

The bronze statue of **Poseidon of Artemision** (450 BC) in room 15 is another of the highlights of the museum. The statue was hauled out of the sea off Cape Artemision in 1928, and shows Poseidon poised to hurl his trident (now missing). More than any other statue of Poseidon, it conveys the god's strength and unlimited power.

Just within the door of this room is a beautiful relief from Eleusis (440 BC). It depicts Demeter, accompanied by her daughter Persephone, giving Triptolemos an ear of wheat to sprout.

Room 16 contains classical grave monuments, most of which were found in Attica. Rooms 17 and 19 contain classical votive sculpture. Room 20 consists mostly of Roman copies of classical Greek statues. At the far end is the statue of Athena Varvakeion, which was made in about 200 BC. It is the most famous copy – much reduced in size – of the statue of Athena Polias by Pheidias that once stood in the Parthenon. Room 18 contains late-5th- and early-4th-century sepulchral monuments.

LATE CLASSICAL & HELLENISTIC SCULPTURE: ROOMS 21 TO 30, 34 & 35

Room 21, the central hall, is dominated by the remarkable 2nd-century bronze statue of the **Horse and Jockey of Artemision**, so named because it was found with the statue of Poseidon. It is a wonderfully animated sculpture – check out the worried look on the jockey's face. Room 22 is devoted solely to sculptures from the excavations in the sanctuary of Asklepios in Epidaurus.

There is an unusual grave monument (540 BC) in the centre of room 24 consisting of a floral column which supports a cauldron decorated with griffins.

Room 25 is mostly devoted to charming diminutive reliefs of nymphs. They are not individually labelled, but there is an explanation in English of their role. On the left, just before room 26, is a highly unusual votive relief of a snake and a huge sandal on which is carved a worshipping figure. It dates from 360 BC and is believed to depict the Hero of the Slipper, who was worshipped near the Theatre of Dionysos.

Room 28 contains some extremely realistic funerary monuments, particularly the Grave Monument of Aristonautes (330 BC), found in the Kerameikos. The large sepulchral relief of a boy attempting to restrain a frisky horse is a powerful and unprecedented piece of realist sculpture, especially the leg muscles of both the horse and boy, and the magnificent drapery. It was found near Larisis Station in 1948, and dates from the second half of the 3rd century.

The famous **Ephebos of Antikythira** (340 BC) stands in the centre of the room. The amazingly lifelike eyes are almost hypnotic. Behind this statue, to the right, is the head of a bronze statue – probably of the Elean boxer Satyros. He certainly looks a nasty piece of work in contrast to the calm 'other world' expressions on the faces surrounding him.

Room 29 is dominated by the statue of Themis (the goddess of justice). Behind her is a head of Alexander the Great with graffitied cheeks (added later), and a head of the orator Demosthenes looking very perplexed.

The comic masks on the right in room 30 provide some light relief, although some of their expressions are as menacing as they are funny. A little way down, in the middle of the room, is a delightful and sensitive sculpture of a naked boy with his hand on a goose – note his gentle smile and the apparent softness of his skin.

Dominating the room is yet another statue of the sea god, Poseidon (140 BC), which was found on Milos in 1877. Behind this statue is the bronze head of a melancholic-looking guy; it was found on Delos. To the right is an amusing sculpture of Pan making amorous advances towards Aphrodite, who is about to clobber him with her sandal.

Room 34 is built to simulate an open-air sanctuary and displays objects from the **Sanctuary of Aphrodite** which existed near Dafni.

ROMAN PERIOD SCULPTURE: ROOMS 31 TO 33

These rooms house sculptures produced in Greece during the period of the Roman occupation from the 1st to the 5th centuries AD.

BRONZE COLLECTION: ROOM 36

The highlight of these rooms is the **Karapanos Collection** of bronzes (room 36) found at the celebrated Sanctuary of Zeus at Dodoni in Epiros. It includes a chariot from the Roman period.

EGYPTIAN COLLECTION: ROOMS 40 & 41

The main point of interest is the collection of elaborately decorated mummy cases in room 40.

TEMPORARY EXHIBITIONS: ROOM 45

Due to renovations room 45 has become the temporary home to an exhibition of the World of Thira and a collection of ancient Greek pottery normally found on the first floor.

THIRA EXHIBITION: ROOM 48A

The rear section of the hall at the top of the stairs houses the celebrated frescoes unearthed by Spyridon Marinatos at the Minoan settlement of Akrotiri on Santorini (Thira) in the late 1960s.

The frescoes are more varied and better preserved than the Minoan frescoes found on Crete. Extremely beautiful and harmonious in both colour and form, they give a comprehensive insight into the everyday life of the Minoans. Scenes depicted in the frescoes include two boxing youths, a youth holding two strings of fish, and women performing religious rites. The most unusual is the one which shows a flotilla of ships sailing from one coastal town to another. The frescoes will remain here until a suitable museum has been built on Santorini.

POTTERY COLLECTION: ROOMS 49 TO 56

These rooms house the world's most comprehensive collection of ancient Greek pottery. The collection traces the development from the Protogeometric and Geometic periods to the 4th century BC.

Flora, fauna and human figures first featured on pottery in the 9th century BC, and mythical scenes appeared a century later. The 7th century BC saw the emergence of the famous Attic black-figured pottery. In about 530 BC, the pots with black figures had been superseded by red-figured pottery, which reached the peak of perfection during Pericles' rule.

OTHER MUSEUMS

The National Archaeological Museum might steal the show, but Athens has lots more in store for keen museum-goers with time on their hands. The following selection has been drawn from a list of 28 (available from the tourist office), covering everything from Byzantine art to old theatre props. See the What's Free in Athens later in this chapter for more information on museums.

BENAKI MUSEUM

Map 6, D2
Vasilissis Sofias 1, Kolonaki ☎ 367 1000
ⓔ benaki@benaki.gr ⓦ www.benaki.gr
☺ 9am-5pm Mon, Wed-Sat, 9am-12am Thur & 9am-3pm Sun ⓢ adult/student 2000/1000 dr
ⓜ Evangelismos

This museum contains the sumptuous and eclectic collection of Antoine Benaki, accumulated during his 35 years of avid collecting in Europe and Asia. In 1931 he turned the family house into a museum and presented it to the Greek nation. The collection includes Bronze Age finds from

Mycenae and Thessaly; two early works by El Greco; ecclesiastical furniture brought from Asia Minor by refugees; pottery, copper, silver and woodwork from Egypt, Asia Minor and Mesopotamia; and a stunning collection of Greek regional costumes.

The Benaki Museum Shop Map 6,D2
Koumbari 1, Kolonaki ☎ 362 7367
⊕ 8.30am-3pm Mon-Fri Ⓜ Evangelismos
The museum's shop, on the ground floor, sells a wide range of books, cards and replicas.

GOULANDRIS MUSEUM OF CYCLADIC & ANCIENT GREEK ART
Map 6, D3
Neofytou Douka 4, Kolonaki ☎ 722 8321
ⓔ info@cycladic-m.gr ⓦ www.cycladic-m.gr
⊕ 10am-4pm Wed-Fri & 10am-3pm Sat
Ⓢ adult/student 1000/500 dr Ⓜ Evangelismos
This private museum houses a collection of Cycladic art, second in importance only to that displayed at the National Archaeological Museum. The museum was custom-built for the collection and the finds are beautifully displayed, lit and labelled. Although the exhibits cover all periods from Cycladic to Roman times, the emphasis is on the Cycladic from 3000 to 2000 BC. Its many exhibits include the marble figurines with folded arms which inspired many 20th-century artists with their simplicity and purity of form.

The museum has now taken over the 19th-century mansion next door, which it uses for temporary exhibitions.

BYZANTINE MUSEUM
Map 6, D5
Vasilissis Sofias 22, Kolonaki ☎ 723 2178,
721 1027 ⓔ protocol@bma.culture.gr
⊕ 8.30am-3pm Tues-Sun Ⓢ adult/student
500/300 dr Ⓜ Evangelismos
This museum has a large collection of Christian art from the 4th to the 19th century, housed in the Villa Ilissia, an attractive, mock-Florentine mansion.

Unfortunately, the museum will be operating at half-capacity until early 2001, as the wing to the right of the courtyard is being completely rebuilt. This wing housed many of the finest frescoes and icons; some are in storage, others have been moved temporarily to Thessaloniki.

The downstairs rooms in the surviving wing are given over to re-creations of churches, starting with a very solemn basilica from the 5th to the 7th century. The reconstruction of an 11th-century Byzantine church is beautiful in its simplicity, in contrast to the elaborate decorations of the post-Byzantine church next door. The bishop's throne in this room was brought to Athens by refugees from Asia Minor. The upstairs rooms contain icons and frescoes.

NUMISMATIC MUSEUM
Map 5, A7
Panepistimiou 12, Syntagma ☎ 364 3774
ⓔ protocol@nm.culture.gr ⊕ 8am-2.30pm Tues-Sun Ⓢ adult/student 1200/600 dr Ⓜ Syntagma
Housed in a magnificent neoclassical mansion, this collection comprises 400,000 coins from ancient Greek, Hellenic, Roman and Byzantine times. The building was once the home of celebrated archaeologist Heinrich Schliemann.

MUSEUM OF GREEK FOLK ART
Map 4, F8
Kydathineon 17, Plaka ☎ 322 9031
ⓔ melt@culture.gr ⊕ 10am-2pm Tues-Sun
Ⓢ adult/student 500/300 dr Ⓜ Syntagma
This museum houses a fine collection of secular and religious folk art, mainly from the 18th and 19th centuries. On the 1st floor is embroidery, pottery, weaving and puppets. On the 2nd floor is a reconstructed traditional village house with paintings by the primitive artist Theophilos of Lesvos (Mytilini). Greek traditional costumes are displayed on the 3rd and 4th floors.

NATIONAL HISTORICAL MUSEUM
Map 5, A6
Stadiou 13, Syntagma ☎ 323 7617
ⓔ nhmuseum@tee.gr ⊕ 9am-2pm Tues-Sun
Ⓢ adult/student 1000/200 dr Ⓜ Syntagma
This museum specialises in memorabilia from the War of Independence, including Byron's helmet and sword. There is also a series of paintings depicting events leading up to the war, Byzantine and medieval exhibits and a collection of photographs and royal portraits.

The museum is housed in the old parliament building. Theodoros Deligiannis, who succeeded Trikoupis as prime minister of

Greece, was assassinated on the steps of the building in 1905.

CITY OF ATHENS MUSEUM

Map 4, B8
Paparigopoulou 7, Syntagma ☎ 324 6164 🕘 9am-1.30pm Wed, Fri-Mon $ adult/student 500/300 dr [M] Panepistimiou

This museum occupies the palace where King Otho and his consort Amalia lived for a few years during the 1830s. It contains some of the royal couple's furniture, costumes and personal mementos, as well as paintings, prints and models of Athens in the 19th century.

JEWISH MUSEUM

Map 4, F9
Nikis 39, Plaka ☎ 322 5582 fax 323 1577 [e] jmg@otenet.gr [w] www.jewishmuseum.gr 🕘 9am-2.30pm Mon-Fri, 10am-2pm Sun $ 500 dr

This museum traces the history of the Jewish community in Greece back to the 3rd century BC through an impressive collection of religious and folk art and documents. It includes a reconstruction of a synagogue. The museum is housed in a 19th-century mansion.

ILIAS LALAOUNIS JEWELLERY MUSEUM

Map 7, A4
Kallisperi 12, Makrigianni ☎ 922 1044 [e] ioannal@acropolis.net [w] www.addgr.com/jewel/lalaounis 🕘 9am-4pm Mon & Thur-Sun, 9am-9pm Wed $ free admission 9am-11am Wed & 3pm-9pm Sat; other times adult/student 800/500 dr; child under 12 free [M] Akropoli

This private museum showcases the talents of celebrity jeweller Ilias Lalaounis. The collection of more than 3000 pieces includes a section featuring works inspired by various periods in Greek history. A highlight is a stunning Hellenistic style gold bracelet in the form of the Knot of Hercules. Copies of some of the works are for sale in the museum shop.

El Greco

PAUL & ALEXANDRA KANELLOPOULOS MUSEUM

Map 4, F5
Panos 2, Plaka ☎ 321 2313 🕘 8am-2.30pm Tues-Sun $ adult/student 500/300 dr [M] Monastiraki

The museum houses the Kanellopoulos family's extensive private collection, donated to the state in 1976.

ART GALLERIES

National Art Gallery Map 8, G1
Vasileos Konstantinou 50, Ilissia ☎ 723 5857, 723 5937 🕘 8.30am-7pm Tues-Sun July-Oct; 9am-3pm Mon-Sat & 6pm-9pm Mon & Wed & 10am-2pm Sun Nov-Jun $ adult/student 2000/1000 dr 🚊 3,13

The emphasis in this gallery is on Greek painting and sculpture from the 19th and 20th centuries. There are also 16th-century works and a few works by European masters, including paintings by Picasso, Marquet and Utrillo and Magritte's sculpture *The Therapist*.

Paintings by the primitive painter Theophilos are displayed on the mezzanine floor and 20th-century works are on the 1st floor. The 2nd floor has mostly 19th-century paintings, with one room of earlier works. It has four El Greco paintings, including *The Crucifixion* and *Symphony of the Angels*.

Greek sculpture of the 19th and 20th centuries is effectively displayed in the sculpture garden and sculpture hall, reached from the lower floor. There are several works by Giannolis Halepas (1851–1937), one of Greece's foremost sculptors.

Athens Municipal Art Gallery Map 4, A3
Piraeus 51, Gazi ☎ 324 0472, 324 3023 🕘 9am-1pm & 5pm-8.30pm Mon-Fri & 9am-1pm Sun $ free 🚊 20 from Omonia

The Athens Municipal Art Gallery houses a permanent collection of Greek art which the municipality has been assembling since 1923. It also features temporary exhibitions by Greek and international artists.

Museum of Traditional Greek Ceramics
Map 4, D5
Areos 1, Monastiraki ☎ 324 2066 🕘 10am-2pm Mon & Wed-Sun $ 500 dr [M] Monastiraki

WHAT'S FREE

Athens has some interesting free museums.

Centre of Folk Arts & Traditions Map 4, F8
Angelika Hatzimihali 6, Plaka ☎ 324 3987 🕘 9am-1pm & 5pm-9pm Tues-Fri, 9am-1pm Sat & Sun $ free [M] Syntagma

The Centre of Folk Arts & Traditions has a good display of costumes, embroideries, pottery and musical instruments.

Museum of Greek Popular Instruments
Map 5, D1
Diogenous 1-3, Plaka ☎ 325 4119
[e] ival@atlas.uoa.gr 🕘 10am-2pm Tues & Thur-Sun, 12pm-6pm Wed $ free [M] Monastiraki

A favourite is the Museum of Greek Popular Instruments. It has displays and recordings of a wide selection of traditional instruments.

Museum of the History of Greek Costume
Map 6, B1
Dimokritou 7, Kolonaki ☎ 362 9513
[e] pelai@netor.gr 🕘 10am-1pm Mon, Wed, Fri, 5.30pm-8.30pm Thur $ free [M] Panepistimiou

The Museum of the History of Greek Costume changes its display every year. The 2000 display featured the costumes of the Northern Sporades and Trkeri.

Theatre Museum Map 4, A10
Akadimias 50, Pefkakia ☎ 362 9430
[e] theatrom@compulink.gr
[w] www.istos.net.gr/theatro/museum
🕘 9am-2.30pm Mon-Fri $ free
[M] Panepistimiou

Aspiring thespians may be interested in visiting this museum, which contains theatre memorabilia from the 19th and 20th centuries. Exhibits include photographs, costumes, props and reconstructions of the dressing rooms of Greece's most celebrated 20th-century actors.

War Museum Map 6, D5
Vassilissis Sofias, Kolonaki ☎ 729 0543/4
🕘 9am-2pm Tues-Sun $ free [M] Evangelismos

The War Museum is a relic of the colonels' junta, and is also an architectural statement of the times. Greece seems to have been at war since time immemorial, and a look around helps to get the country's history in perspective. All periods from the Mycenaean to the present day are covered, and displays include weapons, maps, armour and models of battles.

HILLS OF ATHENS

LYKAVITTOS HILL

The name Lykavittos means 'hill of wolves' and derives from ancient times when the hill was surrounded by countryside and its pine-covered slopes were inhabited by wolves. Today, it is no longer surrounded by countryside nor inhabited by wolves, but rises out of a sea of concrete to offer the finest views in Athens. Pollution permitting, there are panoramic views of the city, the Attic basin, the surrounding mountains and the islands of Salamis and Aegina. A path leads to the summit from the top of Loukianou. Alternatively, you can take the funicular railway to the top of Ploutarhou (500/1000 dr single/return, 9.15am to 11.45pm daily).

There is a cafe halfway up the path and another at the top, as well as a restaurant with a spectacular view over the Acropolis. Also on the summit is the little **Chapel of Agios Giorgios**. The chapel is floodlit at night and from the streets below looks like a vision from a fairy tale. The open-air **Lykavittos Theatre**, to the north-east of the summit, is used for performances of jazz and rock during the Athens Festival.

WEST OF THE ACROPOLIS

The low **Areopagus Hill** lies between the Acropolis and the Ancient Agora. According to mythology, it was here that Ares was tried by the council of the gods for the murder of Halirrhothios, son of Poseidon. The council accepted his defence of justifiable deicide on the grounds that he was protecting his daughter, Alcippe, from unwanted advances.

The hill became the place where murder trials were heard before the Council of the Areopagus, whose jurisdiction by the 4th century had been extended to cover treason and corruption. In AD 51, St Paul delivered his famous 'Sermon – an Unknown God' from Areopagus Hill and gained his first Athenian convert, Dionysos, who became patron saint of the city.

Areopagus Hill is linked to the Acropolis by a saddle and can be climbed by steps cut into the rock. There are good views of the Ancient Agora from the summit. The steps are extremely slippery, and should be tackled with great caution. Don't even consider climbing up in the wet.

Filopappos Hill, also called the Hill of the Muses, is clearly identifiable to the south-west of the Acropolis by virtue of the **Monument of Filopappos** at its summit. The monument was built in AD 114–16 in honour of Julius Antiochus Filopappos, who was a prominent Roman consul and administrator.

There are small paths all over the hill, but the paved path to the top starts next to the Dionysos Taverna on Dionysiou Areopagitou. The pine-clad slopes are a pleasant place for a stroll and offer good views of the plain and mountains of Attica and of the Saronic Gulf. After 250m, the path passes the **Church of Agios Dimitrios**, which contains some fine frescoes. It was sensitively restored in 1951–57.

North of here is the rocky **Hill of the Pnyx**. This was the meeting place of the Democratic Assembly in the 5th century BC. Among the great orators who addressed assemblies here were Aristides, Demosthenes, Pericles and Themistocles.

To the north-west of the Hill of the Pnyx is the **Hill of the Nymphs**, on which stands an observatory built in 1842. It is open to visitors on the last Friday of each month.

PARKS

Athens is sadly lacking in parks. Only three are large enough to warrant a mention.

NATIONAL GARDENS Map 4, E10
These gardens are a delightful shady refuge during the summer months and are the favourite haunt of Athens' many stray cats.

They were formerly the royal gardens and were designed by Queen Amalia.

The gardens contain subtropical trees, ornamental ponds with waterfowl, and a **botanical museum**, which houses interesting drawings, paintings and photographs. There are entrances to the gardens from Vasilissis Sofias and Amalias.

ZAPPEIO GARDENS Map 4, G10
Located just south of the National Gardens, these very formal gardens are laid out in a network of wide walkways around the Zappeio, an imposing neoclassical mansion built in the 1870s with money donated by the wealthy Greek-Romanian benefactor Konstantinos Zappas. It was used as the headquarters of the Olympic Committee for the 1896 Olympics (held at the nearby Roman Stadium). It hosted Council of Europe meetings during Greece's presidency of the EC.

AREOS PARK Map 3, A9
This pleasant park is north of the National Archaeological Museum on Leoforos Alexandras. It is a large park with wide, tree-lined avenues, one of which has a long line of statues of War of Independence heroes.

ATHENS' FIRST CEMETERY Map 7, D9
Athens' First Cemetery (Proto Nekrotafeion Athinon) is not strictly a park, but it bears more than a passing resemblance to one. In the absence of real parks, any patch of greenery is welcome. Athenian families who come to attend the graves of loved ones certainly seem to take this attitude, turning duty into an outing by bringing along a picnic. It's a peaceful place to stroll around and is the resting place of many famous Greeks and philhellenes.

The cemetery is well kept and most of the tombstones and mausoleums are lavish in the extreme. Some are kitsch and sentimental, others are works of art created by the foremost Greek sculptors of the 19th century, such as the *Sleeping Maiden* by Halepas, which is the tomb of a young girl. Someone places a red rose in her hand every day.

Among the cemetery's famous residents are the writers Rangavis (1810–92) and Soutsos (1800–68); the politician Harilaos Trikoupis (1832–96); the archaeologists Heinrich Schliemann (1822–90) and Adolph Furtwängler (1853–1907); the benefactors Antoine Benaki, Georgios Averof and Theodoros Syngros; and War of Independence heroes Sir Richard Church (1784– 1873), Kolokotronis (1770–1843), Makrygiannis and Androutsos. Schliemann's mausoleum is decorated with scenes from the Trojan War. Located near the entrance is a memorial – poignant in its simplicity – to the 40,000 citizens who died of starvation during WWII.

The cemetery is 600m south-east of the Temple of Olympian Zeus at the end of Anapafseos in Mets. You'll know you're getting close when you see all the stonemasons and flower shops. Other shops sell cemetery paraphernalia, ranging from life-size figures of Christ to miniature picture frames – used to put photographs of the deceased on the gravestones.

ACTIVITIES

BEACHES

The best beaches are in the south-east, around the resort district of Glyfada. See the Excursions chapter for details.

Varkiza Beach
Posidionos, Varkiza ☎ 897 2436
🕘 8am-8pm daily $ adult/child 700/350 dr
🚌 115,116,149, A2

Not to be outdone the beach at Varkiza also hires tennis courts (1500/2200 dr per hour day/evening) and volleyball courts (1000/2200 dr per hour day/evening) and has a water slide, children's play area and three snackbars. Catch bus No A2 to Glyfada then catch a connecting bus to Varkiza.

Voula Beach
Alkionidon, Voula ☎ 895 3248 🕘 8am-8pm daily $ adult/child 600/300 dr 🚌 A2

The beach has a tennis court you can hire for 1000/2000 dr per hour in the day/evening. It also has a volleyball court. The bus to Voula stops at the beach.

Vouliagmeni Beach
Posidonos, Vouliagmeni ☎ 896 0906
🕘 8am-8pm daily $ adult/child 700/350 dr
🚌 114,115,116, A2

Vouliagmeni Beach has possibly the best set up of the three beaches. Here you can rent individual cabins for 2000 dr to lounge about in for the day. However, if you are feeling more active you can hire a tennis court for 1500/2200 dr for an hour during the day/evening, or the volleyball court for 1000/2200 dr an hour during the day/evening. The beach also has a children's play area, water slide and a small restaurant. To get to the beach catch bus No A2 to Glyfada then catch a connecting bus to Vouliagmeni.

TENNIS

Visitors are welcome to use the courts at the Glyfada Golf Club.

Otherwise, getting a game involves wangling your way into one of the exclusive clubs.

Athens Tennis Club Map 7, A7
Vasilissis Olgas 2, Zappeio ☎ 923 2872, 921 5630 🕘 7am-10.30pm daily
$ court 5000 dr per hr; lights 800 dr per hr extra; annual membership 165,000 dr; registration 250,000 dr [M] Evangelismos

Athens Tennis Club is an exclusive establishment and also has a gymnasium and squash courts.

Glyfada Golf Club
Glyfada ☎ 894 6820 [e] glyfgolf@compulink.gr
🕘 1pm-sunset Mon, 7.30am-sunset Tues-Sun
$ court 3000 dr per hr 🚌 019

GOLF

Glyfada Golf Course
Glyfada ☎ 894 6820 [e] glyfgolf@compulink.gr
🕘 1pm-sunset Mon, 7.30am-sunset Tues-Sun
$ green fee Mon-Fri 14,000 dr, Sat, Sun & public holidays 18,000 dr; club hire 7000 dr; buggy hire 2000 dr; electric cart hire 9000 dr 🚌 019

The Glyfada Golf Course is Athens' only golf course.

TENPIN BOWLING

Athens Bowling Centre Map 2, A2
28 Oktovriou-Patission 177, Kypseli
☎ 867 3645 🕘 10am-2am daily
$ game Mon-Fri 1500 dr; Sat & Sun 1800 dr
🚎 3,5,13 (from Panepistimiou to the Kallifrona stop on Patission, the first stop after Plateia Amerikis)

The Athens Bowling Centre is not the flashest in the world. It has computerised scoring, but the balls are old and chipped. Still, it's a reasonable option on a wet afternoon. It gets very busy in the evenings.

SKIING

Klaoudatos (ski department) Map 4, A6
Kratinou 3-5, Omonia ☎ 324 1915
🕘 9am-6pm Mon & Wed, 9am-8.30pm Tues, Thur & Fri, 9am-5pm Sat $ bus 3000 dr, skis, bindings, boots and poles 3000 dr, snowboards 4000 dr, toboggans 2000 dr [M] Omonia

The nearest ski fields to Athens are at Mt Parnassos, three hours north-west, where the season lasts from mid-December to March or April. The ski department at Klaoudatos, the big department store on Athinas, in Omonia, organises excursions to the resort of Kelaria. Its buses leave from the stadium in Athens every morning at 4.50 am and get to Kelaria just after 8.30 am. They leave the resort at 4pm.

CHILDREN'S ACTIVITIES

Keeping small children occupied in Athens can be hard work. There is a dire shortage of child-friendly things to do. There are two small amusement parks, both near Kifissia, but they are sorry affairs. It's best not to mention them.

A water park would be ideal in summer: the closest is on the nearby island of Aegina.

One possibility is a visit to the National Gardens, which has a mini zoo with a few goats and assorted fowl.

Children's Museum Map 4, F8
Kydathineon 14, Plaka ☎ 331 2995
🕘 9.30am-1.30pm Mon, Wed & Fri, 5pm-8pm Fri, 10am-1pm Sat & Sun $ free [M] Syntagma

The Children's Museum in Plaka is more of a play group than a museum. It has a games room and a number of 'exhibits', such as a mock-up of a metro tunnel, for children to explore. Parents have to stay and supervise their children.

Museum of Children's Art Map 4, F8
Kodrou 9, Plaka ☎ 331 2621 🕘 10am-2pm Tues-Fri & Sat, 11am-2pm Sun $ free; child attending special programs 200 dr [M] Syntagma

The Museum of Children's Art is more of a gallery than a museum with the majority of its wall space devoted to an exhibition of paintings by primary school children from throughout the country. It runs art courses for children, but these are suitable only for residents. There's also a special room set aside where visiting children can let loose their creative energies. Crayons and paper are supplied.

COURSES

LANGUAGE

If you are serious about learning Greek, an intensive course at the start of your stay is a good way to go about it.

Athens Centre Map 7, C9
Arhimidous 48, Mets ☎ 701 2268
[e] athenscr@compulink.gr
[W] www.athenscentre.gr 🕘 9am-8pm Mon-Fri $ course 150,000 dr 🚎 2,4 or 11

The Athens Centre, in the quiet residential suburb of Mets, has a very good reputation. Its courses cover five levels of proficiency from beginners to advanced. There are eight immersion courses a year for beginners, packing approximately 60 hours of class time into three weeks. The centre occupies a fine neoclassical building.

Hellenic American Union Map 6, A1
Massalias 22, Kolonaki ☎ 362 9886
[e] vioannou@hau.gr [W] www.hau.gr
🕘 9am-5pm daily $ course 92,000-100,000 dr [M] Panepistimiou

Another place offering courses lasting between one and three months covering all levels of proficiency.

DANCE

Dora Stratou Dance Group Map 4, F7
Sholiou 8, Plaka ☎ 324 4395
[e] grdance@hol.gr [W] users.hol.gr/~grdance
🕘 9am-4pm Mon-Fri [M] Akropoli

The celebrated Dora Stratou Dance Group (see the Greek folk dancing section of the Entertainment chapter) also runs occasional dance courses for visitors in summer. The courses run for five days. Check the Dora Stratou Web site for dates and details.

Places to Stay

Athens has a range of accommodation to suit every taste and pocket. Most places are very reasonably priced by European standards, particularly at the middle and lower end of the scale. Rates at the top end have shot up in anticipation of boom times in the lead-up to the 2004 Olympics.

The majority of visitors prefer to stay in the city centre, which is the most convenient place to be if visits to the museums and ancient sites are high on the agenda. It's the best option for the bulk of the year. In summer, though, it's well worth considering the coastal suburbs around Glyfada, or leafy Kifissia in the north. For information about these possibilities see the Excursion chapter.

Hotels everywhere are divided into six categories: deluxe, A, B, C, D and E. They are categorised according to the level of facilities on offer, such as air-con, direct dial phones, hair dryers etc. They don't take into account factors like standards of cleanliness, comfort of the beds and friendliness of staff – all elements which may be of greater relevance to guests. The classification is not often much of a guide to price either: there are good E-class hotels that cost more than some run-down C-class places.

All places to stay are subject to strict price controls set by the tourist police. By law, a notice must be displayed in every room, which states the category of the room and the price charged in each season. These prices include a 4.5% community tax and 8% VAT. At the time of research, many of the city's leading hotels were opting to quote prices in US dollars because of the fall in the value of the drachma against the greenback. This does not mean that the bill must be paid in US dollars. Your bill will be converted into drachma at the day's exchange rate.

The prices quoted in this book are for 2001, listed according to high and low season. Unless stated otherwise, low season covers months October to March, and high season covers April to September. Accommodation owners are entitled to add a 10% surcharge to the listed rates for a stay of less than three nights, but few take up this option. A mandatory charge of 20% is levied if an extra bed is put into a room. Prices for budget accommodation are for rooms without bathrooms, unless otherwise stated. All other prices are for rooms with bathroom.

Bear in mind that these are the maximum rates that can be charged. Some places offer rates well below the official prices, especially between November and February. Not surprisingly, rooms fill up quickly in July and August, so it's important to make a reservation. If you haven't booked, a telephone call can save a fruitless walk. All the hotels listed in this book employ English-speaking receptionists.

Rip-offs rarely occur, but if you suspect you have been exploited by an accommodation owner, report it to either the tourist police or regular police.

PLACES TO STAY – BUDGET

The enormous influx of refugees from neighbouring Albania (in particular) and other Balkan nations has had a major impact on the budget accommodation scene. Some cheap hotels and hostels have become little more than refugee camps, packing in people like sardines.

The budget places recommended in this section all attempt to ensure a secure environment for their guests.

CAMPING

There are no camp sites in central Athens, but there are several possibilities on the coast road to Cape Sounion. (See the Glyfada section of the Excursions chapter for details.)

HOSTELS

Athens International Youth Hostel
Map 3, 4E
Victor Hugo 16, Omonia ☎ 523 4170 fax 523 4015 ⓢ dorms 2850 dr; joining fee 4200 dr; temporary membership 700 dr/day Ⓒ none Ⓜ Metaxourghio

The excellent Athens International Youth Hostel is the only hostel affiliated to Hostelling International (HI). Its location isn't overly salubrious, but otherwise the place is almost too good to be true. It occupies the former C-class Hotel Victor Ougo, which has been completely renovated – it even has double-glazed windows. The spotless rooms, with bathroom, sleep two to four people and include sheets and pillow cases. Facilities include a guest kitchen, laundry, Internet access and free safety deposit boxes. There is no curfew and the reception staff speak English. The hostel is deservedly popular, so call ahead to reserve a bed.

Youth Hostel No 5 Map 2, F4
Damareos 75, Pangrati ☎ 751 9530 fax 751 0616 e y-hostel@otenet.gr Ⓢ dorms 2000 dr C none 🚎 2, 11
The rooms are very basic, with five to nine beds per room, but it's a cheery place. Owner Yiannis is something of a philosopher, and visitors are encouraged to add their jokes or words of wisdom to the hostel noticeboard. Facilities include coin-operated hot showers, a communal kitchen, washing machine (1000 dr) and a TV room. To get there, take trolleybus No 2 or 11 from Syntagma to the Filolaou stop on Frinis, just past Damareos.

XEN (YMCA) Map 4, C10
Amerikis 11, Syntagma ☎ 362 4291 fax 362 2400 e xene7@hol.gr Ⓢ singles 10,000 dr; doubles 12,000 dr; or 9000/11,000 for stays of 2 nights or longer; annual membership 1000 dr C none Ⓜ Syntagma
The XEN is for women only. It's ideally situated right in the centre of town, close to Plateia Syntagmatos. All rooms come with private bathroom. There are also laundry facilities and a snack bar.

GUESTHOUSES
Plaka
Festos Youth & Student Guesthouse Map 4, 9F
Filellinon 18 ☎ 323 2455 fax 321 0907 e consolas@hol.gr Ⓢ singles 8000/7000 dr; doubles 9000/8000 dr; triples 13,000/10,000 dr; dorms 4000/3500 dr C V Ⓜ Syntagma
The Festos has long been a popular place with travellers despite being on one of the noisiest streets in Athens. The main attraction is the

cheapest habitable beds in the Plaka area. A popular feature is the bar on the 1st floor, which also serves meals, including a daily vegetarian dish.

Student & Travellers' Inn Map 4, F8
Kydathineon 16 ☎ 324 4808 fax 321 0065 e students-inn@ath.forthnet.gr Ⓢ singles 10,500/8500 dr with bathroom; doubles 13,500/10,000 dr with bathroom; triples 18,000/13,500 dr; dorms 4000-6000/3500-4500 dr; breakfast 1000-1500 dr C none Ⓜ Syntagma
The Student Inn occupies a converted nursing home, and is a veritable maze of rooms large and small – some with old timber floors. The dorms here are good value. All triple rooms and dorms share communal bathrooms. There's Internet access and a big-screen TV in the courtyard where you can watch satellite coverage of international sporting events. The place stays open all year, and rooms are heated in winter.

North of Omonia
Hostel Argo Map 3, E3
Victor Hugo, Omonia ☎ 522 5939 fax 522 0682 Ⓢ singles 6000/5000 dr; doubles 8000/7000 dr; triples 9000/8000 dr; quads 12,000/11,000 dr; breakfast 1000 dr C none Ⓜ Metaxourghio
This small, privately run hostel offers well-priced clean rooms, all with private bathrooms. While not as atmospheric as its HI neighbour, if it is peace and quiet you are after look no further.

Hostel Aphrodite Map 2, C1
Einardou 12, Victoria ☎ 881 0589 fax 881 6574 e hostel-aphrodite@ath.forthnet.gr Ⓢ singles 9500/8000 dr; doubles 12,000/10,000 dr; triples 13,500/12,000 dr; quads 18,000/14,000 dr; dorms 4000/3500 dr; breakfast 1000-1500 dr C none Ⓜ Viktorias 🚎 1
The popular Hostel Aphrodite, 10 minutes' walk from the train stations, is very clean, with good-sized rooms – many with balconies. It seems to be party time every night at the downstairs bar. In the morning, the bar becomes the breakfast room. The hostel also has Internet access and long-term luggage storage. You can get there on trolleybus No 1, which travels north up Mihail Voda, although the route is not shown on the EOT map. Get off at the Prousis stop, just south of Einardou.

PLACES TO STAY

KEY TO SYMBOLS
☎	telephone number	C	credit cards	Ⓜ	metro station
e	email address	AE	American Express	🚎	trolleybus
w	Web site	V	Visa Card	🚌	bus stop
☺	opening hours	MC	MasterCard	🚉	train station
Ⓢ	prices	JCB	Japan Credit Bureau	⚓	ferry
	(high/low season)	DC	Diner's Club		

Alternatively it's a five minute walk south-east from Viktorias metro station. The hostel is closed from November 1 to February 15.

Zorba's Hotel Map 3, A7
Gilfordiou 10, Victoria ☎/fax 823 4239
ⓔ zorbashotel@hotmail.com ⓢ singles 9000/8000 dr; doubles 12,000/10,000 dr; triples 15,000/12,000 dr; quads 18,000/14,000 dr; dorms 4000/3000 dr; breakfast 1000-1200 dr Ⓒ none ⓜ Viktorias

Zorba's Hotel occupies a quaint old building 100m west of Plateia Viktorias. Following extensive renovations in 1999 all rooms now have bathrooms and newer rooms have been carpeted and have TVs. A downstairs bar with a pleasant outside courtyard has also been added. Other facilities include Internet access and a laundry service.

HOTELS
Syntagma

John's Place Map 5, D4
Patröou 5 ☎ 322 9719 ⓢ singles 8000/5000 dr; doubles 11,000/7000 dr; triples 16,000/10,000 dr Ⓒ none ⓜ Syntagma

John's Place is a small, old-fashioned, family-run place just west of Syntagma. The rooms are large and clean, if simply furnished, and the location is as convenient as you'll find.

Hotel Dioskouros Map 4, G8
Pittakou 6, Plaka ☎ 324 8165 fax 321 0907
ⓔ consolas@hol.gr ⓢ singles 10,000/8000 dr; doubles 11,000/9000 dr; triples 15,000/12,000 dr; quads 20,000/14,000 dr; breakfast from 1000 dr Ⓒ MC, V ⓜ Syntagma

Owned and managed by the same team as the Festos (see previous Hostels section), the Dioskouros is ideally located on a quiet side street on the edge of Plaka. It's an old-style place with timber floors and very high ceilings. The shady courtyard at the back has a snack bar serving breakfast and light meals.

Monastiraki & Thisio

Hotel Tempi Map 5, A1
Eolou 29, Monastiraki ☎ 321 3175 fax 325 4179 ⓔ tempihotel@travelling.gr ⓢ singles 7500/6500 dr, with bath 9500/7500 dr; doubles with bath 12,500/9000 dr; triples with bath 15,000/10,500 dr Ⓒ MC, V ⓜ Monastiraki

The D-class Hotel Tempi is a friendly family-run place on the pedestrian precinct part of Eolou. Owners Yiannis and Katerina keep the place spotless and the rooms at the front have balconies overlooking a little square with a church and a flower market – and views to the Acropolis. There is also a communal kitchen with a refrigerator and facilities for preparing hot drinks and snacks. A washing machine is an added attraction.

Hotel Attalos Map 4, C6
Athinas 29, Monastiraki ☎ 321 2801 fax 324 3124 ⓔ atthot@hol.gr ⓢ singles 15,200/13,500 dr; doubles 19,000/17,000 dr; triples 22,800/20,400 dr; breakfast 2000 dr Ⓒ AE, V ⓜ Monastiraki

The Attalos is a comfortable (if characterless) modern hotel. Its best feature is the rooftop bar which offers wonderful views of the Acropolis by night. All rooms have air-conditioning and TV.

Hotel Carolina Map 5, A2
Kolokotroni 55, Monastiraki ☎ 324 3551/2 fax 324 3550 ⓔ hotelcarolina@galaxynet.gr ⓢ singles 12,000/9000 dr, with bath 15,000/10,000 dr; doubles 15,000/11,000 dr, with bath 16,000/12,000 dr; triples 17,000/13,000 dr, with bath 18,000/14,000 dr; breakfast 1200 dr Ⓒ none ⓜ Monastiraki

The owners of the Carolina have spent a lot of money upgrading this place in the last couple of years, including a fine job on the facade. Work continues inside, and air-conditioning is now available in all rooms.

Hotel Cecil Map 4, B6
Athinas 39, Monastiraki ☎ 321 7079 fax 321 8005 ⓔ cecil@netsmart.gr ⓢ singles 13,500/10,000 dr; doubles 18,000/12,000 dr; triples 23,500/16,000 dr; quads 29,000/20,000 dr; children free; breakfast 1200 dr Ⓒ AE, MC, V ⓜ Monastiraki

If there was a prize for the best restoration job, it should go to the new owners of Hotel Cecil. They have done a magnificent job in reviving this fine old hotel, with its beautiful high, moulded ceilings and polished timber floors. The rooms are tastefully furnished and equipped with air-conditioning and TV.

Hotel Erechthion Map 4, E2
Flammarion 8, Thisio ☎ 345 9606/26 fax 346 2756 ⓢ singles 9000/7000 dr; doubles 14,000/11,000 dr; triples 16,500/13,000 dr; breakfast 1000 dr Ⓒ none ⓜ Thisio

Tourists are something of a rarity at the tiny Hotel Erechthion, hidden away in the back streets of Thisio on the slopes of the Hill of the Pynx. It has spotless single and double rooms with TV and bathroom; the rooms at the front have superb views of the Acropolis. It's one of the few hotels in Athens without an English-speaking receptionist.

Koukaki

Art Gallery Pension Map 7, C3
Erehthiou 5 ☎ 923 8376, 923 1933 fax 923 3025 ⓔ ecotec@otenet.gr ⓢ singles 15,000/10,600 dr; doubles 17,800/12,900 dr; triples 21,300/15,400 dr; quads 25,300/17,800 dr; children under 6 free, cots available; breakfast 1700 dr Ⓒ DC, MC, V ⓜ Syngrou-Fix

PLACES TO STAY

The Art Gallery is one of the best small hotels in town. Run by the brother-and-sister team of Ada and Yannis Assimakopoulos, it's a friendly place that's full of personal touches, like fresh flowers. The rooms are heated in winter, when cheaper long-term rates are available.

Marble House Pension Map 7, D2
Zini 35A ☎ 923 4058 fax 922 6461 $ singles 8000/6000 dr, with bath 10,000/8000 dr; doubles 14,000/12,000 dr, with bath 16,000/14,000 dr; triples 15,000/13,000 dr, with bath 17,000/15,000 dr; air-con extra 3000 dr; children under 2 free; breakfast 900 dr [C] none 🚋 1, 5, 9, 22
Marble House Pension boasts one of the quietest locations in Athens, hidden away at the end of a quiet cul-de-sac off Zini. All rooms have a bar fridge, ceiling fans and safety boxes for valuables. There's a book exchange in the reception area.

Tony's Hotel Map 7, C2
Zaharitsa 26 ☎ 923 0561, 923 6370 fax 923 6370 $ singles 12,000/10,800 dr; doubles 14,000/12,000 dr; triples 17,500/14,800 dr; apartments 16,000/12,000 dr; air-con extra 2000 dr; children under 2 free [C] none [M] Syngrou-Fix
Tony's Hotel is a clean, well-maintained place tucked away on the back streets of Koukaki. All rooms are centrally heated in winter. There is a small communal kitchen downstairs for making tea/coffee and breakfast. Tony also has well-equipped studio apartments next door for long or short term rental. Short term prices are much the same as for rooms at the pension.

Exarhia

Exarhia is off the beaten track as far as hotels go, but there are a couple of good places to be found tucked away at the base of Strefi Hill.

Hotel Orion Map 3, D10
Emmanual Benaki 105 ☎ 382 7362 fax 380 5193 [e] orion-dryades@lycosmail.com $ singles 8000/7000 dr; doubles 10,000/8000 dr; triples 12,000 dr; breakfast 1500 dr [C] none 🚌 230
The Orion is clean and well kept. Bathrooms are shared and Internet access is available. The hotel is to the left at the top of the steps leading off Emmanual Benaki at the junction with Anexartissias. You can save yourself a long uphill trek by catching bus No 230 from Amalias to the Kalidromiou stop on Harilaou Trikoupi.

Hotel Dryades Map 3, D10
Dryades 4 ☎ 382 7362 fax 380 5193 [e] orion-dryades@lycosmail.com $ singles 12,000/10,000 dr; doubles 15,000/12,000 dr; triples 19,500; breakfast 1500 dr [C] none 🚌 230
The entry to Hotel Dryades is on Anehartisias, which skirts the western side of the hill. All rooms have bathrooms and a communal kitchen and laundry are also available. Hotel Dryades and Hotel Orion are managed jointly by a friendly guy who speaks English. Catch bus No 230 from Amalias to the Kalidromiou stop on Harilaou Trikoupi.

PLACES TO STAY – MID-RANGE

PLAKA

Acropolis House Pension Map 4, F8
Kodrou 6-8 ☎ 322 2344 fax 324 4143 $ singles 13,830/11,660 dr, with bath 16,260/13,750 dr; doubles 16,600/13,920 dr, with bath 19,500/16,500 dr; triples with bath 25,100/18,000 dr; children 20% extra; breakfast 1700 dr [C] MC, V [M] Syntagma
Acropolis House Pension is a beautifully preserved 19th-century house where nothing seems to have changed in years. It retains many original features, including some wonderful frescoes in the older section. Another feature of the Acropolis House is that is boasts undoubtedly the most complex pricing structure in Athens, with discounts for stays of three days or more, supplements for air-conditioning and the like.

Hotel Adonis Map 4, F8
Kodrou 3 ☎ 324 9737 fax 323 1602 $ singles 11,500/8300 dr; doubles 20,500/12,000 dr; triples 23,500/18,000 dr; cots available; breakfast included [C] none [M] Syntagma
Hotel Adonis, opposite Acropolis House Pension, is a comfortable modern hotel that represents astonishingly good value for Plaka. All the rooms are equipped with air-conditioning and TV. It has good views of the Acropolis from the 4th floor rooms, and from the rooftop bar.

Hotel Nefeli Map 4, F8
Iperidou 16 ☎ 322 8044 fax 322 5800 $ singles 20,000/13,500 dr; doubles 23,000/15,000 dr; triples 29,000/20,000 dr; children free; breakfast included [C] V [M] Syntagma
The Nefeli is a popular place tucked away in the side streets of Plaka. All the rooms come with air-con and TV. Ask for a room overlooking pedestrian-only Hatzimihali.

Hotel Plaka Map 5, C2
Kapnikareas 7 ☎ 322 2096, 322 2706 fax 322 2412 [e] plaka@tourhotel.gr $ singles 27,000/15,000 dr; doubles 32,000/16,000 dr; triples 36,000/19,000 dr; breakfast 1000 dr [C] AE, MC, V [M] Syntagma
Hotel Plaka is a comfortable modern hotel that is popular with smaller tour groups, particularly in summer when the prices for independent travellers are set unrealistically high. It's good value in the low season. There are good views of the Acropolis from the rooftop bar.

PLACES TO STAY

Hotel Adrian Map 5, D1
Adrianou 74 ☎ 322 1553 fax 325 0461
ⓔ douros@otenet.gr ⓢ singles 26,000/19,300
dr, 30,000/22,500 dr with Acropolis view;
doubles 32,000/26,000 dr, 37,000/30,000 dr
with Acropolis view; triples 39,900/32,700 dr;
all prices inc. breakfast; children under 2 free,
cots available ⓒ AE, MC, V ⓜ Syntagma
The Adrian is ranked by some as the top hotel in
Plaka, although it carries no more than a B classification. The rooms are large and well-appointed.
The best rooms, at the rear of the hotel on the 3rd
floor, have balconies with wonderful views of the
Acropolis.

SYNTAGMA

Hotel Cypria Map 5, B5
Diomeias 5 ☎ 323 8034 fax 324 8792
ⓢ singles 21,000/19,000 dr; doubles
27,500/25,500 dr; triples 36,500/34,500 dr;
quads 42,000/40,000 dr; children under 4 free,
children 4-12 6000 dr, cots available; buffet
breakfast included ⓒ AE, JCB, MC, V
ⓜ Syntagma
Formerly the Hotel Diomeia, the Hotel Cypria
opened in 1998 after a radical remodelling of the
interior and a complete refit. It's now a comfortable, if somewhat sterile, modern hotel, but it's
better value than many of its neighbours around
Syntagma – especially in low season. Expect to
pay around 2000 dr extra for a room with an
Acropolis view.

Hotel Achilleas Map 5, B5
Leka 21 ☎ 323 3197, 322 2706 fax 322 2412
ⓔ achilleas@tourhotel.gr ⓢ singles
25,000/13,500 dr; doubles 28,000/14,500 dr;
triples 33,000/16,000 dr; quads 40,000/
18,000 dr; breakfast 1000 dr ⓒ AE, MC, V
ⓜ Akropoli
Like its stablemate Hotel Plaka, Hotel Achilleas is
popular with small tour groups in summer. It's
great value in winter. The rooms are large and
airy, and those on the top floor open onto garden
terraces.

MAKRIGIANNI

Hotel Hera Map 7, B5
Falirou 9 ☎ 923 6682, 923 5618 fax 924 7334
ⓔ hhera@hol.gr ⓢ singles 29,000/17,000 dr;
doubles 39,000/25,500 dr; triples
48,900/32,500 dr; buffet breakfast included
ⓒ AE, MC, V ⓜ Monastiraki
Hotel Hera, with its comfortable modern rooms,
represents good value for the trendy Makrigianni
district. Air-con and TV are standard in all rooms.

Hotel Philippos Map 7, B4
Mitseon 3 ☎ 922 3611 fax 922 3615
ⓔ philipposhotel@yahoo.com ⓢ singles
US$88/65; doubles US$111/85; triples
US$137/107 dr; children under 2 free; buffet

breakfast included ⓒ DC, JCB, MC, V
ⓜ Monastiraki
The Philippos is a small hotel that's geared towards the well-heeled tourist. The rooms are on
the small side, but well appointed following a recent refit.

Acropolis View Hotel Map 7, A2
Webster 10 ☎ 921 7303/4/5 fax 923 0705
ⓢ singles 29,000/18,500 dr; doubles
39,000/24,000 dr; triples 47,000/29,000 dr;
children under 2 free, cots available; buffet
breakfast included ⓒ MC, V ⓜ Akropoli
The Acropolis View has one of the quietest set-
tings around, nestled below Filopappos Hill just
south of the Theatre of Herodes Atticus. There are
indeed views of the Acropolis from many of the
rooms, although the best views are from the roof
terrace. Other rooms look out over Filopappos
Hill. All rooms have air-con and TV.

Hotel Austria Map 7, B2
Mouson 7 ☎ 923 5151 fax 924 7350
ⓔ austria@hol.gr ⓢ singles 21,400/
16,000 dr; doubles 27,500/21,000 dr; triples
33,600/25,800 dr; children under 2 free, cots
available; breakfast included ⓒ AE, DC, MC, V
ⓜ Akropoli
Hotel Austria occupies a quiet spot on the slopes
of Filopappos Hill, with good views over the city
from its roof garden.

Hotel Acropolis Select Map 7, C4
Falirou 37-39, Koukaki ☎ 921 1611 fax 921
6938 ⓢ singles 24,000 dr; doubles 29,200 dr;
triples 36,500 dr; children under 4 free; buffet
breakfast included ⓒ AE, MC, V ⓜ Syngrou-Fix
Formerly known as Hotel Dimitrios, the B-class
Acropolis Select has just been through a complete
refit. Rooms on the northern side have balconies
with views of the Acropolis.

AROUND OMONIA

Omonia is not really the place to be looking
for upmarket accommodation – you can do
much better for your money elsewhere.
There are a couple of exceptions.

Titania Hotel Map 3, G7
Panepistimiou 52, Omonia ☎ 330 0111
fax 330 0700 ⓔ titania@titania.gr ⓢ singles
29,300 dr; doubles 39,500 dr; triples 49,800 dr;
breakfast included ⓒ AE, DC, JCB, MC, V
ⓜ Omonia
Titania Hotel, with its imposing facade, is a comfortable modern hotel with large rooms all with
satellite TV. There are great views over the city
from the rooftop bar at night.

Hotel Oscar Map 3, B3
Filadelphias 25, Omonia ☎ 883 4215/9
fax 821 6368 ⓔ oscar@oscar.gr ⓢ singles
36,000/23,000 dr; doubles 46,000/32,000 dr;

breakfast included C AE, DC, MC, V
Ⓜ Larisa Ⓡ Larisis
Privately run Hotel Oscar is a late 1970s concrete monolith with a grand lobby. Its spacious rooms have pay TV, air-conditioning and private bath. Other facilities include Internet access, luggage storage, rooftop garden bar and swimming pool.

Hotel Oscar Inn Map 3, C2
Samou 43-45, Omonia ☎ 881 3211/2 fax 882 0818 ⓔ oscar@oscar.gr Ⓢ singles 36,000/ 23,000 dr; doubles 46,000/32,000 dr; breakfast included C AE, DC, MC, V Ⓜ Larisa Ⓡ Larisis
While not as impressive as its sister, the Oscar Inn is just as comfortable. Reservations for either Hotel Oscar or Hotel Oscar Inn made through the Internet get a 15% discount.

KOLONAKI

Athenian Inn Map 6, C4
Haritos 22, Kolonaki ☎ 723 8097, 723 9552 fax 724 2268 Ⓢ singles 22,570/17,600 dr; doubles 33,860/26,780 dr; triples 42,250/ 33,760 dr; apartments 44,065/34,400 dr; breakfast included C DC, MC, V Ⓜ Evangelismos
B-class Athenian Inn is a small but distinguished place on a quiet street in the heart of posh Kolonaki that was reputably a favourite of writer Lawrence Durrell. It has a cosy intimacy which is often lacking in hotels of this category. The rooms are unpretentious but comfortable with air-con and pretty pictures of island scenes on the walls.

PLACES TO STAY – TOP END

CENTRAL ATHENS

Hotel Grande Bretagne Map 5, C7
Vassileos Georgiou 1, Syntagma ☎ 333 0000 fax 322 8034 ⓔ info@hotelgrandebretagneath .gr Ⓢ singles 118,000-140,750 dr; doubles 118,000-140,750 dr; triples extra bed 6800 dr; apartment suites from 192,500 dr; children under 14 free; continental breakfast 6200 dr, American 7500 dr C AE, DC, JCB, MC, V Ⓜ Syntagma
If you are wealthy, *the* place to stay in Athens is – and always has been – the deluxe Hotel Grande Bretagne. Built in 1862 to accommodate visiting heads of state, it ranks among the grand hotels of the world. No other hotel in Athens can boast such a rich history (see the Walking Tour section in the Things to See & Do chapter). It has undergone much expansion since it first became a hotel in 1872, but still has an old-world grandeur. The elegantly furnished rooms have air-con, minibar, satellite TV and video.

NJV Athens Plaza Map 5, B7
Vassilis Georgiou 2, Syntagma ☎ 325 5301 fax 323 5856 ⓔ sales_njv@grecotel.gr Ⓢ singles 75,000-95,000 dr; doubles 85,000-

110,000 dr; suites 160,000-450,000 dr; children under 12 free; breakfast 4500-5500 dr C AE, DC, JCB, MC, V Ⓜ Syntagma
Athens Plaza, next door to the Grande Bretagne, isn't far behind in the luxury stakes following a complete refit and a change of name – it was formerly the Meridien.

Electra Palace Map 5, E5
Nikodimou 18, Plaka ☎ 337 0000 fax 324 1875 ⓔ electrahotels@ath.forthnet.gr Ⓢ singles 47,800/38,600 dr; doubles 57,800/47,400 dr; triples 71,700/59,000 dr; suites 72,800/ 59,400 dr; children under 2 free C AE, DC, MC, V Ⓜ Syntagma
Plaka's smartest hotel is the A-class Electra Palace. Its best feature is the rooftop pool with views over to the Acropolis.

Hotel Parthenon Map 7, A5
Makri 6, Makrigianni ☎ 923 4594 fax 923 5797 ⓔ airotel@netplan.gr Ⓢ singles 67,200/60,600 dr; doubles 79,200/71,200 C AE, DC, JCB, MC, V Ⓜ Akropoli
The Parthenon is geared towards the business traveller, but its convenient location just a couple of minutes' walk from Plaka makes it an ideal base for checking out the sites.

Hotel Herodion Map 7, B4
Rovertou Galli 4, Makrigianni ☎ 923 6832 fax 923 5851 ⓔ herodion@otenet.gr Ⓢ singles US$121/90; doubles US$154/118; triples US$193/149; children under 2 free C DC, JCB, MC, V Ⓜ Akropoli
The Herodion is the upmarket cousin of the nearby Hotel Philippos: bigger, smarter and more expensive. The star feature is the rooftop terrace and bar – perfect for viewing the Acropolis by night.

Novotel Athens Map 3, C4
Mihail Voda 4-6, Omonia ☎/fax 820 0700 ⓔ H0866@accor-hotels.com Ⓢ singles 50,000/40,000 dr; doubles 56,000/45,000 dr; triples 66,000/55,000 dr; breakfast 4000 dr C AE, DC, JCB, MC, V Ⓜ Larisa Ⓡ Larisis

The luxurious Hotel Grande Bretagne

PLACES TO STAY

Novotel Athens has jumped the gun a bit in anticipating the desleazing of this area. The hotel itself, though, is a typical representative of this international chain. There are views over the city to the Acropolis from the rooftop pool and bar area. The hotel is a five-minute walk south-east of Larisis train station and Larisa metro station.

St George Lycabettus Hotel Map 6, B3
Kleomenous 2, Kolonaki ☎ 729 0711/9 fax
729 0439 ⓔ info@sglycabettus.gr
Ⓢ singles 48,000/39,700 dr; doubles
58,500/48,000 dr; triples 71,300/58,800 dr;
suites 107,800/83,300 dr; breakfast 5400 dr
Ⓒ AE, DC, JCB, MC, V 🚐 free shuttle bus
St George Lycabettus Hotel has a prime position at the foot of Lykavittos Hill. No hotel in Athens offers better views, and the rooms are priced accordingly (prices given here are without views; expect to pay around 30% more for rooms with views). A free shuttle bus service operates between the hotel and Plateia Syntagmatos from 7.30am-2.30pm Monday to Saturday.

AMBELOKOPI & ILISSIA

Hotel Andromeda Map 8, C3
Timoleontos Vassou 22, Ambelokopi
☎ 643 7302 fax 646 6361
ⓔ andromeda@otenet.gr Ⓢ singles 95,000-
140,000 dr; doubles 95,000-140,000 dr;
apartments 115,000-140,000 dr;
children under 3 free; breakfast 4800-6000 dr
Ⓒ AE, DC, MC, V ⓜ Megaro Moussikis
The Andromeda is a small, stylish, modern hotel tucked away on a quiet side street close to the US embassy. The rooms are tastefully decorated and offer Internet access through the TV, as well as all the standard comforts expected of a luxury hotel. Rooms at the rear overlook the leafy gardens of the US ambassador's residence.

Hotel Alexandros Map 8, C4
Timoleontos Vassou 8, Ambelokopi ☎ 643
0464, 921 5766 fax 644 1084, 921 5569
ⓔ airotel@netplan.gr Ⓢ singles 74,400/
66,400 dr; doubles 87,800/78,800 dr; buffet
breakfast included Ⓒ AE, DC, JCB, MC, V
ⓜ Megaro Moussikis
The Alexandros was one of the many top-end hotels in the middle of a major refurbishing at the time of research. The finished rooms look a treat, and those on the upper floors have generous balconies and views over the city.

Hotel Riva Map 8, D4
Michalakopoulou 114, Ilissia ☎ 770 6611,
921 5766 fax 770 8137, 921 5569
ⓔ airotel@netplan.gr Ⓢ singles 74,400/
66,400 dr; doubles 87,800/78,800 dr
Ⓒ AE, DC, JCB, MC, V ⓜ Megaro Moussikis
The Riva is an old favourite, although it was looking a bit the worse for wear at the time of research.

That won't be the case for long, with renovators preparing to give the place a facelift.

Holiday Inn Map 8, F3
Mihalakopoulou 50, Ilissia ☎ 727 8000
fax 727 8600 ⓔ holinn@ath.forthnet.gr
Ⓢ singles 98,000/80,000 dr; doubles
123,000/100,000 dr; suites 165,000/135,000
dr; children under 12 free; breakfast 7000 dr
Ⓒ AE, DC, JCB, MC, V ⓜ Megaro Moussikis
The Athens Holiday Inn offers all the facilities business travellers have come to expect from this international chain.

Golden Age Map 8, F3
Mihalakopoulou 57, Ilissia ☎ 724 0861
fax 721 3965 ⓔ goldenage@ath.forthnet.gr
Ⓢ singles 50,000/35,000 dr; doubles
60,000/40,000 dr; triples 75,000/54,000 dr;
children under 5 free; buffet breakfast included
Ⓒ AE, DC, MC, V ⓜ Megaro Moussikis
The architecture may be a far cry from that of the classical city built by Pericles, but the Golden Age represents good value compared with its deluxe neighbours.

Hilton Map 8, G1
Vasilissis Sofias 46, Ilissia ☎ 725 0201
fax 725 3110 ⓔ sales_athens@hilton.com
Ⓢ singles standard/superior/deluxe US$305/
315/330; doubles standard/superior/deluxe
US$335/345/360 dr; club suite US$605
(all plus tax) Ⓒ AE, DC, MC, V 🚇 3, 13
Hilton-hoppers will find their favourite opposite the National Art Gallery. The Athens version is a vast concrete edifice. From the outside, it looks more like a 1950s housing project than a luxury hotel, but inside, no expense has been spared. It has lashings of marble and bronze, public areas with enormous chandeliers and carpets which were especially designed by eminent Greek artists. To get there catch trolleybus No 3 or 13 from the junction of Akadimias and Sina to Plateia Genous Scholi.

SOUTH OF CENTRAL ATHENS
Hotel Athenaeum Inter-Continental
Map 7, G1
Syngrou 89-93, Nea Kosmos ☎ 920 6000
fax 920 6500 ⓔ athens@interconti.com
Ⓢ singles 109,000 dr, 119,000 dr with Acropolis view; doubles 109,000 dr; 119,000 dr with
Acropolis view; suites from 139,000 dr; breakfast 6700 dr per person Ⓒ AE, DC, JCB, MC, V
🚐 shuttle bus
The Athenaeum Inter-Continental is probably the plushest of the city's hotels following recent refurbishment. It has all the facilities expected of a deluxe hotel: business centre, swimming pool, fitness centre, Internet access in all rooms etc. The standard rooms are large, and the suites are very large. All suites have views of the Acropolis.

Hotel Ledra Marriott Map 2, G1
Syngrou 115, Nea Cosmos ☎ 930 0000 fax 935 9153 [e] marriott@otenet.gr $ singles 120,000/83,500 dr; 120,000/83,500 dr; suites from 132,500/97,000 dr; breakfast included [C] AE, DC, JCB, MC, V 🚌 shuttle bus

The Ledra Marriott isn't far behind the Inter-Continental in the luxury stakes. It offers similar facilities: business centre, fitness centre, Internet access etc. Its star attraction is the rooftop swimming pool with a view over to the Acropolis. The Kona Kai Polynesian restaurant has a good reputation.

APARTMENTS

The classified section of the *Athens News* advertise apartments, mostly in Athens.

Αθήνα

Places To Eat

FOOD

Greek food does not enjoy a reputation as one of the world's greatest cuisines. Maybe that's because most travellers have experienced Greek cooking only in tourist resorts. The old joke about the woman who, on summer days, shouted to her husband 'Come and eat your lunch before it gets hot' is based on truth. Until recently food was invariably served lukewarm – which is how Greeks prefer it. Most restaurants that cater to tourist have now cottoned on to the fact that foreigners expect cooked dishes to be hot. Greeks are fussy about fresh ingredients and frozen food is rare.

Athenians eat out regularly. Enjoying life is paramount to them and a large part of this enjoyment comes from eating and drinking with friends.

Plaka is the part of town where most visitors wind up eating. The streets are lined with countless restaurants, tavernas, cafes, patisseries and souvlaki stalls.

There's more to Athens eating than Plaka, though. Every neighbourhood in Athens has its own good eating places, often small unpretentious tavernas tucked away on side streets. Monastiraki is great for souvlaki and cheap eats, and Exarhia's proximity to the university means there are lots of places with prices in tune with the average student's pocket. The waiters may not speak any English, but you'll find tasty food and reasonable prices.

International cuisine is much harder to find, as is vegetarian food. Both categories are listed separately at the end of this section.

WHERE TO EAT
Tavernas

The taverna is usually a traditional place with a rough-and-ready ambience, although some are more upmarket, particularly in Athens, resorts and big towns. In simple tavernas, a menu is usually displayed in the window or on the door, but you may instead be invited into the kitchen to peer into the pots and point to what you want. This is not merely a privilege for tourists; Greeks also do it because they want to see the taverna's version of the dishes on offer. Some tavernas don't open until 8 pm, and then stay open until the early hours. Some are closed on Sunday.

Psistaria

These places specialise in spit roasts and charcoal-grilled food – usually lamb, pork or chicken.

Ouzeria

An *ouzeri* serves ouzo. Greeks believe it is essential to eat when drinking alcohol so, in traditional establishments, your drink will come with a small plate of titbits or mezedes (appetisers) – perhaps olives, a slice of feta and some pickled octopus. Ouzeria are becoming trendy and many now offer menus with both appetisers and main courses.

Kafeneia

Kafeneia are often regarded by foreigners as the last bastion of male chauvinism in Europe. With bare light bulbs, nicotine-stained walls, smoke-laden air, rickety wooden tables and raffia chairs, they are frequented by middle-aged and elderly Greek men in cloth caps who while away their time fiddling with worry beads, playing cards or backgammon, or engaged in heated political discussion.

It was once unheard of for women to enter a kafeneio but in large cities this situation is changing. In rural areas, Greek women are rarely seen inside kafeneia. When a female traveller enters one, she is inevitably treated courteously and with friendship if she manages a few Greek words of greeting. If you feel inhibited about going into a kafeneio, opt for outside seating. You'll feel less intrusive.

Kafeneia originally only served Greek coffee but now most also serve soft drinks, Nescafe and beer. They are generally fairly cheap, with Greek coffee costing about 150 dr and Nescafe with milk 250 dr or less. Most kafeneia are open all day every day, but some close during siesta time (roughly from 3pm to 5pm).

DRINKS

NONALCOHOLIC

Greek coffee is the national drink. It is a legacy of Ottoman rule and, until the Turkish invasion of Cyprus in 1974, the Greeks called it Turkish coffee. It is served with the grounds, without milk, in a small cup. Connoisseurs claim there are at least 30 variations of Greek coffee, but most people only know three – *glyko* (sweet), *metrio* (medium) and *sketo* (without sugar).

The next most popular coffee is instant, called Nescafe (which it usually is). Ask for Nescafe *me ghala* if you want it with milk.

Tea is invariably made with a tea bag.

Tap water is safe to drink in Athens, although sometimes it doesn't taste too good. Many tourists prefer to drink bottled spring water, sold widely in 500mL and 1.5L plastic bottles.

ALCOHOLIC

Beer

Beer lovers will find the market dominated by the major northern European breweries. The most popular beers are Amstel and Heineken, both brewed locally under licence. Other beers brewed locally are Henniger, Kaiser, Kronenbourg and Tuborg.

One of only three local beers is Mythos, launched in 1997 and widely available. It has proved popular with drinkers who find the northern European beers a bit sweet. The other two local beers are Alpha and Vergina.

Imported lagers, stouts and beers are found in tourist spots such as music bars and discos. You might even spot Newcastle Brown, Carlsberg, Castlemaine XXXX and Guinness.

Wine

Don't expect Greek wines to taste like French wines. The varieties grown in Greece are quite different. Some of the most popular and reasonably priced labels include Rotonda, Kambas, Boutari, Calliga and Lac des Roches. Boutari's Naoussa, a dry red wine, is worth looking out for.

More expensive, but of good quality, are the Achaïa-Claus wines from Patras. The most expensive wines are the Kefalonian Robola de Cephalonie, a superb dry white, and those produced by the Porto Carras estate in Halkidiki.

Spirits

Ouzo is the most popular aperitif in Greece. Distilled from grape stems and flavoured with anise, it is similar to the Middle Eastern *arak*, Turkish *raki* and French Pernod. Clear and colourless, it turns white when water is added. A 700mL bottle of a popular brand like Ouzo 12, Olympic or Sans Rival costs about 1200 dr in supermarkets. In an ouzeri, a glass costs from 250 dr to 500 dr.

The second-most popular spirit is Greek brandy, which is dominated by the Metaxa label. Metaxa comes in a wide variety of grades, starting with three star – a high-octane product without much finesse. You can pick up a bottle in a supermarket for about 1500 dr.

PLACES TO EAT – BUDGET

PLAKA

For most people, Plaka is the place to be. It's hard to beat the atmosphere of dining out beneath the floodlit Acropolis. You do, however, pay for the privilege – particularly at the outdoor restaurants around the square on Kydathineon.

KEY TO SYMBOLS					
☎	telephone number	Ⓒ	credit cards	Ⓜ	metro station
⒠	email address	AE	American Express	🚎	trolleybus
☉	opening hours	V	Visa Card	🚌	bus stop
ⓢ	prices	MC	MasterCard	🚊	train station
Ⓥ	restaurant has many	JCB	Japan Credit Bureau	⚓	ferry
	vegetarian options	DC	Diner's Club		

Wine + Pine = Retsina

A holiday in Greece would not be the same without a jar or three of retsina, the famous – some might say notorious – resinated wine that is the speciality of Attica and neighbouring areas of central Greece.

Your first taste of retsina may well leave you wondering whether the waiter has mixed up the wine and the paint stripper, but stick with it – it's a taste that's worth acquiring. Soon you will be savouring the delicate pine aroma, and the initial astringency mellows to become very moreish. Retsina is very refreshing consumed chilled at the end of a hot day, when it goes particularly well with tzatziki.

Greeks have been resinating wine, both white and rosé, for millennia. The ancient Greeks dedicated the pine tree to Dionysos, also the god of wine, and held that land that grew good pine would also grow good wine.

No-one seems quite sure how wine and pine first got together. The consensus is that it was an inevitable accident in a country with so much wine and so much pine. The theory that resin entered the wine-making process because the wine was stored in pine barrels does not convince, since the ancients used clay amphora rather than barrels. It's more likely that it was through pine implements and vessels used elsewhere in the process. Producers discovered that wine treated with resin kept for longer, and consumers discovered that they liked it.

Resination was once a fairly haphazard process, achieved by various methods such as adding crushed pine cones to the brew and coating the insides of storage vessels. The amount of resin also varied enormously. One 19th century traveller wrote that he had tasted a wine 'so impregnated with resin that it almost took the skin from my lips'. His reaction was hardly surprising; he was probably drinking a wine with a resin content as high as 7.5%, common at the time. A more sophisticated product awaits the modern traveller, with a resin content no higher than 1% – as specified by good old EU regulations. That's still enough to give the wine its trademark astringency and pine aroma.

The bulk of retsina is made from two grape varieties, the white *savatiano* and the red *roditis*. These two constitute the vast majority of vine plantings in Attica, central Greece and Evia. Not just any old resin will do; the main source is the Aleppo pine *(Pinus halepensis)*, which produces a resin known for its delicate fragrance.

Retsina is generally cheap and it's available everywhere. Supermarkets stock retsina in a variety of containers ranging from 500mL bottles to 5L casks and flagons. Kourtaki and Cambas are both very good, but the best (and worst) still flows from the barrel in traditional tavernas. Ask for *heema*, which means 'loose'.

Taverna Vizantino (taverna) Map 4, F8
Kydathineon 18 ☎ 322 7368
🕒 6am-1am daily $ breakfast 750 dr; starters 850 dr; mains 1100 dr [C] AE, JCB, MC, V

The Vizantino is the pick of the bunch of restaurants surrounding Plateia Filomousou in the heart of Plaka. There's outdoor seating in the square in summer. It prices its menu more realistically than most and is popular with locals year-round. The daily specials are good value, with dishes like *pastitsio* (1000 dr), stuffed tomatoes (1450 dr) and baked fish with rice (1900 dr).

Ouzeri Kouklis (meze) Map 4, F7
Tripodon 14 ☎ 324 7605 🕒 9am-3am Mon-Fri $ starters 700-1400 dr [C] none [V] [M] Akropoli

Ouzeri Kouklis is an old Plaka institution that's well worth seeking out. It's an old-style ouzeri with an oak-beamed ceiling, marble tables and wicker chairs. It serves only *mezedes*, which are brought around on a large tray for you to take your pick. It gets very busy later in the evening. Flaming sausages and cuttlefish costs 1400 dr, as well as the usual dips at 700 dr. The whole selection, enough for four hungry people, costs 12,000 dr. A litre of draught red wine costs 1000 dr and ouzo is 1000 dr for 250ml.

O Glykos (meze) Map 4, F8
Angelou Geronta 2 ☎ 322 3925
🕒 10.30am-2am daily $ starters 900-1500 dr [C] none [M] Akropoli

Tucked away on a quiet side street between two of the busiest streets in Plaka, O Glykos seems a million miles away from all the tourist hustle and bustle. There's outdoor seating beneath a large jacaranda tree, wine by the litre and a good selection of mezes – all at prices that are very reasonable by Plaka standards.

Taverna Damigos (taverna) Map 4, G8
Kydathineon 41 ☎ 322 5084
⏰ 6pm-2am daily; closed Jul & Aug
Ⓢ starters 500-900 dr; mains 1300-2200 dr
Ⓒ none Ⓜ Akropoli
Opened by the Damigos family in 1865, Taverna Damigos claims to be the oldest taverna in Plaka. It calls itself a *bakaliarakia*, which means that the house speciality is *bakalarios* (cod), fried in a crisp batter. It should be eaten with lashings of *skordalia* (garlic dip) and washed down with plenty of house retsina.

Taverna I Saita (taverna) Map 4, F8
Kydathineon 21 ☎ 322 6671
⏰ 2pm-2am daily; closed Jun-Sep Ⓢ starters 700-1800 dr; mains 1100-2800 dr Ⓒ AE, V Ⓜ Akropoli
A slightly cheaper version of Damigos. The walls are covered with colourful murals of Athenians carousing over a few jars of wine.

Peristeria Taverna (taverna) Map 5, D4
Patröou 5 ☎ 323 4535 ⏰ 8am-1am daily
Ⓢ starters 700-1400 dr; mains 1500-2800 dr
Ⓒ none Ⓜ Syntagma
Peristeria Taverna is a no-frills place serving the usual taverna staples at non-Plaka prices: a large plate of *gigantes* beans (1000 dr), moussaka (1500 dr) or baked veal and potatoes (1600 dr).

SYNTAGMA

Neon Café (Greek/international)
Map 5, D6
Mitropoleos 3 ☎ 324 6873
⏰ 7am-1am Mon-Sat, 8am-1am Sun
Ⓢ breakfast 950-1950 dr; salad bar 900-1150 dr; mains 1150-1950 dr Ⓒ none
Ⓜ Syntagma
Neon Café is a stylish modern cafeteria with a good selection of light meals, as well as coffee and cakes.

You'll find spaghetti or fettucine napolitana for 1150 dr, bolognese or carbonara for 1500 dr. Main dishes include moussaka (1450 dr), roast beef with potatoes (1600 dr) and pork kebab (1950 dr).

Fast Food Heleni (taverna/fast food)
Map 5, B4
Perikleos 30-32 ☎ 323 7361
⏰ 7am-6.30pm Mon-Sat Ⓢ lunch 1000-1300 dr; starters 400-1000 dr; mains 1000-1300 dr Ⓒ none Ⓜ Syntagma
Fast Food Heleni has fast-food favourites like toasted sandwiches and souvlaki as well as a daily selection of taverna dishes, all very reasonably priced.

MONASTIRAKI

Diporto (taverna) Map 4, A5
Theatrou 1 ⏰ 9am-7pm Mon-Sat Ⓢ starters 600-800 dr; mains 1000 dr Ⓒ none
Ⓜ Monastiraki
Eating places don't get any more low-key than Diporto. There's not even a sign, just a smell of cooking wafting up from the cellar beneath the olive shop at the corner of Sokratous and Theatrou, west of the fruit and vegetable markets. There's no menu: Diporto serves only half a dozen dishes, and they haven't changed in years. The house speciality is *revythia* (chickpeas); try a bowl (800 dr), followed by a plate of grilled fish (1000 dr) and a salad (600 dr). This should be washed down with a jug of retsina from one of the giant barrels lining the wall.

Taverna Papandreou (taverna) Map 4, B6
Aristogeitonos 1 ☎ 321 4970
⏰ 24 hours daily Ⓢ starters 600-1200 dr; mains 1400-2200 dr Ⓒ none Ⓜ Monastiraki
The central meat market might sound like a strange place to come for a meal, but the market tavernas are an important part of Athens life, turning out tasty, traditional taverna dishes 24 hours a day. The clientele ranges from hungry market workers in search of a solid meal, to elegant couples emerging from the local clubs and bars at 5am in search of a bowl of steaming *patsas* (tripe soup) or *podarakia* (pig-trotter soup).

PSIRI

O Telis (psistaria) Map 4, A4
Evripidou 86, Koumoundourou ☎ 324 2775
⏰ 8am-2pm Mon-Sat Ⓢ lunch 1500 dr Ⓒ none
Ⓜ Monastiraki, Omonia
The busy O Telis *psistaria* serves only one dish – pork chops and chips. The chops are sold by the kilogram (1900 dr), chargrilled and served with a pile of chips (400 dr).

THISIO

To Steki tou Elia (psistaria) Map 4, D2
Epahalkou 5, Thisio ☎ 345 8052 ⏰ 8pm-1am Mon-Sat Ⓢ starters 600-1000 dr; mains 1500-2000 dr Ⓒ none Ⓜ Thisio
To Steki tou Elia specialises in lamb chops, which are sold by the kilogram (4000 dr). Locals swear that they are the best chops in Athens, and the place has achieved some sort of celebrity status. Eat here with Greek friends, and they will constantly be pointing out famous personalities rolling up their sleeves to tuck into great piles of chops and a few jars of retsina. There are pork chops (2000 dr) and steaks (1500 dr) for those who don't eat lamb, as well as dips, chips and salads.

Ipiros Taverna (taverna) Map 4, D4
Filippou 16, Thisio ☎ 324 5572 ⏰ 9am-6pm

daily $ starters 600-1200 dr; mains 1100-2500 dr [C] none [M] Monastiraki, Thisio
Ipiros Taverna is a popular small taverna on the northern edge of the flea market. The food is cheap and tasty, and the outdoor tables are great for watching the market's hustle and bustle.

MAKRIGIANNI

To 24 Hours (taverna) Map 7, C5
Syngrou 44, Makrigianni ☎ 922 2749
🕘 24 hours daily $ starters 700-1000 dr; mains 1400-2000 dr [C] none [M] Syngrou-Fix
To 24 Hours is something of an institution among Athenian night owls. The place never closes, except on Easter Sunday, and seems to be at its busiest in the wee small hours. The customers are as much of an attraction as the food: you'll be rubbing shoulders with an assortment of hungry cabbies, middle-aged couples dressed for the opera, and leather-clad gays from the area's many bars – all tucking into steaming bowls of the house speciality, *patsas* (tripe soup).

Socrates Prison (Greek/international)
Map 7, A3
Rovertou Galli 17, Makrigianni ☎ 922 3434
🕘 11am-4pm & 7pm-1am Mon-Sat $ starters 700-2100 dr; mains 1500-3800 dr [C] MC, V [M] Akropoli
Socrates Prison is a delightful taverna with an Art Nouveau interior and 19th century Parisian posters on the walls. It also has garden seating in summer. The restaurant is not named after the philosopher, but after the owner (also called Socrates), who reckons the restaurant is his prison. It has an imaginative range of mezedes.

KOUKAKI

Gardenia Restaurant (Greek) Map 7, D2
Zini 31, Koukaki ☎ 922 0583 🕘 11am-10pm Mon-Fri, 11am-6pm Sat & Sun $ starters 500 dr; mains 900-1300 dr [C] none [M] Syngrou-Fix
Gardenia Restaurant claims to be the cheapest taverna in Athens. I wouldn't doubt it. What's more, the food is good and the service is friendly. The owner is an effervescent woman called Gogo who speaks English. A plate of gigantes beans is 650 dr, chicken and potatoes 650 dr, and moussaka 700 dr. A large Amstel beer costs 350 dr, and a litre of draught retsina is 450 dr.

To Meltemi (meze) Map 7, D2
Zini 26, Koukaki ☎ 924 7606 🕘 noon-midnight Mon-Sat $ starters 800-1500 dr; mains 1600-2000 dr [C] none [M] Syngrou-Fix
To Meltemi is a pleasant spot with white stucco walls, marble-topped tables and blue-painted wooden chairs – all of which give a Cycladic island feel. In summer, an outside eating area is shielded from the traffic by large pot plants.

OMONIA

The Omonia area is a place where people clutch at their wallets for safety, not a place to relax over a meal. You'll have to run the gauntlet of junkies and pimps if you want to eat at any of the fast-food outlets around Athinas and Pireos on the southern side of Plateia Omonias.

Neon Cafeteria (Greek/fast food)
Map 3, F6
Plateia Omonias, Omonia 🕘 8am-late daily $ breakfast 950-1100 dr; lunch 750-1050 dr; mains 1500-1950 dr [C] none [M] Omonia
Neon Cafeteria is an oasis of calm on Plateia Omonias occupying a beautiful neoclassical building. It is a stablemate of the Neon at Syntagma and serves the same fare.

Museum Garden (international) Map 3, C7
28 Oktovriou-Patission 44, Moussio ☎ 825 3416 🕘 8am-10pm daily $ breakfast 2500-3100 dr; lunch 1400-1850 dr [C] none 🚋 5
The Museum Garden is a good spot to stop for a light lunch or coffee after visiting the National Archaeological Museum. Its pleasant outdoor terrace overlooks the museum's grounds.

Palmier Bistro Santé (international)
Map 3, A6
Kyriakou 5, Victoria 🕘 8am-1am Mon-Sat $ breakfast 1800-2200 dr; lunch 650-1600 dr; mains 1300-1990 dr [C] none [M] Viktorias
The younger sibling of the Palmier Bistro Santé restaurant chain in Pefkakia with the same menu and prices (see the review under Exarhia).

AROUND THE TRAIN STATIONS

Wherever you choose to eat in this area you will find the lack of tourist hype refreshing – it's a million miles from the strategically placed menus and restaurant touts of Plaka.

O Makis Psistaria (Greek) Map 3, C3
Psaron 48, Larisis ☎ 825 3988 🕘 11am-2pm daily $ starters 450-550 dr; mains 1200-2800 dr [C] none 🚆 Larisa
O Makis Psistaria, opposite the church, is a lively, cheap place. Freshly grilled pork or beef, plus chips, costs 1600 dr. It also does delicious grilled chicken with lemon sauce for 2800 dr.

Dafni Taverna (taverna) Map 3, B5
Ioulianou 65, Victoria ☎ 821 3914
🕘 noon-1am daily $ starters 500-1000 dr; mains 1100-2000 dr [C] none [M] Viktorias
Dafni Taverna, one of Athens's oldest tavernas, offers good value with very tasty food. In summer,

PLACES TO EAT

An *evzone* guarding the monument of the Unknown Soldier

Poster of full moon festivities

Panoramic view of the city of Athens

It's all go in Metaxourghio

The 2nd-century BC Arch of Hadrian lights up a 21st-century night.

Fresco of *Mother of God*, Byzantine Museum

Kouros figure, NAM

Geometric period vase, NAM

16th-century BC frescoes, National Archeological Museum (NAM)

there's outdoor seating in the small courtyard. Gigantes beans cost 900 dr and baked fish with potatoes go for 1500 dr. Wash this down with a bottle of the taverna's own house wine (1000 dr a litre), distilled on the premises.

EXARHIA

Exarhia has lots of small ouzeris and tavernas to choose from, and prices are tailored to suit the pockets of the district's student clientele. It's quite a long hike to the area from Syntagma; or you can catch a No 230 bus from Amalias or Panepistimiou to Harilaou Trikoupi and walk across. It is, however, only a short walk from the National Archaeological Museum to lively Plateia Exarhion. The square (triangle actually) is lined with cafes and snack bars, many with seating under shade.

Most of the better eating places are south of Plateia Exarhion. You'll find a string of small ouzeris on Emmanual Benaki.

Ouzeri I Gonia (ouzeri) Map 3, E9
Emmanual Benaki ☎ 363 9947
🕘 1pm-2am daily $ mains 800-1800 dr [C] none [M] Omonia
The excellent Ouzeri I Gonia has a good range of tasty mezedes and draught wine as well as ouzo. Mezedes cost between 800 dr and 1800 dr, and they also serve 18 types of salad ranging from 500 dr to 900 dr including Russian and Budapest salads.

Karvouras (Greek) Map 3, E8
Themistokleous 64 ☎ 383 8010
🕘 10am-6am daily $ starters 300-1100 dr; mains 1100-1800 dr [C] none [M] Omonia
Karvouras is a favourite haunt of local university students, not least because there is a rembetika club upstairs. Meals are cheap and consist mostly of meat dishes and kebabs.

Taverna Barbargiannis (taverna) Map 3, E9
Emmanual Benaki 94 ☎ 330 0185
🕘 1pm-late daily $ starters 650-1000 dr; mains 950-1800 dr [C] none [M] Omonia
Taverna Barbargiannis is an excellent place with a blackboard list of daily specials (written in Greek). Your best bet is to line up at the counter and ask to have a look. A delicious and generously sized pasta goes for 1200 dr and comes with a portion of fresh crusty bread; tasty bean soup costs 850 dr. Most meat dishes are priced around 1700 dr, and draught retsina is 900 dr for a litre.

Palmier Bistro Santé (international)
Map 4, A10
Solonos, Pefkakia ☎ 364 1794 🕘 8am-1am Mon-Sat $ breakfast 1800-2200 dr; lunch 650-1600 dr; mains 1300-1990 dr [C] none [M] Panepistimiou
At this busy eating establishment the menu says it all: 'eat qualitive food in order to enjoy life'! Dishes range from light snacks to American-style burgers to international dishes such as the 'China Town' (1990 dr).

KOLONAKI

Cheap eats are hard to find around Kolonaki, but not impossible.

Taverna Stiatorion (taverna) Map 6, C2
Plateia Kolonakiou 4 ☎ 361 4033
🕘 9am-midnight daily $ starters 300-1800 dr; mains 1500-2300 dr [C] none [M] Evangelismos
This small taverna is located in a basement just off street level. Dishes are displayed outside, so if you have trouble reading the menu you can always resort to pointing.

Ouzeri Dexameni (Ouzeri) Map 6, B3
Plateia Dexameni ☎ 729 2578
🕘 12.30pm-late daily $ starters 600-1400 dr; mains 1400-2400 dr [C] none [M] Evangelismos
Ouzeri Dexameni is a great spot to stop for a bite. It has a choice of mezedes from 600 dr and a good selection of cold drinks.

PLACES TO EAT – MID-RANGE

Eating out in Athens remains fairly cheap, especially if you're eating Greek. The few places that do charge a bit extra tend to be doing so because of their location rather than the excellence of their cuisine. This is particularly the case in Plaka, where many restaurants charge way over the odds for very average food. A sure way to end up with a large bill is to eat fresh seafood at any of the restaurants on Kydathineon. Psiri is a good place to look if you're happy to pay a bit more for something interesting.

Two people can expect to pay from 10,000 dr to 12,000 dr, plus wine, for a meal at most places in this category.

Restaurant Arheon Gefsis (Ancient Greek)
Map 3, E1
Kodratou 22, Metaxourgio ☎ 523 9661
🕘 12.30pm-2am Mon-Sat $ starters 1700-3700 dr; mains 3500-5900 dr [C] AE, DC, MC, V [M] Metaxourgio
Retro is all the rage in Greece these days, but noone has taken things to quite the lengths of the owners of Restaurant Arheon Gefsis. They have turned the clock back 2500 years to the days of ancient Greece – to a time before the advent of potatoes, rice, tomatoes and many other staples

of the modern Greek diet. Diners are seated at their solid wooden tables by waiting staff dressed in flowing red robes. There are no glasses – the ancients used earthernware cups, and spoons instead of forks. Small portions must also be a modern idea, because the servings here are huge. Not surprisingly, roast meats and fish dominate the menu, served with purees of peas or chickpeas and vegetable. Try the pork stuffed with plums (4500 dr), served with a sweet plum sauce, pea puree and artichoke hearts. Wine, from the barrel, is 2700 dr for a litre. Bookings are essential.

Gerofinikas (Greek) Map 6, C1
Pindarou 10, Kolonaki ☎ 363 6710
🕐 noon-1am daily $ starters 100-2000 dr; mains 1500-4800 dr [C] MC, V [M] Syntagma
Gerofinikas is a smart taverna which aims to please the tourist market. There is an English menu available but the waiters will happily explain all the dishes to you. There is also a 5000 dr set menu available.

Palia Taverna (taverna/international)
Map 7, C9
Markou Mousourou 35, Mets ☎ 752 2396
🕐 7.30pm-1am daily $ starters 300-1800 dr; mains 3000-5000 dr [C] AE, MC, V
The upmarket Palia Taverna, dating to 1896, serves traditional Greek cuisine with a decidedly international flavour to the accompaniment of guitarists.

PLAKA/SYNTAGMA

Taverna O Thespis (Greek) Map 4, G7
Thespidos 18 ☎ 323 8242
🕐 11am-2am daily $ starters 900 dr; mains 1900 dr [C] V [M] Akropoli
Taverna O Thespis has a great setting on the lower slopes of the Acropolis with seating under the trees in the small square outside. The speciality here is *bekri meze* (beef in a spicy tomato sauce) which costs 3000 dr. Thespidos is the south-western extension of Kydathineon, beyond Adrianou, that leads uphill towards the Acropolis.

Restaurant Diogenes (Greek/international) Map 4, G7
Plateia Lysikratous 3 ☎ 322 4845
🕐 11am-midnight daily $ starters 1700 dr; mains 3700-8600 dr [C] AE, DC, MC, V [M] Syngrou-Fix
Restaurant Diogenes has outdoor seating right next to the Monument of Lysicrates. In winter, it moves indoors to Sellev 3.

Restaurant Hermion (Greek/international)
Map 5, D2
Pandrosou 7-15 ☎ 324 6725, 324 7148
🕐 10am-12.30am daily $ starters 1700-3400 dr; mains 2400-4900 dr [C] AE, DC, JCB, MC, V [M] Monastiraki
A tranquil oasis set back from the hustle and bustle of Plaka on a small shady square off Pandrosou.

Estatorio Kentrikon (Greek) Map 5, B6
Kolokotroni 3, Syntagma ☎ 323 2482
🕐 noon-6pm Mon-Fri $ starters 900-4500 dr; mains 1950-6000 dr [C] none [M] Syntagma
The air-conditioned Estatorio Kentrikon, tucked away in a small arcade, is a cool retreat from the city centre crowds that is very popular with local businessmen. The menu is upmarket taverna with a few international touches.

PSIRI

The maze of narrow streets that make up the newly trendy district of Psiri are lined with dozens of small restaurants and ouzeris, particularly the central area between Plateia Agion Anargyron and Plateia Iroön. Most places are open 8pm until late Monday to Saturday, and for Sunday lunch.

Embros (meze) Map 4, B4
Plateia Agion Anargyron 4 ☎ 321 3285
🕐 7pm-3am Mon-Fri, 10am-3am Sat & Sun $ starters 1400-3800 dr [C] none [M] Monastiraki
Embros is a popular spot with summer seating in Plateia Agion Anargyron. It offers a choice of about 50 mezedes, such as cheese croquettes for (1650 dr) and chicken fillets wrapped in bacon (2650 dr). It also has a selection of draft beers on tap, including Stella Artois and Lowenbrau.

Taverna Plateia Iroon (meze) Map 4, C5
Karaiskaki 34 ☎ 321 1915 🕐 2pm-2am daily $ starters 800-4000 dr [C] MC, V [V] [M] Monastiraki
Taverna Plateia Iroon is a popular meeting spot in the heart of Psiri. There's outdoor seating in Plateia Iroon and a cozy interior with music after 9pm every night.

Frourarheio (modern Mediterranean)
Map 4, B5
Agion Anargyron 6 ☎ 321 5220
🕐 9pm-3am Mon-Sat, 1.30pm-7pm Sun $ starters 2500-4000 dr; mains 4500-6500 dr [C] AE, DC, JCB, MC, V [M] Monastiraki
Frourarheio takes its name from the old army barracks it occupies. It's a stylish place, set back from the busy streets of Psiri, with an interesting Mediterranean menu and courtyard seating.

PLACES TO EAT – TOP END

Estiatorion Edodi (International)
Map 7, D1
Veikou 80, Koukaki ☎ 921 3013
🕐 8pm-12.30am Mon-Sat $ lunch 20,000 dr; starters 3900-6200 dr; mains 4900-7000 dr [C] AE, DC, JCB, MC, V [M] Syngrou-Fix

Tucked away in quiet, suburban Koukaki, the tiny Estiatorion Edodi turns out probably the most exciting food in central Athens. Brothers Giorgos and Michalis have come up with a winning combination of clever, creative food and wonderful, stylish presentation. There's no menu as such, just a daily selection of eight or nine starters followed by a similar choice of main courses. Lobster and crayfish feature prominently, as do other delicacies like foie gras, pheasant and ostrich. Dessert eaters face an impossible choice from a mouthwatering line-up. Coffee drinkers can choose between six types of sugar. This is food, and service, to make you smile – perfect for a romantic night out.

Daphne's Restaurant (Greek/International) Map 4, G7
Lysikratous 4, Plaka ☎ 322 7971 ⏰ 7pm-1am daily $ lunch 10,000 dr; starters 2500-3500 dr; mains 4000-5800 dr [C] AE, DC, MC, V [M] Akropoli
Daphne's Restaurant is where former US First Lady Hillary Clinton and daughter Chelsea dined during their one-night stopover in 1996 on their way to light the Olympic flame at Olympia. It's an exquisitely restored 1830s neoclassical mansion decorated with frescoes depicting scenes from Greek mythology. The menu includes regional specialities like rabbit cooked in mavrodaphne wine.

Symposio (modern Greek) Map 7, A3
Erehthiou 46, Makrigianni ☎ 922 5321 ⏰ 8pm-late Mon-Sat $ starters 2500-8700 dr; mains 6400-13,600 dr [C] AE, DC, MC, V [M] Akropoli
Symposio is one of Athens' most elegant restaurants, occupying a beautifully restored 1920s house in the quiet streets south of the Acropolis. The menu is loaded with regional specialities from the Epiros region of north-western Greece, where the restaurant owners raise wild boar and pasture-fed yearling beef. In season, the menu features such delicacies as wild asparagus, wild mushrooms, freshwater crayfish and – occasionally – Lake Ioannina frogs' legs. Symposio's signature dish is fish baked in a salt crust (19,000 dr per kg).

Pil Poule (modern Mediterranean) Map 4, D2
Apostolou Pavlou 51, Thisio ☎ 342 3665, 345 0803 ⏰ 8pm-1.30am Mon-Sat $ lunch 12,000 dr; starters 4000-25,000 dr; mains 6900-16,000 dr [C] AE, DC, JCB, MC, V [M] Thisio
Style is all important at Pil Poule, which occupies a beautifully restored 1920s neoclassical mansion. Snappily clad waiters in black suits and bow ties are obviously used to serving a cast of wealthy businesspeople and foreign dignitaries. The menu is modern Mediterranean with a strong presence, dotted with extravagances like wa foie gras (8500 dr) and Beluga caviar (25,000 dr). In summer, seating moves to the restaurant's rooftop terrace, which boasts fabulous views across to the floodlit Acropolis. It even has a private VIP terrace.

PLACES TO EAT – INTERNATIONAL

International cuisine remains something of a rarity in Athens, although the choice is steadily improving. Most of the non-Greek restaurants that do exist are located in far outer suburbs like Kifissia and Glyfada, but there are a few good places around the city centre. Here are some suggestions.

AMERICAN

Jackson Hall Map 6, C2
Milioni 4, Kolonaki ☎ 361 6098 ⏰ 10am-3am daily $ starters 1100-5900 dr; mains 3300-5900 dr [C] MC, V [M] Evangelismos
If you can't get no satisfaction from the burgers at the fast-food places around town, head to Jackson Hall. It has a selection of sit-down burgers and steaks: burgers with chips and salad cost 3900 dr, and steaks cost from 5600 dr.

ITALIAN

Kolonaki is the area to go to for good Italian food.

La Pasteria Map 6, B2
Tsakalof 18, Kolonaki ☎ 363 2032 ⏰ 1pm-3am daily $ starters 1200-2500 dr; mains 1800-3900 dr [C] none [V]
La Pasteria is a popular spot, offering a choice of pasta served a dozen different ways as well as an array of fresh salads.

Casa di Pasta Map 6, B4
30 Spefsipou, Kolonaki ☎ 723 3348 ⏰ 8.30pm-1.30pm daily $ starters 3000-5000 dr; mains 4000-6000 dr [C] AE, MC, V
Casa di Pasta is rated by many as having the city's best Italian food – meaning that bookings are essential. Expect to pay approximately 10,000 dr per person, plus wine.

ASIAN

Furin Kazan (Japanese) Map 5, D5
Apollonos 2, Syntagma ☎ 322 9170 ⏰ 11am-11pm Mon-Sat $ starters 800-2200 dr; mains 1600-5200 dr [C] JCB, MC, V [M] Syntagma
It's reassuring to see that Furin Kazan is always full of Japanese visitors, obviously enjoying the

…d best Japanese restaurant …election of rice and noodle …d favourites like chicken yaki- …ashimi and sushi trays that steal

Fa… …staurant (Chinese/Korean) Map 5, …
Stadiou 7, Syntagma ☎ 323 4996 🕒 1pm-1am daily $ starters 1450-4950 dr; mains 4500-7950 dr [C] AE, DC, JCB, MC, V [M] Syntagma
Far East Restaurant is a cool, elegant retreat tucked away at the back of the arcade.

Kiku (Japanese) Map 6, B1
Dimokritou 12, Kolonaki ☎ 364 7033 🕒 7.30pm-midnight Mon-Sat $ mains 14,000 dr [C] MC, V [M] Evangelismos
Kiku is the place to go if you want fresh sushi or sashimi, but you'll pay for the privilege.

CURRY

Until very recently, curries were virtually unobtainable in Athens. Suddenly there's a cluster of tiny curry restaurants in the streets between Plateia Koumoundourou and Plateia Omonias. It's hardly the most salubrious part of town, but it's the place to go for a good cheap curry.

Bengal Garden (Bangladeshi) Map 4, A4
Korinis 12, Psiri ☎ 325 3060 🕒 10am-8pm daily $ starters 100-500 dr; mains 600-1400 dr [C] none [M] Omonia
This is one of the cheapest places to eat in Athens, turning out a large plate of curry and rice for just 800 dr. There's no menu: just walk up to the serving counter and check out what's on offer (but don't look at the kitchen too closely!). The day's dishes normally include either chickpeas or dahl (500 dr) as well as a choice of chicken curry (600 dr) or beef curry (800 dr). It also has chapatis and delicious spicy vegetable pakoras (both 100 dr). Takeaways are available.

Tandoori Sizzler (Indian) Map 4, A4
Sapfous 5, Omonia ☎ 325 4216, 323 5346 🕒 2pm-2am daily $ starters 500-1100 dr; mains 2000-2900 dr [C] none [M] Omonia
More refined surroundings than the Bengal Garden, and a chicken vindaloo with enough kick to warrant a second beer.

Pak Bangla Indian Restaurant (Indian) Map 4, A5
Menandrou 13, Psiri ☎ 321 9412 🕒 11am-2am daily $ starters 500-1500 dr; mains 2500-4000 dr [C] AE, DC, MC, V [M] Omonia
The most upmarket of this neighbourhood's cluster of curry restaurants, but still a bargain.

PIZZA

Pizza is widely available from a number of restaurants and fast-food outlets.

Brooklyn Pizza Map 5, D5
Voulis 31-33, Syntagma ☎ 323 2727, 321 3200 🕒 noon-midnight daily, closed Sun Nov-Apr $ mains 950-5000 dr [C] V [M] Syntagma
Brooklyn Pizza was opened by a local guy who wanted pizza like the pizza he'd eaten when he was in New York, and set about doing just that. You'll find pizzas to eat in or take away, as well as calzones, hot dogs and other favourites.

PLACES TO EAT – VEGETARIAN

Vegetarian restaurants are very thin on the ground in Athens.

Vegetarian Fast Food Map 3, G7
Panepistimiou 57, Omonia ☎ 321 0966 🕒 8am-8pm Mon-Fri, 8am-9pm Sat, 10am-4pm Sun $ buffet 1050 dr [C] none [V] [M] Omonia
Vegetarian Fast Food offers a choice of three dishes from its buffet, as well as portions of wholemeal pizza and pies (750 dr). There is also fresh orange and carrot juice for 400 dr, and a well stocked health-food shop which carries a small range of biodynamic produce.

Eden Vegetarian Restaurant Map 5, E1
Lyssiou 12, Plaka ☎ 324 8858 🕒 noon-midnight Mon, Wed-Sun $ starters 1000-2250 dr; mains 2000-2900 dr [C] AE, DC, JCB, MC, V [V] [M] Akropoli
The Eden is unchallenged as the best vegetarian restaurant in Athens. It's been around for years, substituting soya products for meat in tasty vegetarian versions of moussaka (1600 dr) and other Greek favourites. You'll also find vegie burgers (1800 dr) and mushroom stifado (2300 dr), as well as organically produced beer and wine.

PLACES TO EAT – CAFES & PASTRY SHOPS

Brazil Coffee Shop (cafe) Map 5, B7
Voukourestiou 1, Syntagma ☎ 323 5463 🕒 7am-8.30pm Mon-Fri, 8am-4pm Sat [C] none [M] Syntagma
It's very hard to ignore the delicious aromas emanating from Brazil Coffee Shop. It offers a range of coffees, including Greek coffee (500 dr), cappuccino and filter coffee (both 600 dr). Cakes and croissants start at 350 dr.

Flocafe Expresso Bar Map 3, A6
3 Septemvriou 87, Victoria ☎ 822 2815 🕒 8am-midnight daily [C] none [M] Viktorias
The Flocafe Expresso Bar is a good spot to stop for a strong coffee, gooey cakes or light snacks. A

frothy cappuccino is 850 dr, Danish pastries are 450 dr, crepes are 1250 dr and sandwiches 800 dr.

Flocafe (cafe) Map 3, C7
Stadiou 5, Syntagma ☎ 324 4808 ⊘ 7am-2pm daily ⓒ none ⓜ Syntagma
Coffees cost from 700 dr to 1150 dr, plus it also has a range of cakes and ice creams.

Kotsolis (pastry shop) Map 4, F7
Adrianou 112, Plaka ☎ 322 1164 ⊘ 9am-11pm daily ⓒ none ⓜ Monastiraki
Kotsolis is a smart pastry shop with a mouth-watering array of goodies. They include such traditional Greek favourites as galaktoboureko (900 dr), baklava and kataifi (both 850 dr).

Hydria (cafe) Map 5, D1
Adrianou 68, Plaka ☎ 325 1619 ⊘ 9am-2pm daily ⓢ breakfast 1200-1900 dr; starters 1600-3800 dr; mains 3000-4800 dr ⓒ AE, MC, V ⓜ Monastiraki
This smart cafe has outdoor seating in shady Plateia Paleo Agora.

PLACES TO EAT – FAST FOOD

PLAKA

Plaka Psistaria (psistaria) Map 4, F8
Kydathineon 28 ☎ 324 6229 ⊘ 9am-midnight daily ⓒ none ⓜ Akropoli
Plaka Psistaria has a range of gyros and souvlaki to eat there or take away. The dash of paprika and extra-garlic tzatziki gives this place the edge over dozens of similar places around town. Try their chicken souvlaki wrapped in pitta bread (450 dr) or pork gyros (400 dr), and ask for apola – with the lot!

Souvlaki tou Hasepi (psistaria) Map 5, D5
Apollonos 3, Syntagma ⊘ 10am-4pm Mon-Fri ⓒ none ⓜ Syntagma
Meat is the only item on the menu at the tiny Souvlaki tou Hasepi (The Butcher's Souvlaki). There's pork souvlaki for 200 dr or grilled bifteki (beef patties) for 250 dr. A large cold beer costs 350 dr.

MONASTIRAKI

There are some excellent cheap eats around Plateia Monastirakiou, particularly for gyros and souvlaki fans.

Thanasis (Greek) Map 4, D6
Mitropoleos 69 ☎ 324 4705 ⊘ 9am-2am daily ⓒ none ⓜ Monastiraki
Thanasis is famous for its special souvlaki, made to a traditional house recipe that combines minced lamb, minced beef and seasonings. The place is always packed out and the service is pure theatre – at times the waiters have to run to keep up with the demand. Thanasis charges 350 dr for takeaway souvlaki wrapped in a small pitta bread,

or 1400 dr to sit down to a plate of four souvlaki and a large pitta bread.

Savas (Greek) Map 4, D6
Mitropoleos 86 ☎ 324 5048 ⊘ 11am-2am daily ⓒ none ⓜ Monastiraki
Opposite Thanasis is Savas, which specialises in gyros. It has a takeaway stall and a restaurant (there's a shop in between) with seating in the square opposite. Savas turns out tasty chicken gyros (350 dr) as well as pork or minced beef (both 300 dr).

PLACES TO EAT – SELF-CATERING

MARKETS

You'll find the widest range of whatever's in season and the best prices at the main *fruit & vegetable market* on Athinas, opposite the *meat market*. The stretch of Athinas between the meat market and Plateia Monastirakiou is the place to shop for nuts and nibblies.

SUPERMARKETS

Vasilopoulou Map 4, B8
Stadiou 18, Syntagma ☎ 322 2405 ⊘ 8am-8pm Mon-Fri, 8am-3.30pm Sat ⓒ none ⓜ Panepistimiou
Vasilopoulou is a large, well-stocked delicatessen that almost qualifies as a supermarket. It has an excellent selection of cheeses and cold meats, and an imported food section where you'll find such treasured items as Marmite – but not Vegemite!

Papageorgiou Map 7, D2
Dimitrakopoulou 72, Koukaki ☎ 921 3043 ⊘ 8am-8pm Mon-Fri, 8am-6pm Sat ⓒ none ⓜ Syngrou-Fix

Veropoulos Map 7, C3
Parthenonos 6, Koukaki ☎ 924 7169 ⊘ 8am-8pm Mon-Fri, 8am-6pm Sat ⓒ none ⓜ Syngrou-Fix

Sofos Supermarket Map 5, C1
Mitropoleos 78, Monastiraki ☎ 322 6677 ⊘ 7am-10pm Mon-Sat, 9am-10pm Sun ⓒ none ⓜ Monastiraki
Sofos is small but convenient, and open long hours.

Marinopoulos Map 3, G5
Athinas 60, Omonia ☎ 989 8120 ⊘ 8am-9pm Mon-Fri, 8am-6pm Sat ⓒ none ⓜ Omonia
Omonia is better served than most areas. There is a branch of the Marinopoulos chain, with the food section downstairs.

Bazaar Discount Supermarket Map 3, F6
Eolou 104, Omonia ☎ 324 8290 ⊘ 8am-9pm Mon-Fri, 8am-6pm Sat ⓒ none ⓜ Omonia
The Bazaar Discount Supermarket stocks most general supplies.

PLACES TO EAT

Entertainment

The best source of entertainment information is the weekly listings magazine *Athenorama*, but you'll need to be able to read some Greek to make much sense of it. It costs 500 dr and is available from *periptera* all over the city.

English-language listings appear daily in the Kathimerini supplement that accompanies the *International Herald Tribune*, while Friday's edition of the *Athens News* carries a 16-page entertainment guide.

Another useful source of information is the quarterly magazine *Welcome to Athens*, available free from the tourist office. It has details of theatre, dance, classical music concerts and art exhibitions.

PUBS & BARS

Athens has a good selection of pubs and bars bound to satisfy all tastes. There are the inevitable English and Irish themed bars full of expats as well as some fun local bars and a growing number of German-style beer halls.

Brettos Map 4, G8
Kydathineon 41, Plaka ☎ 323 2110
☉ 10am-midnight daily ⓜ Akropoli
Brettos is a delightful little place right in the heart of Plaka. Very little has changed here in years, except that being old-fashioned has suddenly become very fashionable. It's a family-run business which acts as a shop-front for the family distillery and winery in Kalithea. Huge old barrels line one wall, and the shelves are stocked with a colourful collection of bottles, backlit at night. Shots of Brettos brand spirits (ouzo, brandy and many more) cost 500 dr, while Brettos wine sells at 600 dr per tumbler. Cold beers are 700 dr.

Stavlos Map 4, E2
Iraklidon 10, Thisio ☎ 345 2502
Ⓦ www.stavlos.gr ☉ 11am-5am, rock bar 11pm-midnight, Ⓢ free ⓜ Thisio
Stavlos occupies an amazing old rabbit warren of a building. It has a rock bar playing mainly alternative British music, and more mellow sounds in the cafe/brasserie outside. Large beers go for 1600 dr, spirits are 2000 dr and cocktails 2500 dr.

Berlin Club Map 4, E2
Iraklidon 8, Thisio ☎ 671 5455 Ⓔ berlin@otenet.gr Ⓦ www.berlin.gr ☉ 10am-4am Wed-Sun Ⓢ 2500 dr (includes free drink) ⓜ Thisio

Cafe by day and rock 'n' roll bar by night, Berlin is known for its special theme nights, which you'll see advertised around town. Most drinks are 2000 dr, cocktails 2200 dr to 2500 dr.

Mike's Irish Bar Map 8, C5
Sinopsis 6, Ambelokopi ☎ 777 6797
☉ 8pm-4am Mon-Thur & Sat, Sun, 5pm-late Fri Ⓢ free ⓡ 3,13
Mike's Irish Bar is a long-time favourite of Athens' expatriate population, who come here to play a few games of darts and sup pints of Guinness or Murphy's stout (2000 dr).

DISCOS

Discos operate in Athens only between October and April. In summer, the action moves to the coastal suburbs of Ellinikon and Glyfada (see Excursions chapter).

Lava Bore Map 4, F9
Filellinon 25, Syntagma ☎ 324 5335
☉ 10pm-5am daily Ⓢ 2000 dr ⓜ Syntagma
Lava Bore is always on the move. Filellinon 23 is its third address in five years, but the formula remains much the same: a mixture of mainstream rock and techno and large beers for 1000 dr.

Soda Map 4, C1
Ermou 161, Thisio ☎ 345 6187 ☉ 11pm-4am Tues-Thur, 11pm-6am Fri-Sun Ⓢ 3000 dr (includes free drink) ⓜ Thisio
Soda's winter address in Thisio boasts an enormous dance floor and a cast of glamour DJs turning out a diet of techno, trance and psychedelia for an energetic crowd of under-25s.

LIVE MUSIC

Top-name international acts play at a variety of venues, including the spectacular Lykavittos Theatre on Lykavittos Hill, and the Panathinaïkos football stadium.

Rodon Club Map 3, D6
Marni 24, Moussio ☎ 524 7427
☉ from 10.30pm ⓡ 5
Athens' main rock venue is the Rodon Club, in a converted movie theatre north of Plateia Omonias. It has bands most Fridays and Saturdays.

AN Club Map 3, E8
Solomou 20, Exarhia ☎ 363 9217
☉ 10.30pm-late ⓜ Omonia
AN Club is a popular venue for rock music and most nights it hosts rave parties after 1am.

Half Note Jazz Club Map 7, C7
Trivonianou 17, Mets ☎ 921 3310
ⓔ halfnote@otenet.gr ⓦ www.megafon.com
⊘ 11pm-late daily ⓢ 4000-7000 dr
Jazz enthusiasts should check out what's happening at the Half Note Jazz Club. The club plays host to many leading international jazz and blues artists.

GAY & LESBIAN VENUES

The greatest concentration of gay bars is to be found in Makrigianni, south of the Temple of Olympian Zeus. You'll find more information, and opinions, about the bars featured in this section on the Internet at ⓦ communities.msn.com/man2maningreece.

The Guys Map 7, B5
Lembesi 8, Makrigianni ☎ 921 4244
⊘ 10pm-3.30am Sun-Thur, 10pm-5am Fri & Sat
ⓢ entry free; drinks 1200-2000 dr ⓜ Akropoli
The Guys is a small, laid-back bar that is a popular meeting point for the over-40s crowd with music at a volume that still permits conversation – just.

Granazi Bar Map 7, B6
Lembesi 20, Makrigianni ☎ 924 4185
⊘ 11pm-4am Mon-Thur, 11pm-6am Fri-Sun
ⓢ 1000 dr (goes towards first drink) ⓜ Akropoli
The Granazi has long been at the forefront of the gay scene. These days, the ambience is Pet Shop Boys played at a volume that permits only body language. It's popular with the under-35 crowd, who come to party.

E-Kai Map 7, B6
Iossif Rogon 12, Makrigianni ☎ 922 1742
⊘ 10.30pm-3am Sun-Thur, 10.30pm-5am Fri & Sat ⓢ entry free; drinks 1000-1500 dr ⓜ Akropoli
Supposedly popular with older gays, E-Kai was empty at the time (2am) of research, although the surrounding bars were full.

Lamda Club Map 7, B6
Lembesi 15, Makrigianni ☎ 922 4202 ⊘ 11pm-5am daily ⓢ 2500 dr (includes free drink)
ⓜ Akropoli
The Lamda is the most risque of Makrigianni's bars, with chunky chains adorning the walls, and murals of well-muscled guys strutting their stuff. There's a dance floor upstairs, playing a mixture of Greek and mainstream Western rock, and various other rooms.

Alexander Club Map 6, B2
Anagnostopoulou 44, Kolonaki ☎ 364 6660

⊘ 9pm-late daily, drag shows from 2am Wed, Sat & Sun ⓢ 1000 dr ⓜ Syntagma
The popular Alexander Club is a lively place that draws mostly younger gays. There's a cruising bar upstairs and a disco downstairs. The club also hosts drag shows at 2 am every Wednesday, Saturday and Sunday.

Alekos Island Map 6, B2
Tsakalof 42, Kolonaki ☎ 364 0249
ⓔ doxa13@hotmail.com ⊘ 10.30pm-3.30am daily ⓢ 1000 dr ⓜ Syntagma
Coming highly recommended by no less an authority than Spartacus, this relaxing, friendly bar is frequented by a more sedate, older crowd of gays.

Koukles Club Map 7, E2
Zan Moreas 32, Koukaki ☎ 921 3054 ⊘ 11pm-5am daily, drag shows from 2.30am Fri & Sat
ⓢ 2000 dr (includes free drink) ⓜ Syngrou-Fix
The Koukles Club is the favoured venue of Athens' surprisingly large transsexual community. It stages a drag show on Friday and Saturday nights, starting at about 2.30 am.

Teleia & Pavla Map 2, C4
Alexandras 98, Exarhia ☎ 643 0960 ⊘ 10pm-4am daily ⓢ 2000 dr (includes free drink) ⓠ 230
Teleia & Pavla, which translates as Dot & Dash, is a popular lesbian meeting point on the northern edge of Exarhia. The place doesn't start to warm up until after midnight. The bar charges a standard 1000 dr for shots, 1500 dr for beers and 2000 dr for spirits.

To Lizard Map 4, E3
Apostolou Pavlou 31, Thisio ☎ 346 8670
⊘ 11pm-5am Fri-Sun ⓢ 2000 dr (includes free drink) ⓜ Thisio
Lively bar where the action kicks on into the wee small hours. The crowd is a mix of gays and lesbians, with the occasional straight as well.

Mistagogia Map 8, A1
Alexandras 115, Ambelokipi ☎ mobile 097-252 9261 ⊘ 11.30pm-5am Sun-Thur, midnight-7am Sat & Sun ⓢ 2500 dr; drinks 2500-2800 dr ⓜ Ambelokipi
Mistagogia is a place for partying long and hard. It draws a mixed crowd, predominantly gay.

Bee Map 4, C5
Miaouli 6, Psiri ☎ 321 2624 ⊘ 8pm-3am Mon-Fri, noon-4am Fri & Sat ⓢ free; drinks 1000-2000 dr. ⓜ Monastiraki
The Bee is a lively new bar that draws a mixed crowd: mainly straight until midnight; mainly gay

KEY TO SYMBOLS
☎	telephone number	ⓢ	prices	ⓠ	bus stop
ⓔ	email address	ⓜ	metro station	ⓡ	train station
ⓦ	Web site	ⓣ	trolleybus	⚓	ferry
⊘	opening hours				

euro currency converter 1000 dr = €2.93

ENTERTAINMENT

for the rest of the night. The restaurant turns out a selection of light meals priced from 2100 dr to 3500 dr.

Fairytale Map 3, E8
Kolleti 25, Exarhia ☎ 330 1763 🕘 10pm-3.30am Tues-Sun $ free [M] Omonia
This intimate hole-in-the-wall bar is the favourite haunt of young lesbians.

CINEMA

Athenians are avid cinema-goers. Most cinemas show recent releases from Britain and the USA in English. Two areas with the highest number of cinemas are the main streets between Syntagma and Omonia, and the 28 Oktovriou-Patission and Plateia Amerikis area.

Apollon Map 4, B8
Stadiou 19, Syntagma ☎ 323 6811 $ 2000 dr [M] Akropoli

Astor Map 4, B8
Stadiou 28, Syntagma ☎ 323 1297 $ 2000 dr [M] Panepistimiou

Asty Map 4, B9
Koraï 4, Syntagma ☎ 322 1925 $ 1800 dr [M] Akropoli
The Asty shows mostly avant-garde films.

Cine Paris Map 4, F8
Kydathineon 22, Plaka ☎ 322 0721 🕘 May-Oct $ 1900 dr [M] Akropoli
One of the last of the old outdoor cinemas still in operation – summer only.

Ideal Map 3, G7
Panepistimiou 46, Omonia ☎ 382 6720 $ 2000 dr [M] Omonia

Titania Map 3, G7
Panepistimiou, Omonia ☎ 381 1147 $ 2000 dr [M] Omonia

THEATRE

Athens has a dynamic theatre scene, but, as you'd expect, most performances are in Greek. If you're a theatre buff you may enjoy a performance of an old favourite, provided you know the play well enough. The listings in the publications described at the start of this chapter mention when a performance is in English – which happens occasionally.

FOLK MUSIC

TRADITIONAL MUSIC TAVERNAS

There are a number of tavernas around Plaka that put on displays of Greek music and dancing.

Taverna Kalokerinos Map 4, F8
Kekropos 10, Plaka ☎ 323 2054, 322 1679 🕘 8.30am-12.30am daily $ 3500 dr [M] Akropoli
Like all the music tavernas in Plaka, the fare at the Kalokerinos is strictly for the tourist market. The music starts at 9pm, with displays of folk dancing through the evening. Meals are relatively expensive, with starters priced from 1800 dr to 3900 dr and mains from 3700 dr to 6500 dr.

REMBETIKA CLUBS

Athens has a good number of rembetika clubs, but most close down from May to September. Performances in these clubs start at around 11.30pm; most places do not have a cover charge but drinks are expensive. Clubs open up and close down with great rapidity – telephone to check if a club is still open. The biggest concentration of clubs is in and around Exarhia.

Karvouras Map 3, E8
Themistokleous 64, Exarhia ☎ 381 0202 🕘 11.30pm-5am Mon-Sat $ 1500 dr inc. first drink [M] Omonia
Karvouras is the current *in* club with Athens' hip young things. The club is fairly small and is always packed so get in early if you want a seat. Drinks are a pricey 12,000 dr for a bottle of wine and 20,000 dr for a bottle of whisky.

Rembetika Istoria Map 2, C4
Ippokratous 181, Exharhia ☎ 642 4937 🕘 10pm-6am Tues-Sun $ free
Old vinyl records and black-and-white pictures of rembetika greats adorn the walls of this club. The music is good and the atmosphere relaxed. Spirits range between 1500 dr and 2000 dr per glass and wine is between 600dr and 900 dr per glass.

Rembetika Stoa Athanaton Map 4, A6
Sofokleous 19, Monastiraki ☎ 321 4362 🕘 3.30pm-6pm & 11pm-6am Mon-Sat; closed Jun-Nov $ free [M] Monastiraki
Rembetika Stoa Athanaton is one of the city's oldest and best known rembetika clubs. It also boasts the most unusual location, a large timber-beamed hall above the meat market. Admission may be free, but the food and drink are expensive: 8900 dr for a plate of mixed meze, and 10,900 dr for the cheapest bottle of wine.

GREEK FOLK DANCING

Dora Stratou Dance Company Map 2, F1
Filopappos Hill, Filopappou ☎ 921 6650 [e] grdance@hol.gr [w] users.hol.gr/~grdance 🕘 10.15pm Tues & Thur-Sat, 8.15pm Wed & Sun May-Oct $ adult/student 4000/2000 dr 🚌 230
Folk dancing at the Dora Stratou Theatre on Filopappos Hill is one of the highlights of the

Rembetika – The Greek Blues

Rembetika music – the Greek equivalent of the American blues – is today the most popular form of musical entertainment for Greeks of all ages. Its controversial past and soulful lyrics have only heightened its appeal among this new generation of followers.

Opinions differ as to the origins of rembetika – believed to have been derived from the Turkish word *rembet* meaning outlaw – but it is probably a hybrid of several different types of music. One source was the music that emerged in the 1870s in 'low life' cafes, called *tekedes* (hashish dens), in urban areas and especially around ports. Another source was the Arabo-Persian music played in sophisticated Middle Eastern music cafes *(amaneded)* in the 19th century. Rembetika was popularised in Greece by the refugees from Asia Minor.

The songs which emerged from the tekedes had themes concerning hashish, prison life, gambling, knife fights etc, whereas cafe *aman* music had themes which centred around erotic love. These all came together in the music of the refugees, from which a subculture of rebels, called *manges*, emerged. It was in a tekes in Piraeus that Markos Vamvakaris, now acknowledged as the greatest *rembetis*, was discovered by a recording company in the 1930s.

Although hashish was illegal, the law was rarely enforced until Metaxas did his clean-up job in 1936. His censorship meant that themes of hashish, gambling and the like disappeared from recordings of rembetika in the late 1930s, but continued clandestinely in some tekes. This polarized the music, and the recordings, stripped of their 'meaty' themes and language, became insipid and bourgeois; recorded rembetika even adopted another name – *Laïko tragoudi* – to disassociate it from its illegal roots.

Whilst WWII brought a halt to recording, a number of composers emerged at this time. They included Apostolos Kaldaras, Yannis Papaïoanou, Georgos Mitsakis, Manolis Hiotis and Sotiria Bellou, one of the greatest female rembetika.

Throughout the 1950s and 1960s rembetika became increasingly popular, but less and less authentic. Much of the music was glitzy and commercialised.

During the junta years, many rembetika clubs were closed down, but interest in the genuine rembetika revived in the 1980s – particularly among students and intellectuals. Today there are a number of rembetika clubs in Athens.

summer entertainment scene. The dances are performed by the excellent Dora Stratou Dance Company, which has an international reputation for authenticity and professionalism. Tickets can be bought at the door. The theatre is signposted from the western end of Dionysiou Areopagitou. The company also runs folk dancing workshops in summer – see Courses in the Thing to See & Do chapter.

CLASSICAL MUSIC, OPERA & BALLET

Megaron Moussikis Map 8, D3
Vasilissis Sofias 89, Ilissia ☎ 728 2333
[e] webmaster@admin.megaron.gr
[w] www.megaron.gr ⌚ performances 9pm; box office 10am-8.30pm Mon-Fri, 10am-2pm & 6pm-8.30pm Sat, 6pm-8.30pm Sun 🚎 8

There are frequent classical music concerts, by both international and Greek performers, at the Athens Concert Hall. You can also buy tickets at the Megaron's city centre box office, 26 Stoa Spyrou Milou, which is in the arcade between Voukourestiou and Amerikis. The office is open 10am-4pm from Monday to Friday.

Olympia Theatre Map 3, G8
Akadimias 59, Exarhia ☎ 361 2461
[M] Panepistimiou

The Olympia Theatre has performances by the National Opera (Ethniki Lyriki Skini), and also stages ballet.

SON ET LUMIÉRE

Hill of the Pnyx Theatre Map 4, G3
Hill of the Pnyx ☎ 322 1459 ⌚ 8pm-11pm daily Apr-Oct $ adult/child 3000/1500 dr 🚌 230

The 'sound and light' spectacle at the Hill of the Pnyx Theatre is not one of the world's best, but it is an enduring and integral part of the Athens tourist scene. There are shows in English every night at 9pm from the beginning of April until the end of October. There are shows in French at

10pm every night except Tuesday and Friday, when the show is in German. During the performance, the monuments of the Acropolis are lit up in synchronisation with accompanying music, sound effects and historical narration. The lights are the most exciting part of the performance.

ATHENS FESTIVAL

Hatzihristou 23, Makrigianni, ☎ 928 2900 fax 928 2933 ⏲ 8am-2pm Mon-Fri ⓔ pr@greekfestival.gr ⓦ www.greekfestival.gr Ⓜ Akropoli

The annual Athens Festival is the city's most important cultural event, running from mid-June to late September. It features a line-up of international music, dance and theatre at the Theatre of Herodes Atticus. The setting is superb, backed by the floodlit Acropolis.

The festival has been going from strength to strength in recent years. The 2000 line-up featured performances by the renowned Vienna Boys Choir, super tenor Placido Domingo, rock star Elton John and flamenco wizard Joaquim Cortes, as well as a mix of opera, modern dance and theatre both ancient and modern.

The festival also features performances of ancient Greek drama at the famous Theatre of Epidaurus in the Peloponnese, 2½ hours west of Athens. There are performances in Epidaurus every Friday and Saturday night during July and August. See the Epidaurus section of the Excursions chapter for more information.

Organisers plan to use the Lykavittos Theatre, on top of Lykavittos Hill, as an additional venue for future festivals.

The festival program should be available on the Internet from the beginning of February.

BUYING TICKETS

Athens Festival Box Office Map 5, A7 **Stadiou 4, Syntagma ☎ 322 1459 ⏲ 8.30am-4pm Mon-Fri, 9am-2.30pm Sat ⓔ grammateia@greekfestival.gr ⓦ www.greekfestival.gr Ⓜ Syntagma**

The festival box office sells tickets for all festival performances, including those at Epidaurus. It opens three weeks before the first performance. Tickets sell out quickly, so try to buy yours as soon as possible. They are priced according to seating; the cheapest seats are in the upper tier, and the most expensive – called distinguished class – are right in front of the stage. Zone A, just behind the best seats, is a good compromise. Students qualify for a 50% discount on all seats except distinguished class on production of an ISIC student card.

Tickets can also be bought on the day at theatre box offices, but queues can be very long.

SPECTATOR SPORTS

SOCCER

Athens and Piraeus supply almost half the teams in the Greek first division, seven out of 18 teams at the time of writing. They are Athinaikos, AEK, Ionikos, Panathinaïkos and Panionios from Athens; and Ethnikos Asteras and Olympiakos from Piraeus. Two other clubs, Apollon Athens and Proödeftiki Piraeus, fluctuate between the first and second divisions.

Greek soccer is dominated by the intense rivalry between Olympiakos and Panathinaïkos, which are the nation's two best-supported teams. Both have enthusiastic supporters' clubs nationwide. Olympiakos has dominated on the domestic front; its success in the 1999/2000 Greek championship was its 29th in 75 years. Panathinaïkos, however, has enjoyed the greater success on the European stage, reaching the semifinals of the European club championship in 1996 – the best result achieved by a Greek team.

The supremacy of the big two is occasionally challenged by AEK Athens, another club to perform well in Europe. AEK reached the last 16 of the 2000/2001 UEFA Cup after downing German champions Bayer Leverkusen 6-4.

Olympiakos normally plays its home matches at the Karaiskaki stadium in Piraeus, but the stadium was closed for upgrading at the time of writing. Home games had been transferred to the Olympic Stadium in Maroussi, five-minutes walk from Irini metro station.

Panathinaïkos plays the majority of its home games at the Panathinaikou stadium on Leoforos Alexandras, five-minutes walk from Ambelokopi metro station. Games likely to draw huge crowds are transferred to the Olympic Stadium.

AEK plays at the Nikos Goumas Stadium in Nea Philadelphia; Panionios at Nea Smyrni; and Proödeftiki at the Korydalos Stadium in Piraeus. First division matches are played on Sunday and cup matches on Wednesday. They are often televised. The soccer season lasts from September to the middle of May. Fixtures and results are given in the *Athens News*.

Shopping

The Athens shopping scene is alive with colour and variety. Markets and stalls abound and bargains are aplenty. Specialities include gold and silver jewellery, flokati rugs, hand-painted icons, pottery, embroideries, wall hangings and leather goods.

Also on offer are a delectable range of culinary delights that will fill your senses. Pots of thick amber honey, jars of plump olives, traditional Greek coffee and bottles of olive oil all make lovely gifts – providing you can take them home.

ANTIQUES

It is illegal to buy, sell, possess or export antiquity in Greece (see the Customs section in Facts for the Visitor chapter). However, there are antiques and 'antiques'; a lot of them only a century or two old are regarded as junk, rather than part of the national heritage. These items include handmade furniture and odds and ends from rural areas in Greece, ecclesiastical ornaments from churches and items brought back from far-flung lands. Good hunting grounds for this 'junk' are Monastiraki, Kolonaki, the flea market in Athens and the Piraeus market held on Sunday morning.

Michael Mihalakos Map 6, B1
Solonos 32, Kolonaki ☎ 362 6182 ⊘ 8.30am-8.30pm Tues, Thur & Fri, 8.30am-3pm Mon, Wed & Sat
Michael Mihalakos' is a good place to start your hunting with lots of collectables to search through including china, prints, paintings, silver and furniture items.

Antiquarius Map 6, C2
Anagnostopoulou 8, Kolonaki ☎ 360 6454 ⊘ 10am-2pm & 5.30pm-8.30pm Tues, Thur & Fri, 10am-3pm Mon, Wed & Sat
This small, long-established shop specialises in imported antique gift items mostly from the UK and France. Items include old books, prints, silver, crystal, embroideries and small furniture items.

JEWELLERY

Although gold is good value in Greece, and designs are of a high quality, it is priced beyond the capacity of most tourists' pockets. If you prefer something more reasonably priced, go for the filigree silver jewellery. For those with money to spare, the area to head to is around Stadiou and Voukourestiou streets in Syntagma, which are home to quality jewellery stores such as Ilias Lalaounis, Kessaris and Bvlgari.

Tresor Map 5, A6
Stadiou 4, Syntagma ☎ 323 2336 ⊘ 9am-3pm Mon, Wed & Sat, 9am-8pm Tues, Thur & Fri Ⓜ Syntagma
One of Greece's most reputable jewellery stores, Tresor is part of the Ilias Lalaounis jewellery chain which has shops as far afield as London and Hong Kong. The store specialises in reproductions of ancient jewellery designs. Ilias Lalaounis also runs the Jewellery Museum at the base of the Acropolis (see the Things to See & Do chapter for details).

ART GALLERIES

Artworks available vary from traditional paintings and sculptures to contemporary works of art in every imaginable medium. Both galleries listed avidly promote their art works through the Internet, where works can be viewed, purchased and even delivered to your door. The Web site and email address for both are ⓦ www.athensgallery.gr and ⓔ info@athensgallery.gr.

Gallerie Areta Map 5, C1
Pandrosou 31, Plaka ☎ 324 3397, 324 6942 ⊘ 10am-7pm Mon-Sat 10am-2pm Sun Ⓜ Monastiraki
Gallerie Areta sells contemporary pieces such as sculptures and paintings by talented local artists. There is a second shop at the Hilton Hotel and another on Amalias.

The Athens Gallery Map 5, C1
Pandrosou 14, Plaka ☎ 324 6942 ⊘ 9.30am-10pm daily Ⓜ Monastiraki
The Athens Gallery also supports and promotes local artists.

BOOKSHOPS

Athens has a good choice of English-language bookshops. Ippokratous, in the student suburb of Exarhia, is packed solid with bookshops.

Eleftheroudakis Map 4, C9
Panepistimiou 17, Syntagma ☎ 331 4180
🕘 9am-8pm Mon-Fri, 9am-5pm Sat
[M] Syntagma
This seven-storey building is the headquarters of the Eleftheroudakis group, which operates a chain of stores around Athens. There's a floor devoted to English-language books, as well as a large map section.

Eleftheroudakis Map 5, D6
Nikis 20, Syntagma ☎ 322 1401 🕘 9am-5pm Mon, Wed & Sat, 9am-8pm Tues, Thur & Fri [M] Syntagma

Eleftheroudakis Map 8, C5
Sinopsis 2, Ambelokopi ☎ 770 8007
🕘 9am-5pm Mon, Wed & Sat, 9am-8pm Tues, Thur & Fri [M] Syntagma

Compendium Map 5, E6
Nikis 28, Plaka ☎ 322 1248 🕘 9am-5pm Mon & Wed, 9am-8pm Tues, Thur & Fri, 9am-3pm Sat [M] Syntagma
Compendium is an old-fashioned place specialising in English-language books. It stocks a good overall selection, strong on history and literature. It also has a second-hand section with plenty of cheap detective novels for reading on long flights. The English-language notice board outside has information about jobs, accommodation and courses in Athens.

Pantelides Books Map 4, C10
Amerikis 9-11, Syntagma ☎ 362 3673
🕘 9am-4pm Mon, Sat, 9am-8pm Tues-Fri
[M] Syntagma
Pantelides also specialises in English-language books. It has a range of feminist books as well as paperbacks, travel guides, maps etc.

Kauffmann Map 4, B8
Stadiou 28, Syntagma ☎ 322 2160
🕘 9am-5pm Mon, Wed & Sat, 9am-8pm Tues, Thur & Fri [M] Syntagma
Kauffmann stocks books in English and French.

The Booknest Map 4, B9
Panepistimiou 25-29, Syntagma
☎ 323 1703, 322 9560 🕘 9am-5pm Mon & Wed, 9am-8.30pm Tues, Thur & Fri, 9am-4pm Sat [M] Panepistimiou
This shop stocks books in English, French, German, Italian, Spanish and Russian. Booknest has a small shopfront on the ground floor of the arcade, but the main store in on the mezzanine level.

Road Editions Map 3, G9
Ippokratous 39, Exarhia ☎ 361 3242
🕘 8.30am-3pm Mon, Wed & Sat, 8.30am-2.30pm & 5.30pm-8.30pm Tues, Thur & Fri
[M] Panepistimiou
This map specialist is where you'll find a wide range of travel literature as well as a complete selection of maps.

Xenoglosso Vivlopoleio Map 3, G9
Ippokratous 10-12, Exarhia ☎ 362 6028
🕘 8am-9pm Mon-Sat [M] Panepistimiou
This foreign-language bookshop stocks books in English, French, Italian and German.

TRADITIONAL HANDICRAFTS

Greece produces a vast array of handicrafts.

The National Welfare Organisation's Hellenic Folk Art Gallery Map 5, D4
Ipatias 6, Plaka ☎ 325 0524 🕘 9am-8pm Tues-Fri, 9am-3pm Mon & Sat [M] Monastiraki
The National Welfare Organisation's Hellenic Folk Art Gallery is a good place for handicrafts. It has top-quality merchandise and the money goes to a good cause – the preservation and promotion of traditional Greek handicrafts. It has a wide range of knotted carpets, kilims, flokatis, needle-point rugs and embroidered cushion covers as well as a small selection of pottery, copper and woodwork.

The Centre of Hellenic Tradition Map 5, C1
Pandrosou 36, Plaka ☎ 321 3023 🕘 10am-7.30pm daily [M] Monastiraki
The Centre of Hellenic Tradition has a display of traditional and modern handicrafts from each region of Greece. Most of the items, including furniture, icons, pottery, antiques and embroideries, are for sale.

Mado Map 4, G7
Sellev 6, Plaka ☎ 322 3628 🕘 noon-8pm Mon-Sat
Mado is a small workshop that turns out beautiful, hand-woven wall hangings. Many depict island scenes.

RUGS & CARPETS

Acropolis Rugs Map 5, D5
Voulis 31-33, Plaka ☎ 322 4932 🕘 9am-5pm Mon & Wed, 9am-8.30pm Tues, Thur & Fri, 9am-4pm Sat [M] Syntagma
Acropolis Rugs has the largest selection of flokati rugs in town.

KEY TO SYMBOLS

☎	telephone number	[$]	prices	🚌	bus stop
[e]	email address	[M]	metro station	🚆	train station
[w]	Web site	🚎	trolleybus	⛴	ferry
🕘	opening hours				

Fancy a Flokati?

There are few better souvenirs of a visit to Greece than the luxuriant woollen flokati rugs, produced in the mountain areas of central and northern Greece.

The process by which these rugs are produced has changed little over the centuries. The first step is to weave a loose woollen base. Short lengths of twisted wool are then looped through it, leaving the two ends on the top to form the pile – the more loops the denser the pile.

At this point, the rugs look like a scalp after stage one of a hair transplant – a series of unconvincing tuffs. The twisted threads can easily be pulled through.

A transformation takes place during the next stage, the 'waterfall treatment'. The rugs are immersed in fast-running water for between 24 and 36 hours, unravelling the twisted wool and shrinking the base so that the pile is held fast. They can then be dyed.

The main production areas are the villages of Epiros, around the town of Tripolis in the Peloponnese, and around the towns of Trikala and Karditsa in Thessaly. All these villages have plenty of running water required for the waterfall treatment.

The rugs are sold by weight. A rug measuring 150x60cm will cost from 12,000 dr to 45,000 dr, depending on the length of the pile.

National Organisation of Greek Handicrafts
Mitropoleos 9, Plaka ☎ 323 0408 ☺ 8.30am-2pm Mon & Wed, 8.30am-8pm Tues, Thur & Fri, 9.30am-2.30pm Sat ⓜ Syntagma
The National Organisation of Greek Handicrafts sells beautiful hand-woven rugs and operates some 32 workshops throughout the country on the art of traditional carpet weaving.

LEATHER

There are plenty of leather goods for sale in Athens ranging from expensive boutique shoes and handbags to simple handmade items.

Stavros Melissinos Map 4, D6
Pandrosou 89, Monastiraki ☎ 321 9247
☺ 10am-2pm & 4pm-7pm Mon-Sat, 10am-2pm Sun ⓜ Monastiraki

Good-quality leather sandals may be bought from Stavros Melissinos. The 'poet sandal-maker' of Athens names the Beatles, Rudolph Nureyev and Jackie Onassis as past customers, but he still makes the best-value sandals in Athens at 4000 dr to 6000 dr per pair.

MUSIC & INSTRUMENTS
Pandora Music Shop Map 3, F10
Mavromihali 51, Pefkakia ☎ 361 9924
☺ 11am-2pm & 5.30pm-8pm Tues, Thur & Fri
The Pandora Music Shop is the place to go for beautifully crafted hand-made traditional Greek and ethnic instruments. The store specialises in *Lutes* including Continental and Cretan and also sells *Bouzoukis* and *Tanburas*.

MUSIC SHOPS
Virgin Megastore Map 5, A6
Stadiou 7-9, Syntagma ☎ 331 4788 ☺ 9am-8pm Mon-Fri, 9am-7pm Sat & Sun ⓜ Syntagma
Virgin has the biggest selection of music in town. It has a large section devoted to Greek music, as well as sections for mainstream Western rock, heavy metal, world music, classical and various other styles.

Metropolis Map 3, F6
Panepistimiou 64, Omonia ☎ 383 0404
fax 384 5523 e metropolis@otenet.gr
☺ 9am-9pm Mon-Fri, 9am-6pm Sat ⓜ Omonia
Metropolis specialises in Greek music, but also has a good selection of mainstream Western music.

FOOD

Street vendors are a great place to begin your culinary journey in Athens. On sale on almost every street corner you'll find locally grown nuts such as pistachios *(ta fistikia)*, walnuts *(ta karidhia)* and almonds *(ta amighdhala)*. For fresh olives and herbs look no further than the Central Market on Athinas (Map 4, B6).

Attiki Alexandros Pittas
Arkadias 18, Peristeri ☎ 575 1896
☺ 10am-5pm Mon-Fri 🚌 12
Greek honey is renown for its flavour and distinctive aroma. Attiki Alexandros Pittas sells honey in jars, tins and gift packs. Also available is royal jelly and various flavoured honeys including thyme and orange blossom.

Brazita Coffee Shop Map 3, F6
Plateia Omonias 6, Omonia ☎ 524 8558
☺ 8am-8pm Mon-Fri, 8am-3pm Sat ⓜ Omonia
Brazita stocks the best range of freshly ground coffees in Athens, and a good selection of coffee-making equipment.

Choosing Music

It's so easy and tempting to buy one of those neatly packaged and marketed CDs or tapes containing the 'Best of Zorba the Greek', or a selection of 'Syrtaki Serenades'. What sounded so romantic over a candlelit dinner in Plaka may just sound tinny and tacky when played on your home stereo system. Avoid the temptation to take home yet another worthless musical souvenir from a streetside stall or tourist shop. Be brave, go where only Greeks usually dare to tread and seek out some real Greek music.

Find yourself a record store where Greeks buy their music. It won't be in Monastiraki or Plaka, but it won't be far away. If you don't see tourist CD covers in the window, you are probably on the right track. The best selling domestic Greek albums are usually displayed in their own rack. If the cover displays a singer's portrait it's more likely to be a showcase of that singer's vocal talent – which you may or may not like. If the cover is more subtle, with abstract artwork, it is more likely to be the music of a composer that is showcased, with the singers being merely interpreters of the composer's and lyricist's music and words. Although it's only a rough guide, CDs packaged in fancy cardboard presentations tend to contain good quality works. A full-priced, current Greek CD will cost between 5000 dr and 6000 dr.

Contemporary singers or singer-songwriters to look out for include Nikos Xydakis, Sokratis Malamas, Melina Kana and Eleftheria Arvanitaki who specialise in the so-called *entehno* 'artistic' style. Giannis Parios, Haris Alexiou, Georgos Dalaras and Glykeria lean more towards the *laïko* (popular) style with frequent crossovers to the *dimotiko* (folk), *nisiotiko* (island) or contemporary pop modes.

For traditional *paradosiako* music look for Psarandonis, Haïnides, or Ross Daly who delve deep into Cretan and Middle Eastern musical roots for their works. For the truly eclectic, *entehno paradosiako* (artistic traditional), look out for the albums by En Hordais, a talented musical ensemble from Thessaloniki, or Loudovikos ton Anogeion a truly multi-talented artist from Crete.

Fans of the 'Greek blues' *rembetiko* could ask for albums by Nikos Papazoglou or the long-time favourite Grigoris Bithikotsis. Raw roots traditional *dimotiko* music is exemplified by the recordings of veteran female singer Domna Samiou.

For contemporary Greek rock and blues check out Pyx Lax, Lavrendis Maheritsas, Dionysis Tsaknis or Vasilis Papakonstandinou who prove that Greek rock stands on its own without need for instrumental support from the bouzouki or lyre.

Works by composers Mikis Theodorakis, Giannis Markopoulos and the evergreen Manos Hatzidakis are all revered by Greek audiences.

CLINT CURÉ

Paul Hellander

WHERE TO SHOP

Athens has no one central shopping district, but instead numerous shopping areas each with its own distinctive character.

ERMOU

One of the most popular shopping areas for fashion-conscious Athenians is the pedestrian end of Ermou, which leads from the southern end of Plateia Syntagma to Monastiraki. Lining its path you'll find large department stores, such as Marks & Spencer, alongside small boutiques and stylish shoe stores. On Saturdays it is often hard to negotiate your way through the throng of crazed shoppers, street vendors and entertainers.

PANDROSOU

If you really must have that mini statue of Athina or the compulsory 'I've been to Greece' T-shirt then look no further than Pandrosou. Along this pedestrianised street, which runs from the Monastiraki flea market north to Plateia Mitropoleos, you'll find numerous souvenir shops.

ATHINAS

The busy Athinas runs from Plateia Omonia south to Monastiraki. Along its path are a variable array of shops and markets. Midway along you'll find the central meat markets, opposite which is the fresh fruit and vegetable market. Farther south are shops selling every imaginable cooking utensil and various household items. As you approach Monastiraki the scene changes to specialist machinery and hardware shops.

KOLANAKI

Kolanaki is central Athens' most stylish shopping district. The greatest concentration of shops can be found in the streets surrounding Plateia Kolanaki. Here the streets are lined with upmarket boutiques selling designer fashions, shoes and accessories, quaint antique shops, art galleries and chic home furnishing stores.

KIFISSIA

If it is elegant haute couture houses that you are looking for then head straight to Kifissia, Athens' exclusive northern suburb. Its beautiful tree-lined streets tout all the famous designer names including Valentino, Ralph Lauren, Cartier and Hugo Boss. The clothing is expensive, but it is worth coming here just to window shop!

OPENING HOURS

Most shops tend to open from 9am to 3pm on Monday, Wednesday and Saturday, and from 9.30am to 1.30pm, then again from 5.30pm to 8.30pm on Tuesday, Thursday and Friday. Stores are closed on Sunday, except for those in tourist areas.

MARKETS

FLEA MARKETS
Athens Flea Market Map 4, D5
Plateia Monastirakiou ☼ 8am-1pm Sun

This market is the first place which springs to most people's minds when they think of shopping in Athens. The flea market is the commercial area, which stretches both east and west of Plateia Monastirakiou, and consists of shops selling goods running the whole gamut from high quality to trash. However, when most people speak of the Athens flea market, they are referring to the Sunday morning outdoor flea market. This market spills over into Plateia Monastirakiou and onto Ermou.

A visit to Athens isn't complete without a visit to this market. All manner of things – from new to fourth-hand – are on sale. There's everything from clocks to condoms, binoculars to bouzoukis, tyres to telephones, giant evil eyes to jelly babies, and wigs to welding kits. Wandering around the market, you'll soon realise that Greece is top of the league of European countries when it comes to mass-produced kitsch. If you're looking for a plastic jewellery box with a psychedelic picture of the Virgin Mary on the lid, which plays 'Never on a Sunday' when you open it, you might just be in luck at the flea market.

Piraeus Flea Market Map 9, B3
Alipedou , Great Harbour ☼ 7am-2pm Sun
Ⓜ **Piraeus**

Many locals will tell you that the Piraeus Flea Market is infinitely better than its famous counterpart in Athens. As well as stalls selling junk, there are small shops selling high-quality jewellery, ceramics and antiques.

Αθήνα

Excursions

Within easy reach of Athens opportunities abound for one- or two-day excursions to explore greater Greece. The suburbs of Piraeus, Glyfada and Kifissia offer a different take on the Athens experience. Interesting side trips outside of Athens include the monasteries of Dafni and Kaissarianis, the Apollo Coast beach resorts, historic Marathon, and the idyllic Saronic Gulf Islands.

For more information on these destinations than is presented in this chapter, see Lonely Planet's *Greece* guide.

Attica

PIRAEUS

Πειραιάς

☎ 01 • postcode 185 01 • pop 171,000

Piraeus is the port of Athens, the main port of Greece and one of the Mediterranean's major ports. It's the hub of the Aegean ferry network, the centre for Greece's maritime export-import and transit trade and the base for its large merchant navy. Nowadays, Athens has expanded sufficiently to meld imperceptibly into Piraeus. The road linking the two passes through a grey, urban sprawl of factories, warehouses and concrete apartment blocks. Piraeus is as bustling and traffic-congested as Athens. It's not a place in which many visitors want to linger; most come only to catch a ferry.

HISTORY

The histories of Athens and Piraeus are inextricably linked. Piraeus has been the port of Athens since classical times, when Themistocles transferred his Athenian fleet from the exposed port of Phaleron (modern Faliro) to the security of Piraeus. After his victory over the Persians at the Battle of Salamis in 480 BC, Themistocles fortified Piraeus' three natural harbours. In 445 BC Pericles extended these fortifying walls to Athens and Phaleron. The Long Walls, as they were known, were destroyed as one of the peace conditions imposed by the

Spartans at the end of the Peloponnesian Wars, but were rebuilt in 394 BC.

Piraeus was a flourishing commercial centre during the classical age, but by Roman times it had been overtaken by Rhodes, Delos and Alexandria. During medieval and Turkish times Piraeus diminished to the size of a tiny fishing village, and by the time Greece became independent, it was home to fewer than 20 people.

Its resurgence began in 1834 when Athens became the capital of independent Greece. By the beginning of the 20th century Piraeus had superseded the island of Syros as Greece's principal port. In 1923 its population was swollen by the arrival of 100,000 refugees from Turkey. The Piraeus which evolved from this influx had a seedy but somewhat romantic appeal with its bordellos, hashish dens and rembetika music – all vividly portrayed in the film *Never on a Sunday*.

These places have long since gone and beyond its facade of smart, new shipping offices and banks, much of Piraeus is now just plain seedy. The exception is the eastern quarter around Zea Marina and Mikrolimano, where the seafront is lined with seafood restaurants, bars and discos.

ORIENTATION

Piraeus is 10km south-west of central Athens. The largest of its three harbours is the Great Harbour (Megas Limin), on the western side of the Piraeus Peninsula. All ferries leave from here. Zea Marina (Limin Zeas), on the other side of the peninsula, is the port for hydrofoils to the Saronic Gulf Islands (except Aegina) as well as being the place where millionaires moor their yachts. North-east of here is the picturesque Mikrolimano (small harbour), brimming with private yachts.

The metro line from Athens terminates at the north-eastern corner of the Great Harbour on Akti Kalimassioti. Most ferry departure points are a short walk from here. A

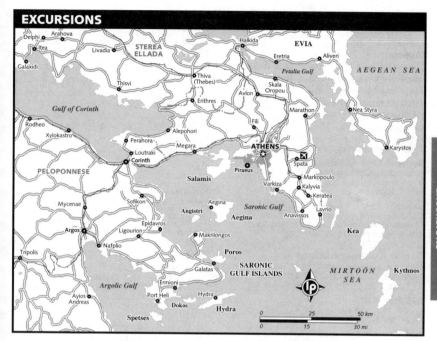

EXCURSIONS

left turn out of the metro station leads, after 250m to Plateia Karaïskaki, which is the terminus for buses to the airport. Jutting out into the harbour behind the square is Akti Tzelepi with its mass of ticket agencies.

South of Plateia Karaiskaki, the waterfront becomes Akti Poseidonos, which leads into Vasileos Georgiou beyond Plateia Themistokleous. Vasileos Georgiou is one of the two main streets of Piraeus, running south-east across the peninsula; the other main street is Iroön Polytehniou, which runs south-west along the ridge of the peninsula, meeting Vasileos Georgiou by the main square, Plateia Korai.

INFORMATION

Most major services, such as banks and the post and telephone offices, can be found around the Great Harbour and are within easy access of the Piraeus metro station. The most notable exception is the EOT office which is rather inconveniently located at Zea Marina.

Piraeus EOT Map 9, E4
Dikitirio, Zea Marina ☎ 452 2586/91 fax 452 2586 ⏲ 8am-3pm Mon-Fri 🚌 904,905
Thanks to some kind of bureaucratic bad joke, the Piraeus EOT is at Zea Marina. Why it should be here and not at the Great Harbour defies imagination. To get there catch bus No 904 or 905 from outside the metro to Zea Marina.

KEY TO SYMBOLS

☎	telephone number	Ⓒ	credit cards	Ⓥ	restaurant has many
ⓔ	email address	AE	American Express		vegetarian options
ⓦ	Web site	V	Visa Card	Ⓜ	metro station
⏲	opening hours	MC	MasterCard	🚌	bus stop
ⓢ	prices	JCB	Japan Credit Bureau	🚃	train station
	(high/low season)	DC	Diner's Club	⚓	ferry

Piraeus port police
Akti Miaouli, Great Harbour ☎ 412 2501
⏰ 8am-11pm daily

Money

There are lots of places to change money at Great Harbour, including virtually all the ticket and travel agencies. The three banks listed all have 24-hour automatic exchange machines.

Emporiki Bank
Antistaseos, Great Harbour ☎ 417 4301
⏰ 8am-2pm Mon-Thur, 8am-1.30pm Fri

National Bank of Greece Map 9, B3
Antistaseos, Great Harbour ☎ 417 4101
Ⓦ www.ethniki.gr ⏰ 8am-2pm Mon-Thur, 8am-1.30pm Fri

National Bank of Greece Map 9, E3
Moutsoupoulou 14, Zea Marina ☎ 414 4273
Ⓦ www.ethniki.gr ⏰ 8am-2pm Mon-Thur, 8am-1.30pm Fri 🚌 904, 905

Post & Communications

Main post office Map 9, B4
Tsamadou, Great Harbour ☎ 417 7489
⏰ 7.30am-8pm Mon-Fri, 7.30am-2pm Sat

OTE Map 9, B4
Karaoli 19, Great Harbour ☎ 417 1699,
⏰ 24 hrs daily

Surf Internet Café Map 9, C3
Platanos 3, Great Harbour ☎ 422 7478
ⓔ surfin@forthnet.gr Ⓦ www.surfin.gr
⏰ 8am-9pm Mon-Fri, 8am-3pm Sat

Dios Internet Café Map 9, C4
Androutsou 170, Great Harbour ☎ 412 4220
ⓔ dios@dios.gr Ⓦ www.geocities.com/dios.gr
⏰ 9.30am-midnight daily

PLACES TO STAY – BUDGET

There's no reason to stay at any of the shabby cheap hotels around Great Harbour when Athens is so close. The cheap hotels are geared more towards accommodating sailors than tourists. Whatever happens, don't attempt to sleep out – Piraeus is the most dangerous place in Greece to do so.

Hotel Acropole Map 9, B3
Gounari 7, Great Harbour ☎ 417 3313 fax 988 2726 ⓔ ahotel@otenet.gr Ⓢ singles 6000 dr; doubles 9000 dr; dorms 3500 dr Ⓒ AE,V
Hotel Acropole is on Gounari, the main thoroughfare running inland from Plateia Karaïskaki. Newly renovated rooms are neat and clean and all have bathrooms. Other facilities include long-term luggage storage and a security safe for valuables.

Hotel Delfini Map 9, B3
Leoharous 7, Great Harbour ☎ 412 9779 fax 417 3110 Ⓢ singles 9000/7000 dr; with air-con 12,000/9000 dr; doubles 12,000/10,000 dr; with air-con 16,000/12,000 dr Ⓒ none
The C-class Hotel Delfini is a bit smarter. Make sure you don't get taken there by one of the touts who hang around the port or you will wind up paying more.

PLACES TO STAY – MID-RANGE

The best hotels are to be found around the Mikrolimano. There are three reasonable B-class options on Vasileos Pavlou, which runs around the hillside above the harbour.

Hotel Castella Map 9, C6
Vasileos Pavlou 75, Kastella ☎ 411 4735 fax 417 5716 Ⓢ singles 24,000 dr; doubles 37,000 dr; triples 46,000 dr Ⓒ AE,MC, V
The pick of Piraeus' hotels is Hotel Castella which has rooms with air-con and good views of the harbour.

Hotel Mistral Map 9, D6
Vasileos Pavlou 105, Kastella ☎ 411 7675 fax 412 2096 Ⓢ singles 23,500/20,000 dr; doubles 29,500/25,000 dr; triples 35,250/30,000 dr; apartments 43,000/38,000 dr Ⓒ AE,MC, V
The rooms at Hotel Mistral have views of the harbour, are fully air-conditioned and have double-glazed sound proof windows.

Hotel Cavo d'Oro Map 9, D5
Vasileos Pavlou 19, Kastella ☎ 411 3744 fax 412 2210 Ⓢ singles 25,000/21,000 dr; doubles 32,000/27,000 dr; triples 38,000/32,000 dr Ⓒ AE, DC, MC, V
Piraeus' friendliest hotel would have to be Hotel Cavo d'Oro. Its comfortable rooms have air-con, private bathroom and sea views. The hotel also has a swimming pool and rooftop garden.

PLACES TO STAY – FALIRO BAY

Most of the hotels around Faliro Bay, 2km east of Piraeus, are simple C-class hotels geared towards short-stay guests (the three hour type) and have little interest in accommodating tourists.

Miami Hotel
Diakou 6, Moschato ☎ 940 2131, 941 4298 fax 941 4298 Ⓢ singles 11,000 dr; doubles 13,000 dr Ⓒ none 🚌 040
While not very appealing from the outside, or the drab reception, the Miami's rooms are a pleasant surprise. Each room has a private bathroom and a small balcony. To get to the hotel catch bus No 040

from central Athens to the Tivoli Amusement Park on Posidonos. The hotel is 800m east of the park.

Delfini Hotel
Smirnis 12-14, Moschato ☎ 941 5364 fax 941 5373 Ⓢ singles 11,500 dr; doubles 13,200 dr; triples 15,800 dr Ⓒ none ☒ 040
This bland seventies relic has adequate rooms, all with balconies, air-con, TV and private bath. Bus No 040 from central Athens stops 850m east of the hotel at the Tivoli Amusement Park on Poseidonos.

Metropolitan Hotel
Syngrou 385, Nea Smarni ☎ 947 1000 fax 947 1010 Ⓔ metropolitan@chandris.gr Ⓢ singles & doubles 75,000-130,000 dr; apartments 160,000-240,000 dr, breakfast 5500 dr Ⓒ AE, DC, MC, JCB, V
Boasting views of the Acropolis and the Saronic Gulf the Metropolitan Hotel is by far the best hotel around Faliro Bay. It has first-class rooms with all the mod cons and is well adorned with services including an on call doctor, baby sitter, luggage storage, currency exchange, laundry service and wheelchair access. If that's not enough there is also a fitness centre, rooftop pool and a grand ballroom.

PLACES TO EAT
Great Harbour
There are dozens of cafes, restaurants and fast-food places along the waterfront. If you want to stock up on supplies before a ferry trip, head for the area just inland from Poseidonos. There are **markets** on Demosthenous where you'll find fresh fruit and vegetables.

Pairaikon supermarket Map 9, B3
Piraeus ☎ 413 1197 ◷ 8am-8pm Mon-Fri, 8am-4pm Sat

Restaurant I Folia (Greek) Map 9, B3
Akti Poseidonos, Piraeus ◷ 8am-late daily Ⓒ none
The tiny Restaurant I Folia, opposite Plateia Karaïskaki on Akti Poseidonos, is a rough and ready place. Gigantes beans go for 600 dr, calamari for 750 dr and moussaka for 850 dr.

Zea Marina
Numerous cafes – along with every imaginable fast-food outlet – line Akti Moutsoupoulou, which runs around Zea Marina.

Collection Barbeque Caffee Map 9, D4
Moutsoupoulou 10, Zea Marina ☎ 429 7581 ◷ 8am-late daily Ⓢ starters 900-1400 dr; mains 1800-4400 dr Ⓒ none ☒ 904,905
Collection Barbeque Caffee is a large and lively restaurant-cum-bar overlooking the marina. Its menu, consisting of burgers, steaks and salads, will delight diehard carnivores.

La Tradizione (Italian) Map 9, E3
Akti Moutsoupoulou, Zea Marina ☎ 451 7519 ◷ 11.30am-1am Mon-Fri, 6pm-1am Sat & Sun Ⓢ lunches 900 dr; starters 400-1000 dr; mains 1400-2300 dr Ⓒ none ☒ 904,905
La Tradizione, a small Italian restaurant with outdoor seating overlooking Zea Marina, serves well-portioned pasta dishes and delicious pizzas.

Kastella & Mikrolimano
The setting around the Kastella and Mikrolimano is rather more relaxed, with a string of seafood restaurants overlooking the bay and right on the waterfront.

Restaurant Arheon Gefsis (Greek)
Map 9, D6
Epidavrou 10, Kastella ☎ 413 8617 ◷ 12.30pm-2am daily Ⓢ starters 1700-3700 dr; mains 3500-5900 dr Ⓒ AE, DC, MC, V
The second of the ancient Greek inspired Arheon Gefsis chain is much better positioned than its Athenian counterpart. Tucked away in a quiet street overlooking Mikrolimano the restaurant serves up large portioned meat and fish-based dishes amid an air of yesteryear. See the Places to Eat chapter for more details. Bookings are essential.

ENTERTAINMENT
Hard Rock Cafe Map 9, A2
Etolikou 28 ☎ 413 6750 Ⓔ hard-rock@united-hellas.com ◷ 11am-3am Sun-Thur, 11am-4am Fri, 11am-5am Sat Ⓢ free
The location isn't the greatest, but this is the place to come for aficionados in search of Hard Rock Cafe Piraeus T-shirts and other souvenirs. As well as beers, the bar menu also has a choice of burgers (1500 dr to 2500 dr) and salads.

Cinemas
Zea Cinema Map 9, D4
Trikoupi 37, Zea Marina ☎ 452 1388 Ⓢ 1600-2000 dr ☒ 904, 905

GETTING THERE & AWAY
Air
Olympic Airways Map 9, C3
Akti Miaouli 27, Great Harbour ☎ 926 7560, 966 6666 Ⓔ telsales@Olympic-airways.gr Ⓦ www.Olympic-airways.gr ◷ 9.15am-4.30pm Mon-Fri

Bus
There are no intercity buses to or from Piraeus. There are buses to central Athens,

EXCURSIONS

to the airport and to the coastal suburbs of Glyfada and Voula, south of the airport.

Special buses (Nos 040 and 049) operate 24 hours a day between Piraeus and central Athens; they run every 20 minutes from 6am until midnight and then hourly. No 040 runs between Akti Xaveriou in Piraeus and Filellinon in Athens; the most convenient stop is outside the Hotel Savoy on Iroön Polytehniou. No 049 runs between Akti Xaveriou in Piraeus and Plateia Omonias in Athens. The fare is 150 dr on each service. Blue bus No A1 runs from Akti Xaveriou to Glyfada and Voula every 15 minutes (150 dr).

Metro

The metro (250 dr) is the fastest and easiest way of getting from the Great Harbour to central Athens (see the Getting Around chapter). The station (Map 9, E1) is at the northern end of Akti Kalimassioti.

Train

Piraeus also has train stations for both northern Greece and the Peloponnese. Piraeus' train station (Map 9, E1) is one block north of the metro. All the railway services to the Peloponnese (see the Getting There & Away chapter) actually start and terminate at Piraeus, although most schedules don't mention it. The single service from the northern line train station (via Larisis train station) is of purely academic interest, leaving at 1.30pm and taking more than seven hours to crawl to Volos, stopping all stations. The station for northern Greece (Map 9, F1) is at the western end of Akti Kondyli.

GETTING AROUND

Piraeus has its own network of buses and trams, but the only services likely to be of much interest to travellers are the buses (No 904 or 905) which run between Zea Marina and the bus stop next to the metro.

GLYFADA

Γλυφάδα

☎ 01 • postcode 166 75

The first place you'll encounter travelling south is Glyfada, Attica's largest resort. The place is overrun with package tourists in summer, and they are joined by half the population of Athens at weekends. In addition, Glyfada has a permanent population of wealthy expatriates. Loads of bars and discos complete the picture.

ORIENTATION

Most buses from Athens drop you off at Plateia Katraki Vasos at the northern end of Glyfada. The bulk of Glyfada's shops and restaurants are centred around this square or are within easy walking distance.

Posidonos, the major road which runs from Athens in the north, follows Glyfada's coastline and continues south through Voula, Vouliagmeni and Varkiza.

INFORMATION

Tourist Police
Dousmani 22 ☎ 898 2596 🕒 telephone service 8am-11pm daily, office 8am-1.30pm daily

Money

Piraeus Bank
Metaxa ☎ 894 0350 [W] www.piraeusgroup.gr 🕒 8am-2pm Mon-Thur, 8am-1.30pm Fri
The bank has a 24-hour automatic exchange machine.

National Bank of Greece
Metaxa 13 ☎ 894 7523 [W] www.ethniki.gr 🕒 8am-2pm Mon-Thur, 8am-1.30pm Fri
The National Bank of Greece also has a 24-hour automatic exchange machine.

Post & Communications

Glyfada Post Office
Karageorga Saki ☎ 894 5684 🕒 7.30am-2pm Mon-Fri

Xplorer Internet Café
Plateia Chorion 4 ☎/fax 968 0620 [e] xplorer@welcome.to [W] www.welcome.to/xplorer 🕒 10am-1am daily

PLACES TO STAY – BUDGET

Hotel Ilion
Kondyli 4 ☎ 894 6011 $ singles 8500/5000 dr with/without bathroom; doubles 10,500/7000 dr with/without bathroom [C] none
The cheapest rooms in Glyfada are at the not-so-cheerful Hotel Ilion on the corner of the main square. The rooms here are OK but not overly enticing.

Hotel Blue Sky
Eleftherias 26 ☎ 894 5664 fax 894 3445 [e] bluesky@otenet.gr $ singles 9000/8000 dr;

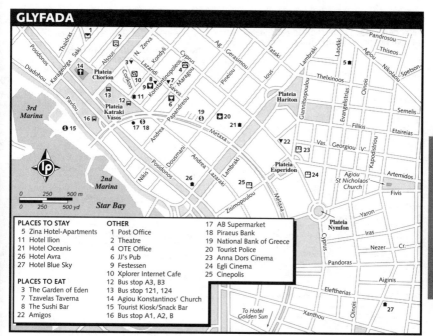

GLYFADA

3rd Marina

2nd Marina

Star Bay

PLACES TO STAY
5 Zina Hotel-Apartments
11 Hotel Ilion
21 Hotel Oceanis
26 Hotel Avra
27 Hotel Blue Sky

PLACES TO EAT
3 The Garden of Eden
7 Tzavelas Taverna
8 The Sushi Bar
22 Amigos

OTHER
1 Post Office
2 Theatre
4 OTE Office
6 JJ's Pub
9 Festessen
10 Xplorer Internet Cafe
12 Bus stop A3, B3
13 Bus stop 121, 124
14 Agiou Konstantinou' Church
15 Tourist Kiosk/Snack Bar
16 Bus stop A1, A2, B

17 AB Supermarket
18 Piraeus Bank
19 National Bank of Greece
20 Tourist Police
23 Anna Dors Cinema
24 Egli Cinema
25 Cinepolis

EXCURSIONS

doubles 14,000/10,000 dr; triples 16,000/12,000 dr; quads 20,000/16,000 dr C none 🚌 129
Worth making the trip from Glyfada's centre is the excellent Hotel Blue Sky. Its decent-sized rooms all have newly renovated bathrooms, TV and air-con. Other facilities include a common room, laundry and kitchen (for long stay guests). To get to the hotel catch bus No 129 from Plateia Katraki Vasos. The bus stops on Zamanou, 100m from the hotel.

PLACES TO STAY – MID-RANGE

Hotel Oceanis
Lambraki 23 ☎ 894 4038 fax 898 1746 Ⓢ singles 16,000 dr; doubles 22,000 dr; triples 25,000 dr C none
The C-class Hotel Oceanis is a friendly establishment with loads of character. With advance notice, group meals can be provided in the breakfast-only restaurant.

Zina Hotel-Apartments
Evangelistrias 6 ☎ 960 3872 fax 960 4004 Ⓢ apartments 25,000/22,000 dr; 28,000/ 25,000 dr C V
If your budget permits, a good choice is the quiet Hotel Zina. It has spacious, well-equipped apartments with kitchen, lounge and TV.

Hotel Avra
Lambraki 5 ☎ 894 7185, 894 6264 fax 898 1161 ⓔ avrahti@hol.gr Ⓢ singles 22,500/ 18,000 dr; doubles 30,000/22,000 dr; triples 36,000/25,000 dr C MC, V
Just 300m from the beach, Hotel Avra' s rooms have pleasant Marina views. The hotel also has a sauna and gym, and a pool which is available to non-guests for 2500 dr per person.

Golden Sun Hotel
Metaxa 72 ☎ 898 1353 fax 898 1090 ⓔ goldnsun@otenet.gr Ⓢ singles 28,300/ 22,000 dr; doubles 36,250/29,000 dr; triples 45,300/37,380 dr; apartments 54,350/ 45,110 dr C AE, DC, MC, V
One of the nicest places to stay in Glyfada is the modern Golden Sun Hotel. Its comfortable rooms all have private bath, TV, telephone and air-con.

PLACES TO STAY – SOUTH OF GLYFADA

The beach-resort belt continues south through Voula, Vouliagmeni and Varkiza where there are a number of pleasant B- and C-class hotels.

euro currency converter 1000 dr = €2.93

Hotel Parthenis
Alkionidon 21, Voula ☎ 895 6072 fax 895 3495 $ singles 13,000/10,000 dr; doubles 16,000/13,000 dr; apartments 32,000/28,000 dr C V 🚌 A2

The Hotel Parthenis is a small, better-than-average private hotel. All rooms have private bath, air-con and balcony.

Plaza Hotel
Alkionidon, Voula ☎ 899 1079 fax 899 1662 $ singles 19,800/17,600 dr; doubles 23,000/19,800 dr; apartments 28,600/22,000 dr C MC, V 🚌 A2

A bright option is the smart Plaza Hotel, a few doors down from Hotel Parthenis. It has comfortable air-conditioned rooms with soundproof, double glazed windows. The hotel's restaurant is only open upon request.

Hotel Armonia
Armonias 1, Vouliagmeni ☎ 896 0030, 896 3184 fax 967 1308 e armonia@armonia.gr $ singles 43,000/25,000 dr; doubles 52,000/30,000 dr; triples 59,000/35,000 dr; Paradise singles/doubles/triples 35,000/42,000/48,000 dr high; apartments 75,000/45,000 dr; C AE, DC, MC, V 🚌 114,115,116

This large hotel offers well-priced rooms in two locations. The Armonia's main building houses the more upmarket rooms, while the adjoining Paradise building's rooms, which have the same facilities, are marginally cheaper.

Plaza Hotel
Letous 14, Vouliagmeni ☎ 896 0066 fax 967 0139 $ singles 45,000/24,000 dr; doubles 52,000/29,000 dr; triples 59,000/35,000 dr C AE, DC, JCB, MC, V 🚌 114,115,116

Set close to the beach, the Plaza Hotel's rooms are light and breezy. Other facilities include car hire, a laundry service and a cocktail bar on the sixth floor.

PLACES TO EAT

The streets around Glyfada's main square are filled with representatives of every fast-food chain operating in Greece. Konstantinopoleos, which runs inland from the main square, is packed solid with bars and tavernas.

AB Supermarket
Metaxa 2 ☎ 894 3491 ⌚ 8am-9pm Mon-Fri, 8am-6pm Sat

This large chain supermarket sells everything from tinned goods to homewares.

The Sushi Bar (Japanese)
Konstantinopoleos 15 ☎ 894 2200 ⌚ noon-12.30am daily $ starters 1200-1850 dr; mains 1300-2200 dr C MC, V V

The popular Sushi Bar is great value. There is plenty of variety on offer including an excellent range of vegetarian rolls, soups and sashimi dishes.

The Garden of Eden (Lebanese)
Zerva 12 ☎ 898 0754 ⌚ 9pm-midnight Mon-Sat, 1pm-4am Sun $ starters 850-1200 dr; mains 1000-2800 dr C DC, V V

For authentic Lebanese head straight to The Garden of Eden. Try the delicious *makdous* (eggplant stuffed with walnuts and spices; 850 dr) or the *hommos snouber* (hommos with pine nuts; 1200 dr).

Tzavelas Taverna (Greek)
Konstantiopleos 16 ☎ 894 4125 ⌚ 12.30pm-late daily $ starters 1000-2000 dr; mains 1600-4000 dr C none

Tzavelas Taverna is away from the main pack of eateries on Konstantinopoleos and has the best prices.

Amigos (Mexican)
Kyprou 51 ☎ 898 3167 ⌚ 7pm-12.30am daily $ mains 1700-4900 dr C MC, V

A fun place for a night out is the cheery Amigos Mexican restaurant, hidden behind a large shady garden. Meals are a little on the overpriced side but the food is good and filling. A plate of chilli concarne costs 3600 dr and the super nachos costs 3100 dr.

PLACES TO EAT – SOUTH OF GLYFADA

Heading south from Glyfada there are a couple of restaurants that are worth the drive.

The Nest of the Hunters (Traditional Greek)
Varis 31, Vari ☎ 895 2445 ⌚ 11.30am-4pm daily $ starters 500-650 dr; mains 900-2900 dr C none

The Nest of the Hunters is first in line of the well-known psistaria restaurants that line the main street of Vari, 8km south-east of Glyfada. All restaurants along the strip employ touts dressed in traditional costumes who sit outside and wave in customers as they drive by. The restaurant's specialities include spit roasted meats such as goat and pork all prepared before your eyes.

Lake Vouliagmeni Cafe (Cafe)
Poseidonos, Vouliagmeni ☎ 967 0617 ⌚ 6am-4am daily summer, 8am-5pm daily winter $ starters 500-2500 dr; mains 2500-4500 dr C none 🚌 114,115,116

Positioned on the edge of a 12m deep natural lake, Lake Vouliagmeni Cafe is a relaxing place to wile away a long hot summer's evening. The menu, while not overly stimulating, is fairly substantial. Before you eat take a dip in the lake

(1300 dr all day) whose waters are never under a pleasant 22 degrees.

ENTERTAINMENT

Pubs

JJ's Pub
Maragou 8 ☎ 898 3600 🕒 11am-late daily
JJ's Pub is the favourite haunt of the expatriate community and has a large range of imported British and continental beers.

Festessen
Konstantinopoleos 13 ☎ 968 1225, 894 7358 🕒 8pm-1.30am Mon-Thur, 8pm-2.30am Fri, noon-2.30am Sat, noon-1.30am Sun
Decked out in true German style, Festessen lives up to its name and delivers a lively and boisterous beer-hall atmosphere.

Cinemas

Cinepolis
Zisimopoulou 7 ☎ 898 3238 $ 2000 dr

Egli Cinema
Cyprus 57 ☎ 898 2929 $ 2000 dr

Anna Dors Cinema
Plateia Esperidon ☎ 894 6617 $ 2000 dr

GETTING THERE & AWAY

Blue city buses can take you as far south as Voula for 150 dr. There are buses from Syntagma in Athens to Glyfada (A2, A3 & B3). Buses A3 and B3 terminate at Glyfada. Bus A2, which is much faster, continues on to Voula. From Glyfada connecting buses will take you farther south: Vari (No 149) Varkiza (Nos 115, 116, 149) and Vouliagmeni (Nos 114, 115, 116).

If your destination is Sounion, take one of the *paraliako* (coastal) buses which leave Athens hourly, on the half-hour (two hours, 1200 dr), from the Mavromateon bus terminal (see the Getting Around chapter for details). These buses also stop on Filellinon, on the corner of Xenofontos, 10 minutes later, but by this time they're usually very crowded.

KIFISSIA

Κηφισιά
☎ 01 • postcode 145 62

The posh leafy northern suburb of Kifissia is 12km north of central Athens, at the end of the metro's line one branch. It's cooler climate, beautiful tree-lined streets and immaculately tended gardens have long assured Kifissia's position as Athens' most enviable address. On weekends expensive foreign cars jam the streets as well-to-do Athenians descend upon the suburb to shop in its exclusive stores or unwind over coffee in one of its many outdoor cafes.

ORIENTATION

Kifissia's metro station, on Dragoumi, is a five-minute walk west of the centre. From the station, cross over Dragoumi and walk straight through Kifissia Park to Plateia Platanou, Kifissia's central departure point for buses to Athens. Beyond Plateia Platanou is Kifissias, the main street which runs north to south bordering the central shopping district.

INFORMATION

Kifissia's post office and major banks are in the main shopping centre close to the bus stop. The telephone office and tourist police are a little farther north, but still only a short walk.

Tourist Police
Othonos 94 ☎ 808 1464 🕒 telephone service 8am-11pm daily, office 8am-1.30pm daily

National Bank of Greece
Kifissias 178 ☎ 672 6350 [W] www.ethniki.gr 🕒 8am-2pm Mon-Thur, 8am-1.30pm Fri
The bank has an easy access 24-hour automatic exchange machine.

Citibank
Levidou 16 ☎ 801 8346 [W] www.citibank.com 🕒 8am-2pm Mon-Thur, 8am-1.30pm Fri
There is a 24 hour automatic exchange machine available.

Post & Communications

Post Office
Levidou 3a ☎ 623 3280 🕒 7.30am-2pm Mon-Fri

OTE Kifissia
Papadiamanti 8 ☎ 623 2899 🕒 7.40am-2pm Mon-Fri

Cyberian Monkey Internet Cafe
Drosini 14 ☎ 623 3831 fax 623 3830 [e] info@cyberianmonkey.com [W] www.cyberianmonkey.com 🕒 11am-11pm Mon-Sat, 3pm-11pm Sun
Not far from the cinema, this cybercafe is a good place to hang out. Printing facilities are also available.

EXCURSIONS

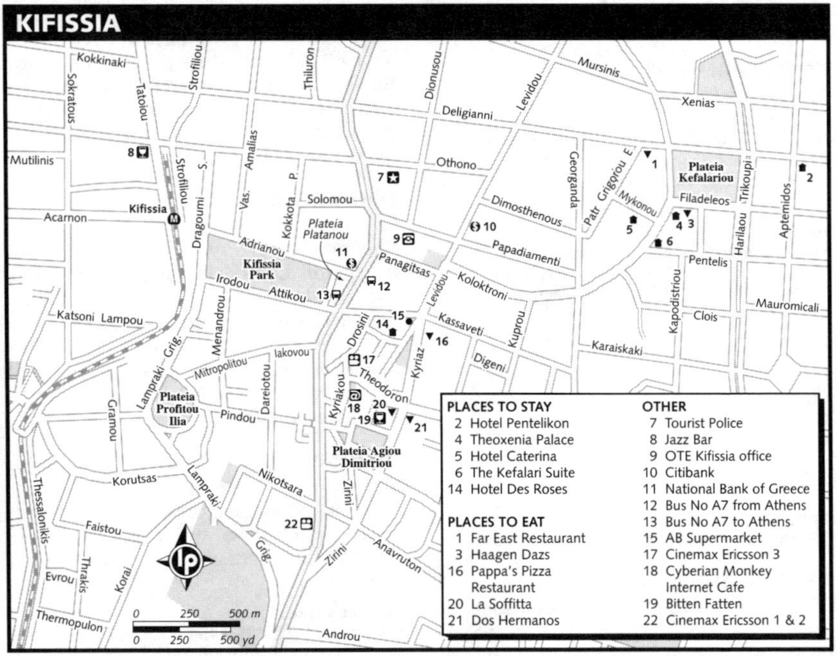
KIFISSIA
Kokkinaki
Sokratous
Tatoiou
Strofiliou
Thiluron
Dionusou
Levidou
Mursinis
Xenias
Deligianni
Mutilinis
Strofiliou
Dragoumi S.
Vas. Amalias
Kokkota P.
Othono
Georganda
Patr Grigoriou E.
Mykonou
Plateia Kefalariou
Trikoupi
Aptemidos
Filadeleos
Kifissia
Acarnon
Solomou
Plateia Platanou
Dimosthenous
Papadiamenti
Adrianou
Kifissia Park
Panagitsas
Koloktroni
Pentelis
Harilaou
Irodou
Attikou
Levidou
Kapodistriou
Maurmicali
Clois
Katsoni Lampou
Menandrou
Kassaveti
Kuprou
Karaiskaki
Lampraki Grig.
Mitropolitou
Iakovou
Drosini
Kyriaz
Digeni
Dareiotou
Theodoron
Plateia Profitou Ilia
Gramou
Pindou
Kyriakou
Plateia Agiou Dimitriou
Korutsas
Lampraki
Nikotsara
Zirini
Thessalonikis
Faistou
Grig.
Zirini
Anavruton
Evrou
Thrakis
Korai
Thermopulon
0 250 500 m
0 250 500 yd
Androu
PLACES TO STAY
2 Hotel Pentelikon
4 Theoxenia Palace
5 Hotel Caterina
6 The Kefalari Suite
14 Hotel Des Roses
PLACES TO EAT
1 Far East Restaurant
3 Haagen Dazs
16 Pappa's Pizza Restaurant
20 La Soffitta
21 Dos Hermanos
OTHER
7 Tourist Police
8 Jazz Bar
9 OTE Kifissia office
10 Citibank
11 National Bank of Greece
12 Bus No A7 from Athens
13 Bus No A7 to Athens
15 AB Supermarket
17 Cinemax Ericsson 3
18 Cyberian Monkey Internet Cafe
19 Bitten Fatten
22 Cinemax Ericsson 1 & 2

PLACES TO STAY – MID-RANGE

Kifissia is laden with luxury hotels. Two of the less expensive options are as follows:

Des Roses
Miltiadou 4 ☎ 801 9952 fax 801 8074
$ singles 15,000 dr breakfast 17,000 dr; doubles 19,000 dr breakfast 23,000 dr; triples 22,800 dr breakfast 28,800 dr
[C] none

A quick 200m walk south-east from the A7 Bus stop on Kifissias, Hotel Des Roses is the most downmarket in the area. Its modest rooms all have private bath, TV, telephone and air-con.

Nafsika
Pellis 6 ☎ 623 4034, 801 8027 fax 801 3556
[e] info@nafsika.gr $ singles 16,500 dr; doubles 22,700 dr; triples 28,140 dr [C] MC, V

While not in the centre, this small hotel offers good value rooms in a quiet location. Renovated in 1991 all rooms have private bath, but surprisingly no air-con.

Hotel Caterina
Mykonou 3 ☎ 801 8495 fax 801 5218
$ singles 30,000 dr; doubles 37,000 dr; apartments single/double/triple 47,000/52,000/55,000 dr [C] A, DC, MC, V

The well-appointed Hotel Caterina mainly caters to suitably attired businesspeople. Rooms have all the mod cons including modem connection, foreign newspapers are provided and there is even a secretarial service available.

PLACES TO STAY – TOP END

Theoxenia Palace
Filadeleos ☎ 623 3622 fax 623 1675 $ singles 52,000 dr; doubles 65,000 dr [C] AE, DC, MC, V

From its superb location, opposite Kefalariou Park, the Theoxenia Palace is a charming combination of old-world elegance and modern city comforts. Its stylish rooms all have private bath, TV and telephone. Other facilities include Internet access, pool and gym.

The Kefalari Suites
Pentelis 1 ☎ 623 3333 fax 623 3330
[e] info@kelalarisuites $ apartments 85,000-10,5000 dr [C] AE, DC, MC, V

Fancy a night dreaming of some far-off exotic destination? Then the Kefalari Suites might be just what you are searching for. All of the luxury suites are tastefully decorated to reflect their individual themes including Africa, Jaipur (think Arabian nights) and Saddle (you get the picture).

Hotel Pentelikon
Deligianni 66 ☎ 623 0650 fax 801 0314 $ singles 90,000 dr; doubles 105,000 dr; triples 118,000 dr; apartments 130,000-195,000 dr [C] AE, DC, MC, V
The pick of the luxury hotels is the deluxe Hotel Pentelikon. It's an exquisite place built in traditional style with a swimming pool and a lovely garden. All of the beautifully furnished rooms have minibar and satellite TV.

PLACES TO EAT

Kifissia, as to be expected, boasts mostly expensive internationally flavoured restaurants. The cheapest places to eat are the fast-food outlets lining Kassaveti and Levidou.

AB Supermarket
cnr Levidou & Kassaveti ☎ 808 2812 🕒 8am-9pm Mon-Fri, 8am-6pm Sat
This large, multilevelled supermarket sells every food item imaginable. The basement level has a well-stocked deli full of meats, fish and cheeses, the middle, entry level has a sizable fruit and vegetable section as well as shelves upon shelves of tinned goods and dry products; and the top level is home to cleaning products, stationary and homewares supplies.

Häagen Dazs (cafe)
Filadeleos ☎ 621 7070 🕒 11am-1am Mon-Thur & Sun, 11am-2am Fri & Sat
Häagen Dazs is the place to come to satisfy your sweet tooth. On offer are a decadent array of ice creams, sundaes, crepes and cakes. Forget the diet and try the Caramel Explosion for 1900 dr, or one of the 17 richly flavoured ice creams including Bailey's, Malibu and Chocolate Midnight Cookies from 850 dr a scoop.

Pappa's Pizza Restaurant (Italian)
Kyriazi 40 ☎ 801 8463 🕒 8am-midnight daily $ starters 850-2450 dr; mains 1500-3500 dr [C] V
Pappa's is one of the more casual places to dine in Kifissia. The menu is an ode to pizza and pasta with a sampling of meat and seafood dishes thrown in. Pizza varieties include the scrumptious Greek Pizza at 3100 dr and Pappa's Super Special Vegetarian Pizza at 3300 dr.

Dos Hermanos (Mexican)
Kyriazi 24 ☎ 808 7906 🕒 noon-12.30am Tues-Fri, noon-1.30am Sat & Sun $ starters 1700-2700 dr; mains 2200-4200 dr [C] DC, V
Mexican food is gaining in popularity in Athens, as can be ascertained from the hip young crowd that frequent Dos Hermanos. All your standard Mexican fare is on offer, although it is accompanied by not so authentic prices.

Far East (Oriental)
Deligianni 54 ☎ 623 3140 🕒 noon-2am daily $ lunches 9000 dr; starters 1750-6950 dr; mains 4950-9000 dr [C] AE, DC, MC, V
The second of the Far East restaurant chain offers a large all-you-can-eat buffet, including soft drinks and deserts, as well as a lengthy à la carte menu.

La Soffita (Italian)
Kyriazi 11 ☎ 801 4800 🕒 8.30am-1.30am daily $ starters 1000-4000 dr; mains 4000-5000 dr [C] MC, V
For a more formal dining experience head to the upmarket La Soffita Italian restaurant, where both quality and hefty prices are assured. Call ahead to reserve a table, especially on weekends.

ENTERTAINMENT

Pubs & Bars

Bitten Fatten
Ag Dimitriou 17 ☎ 801 1065 🕒 8pm-1.30am Mon-Thur, 8pm-2.30am Fri, noon-2.30am Sat, noon-1.30am Sun
This shady German beer garden is an excellent spot to cap off your Sunday afternoon and quaff a beer or two. On offer are a staggering list of 33 types of international beers including Australian, American, Irish and Cuban. Meals are also served.

Jazz Bar
Tatoiou 15 ☎ 801 4036 🕒 9pm-3am daily $ 2000 dr
The small out-of-the-way Jazz Bar is a friendly place which has live jazz on Monday, Tuesday and Wednesday nights.

Cinemas

Cinemax Ericsson 1 & 2
Kifissias 245 ☎ 623 3567, 623 2808 $ 2000 dr

Cinemax Ericsson 3
Drosini 16 ☎ 623 1601, 623 1933 $ 2000 dr

GETTING THERE & AWAY

To get to Kifissia catch the blue A7 city bus (150 dr) from the junction of Kaningos and Halkokondili to the main stop opposite the National Bank of Greece on Kifissias. The return bus to Athens departs from the stop, on the opposite side of the road, at the western end of Kifissia Park.

A quicker and more convenient alternative is the metro, with the Kifissia station at the northern end of line one.

EXCURSIONS

AROUND ATHENS

MONI DAFNIOU

Μονή Δαφνίου

Haidari ☎ 581 1558 [W] www.culture.gr
🕘 8.30am-3pm daily $ adult/student 800/400 dr

Moni Dafniou is Attica's most important Byzantine monument, and is on Unesco's World Heritage List. Built in the 11th century, the history of the site dates more than 2500 years. It stands on the site of an ancient Sanctuary of Apollo along the route of the Sacred Way which ran from Elefsina (ancient Eleusis) to the Acropolis in Athens. Its name derives from the daphne laurels which were sacred to Apollo. The temple was destroyed by the Goths in AD 395, although a single Ionic column survives in the narthex of the church.

The church contains some of Greece's finest **mosaics**, created at a time when the artistic and intellectual achievements of Byzantium had reached unprecedented heights.

The monastery was sacked in 1205 by the renegades of the Fourth Crusade who had earlier captured Constantinople. It was rebuilt and occupied by monks until the time of the War of Independence, after which it was used as army barracks and as a hospital for the mentally ill.

The mosaics on the church walls depict saints and monks, while the ones on the dome depict apostles, prophets and guardian archangels. Exquisite though these mosaics are, they fade into insignificance once the visitor has gazed upon the Christos Pantokrator (Christ in Majesty) which occupies the centre of the dome.

Unfortunately the monastery was badly damaged by the earthquake that struck Athens on September 14, 1999. It was cloaked in scaffolding at the time of research, and unlikely to reopen before the beginning of 2002.

Bus No A16 runs from Plateia Koumoundourou to the Venzini stop, which is right outside the monastery. The buses run every 20 minutes and take about 30 minutes in reasonable traffic.

ELEFSINA

Ελευσίνα

Modern Elefsina is one of the least attractive towns in Greece. It has become an industrial extension of Athens, surrounded by oil refineries and factories. The only reason to visit is to check out the site of ancient Eleusis.

Ancient Eleusis

Elefsina ☎ 554 6019 [W] www.culture.gr
🕘 8.30am-3pm Tues-Sun $ adult/concession 500/300 dr

It's hard to imagine how Eleusis must have been in ancient times. Doubtless, like all the great spiritual centres of ancient Greece, the place had a special feel about it, nestled on the slopes of a low hill close to the shore of the Saronic Gulf. The modern setting is far from inspiring, surrounded by heavy industry – which encroaches on the western edge of the site.

The ancient city of Eleusis was built around the **Sanctuary of Demeter**. The site dates back to Mycenaean times, when the cult of Demeter began. The cult became one of the most important in ancient Greece. By classical times it was celebrated with a huge annual festival, which attracted thousands of pilgrims wanting to be initiated into the Eleusian mysteries. They walked in procession from the Acropolis to Eleusis along the Sacred Way, which was lined with statues and votive monuments. Initiates were sworn to secrecy on punishment of death, and during the 1400 years that the sanctuary functioned its secrets were never divulged. The sanctuary was closed by the Roman emperor Theodosius in the 4th century AD.

A visit to the site's **museum** first will help to make some sense of the scattered ruins. The museum has models showing how the city looked in classical times and in Roman times.

Take Bus A16 from Plateia Koumoundourou to the final stop in Elefsina. The buses run every 20 minutes and take about 45 minutes in reasonable traffic. The site is five-minutes walk from the bus stop.

MONI KAISSARIANIS

Μονή Καισσαριανής

Alimou-Katehaki, Kaissarianis ☎ 723 6619
🕘 grounds open until sunset daily, monastery 8am-2.30pm Tues-Sun $ 800 dr

This 11th-century monastery, 5km east of Athens, is set amid pines, plane and cypress trees on the slopes of Mt Hymettos. The air is permeated with the aroma of herbs which grow on the mountain.

The source of the river Ilissos is on the hill above the monastery. Its waters were once believed to cure infertility and were sacred to Aphrodite; a temple dedicated to her stood nearby. The spring feeds a fountain on the eastern wall of the monastery, where the water gushes from a marble ram's head (this is a copy – the 6th-century original is in the National Archaeological Museum).

Surrounding the courtyard of the monastery are a mill, bakery, bathhouse and refectory. The church is dedicated to the Presentation of the Virgin and is built to the Greek-cross plan. Four columns taken from a Roman temple support its dome. The 17th-century frescoes in the narthex are the work of Ioannis Ipatos. Those in the rest of the church date from the 16th century, and were painted by a monk from Mt Athos.

The monastery is best visited during the week – it's swarming with picnickers at weekends. To get to the monastery take bus No 224 from Plateia Kaningos (at the north end of Akadimias), or from the junction of Akadimias and Sina, to the terminus at the Kaissariani cemetery. From here it's a walk of about 30 minutes to the monastery.

MT PARNITHA

Πάρνηθα

Mt Parnitha National Park lies just 20km north of the city centre and is a popular weekend escape for Athenians. At an altitude of more than 1000m, the air is delightfully fresh. The nights can be decidedly cool, even in summer.

Mt Parnitha itself comprises a number of smaller peaks, the highest of which is Mt Karavola at 1413m – high enough to get snow in winter. The park is crisscrossed by numerous walking trails, marked on the Road Editions trekking map of the area.

There's a road up the mountain, clearly signposted (Mt Parnitha) from National Road 1, but most visitors access the park by cable car, known as *teleferik*. You can get to the cable car station at the base of the mountain on bus No 714 from the southern end of Aharnon, near Plateia Omonias.

Casino Mt Parnes
☎ 246 9111 🕘 7pm-3.30am daily

Athens' only casino is fairly lacklustre by international standards. Casino connoisseurs prefer the set-up at Loutraki, near Corinth. If you want to enter the gaming rooms, you will need to bring your passport or identity card for registration. You will also need to be properly attired: no jeans and no T-shirts.

Hotel Mt Parnes
☎ 246 9111 fax 246 0768 $ singles 19,000 dr; doubles 26,000 dr; triples 32,000 dr [C] AE,MC, V

Unfortunately for a place with such a magnificent setting, the shabby Hotel Mt Parnes is typical of many places run by the National Tourist Organisation: an ageing concrete monstrosity where nothing quite works.

CAPE SOUNION

Ακρωτήριο Σούνιο

INLAND ROAD TO CAPE SOUNION

The inland road to Cape Sounion passes through the Mesogeia (middle land) region, renowned for the fine olives and grapes grown on its red soil.

Peania, a village 18km east of Athens in the eastern foothills of Mt Hymettos, was the birthplace of the orator Demosthenes (384–322 BC).

Vorres Museum
Diadohou Konstantinou 1, Peania ☎ 01-664 2520, 664 4771 🕘 10am-2pm Sat & Sun $ 1000 dr

Little remains of the ancient town, but visitors come today not for the ruins, but to look around the **Vorres Museum**, which houses folkloric items, prints and pictures, and an impressive collection of contemporary Greek paintings. Modern sculptures stand in the courtyard.

The museum is a fair hike from the bus stop on Peania's main square, Plateia Vasileos Konstantinou. Walk down Demosthenous (which has the New Democracy building on the corner and the post office next to it) and turn right onto Dimihounta at the bottom. Walk to the top of Dimihounta, and turn left onto Diadohou Konstantinou – where you'll soon find a reassuring sign pointing straight ahead to the museum.

EXCURSIONS

Peania Caves
☎ 01-664 2108 🕘 9am-4.30pm daily $ adult/child 1500/800 dr

The Peania Caves, 4km west of Peania on the slopes of Mt Hymettos, have an impressive array of stalactites and stalagmites that are very effectively lit. The caves were discovered in 1926 when a shepherd saw a lamb disappear down the tiny crevice that is the only natural entrance. The temperature inside the caves is a constant 17°C all year, making them a pleasant retreat from the heat of summer. The caves are signposted from Peania, but there is no public transport.

The largest of the villages of Mesogeia is **Koropi**, a lively market town 7km south of Peania. Its Church of the Transfiguration, on the road to Markopoulo, is one of the oldest churches in Attica and contains the remains of 10th-century frescoes.

The road continues to **Markopoulo** – home of the Kourtaki company, producer of Greece's most popular bottled retsina. The road south continues to Lavrio and Cape Sounion.

Getting There & Away

There is an Athens suburban blue bus to Peania and Koropi from Eptahalkou, just south of the metro line at Thisio. Bus No 308 terminates at Koropi.

There are also *mesogiaki* (inland) buses to Cape Sounion (2¼ hours, 1250 dr) from the Mavromateon terminal in Athens. They stop at both Peania and Koropi and continue south via Markopoulo and Lavrio.

TEMPLE OF POSEIDON

☎ 0292-39 363 🕘 8am-sunset daily summer, 10am-sunset winter $ 800 dr

The ancient Greeks chose their temple sites carefully, with the prime considerations being a site's natural beauty and its appropriateness to the god in question. Nowhere is this more evident than at Cape Sounion, where the Temple of Poseidon stands on a craggy spur that plunges 65m to the sea. The temple was built in 444 BC at the same time as the Parthenon. It is constructed of local marble from Agrilesa and its slender columns – of which 16 remain – are Doric. It is thought that the temple was built by Ictinus, the architect of the Temple of Hephaestus in Athens' Ancient Agora.

The temple looks gleaming white when viewed from the sea and is discernible from a long distance. It gave great comfort to sailors in ancient times; they knew they were nearly home. The views from the temple are equally impressive. On a clear day, you can see Kea, Kythnos and Serifos to the south-east, and Aegina and the Peloponnese to the west. The site also contains scanty remains of a propylon, a fortified tower and, to the north-east, a 6th-century temple to Athena.

Visit early in the morning before the tourist buses arrive if you wish to indulge the sentiments of Byron's lines from *Don Juan*:

Place me on Sunium's marbled steep,
Where nothing save the waves and I,
May hear our mutual murmurs sweep ...

Byron was so taken by Sounion that he carved his name on one of the columns – many others have followed suit.

PLACES TO STAY

Camping Bacchus
☎ 0292-39 571/2 fax 39 572 [e] linosP@panafonnet.gr $ 1600 dr plus 1400 dr for tent; caravan 8000 dr [C] A,DC,MC, V

Well-located Camping Bacchus' facilities include a mini market and a laundry service (1500 dr per load). The bus to Sounio stops at the site.

Hotel Saron
☎ 0292-39 144 fax 39 045 $ singles 13,000 dr; doubles 14,000 dr; breakfast 2000 dr [C] MC, V

Set amid pines the friendly Hotel Saron has well-priced comfortable rooms. The hotel also has a pool.

PLACES TO EAT

The cafe at the cape is expensive, so it's a good idea to bring along something to eat and drink. The nearest tavernas are on the waterfront below the Temple or at Sounio Beach on the way to Lavrio.

Taverna Akrogiali (Traditional Greek)
☎ 0292-39 107 🕘 10am-1am daily summer, 10am-1am Sat & Sun winter $ starters 200-2000 dr; mains 1900-5000 dr [C] none

The small family run Taverna Akrogiali oozes with charm and history. The crisp blue and white painted taverna, dating to 1887, boasts such famous guests as Jackie Kennedy – ask to see the her framed letter of thanks sent from the White House – and Sophia Loren. The mostly seafood menu is simply delicious!

GETTING THERE & AWAY

You can take either the inland or coastal bus to Cape Sounion. For details on the inland road bus see the preceding section. The coastal bus (1350 dr) departs every hour from the Mavromateon terminal in Athens.

EAST COAST

RAFINA

Ραφήνα

☎ 0294 • postcode 190 09 • pop 10,000

Rafina, on Attica's east coast, is Athens' main fishing port and second-most important port for passenger ferries. The port is much smaller than Piraeus and less confusing – and bus fares are about 20% cheaper, but you have to spend an hour on the bus and 460 dr to get there.

The quay is lined with fish restaurants and ticket agents. The main square, Plateia Plastira, is at the top of the ramp leading to the port.

There's no reason to hang about in Rafina and there are frequent bus connections with Athens. If, however, you want to stay the night and catch an early ferry or hydrofoil, your choices are limited.

Hotel Koralli
Plateia Plastira ☎ 22 477 $ singles 6000 dr; doubles 9000 dr; triples 14,000 dr [C] none
The D-class Hotel Koralli is reasonable. Facilities are shared.

Getting There & Away

Bus

There are frequent buses from the Mavromateon terminal in Athens to Rafina (one hour, 550 dr) between 5.40am and 10.30pm. The first bus leaves Rafina at 5.50am and the last at 10.15pm.

Ferry

Minoan Lines and Strintzis Lines both operate ferries to the Cycladic islands of Andros (two hours, 2400 dr), Tinos (3½ hours, 3600 dr) and Mykonos (4½ hours, 4100 dr). Strintzis has departures to all three, every morning at 8.00am, and a 7.15pm service (except Friday) to Andros only. Minoan has departures to Andros, Tinos and Mykonos at 7.15am every day except Wednesday. The Tuesday service continues from Mykonos to Syros (5¾ hours, 3400 dr), Paros (7¼ hours, 4100 dr), Naxos (8½ hours, 4200 dr) and Amorgos (11¾ hours, 4700 dr), returning the next day.

The Maritime Company of Lesvos has four boats weekly to Limnos (10 to 13 hours, 5540 dr), two of them stopping at Lesvos (8½ hours, 4540 dr).

There are also ferries to the ports of Karystos and Marmari on the island of Evia. There are three services daily to Marmari (1¼ hours, 1240 dr) and two to Karystos (1¾ hours, 1770 dr).

Catamaran

High-speed catamarans have almost completely taken over from hydrofoils on the routes from Rafina to the western Cyclades. Strintzis Lines' *Seajet I* leaves at 8.15am daily for Syros (1¾ hours, 6900 dr), Paros (2½ hours, 8200 dr), Naxos (3¼ hours, 8500 dr), Ios (four hours, 8200 dr) and Santorini (4¾ hours, 9600 dr). Strintzis also operates the *Seajet II* to Tinos (1½ hours, 7200 dr) and Mykonos (two hours, 8200 dr) at 7.40am and 2.15pm daily except Tuesday. The Tuesday morning service also calls at Andros (one hour, 4700 dr), and continues from Mykonos to Syros (three hours, 6900 dr), Paros (3¾ hours, 8200 dr), Naxos (4¼ hours, 8500 dr) and finally Amorgos (5½ hours, 9500 dr).

Minoan Flying Dolphins operates hydrofoils to Tinos and Mykonos at 8am and 4.15pm daily. The Thursday morning service calls at Andros, and continues from Mykonos to Paros, Naxos and Amorgos.

VRAVRONA (BRAURON)

Βραυρώνα

Sanctuary of Artemis

☎ 0299-27 020 🕐 8am-3pm Tues-Sun
$ 500 dr

The ruins of the ancient city of Brauron lie just outside the small village of Vravrona (vrah-**vro**-nah), 40km east of Athens. Brauron belonged to King Cecrops' league of 12 cities (King Cecrops was the mythical founder of Athens). Remains dating back to 1700 BC have been found at the site, but it is best known for the Sanctuary of Artemis.

According to mythology, it was to Brauron that Iphigenia and Orestes brought the *xoanon* (sacred image) of Artemis that they removed from Tauris. The site became a sanctuary to Artemis during the time of the tyrant Peisistratos, who made the worship of Artemis the official religion of Athens.

The cult centred around a festival, held every five years, at which girls aged between five and 10 performed a ritual dance that imitated the movements of a bear. The ruins of the dormitories where the girls stayed can be seen at the site.

The sanctuary's Doric temple, of which only a small section still stands, was built in the 5th century BC on the site of an earlier temple that was destroyed by the Persians. The site's **museum** houses finds from the sanctuary and the surrounding area.

Getting There & Away

Extremely early risers can follow the tourist office's advice and catch the 5.50am bus from Mavromateon to Cape Sounion as far as Markopoulo, where you take the 6.50am bus to Vravrona. A less painful option is to catch a regular A5 bus from the junction of Sina and Akadimias to the ERT (radio and TV) office at Agia Paraskevi on the outskirts of Athens. There are buses to Vravrona (150 dr) from here every 20 minutes.

MARATHON REGION

MARATHON

Μαραθώνας

☎ 0299 • postcode 180 10 • pop 10,000

The plain surrounding the unremarkable small town of Marathon, 42km north-east of Athens, is the site of one of the most celebrated battles in world history. In 490 BC, an army of 9000 Greeks and 1000 Plataeans defeated the 25,000-strong Persian army, proving that the Persians were not invincible. The Greeks were indebted to the ingenious tactics of Miltiades, who altered the conventional battle formation so that there were fewer soldiers in the centre, but more in the wings. This lulled the Persians into thinking that the Greeks were going to be a pushover. They broke through in the centre, but were then ambushed by the soldiers in the wings. At the end of the day, 6000 Persians and only 192 Greeks lay dead. The story goes that after the battle a runner was sent to Athens to announce the victory. After shouting *'Enikesame!'* ('We won!') he collapsed in a heap and never revived. This is the origin of today's marathon foot race.

MARATHON TOMB & MUSEUM

Plataion 114 ☎ 55 155, 55 462 🕘 8.30am-3pm Tues-Sun $ 500 dr

This burial mound, 4km before the town of Marathon, stands 350m from the Athens-Marathon road. In ancient Greece, the bodies of those who died in battle were returned to their families for private burial, but as a sign of honour the 192 men who fell at Marathon were cremated and buried in this collective tomb. The mound is 10m high and 180m in circumference. The tomb site is signposted from the main road. The **museum** is nearer to the town.

LAKE MARATHON

This huge dam, 8km west of Marathon, was Athens' sole source of water until 1956. The massive dam wall, completed in 1926, is faced with the famous Pentelic marble that was used to build the Parthenon. It's an awesome sight, standing over 50m high and stretching for more than 300m.

RAMNOUS

Ραμνούς

☎ 0299-63 477 🕘 7am-5pm Mon-Sat summer, 8am-5pm Sun summer $ 500 dr

It's an evocative, overgrown and secluded little site, standing on a plateau overlooking the sea. Among the ruins are the remains of a Doric **Temple of Nemesis** (435 BC), which once contained a huge statue of the goddess. Nemesis was the goddess of retribution and mother of Helen of Troy. There are also ruins of a smaller 6th-century temple dedicated to Themis, goddess of justice.

SHINIAS

Σχοινιάς

The long, sandy, pine-fringed beach at Shinias, south-east of Marathon, is the best in this part of Attica. It's also very popular, particularly at weekends.

PLACES TO STAY

Camping Ramnous
Leoforos Posidonos 174 ☎ 0299-55 855, 55 244 fax 55 244 [e] ramnous@otenet.gr $ tent 1900 dr plus 1700 dr per person; caravan 2300 dr plus 1700 dr per person [C] none
The well-maintained Camping Ramnous is on the way to the beach. Its shared shower and kitchen facilities are kept spotlessly clean. The camp site also has a childrens' playground and waterslide (1700/1000 dr adult/child per half hour). The bus to Marathon stops at the entrance to the camp.

GETTING THERE & AWAY

There are hourly buses from Athens' Mavromateon terminal to Marathon (1¼ hours, 800 dr). The tomb, the museum and Shinias Beach are all within short walking distance of bus stops (tell the driver where you want to get out). There are no buses to Lake Marathon or Ramnous; you need your own transport.

Peloponnese

CORINTH

Κόρινθος

☎ 0741 • postcode 201 00 • pop 27,400

Ancient Corinth was one of the great cities of classical Greece. Modern Corinth (in Greek, Korinthos; **ko**-rin-thoss), however, is little more than a dull administrative centre. The city was rebuilt in its present location on the shores of the Gulf of Corinth after the old town was destroyed by an earthquake in 1858. The new town was wrecked by another, equally violent, earthquake in 1928 and badly damaged again in 1981. As a result, Corinth is dominated by concrete buildings built to withstand future earthquakes.

The main attraction is Ancient Corinth, which lies 7km south-west of town. Old Corinth is a mere village near the ancient site.

ORIENTATION & INFORMATION

It is not difficult to negotiate Corinth, which is laid out on a grid of wide streets stretching back from the waterfront. Social activity centres around the large square by the harbour, Plateia El Venizelou, while transport and administrative activity is based around the small park 200m inland on Ethnikis Antistaseos.

There is no EOT in Corinth. The tourist police (☎ 23 282), located next to the park at Ermou 51, are open 8am to 2pm and 5pm to 8pm daily between May and October. The regular police (☎ 22 143) are in the same building. The National Bank of Greece is one of several banks on Ethnikis Antistaseos, the post office is on the edge of the park at Adimantou 33, and the OTE is nearby on the corner of Kolokotroni and Adimantou.

ANCIENT CORINTH & ACROCORINTH

☎ 31 443 [W] www.culture.gr 🕘 8am-7pm daily Apr-Oct, 8am-5pm daily Nov-Mar $ adult/student 1200/600 dr; Acrocorinth free
The sprawling ruins of ancient Corinth are 7km south-west of modern Corinth. Towering 575m above them is the massive, fortified bulk of Acrocorinth.

Allow a day to see both ancient Corinth and Acrocorinth. Most people come on day trips from modern Corinth, but there are ***tavernas*** and a few ***domatia*** in the village near the ancient site. Look for the signs.

History

During the 6th century BC, Corinth was one of ancient Greece's richest cities. It owed its wealth to its strategic position on the Isthmus of Corinth, which meant it was able to build twin ports, one on the Aegean Sea (Kenchreai) and one on the Ionian Sea (Lecheon), and it traded throughout the Mediterranean. It survived the Peloponnesian Wars and flourished under Macedonian rule, but it was sacked by the Roman consul Mummius in 146 BC for rebelling against Roman rule. In 44 BC, Julius Caesar began rebuilding the city and it again became a prosperous port.

During Roman times, when Corinthians weren't clinching business deals, they were paying homage to the goddess of love, Aphrodite, in a temple dedicated to her (which meant they were having a rollicking time with the temple's sacred prostitutes, both male and female). St Paul, perturbed

EXCURSIONS

by the Corinthians' wicked ways, spent 18 fruitless months preaching here.

Earthquakes and sackings by a series of invaders have left little standing in ancient Corinth. The remains are mostly from Roman times. An exception is the 5th-century-BC Doric **Temple of Apollo**, the most prominent ruin on the site. To the south of this temple is a huge **agora**, or forum, bounded at its southern side by the foundations of a **stoa**. This was built to accommodate the bigwigs summoned here in 337 BC by Philip II to sign oaths of allegiance to Macedon. In the middle of the central row of shops is the **bema**, a marble podium from which Roman officials addressed the people.

At the eastern end of the forum are the remains of the **Julian Basilica**. To the north is the **Lower Peirene fountain** – the Upper Peirene fountain is on Acrocorinth. According to mythology, Peirene wept so much when her son Kenchrias was killed by Artemis that the gods, rather than let all the precious water go to waste, turned her into a fountain. In reality, it's a natural spring which has been used since ancient times and still supplies old Corinth with water. The water tanks are concealed in a fountain house with a six-arched facade. Through the arches can be seen the remains of frescoes.

West of the fountain, steps lead to the **Lecheon road**, once the main thoroughfare to the port of Lecheon. On the east side of the road is the **Peribolos of Apollo**, a courtyard flanked by Ionic columns, some of which have been restored. Nearby is a **public latrine**. Some seats remain. The site's **museum** houses statues, mosaics, figurines, reliefs and friezes.

In times of danger, Corinthians retreated to **Acrocorinth**, a massive limestone outcrop which was one of the finest natural fortifications in Greece. The original fortress was built in ancient times, but it has been modified many times over the years by a string of invaders. The ruins are a medley of imposing Roman, Byzantine, Frankish, Venetian and Turkish ramparts, harbouring remains of Byzantine chapels, Turkish houses and mosques.

On the higher of Acrocorinth's two summits is the **Temple of Aphrodite** where the sacred courtesans, who so raised the ire of St Paul, catered to the desires of the insatiable Corinthians. Little remains of the temple, but the views are tremendous.

CORINTH CANAL

The concept of cutting a canal through the Isthmus of Corinth to link the Ionian and Aegean seas was first proposed by the tyrant Periander, founder of ancient Corinth. The magnitude of the task defeated him, so he opted instead to build a paved slipway across which sailors dragged small ships on rollers – a method used until the 13th century.

In the intervening years, many leaders, including Alexander the Great and Caligula, toyed with the canal idea, but it was Nero who actually began digging in AD 67. In true megalomaniac fashion, he struck the first blow himself using a golden pickaxe. He then left it to 6000 Jewish prisoners to do the hard work. The project was soon halted by invasions by the Gauls. Finally, in the 19th century (1883–93), a French engineering company completed the canal.

The Corinth Canal, cut through solid rock, is over 6km long and 23m wide. The vertical sides rise 90m above the water. The canal did much to elevate Piraeus' status as a major Mediterranean port. It's an impressive sight, particularly when a ship is passing through it. Any bus or train between Corinth and Athens will also pass over the canal. The canal can be reached on a Loutraki bus from modern Corinth to the canal bridge.

PLACES TO STAY

Hotel Ephira
Ethnikis Antistaseos 52 ☎ 24 022, 22 434 fax 24 514 Ⓢ singles 10,500/10,000 dr; doubles 17,000/15,000 dr; triples 19,000/17,000 dr; apartments 40,000/60,000 dr; breakfast 1200 dr Ⓒ V
The best deal in town is at the Hotel Ephira, a comfortable C-class hotel right in the heart of town. All the rooms have air-con and TV.

PLACES TO EAT

Taverna O Theodorakis (Fish taverna)
Seferi 8 ☎ 22 578 ⏱ 11.30am-2am daily Ⓢ starters 500-1000 dr; mains 1000-3000 dr Ⓒ none

Pilgrims would trek miles to worship Athena Pronaia at the *tholos* at Delphi's Sanctuary of Athena.

Corinth Canal links the Ionian and Aegean Seas.

The Sanctuary of Artemis, Vravrona

Peaceful Pireaus – watch out for the ferries.

View of Nafplio's narrow promontory from the imposing Palamidi Fortress, Peloponnese

Lion Gate, entry to the Citadel of Mycenae

Corinthian grapes on sale at Glyfada street market

A quiet word in Hydra, Saronic Gulf Islands

Taverna O Theodorakis is a lively place run by the eccentric Vangelis and his wife Kathanasia. It specialises in fresh grilled fish, priced from 7000 dr per kilogram. You can have a plate of sardines for 1000 dr, a large Greek salad for 1000 dr and a litre of retsina for 800 dr. It's open all year, with outdoor seating in summer.

Neon Cafeteria (Greek)
Ethnikis Antistaseos ☎ 84 950 🕗 8am-2am daily $ starters 800-1150 dr; mains 1400-1900 dr [C] none
Neon is a popular cafeteria with a good range of daily specials like macaroni with octopus (1450 dr) or veal with rice (1650 dr) as well as a salad bar (1150 dr).

GETTING THERE & AWAY

Bus

Buses to Athens (1½ hours, 1850 dr) leave every half-hour from the bus terminal on the corner of Ermou and Koliatsou. Buses to Argos (one hour, 1000 dr) and Nafplio (1¼ hours, 1550 dr) leave from the Argolis bus terminal on the corner of Aratou and Ethnikis Antistaseos. They also stop at Fihtio (45 minutes, 850 dr), on the main road 2km from Mycenae.

Train

There are 12 trains a day to Athens. Most of these are slow trains, which take 1¾ hours and cost 1100 dr. The intercity trains are only 15 minutes faster, but they are much more comfortable. Intercity services cost 1800 dr in 2nd class, 2400 dr in 1st class.

The Peloponnese rail network divides at Corinth, with seven trains a day heading along the north coast to Patras. It's worth checking the timetable before you set out – journey times to Patras range from under two hours on intercity trains to 3½ hours on the slowest slow train.

There are also five trains a day south to Argos, where the line forks again. Two trains a day travel east around the shores of the Argolic Gulf to Nafplio, while three head south-west to Tripolis and Kalamata. All these trains are slow services, which allows plenty of time for travellers to enjoy the scenery along the way. The trains to Nafplio take 1¼ hours and cost 810 dr. Trains between Corinth and Argos stop at Fihtio, 2km from Mycenae.

GETTING AROUND

Bus

Buses to ancient Corinth (20 minutes, 270 dr) leave Corinth hourly on the hour, returning on the half-hour. They leave from the bus stop north-west of the central park on Koliatsou. There is no public transport between ancient Corinth and Acrocorinth.

MYCENAE

Μυκήνες

☎ 0751 • postcode 212 00 • pop 450

The modern village of Mycenae (in Greek, Mikines; mih-**kee**-ness) is 12km north of Argos, just east of the main Argos-Corinth road. The village is geared towards the hordes of package tourists visiting ancient Mycenae, and has little to recommend it other than its proximity to the ancient site, 2km to the north. There are hotels along its single street, Hristou. There's no bank, but there is a mobile post office with a currency exchange service at the ancient site.

ANCIENT MYCENAE

☎ 76 585, 76 801 [W] www.culture.gr 🕗 8am-7pm daily Apr-Oct, 8am-6pm daily Nov-Mar $ adult/student 1500/800 dr

In the barren foothills of Mt Agios Ilias (750m) and Mt Zara (600m) stand the sombre and mighty ruins of ancient Mycenae, vestiges of a kingdom which, for 400 years (1600–1200 BC), was the most powerful in Greece, holding sway over the Argolid (the modern-day prefecture of Argolis) and influencing the other Mycenaean kingdoms.

History & Mythology

Mycenae is synonymous with Homer and Schliemann. In the 9th century BC, Homer told in his epic poems, the *Iliad* and the *Odyssey*, of 'well-built Mycenae, rich in gold'. These poems were, until the 19th century, regarded as no more than gripping and beautiful legends. But in the 1870s, the amateur archaeologist Heinrich Schliemann (1822–90), despite derision from professional archaeologists, struck gold, first at Troy then at Mycenae.

In Mycenae, myth and history are inextricably linked. According to Homer, the

EXCURSIONS

city of Mycenae was founded by Perseus, the son of Danaë and Zeus. Perseus' greatest heroic deed was the killing of the hideous snake-haired Medusa, whose looks literally petrified the beholder. Eventually, the dynasty of Perseus was overthrown by Pelops, a son of Tantalus. The Mycenaean Royal House of Atreus was probably descended from Pelops, although myth and history are so intertwined, and the genealogical line so complex, that no-one really knows. Whatever the bloodlines, by Agamemnon's time the House of Atreus was the most powerful of the Achaeans (Homer's name for the Greeks). It eventually came to a sticky end, fulfilling the curse which had been cast because of Pelops' misdeeds.

The historical facts are that Mycenae was first settled by Neolithic people in the 6th millennium BC. Between 2100 and 1900 BC, during the Old Bronze Age, Greece was invaded by people of Indo-European stock who had crossed Anatolia via Troy to Greece. The invaders brought an advanced culture to the then-primitive Mycenae and other mainland settlements. This new civilisation is now referred to as the Mycenaean, named after Mycenae, its most powerful kingdom. The other kingdoms included Pylos, Tiryns, Corinth and Argos in the Peloponnese. Evidence of Mycenaean civilisation has also been found at Thiva (Thebes) and Athens.

The city of Mycenae consisted of a fortified citadel and surrounding settlement. Due to the sheer size of the walls of the citadel (13m high and 7m thick), the ancient Greeks believed they must have been built by a Cyclops, one of the giants described by Homer in the *Odyssey*.

Archaeological evidence indicates that the palaces of the Mycenaean kingdoms were destroyed around 1200 BC. It was long thought that the destruction was the work of the Dorians, but later evidence indicates that the decline of the Mycenaean civilisation was symptomatic of the general turmoil around the Mediterranean at the time. The great Hittite Empire in Anatolia, which had reached its height between 1450

and 1200 BC, was now in decline, as was the Egyptian civilisation.

The Mycenaeans, Hittites and Egyptians had all prospered through their trade with each other, but this had ceased by the end of the 1200s. Many of the great palaces of the Mycenaean kingdoms were destroyed 150 years before the Dorians arrived.

Whether the destruction was the work of outsiders or due to internal division between the various Mycenaean kingdoms remains unresolved.

Exploring the Site

The **Citadel of Mycenae** is entered through the **Lion Gate**, so called because of the relief above the lintel of two lionesses supporting a pillar. This motif is believed to have been the insignia of the Royal House of Atreus.

Inside the citadel, you will find **Grave Circle A** on the right as you enter. This was the royal cemetery and contained six grave shafts. Five were excavated by Schliemann in 1874–76 and the magnificent gold treasures he uncovered are in the National Archaeological Museum in Athens. In the last grave shaft, Schliemann found a well-preserved gold death mask with flesh still clinging to it. Fervently, he sent a telegram to the Greek king stating, 'I have gazed upon the face of Agamemnon'. The mask turned out to be that of an unknown king who had died some 300 years before Agamemnon.

To the south of Grave Circle A are the remains of a group of houses. In one was found the famous **Warrior Vase** which Schliemann regarded as one of his greatest discoveries.

The main path leads up to **Agamemnon's palace**, centred around the **Great Court**. The rooms to the north were the private royal apartments. One of these rooms is believed to be the chamber in which Agamemnon was murdered. Access to the **throne room**, west of the Great Court, would originally have been via a large staircase. On the south-eastern side of the palace is the **megaron** (reception hall).

On the northern boundary of the citadel is the **Postern Gate** through which, it is said, Orestes escaped after murdering his mother. In the far north-eastern corner of the citadel is the **secret cistern**. It can be explored by torchlight, but take care – the steps are slippery.

Treasury of Atreus

☎ 76 585, 76 801 Ⓦ www.culture.gr
⏱ 8am-7pm daily Apr-Oct, 8am-6pm daily Nov-Mar ⓢ adult/student 1500/800 dr

The **Treasury of Atreus** is an immense beehive-shaped chamber built into the hillside to the west of the road connecting modern and ancient Mycenae. Many visitors rate this extraordinarily well-preserved monument as the highlight of their visit to Mycenae. The name is misleading, because no treasure was found here during excavations. Any treasure that might have been buried had disappeared long before the archaeologists arrived. It's also known as the Tomb of Agamemnon.

Either way, it's the finest known example of the *tholos* tomb, a style of royal burial that evolved in about 1500 BC, replacing the previous system of burying royal dead in shaft graves. The tholos tomb is so-called because of its beehive shape. It was built on a circular base, with walls that curved in to meet at a central peak – held together with a keystone. The tholos was dug into a hillside, and covered with the earth to create a larger hill than existed previously. Examples have been found almost everywhere that Mycenaean culture flourished, particularly in the Peloponnese.

None, however, can match the impressive dimensions and remarkable condition of the Treasury of Atreus, which was constructed in about 1300 BC when tholos design was at its most sophisticated. Entry is via a 40m-long *dromos*, a stone-walled passage that leads to a suitably oversized square entrance gate. The triangular section above the gate was a refinement designed to spare the lintel from the full weight of the structure.

Step inside and allow a couple of minutes for your eyes to adjust to the light before studying the astonishing stonework of the interior. Starting with mighty blocks for foundations, the size of the blocks steadily diminishes as the walls rise and taper to a peak 13.5m high.

PLACES TO STAY & EAT

Most people prefer to use nearby Nafplio as a base for visiting Mycenae, but there are several hotels along the main street. They are worth considering if you want to visit the ancient site early, or late.

Hotel Belle Helene

Christou Tsounta 15 ☎ 76 225 fax 76 179
ⓢ singles 9000 dr; doubles 13,000 dr; breakfast 1200 dr Ⓒ AE, DC, MC, V

The renowned archaeologist Heinrich Schliemann stayed here while excavating at ancient Mycenae. Other famous guests have included Claude Debussy and Virginia Woolf.

La Petit Planete

Christou Tsounta ☎ 76 240 fax 76 610
ⓢ singles 15,000 dr; doubles 20,000 dr; triples 25,000 dr; breakfast 2000 dr Ⓒ AE, MC, V

The best address these days is the Hotel La Petit Planete, set back on a hillside between the village and the ancient site. Facilities here include a swimming pool, a restaurant and bar.

GETTING THERE & AWAY

There are buses to Mycenae from Nafplio (one hour, 650 dr, three daily) and Argos (30 minutes, 360 dr, six daily). The buses stop at the village and the ancient site.

Other bus services, such as Athens-Nafplio, advertise a stop at Mycenae but they actually go no closer than the village of Fihtio on the main road, leaving you 3km from Mycenae village.

NAFPLIO

Ναύπλιο

☎ 0752 • postcode 211 00 • pop 11,900

Nafplio, 12km south-east of Argos on the Argolic Gulf, is one of Greece's prettiest towns. The narrow streets of the old town are filled with elegant Venetian houses and gracious neoclassical mansions. The setting is dominated by the towering Palamidi Fortress.

Nafplio was the first capital of Greece after independence and has been a major port since the Bronze Age. So strategic was its position that it had three fortresses – the massive principal fortress of Palamidi, the smaller Akronafplia and the diminutive Bourtzi on an islet west of the old town.

Removed from the spotlight as capital of Greece after Kapodistrias' assassination by the Maniot chieftains Konstantinos and

EXCURSIONS

Georgos Mavromihalis, Nafplio has settled into a more comfortable role as a peaceful seaside resort. With good bus connections, the city is an absorbing base from which to explore many ancient sites.

ORIENTATION

The old town occupies a narrow promontory with the Akronafplia Fortress on the southern side and the promenades of Bouboulinas and Akti Miaouli on the north side. The principal streets of the old town are Amalias, Vasileos Konstantinou, Staïkopoulou and Kapodistriou. The old town's central square is Plateia Syntagmatos, at the western end of Vasileos Konstantinou.

The bus station is on Syngrou, the street separating the old town from the new. The main street of the new town, known to locals as Neapolis, is 25 Martiou – an easterly continuation of Staïkopoulou.

INFORMATION

Nafplio's municipal tourist office (☎ 24 444) is on 25 Martiou. It's open 9am to 1pm and 4pm to 8pm daily. The tourist police (☎ 28 131) can be found at the western end of 25 Martiou, sharing an office with the regular police (☎ 22 100). The post office is on Syngrou, and the OTE is on 25 Martiou opposite the tourist office. All the major banks have branches in town, including the National Bank of Greece on Plateia Syntagmatos and the Ionian Bank at the western end of Amalias.

There is a laundrette at 22 Papanikolaou. For Internet access head to the Diplo Internet Cafe, Bouboulinas 43, open 8am until late.

PALAMIDI FORTRESS

☎ 28 036 ◷ 8am-6.30pm daily Apr-Oct, 8am-5pm daily Nov-Mar Ⓢ adult/student 800/500 dr

This vast citadel stands on a 216m-high outcrop of rock. Within its walls stand three separate Venetian fortresses, built between 1711 and 1714, but seized by the Turks only a year after completion. Above each of the gates of the citadel is the Venetian emblem of the Lion of St Mark. During the War of Independence, the Greeks, under the leadership of the venerable *klepht* (mountain

fighter) chief, Theodoros Kolokotronis, besieged the citadel for 15 months before the Turks surrendered.

The fortress affords marvellous views. The energetic can tackle the seemingly endless 999 steps that begin south-east of the bus station, off the road to Aravita beach. Climb early and take water. There's also a road to the fortress. It loops around to the north, stopping at a car park outside the top gate. A taxi costs 1000 dr one way.

AKRONAFPLIA FORTRESS

The Akronafplia Fortress, which rises above the old part of town, is the oldest of Nafplio's three castles. The lower sections of the walls date back to the Bronze Age. Up until the arrival of the Venetians, the town was restricted to within its walls. The Turks called it İç Kale (meaning 'inner castle'). It was used as a political prison from 1936–56. It now houses a hotel complex.

There's a lift up to the fortress from Plateia Poliko Nosokomiou at the western edge of town – look for the flags at the entrance of the tunnel leading to the lift. The old gateway to the fortress, crowned with a fine Venetian lion emblem, is at the top of Potamianou, the stepped street that heads uphill off Plateia Agios Spridonos.

BOURTZI

This small island fortress lies about 600m west of the port. Most of the existing structure was built by the Venetians. Boats to the island leave from the north-eastern end of Akti Miaouli. The trip costs 2000 dr for up to four passengers.

BEACHES

Aravanitia Beach is a small pebble beach just 10-minutes walk south of town, tucked beneath the Palamidi Fortress. If you're feeling energetic, you can follow a path east around the coast to sandy **Karathona Beach**, at the far side of the Palamidi Fortress. The walk takes about an hour.

TIRYNS

Τίρυνθα
☎ 22 657 ◷ 8am-8pm daily summer, 8am-2.30pm daily winter Ⓢ 500 dr

The ruins of Homer's 'wall-girt Tiryns' are 4km north-west of Nafplio. The walls of Tiryns are the apogee of Mycenaean architectural achievement (or paranoia), being even more substantial than those at Mycenae. In parts, they are 20m thick. The largest stones are estimated to weigh 14 tonnes. Within the walls there are vaulted galleries, secret stairways, and storage chambers. Frescoes from the palace are in Athens' National Archaeological Museum. Tiryns' setting is less awe-inspiring than Mycenae's and much less visited. The ruins stand to the right of the Nafplio-Argos road. Any Nafplio-Argos bus can drop you outside the site.

PLACES TO STAY

Most people head for the old town, which is the most interesting place to be. There are no cheap hotels, but there are plenty of domatia dotted around the maze of narrow, stepped streets between Staïkopoulou and the Akronafplia.

Accommodation can be very hard to find at weekends, when all the better places are normally booked out by visiting Athenians. Reservations are important if you plan to stay on Friday or Saturday nights. Finding a room should be no problem at other times.

Dimitris Bekas Rooms
Efthimiopoulou 26 ☎ 24 256 $ singles 5000 dr; doubles 6500 dr; triples 7500 dr [C] none

Dimitris Bekas is the best budget option around for those who are happy to forego the luxury of a private bathroom. Dimitris has a great location overlooking the old town from the northern slope of the Akronafplia. He normally charges less than his official rates for midweek visitors.

Pension Marianna
Potamianou 9 ☎ 24 256 fax 21 783 [e] marianna@otenet.gr $ singles 12,000 dr; doubles 14,000 dr; triples 16,000 dr; quads 18,000 dr; breakfast 1000-1200 dr [C] MC, V

The Pension Marianna is another place with great views, perched high above the town at the top of Potamianou. It's a family business run by brothers Panos, Petros and Takis, who have named the business after their mother. All the rooms come with private bathroom, air-con and TV.

Hotel Byron
Platanos 2 ☎ 22 351 fax 26 338 [e] byronhotel@otenet.gr $ singles 13,000 dr; doubles 16,000-24,000 dr; triples 22,000-26,000 dr; breakfast 1800 dr [C] AE,MC, V

The Hotel Byron is a beautifully furnished traditional hotel, although some of the cheaper rooms are a bit gloomy. All rooms have private bathroom and air-con. Some also have TV, and some have good views. They are priced accordingly. Reservations are important if you want a room with a view.

PLACES TO EAT

The streets of the old town are filled with dozens of restaurants. Staïkopoulou, in particular, is one long chain of restaurants; it would take weeks to eat at all of them. Most of these places close down in winter, and the choice shrinks to a few long-standing favourites.

O Noulis (Mezedopoleio)
Moutzouridou 21 ☎ 25 541 🕘 9am-3pm & 8pm-11.30pm summer, 8am-4pm winter $ starters 500-2500 dr [C] none

O Noulis serves a fabulous range of *mezedes* (snacks) which can easily be combined to form a meal. Prices start at 500 dr for tzatziki and other dips, and range up to 2500 dr for seafood. Check out the spectacular *saganaki flambé* (1100 dr), ignited with Metaxa (brandy) as it reaches your table. Noulis also offers unusual dishes like snails in red wine (1400 dr) and a good selection of seafood.

Taverna O Vassilis (Greek taverna)
Staikopoulou 20-24 ☎ 25 334 🕘 12.30pm-midnight daily $ starters 600-1200 dr; mains 1300-2600 dr [C] AE, DC, JCB, MC, V

O Vassilis is a popular family-run place at the heart of the restaurant strip on Staikopoulou. It has a large choice of starters, and a good selection of main dishes – including a very tasty rabbit *stifado* (stew) for 1650 dr.

ENTERTAINMENT

Nafplio seems to have almost as many nightclubs and bars as it has restaurants. Most of them are on Bouboulinas – just cruise along until you find a sound that you like at a volume you can handle.

SHOPPING

The Museum of the Komboloi
Staïkopoulou 25 $ 500 dr

Really more of a shop, this museum sells a wide range of *komboloi* (worry beads), evil eye charms and amulets. The upstairs museum has a collection of ancient beads assembled by owner Aris Evangelinos.

To Enotio
Staïkopoulou 40

Produces and sells Greek shadow puppets, traditional and modern. Prices start at 2000 dr.

GETTING THERE & AWAY

Bus

There are buses to Athens (2½ hours, 2800 dr) every hour, travelling via Corinth (1¼ hours, 1550 dr). Other useful service include three buses a day to Mycenae (one hour, 650 dr) and four a day to Epidaurus (40 minutes, 650 dr). There are also two buses a day to Galatas (two hours, 1750 dr), opposite the Saronic Gulf island of Poros.

Train

Train services from Nafplio are of little more than academic interest. There are trains to Athens (three hours, 1400 dr) leaving at 6.10am and 6.30pm daily. The station is by the port on Bouboulinas. An old train has been converted into the ticket office and *kafeneio*.

GETTING AROUND

There are several car hire places in town, so it pays to shop around. Two places worth checking out are Auto Europe (☎ 24 160-1, fax 24 164), Bouboulinas 51, and Safe Way Rent a Car (☎ 22 155, fax 25 738), Agiou 2. Moto Rent (☎ 21 407, fax 25 642), Polizoidou 8, also has a motorcycles.

EPIDAURUS

Επίδαυρος

Ancient Epidaurus

☎ 0753-23 009, 22 666 [W] www.culture.gr ⌚ 8am-7pm daily Apr-Oct, 8am-5pm daily Nov-Mar $ adult/student 1500/800 dr

Epidaurus (eh-pee-dahv-ross) is one of the most renowned of Greece's ancient sites, as reflected by its listing as a World Heritage Site. Epidaurus was a sanctuary of Asclepius, the god of medicine. The difference in the atmosphere here, compared with that of the war-orientated Mycenaean cities, is immediately obvious. Henry Miller wrote in *The Colossus of Maroussi* that Mycenae 'folds in on itself', but Epidaurus is 'open, exposed...devoted to the spirit'. Epidaurus seems to emanate joy, optimism and celebration.

HISTORY & MYTHOLOGY

Legend has it that Asclepius was the son of Apollo and Coronis. While giving birth to Asclepius, Coronis was struck by a thunder bolt and killed. Apollo took his son to Mt Pelion where the physician Chiron instructed the boy in the healing arts.

Apollo was worshipped at Epidaurus in Mycenaean and Archaic times but, by the 4th century BC, he had been superseded by his son. Epidaurus became acknowledged as the birthplace of Asclepius. Although there were sanctuaries to Asclepius throughout Greece, the two most important were at Epidaurus and on the island of Kos. The fame of the sanctuary spread, and when a plague was raging in Rome, Livy and Ovid came to Epidaurus to seek help.

It is believed that licks from snakes were one of the curative practices at the sanctuary. Asclepius is normally shown with a serpent, which – by renewing its skin – symbolises rejuvenation. Other treatments provided at the sanctuary involved diet instruction, herbal medicines and occasionally even surgery. The sanctuary also served as an entertainment venue. Every four years the Festival of Asclepieia took place at Epidaurus. Dramas were staged and athletic competitions were held.

THEATRE

Today it is the site's superb theatre, not the sanctuary, that pulls the crowds to Epidaurus. Built at the end of the 4th century BC, it ranks as one of the best preserved of Greece's many classical buildings, renowned for its amazing acoustics. A coin dropped in the centre can be heard from the highest seat. Built of limestone, the theatre seats up to 14,000 people. Its entrance is flanked by restored Corinthian pilasters. You can experience the acoustics in action during July and August, when the theatre is used for performances during the Festival of Epidaurus (see the following Entertainment section for details).

MUSEUM

The museum, between the sanctuary and the theatre, houses statues, stone inscriptions recording miraculous cures, surgical instruments, votive offerings and partial reconstructions of the sanctuary's once-elaborate tholos. After the theatre, the tholos is considered to have been the site's most impressive building and fragments of beautiful, intricately carved reliefs from its ceiling are also displayed.

SANCTUARY

The vast ruins of the sanctuary are less crowded than the theatre. In the south is the huge **katagogeion**, a hostelry for pilgrims and patients. To the west is the large **banquet hall** in which the Romans built an **odeum**. It was here that the Festival of Asclepieia took place. Opposite is the **stadium**, venue for the festival's athletic competitions.

To the north are the foundations of the **Temple of Asclepius** and next to them is the **abaton**. The therapies practised here seemed to have depended on the influence of the mind upon the body. It is believed that patients were given a pep talk by a priest on the powers of Asclepius then put to sleep in the abaton to dream of a visitation by the god. The dream would hold the key to the healing process.

East is the **Sanctuary of Egyptian Gods**, which indicates that the cult of Asclepius was an adaptation of the cult of Imhotep, worshipped in Egypt for his healing powers. To the west of the Temple of Asclepius are the remains of the **tholos**, built in 360–320 BC; the function of which is unknown.

ENTERTAINMENT

The theatre is used to stage performances of ancient Greek dramas during the Athens Festival in July and August. Performances are held on Friday and Saturday night, starting at 9pm. Tickets can be bought in Epidaurus at the site office (☎ 22 006) from 9am to 1pm and 5pm to 8pm from Sunday to Thursday, and from 9am to 9pm on performance days. Tickets can also be bought at the Athens box office (see the Athens Festival section of the Entertainment chapter for details). Tickets are priced from 4000 dr to 10,000 dr, according to seating. Student discounts are available for all but the best seats. There are special bus services to the festival from both Athens and Nafplio.

GETTING THERE & AWAY

There are three buses a day from Nafplio (40 minutes, 600 dr), and two buses a day from Athens (2½ hours, 2250 dr).

DELPHI

Δελφοί

☎ 0265 • postcode 330 54 • pop 2400

The setting is quite stunning, perched at an altitude of more than 1000m overlooking the Gulf of Corinth. The modern village of Delphi, though, seems to be comprised almost entirely of hotels, restaurants and shops catering to the tourist trade. As well as catering for the thousands who come to visit the nearby ancient site, Delphi is also popular with winter sports enthusiasts who come for the skiing on Mt Parnassos.

The bus station, post office, OTE, National Bank of Greece and tourist office (☎ 82 900) are all on the main street, Vasileon Pavlou. The tourist office, at No 44, is open Monday to Friday from 7.30am to 2.30pm. The ancient site is 1.5km east of modern Delphi.

ANCIENT DELPHI

Αρχαίοι Δελφοί

Sanctuary of Apollo

☎ 82 312 [W] www.culture.gr 🕒 7.30am-6.45pm daily Apr-Oct, 8.30am-2.45pm daily Nov-Mar $ adult/student 1200/600 dr

Of all many the ancient sites in Greece, Delphi is the one with the most potent 'spirit of place'. Built on the slopes of Mt Parnassos, Delphi's allure lies both in its stunning setting and its awe-inspiring ruins. The ancients regarded Delphi as the centre of the world; according to mythology, Zeus released two eagles at opposite ends of the world and they met here at Delphi.

History

During early Mycenaean times, the earth goddess, Gaea, was worshipped at Delphi, and it is believed the oracle originated at that time. Later Delphi became a sanctuary to Themis, then Demeter and later Poseidon, but by the end of the Mycenaean period, Apollo had replaced the other deities.

Delphi reached its height in the 4th century BC, when multitudes of pilgrims bearing expensive votive gifts came to ask advice of its oracle, believed to be Apollo's mouthpiece.

Delphi was protected by a federation of Greek states called the Amphyctionic Council. However, the surrounding territory belonged to the city of Krisa, which took advantage of this by charging visitors an exorbitant fee for the privilege of disembarking at its port of Kirrha. This angered the city-states, especially Athens, who called upon the Amphyctionic Council to do something about it. The result was the First Sacred War (595–586 BC), which resulted in the council destroying Krisa and its port.

The council now took control of the sanctuary, and Delphi became an autonomous state. The sanctuary enjoyed great prosperity, receiving tributes from numerous benefactors, including the kings of Lydia and Egypt. Struggles for its control ensued, and Delphi passed from one city-state to another, resulting in further sacred wars.

The Third Sacred War was precipitated by a dispute between Thebes and the district of Phocis, in 356 BC, over control of the sanctuary. Philip II, the king of Macedon, seized the opportunity to exert power over the city-states by acting as arbitrator in this war. He brought an end to the conflict and, in 346 BC, the sanctuary again came under the protection of the Amphyctionic Council. Philip now took Phocis' place in the council, which had probably been his intention all along.

The Fourth Sacred War broke out in 339 BC when the Amphyctionic Council declared war on Amfissa because it had staked a claim to the sanctuary. The council appealed to Philip for help. Philip saw this as an opportunity to bring his formidable army into Greece and, in so doing, not only destroyed Amfissa, but fought, and defeated, a combined army of Athenians, Thebans and their allies in the Battle of Khaironeia, in Boeotia (north-west of Athens). He had now achieved his ambition – control of Greece.

In 191 BC, Delphi was taken by the Romans and the oracle's power dwindled. It was consulted on personal, rather than political issues. Along with the country's other pagan sanctuaries, it was abolished by Theodosius in the late 4th century AD.

Exploring the Site

The **Sanctuary of Apollo** is on the left of the main road as you walk towards Arahova and Athens. From the main entrance, at the site of the old **Roman agora**, steps lead to the **Sacred Way**, which winds up to the foundations of the Doric **Temple of Apollo**.

Once you have entered the site, you will pass on your right the pedestal which held the statue of a bull dedicated by the city of Kerkyra (Corfu). Farther along are the remains of monuments erected by the Athenians and Lacedaemonians. The semicircular structures on either side of the Sacred Way were erected by the Argives (people of Argos). The one to the right was the **King of Argos Monument**, built in the 4th century BC.

In ancient times the Sacred Way was lined with treasuries and statues given by grateful city-states, including Thebes, Siphnos, Sikyon, Athens and Knidos, in thanks to Apollo for helping them win battles. The **Athenian treasury** has been reconstructed. To the north of this treasury are the foundations of the **bouleuterion** (council house).

The 4th-century-BC Temple of Apollo dominated the entire sanctuary. Inside the cella was a gold statue of Apollo and a hearth where an eternal flame burned. On the temple architrave were inscriptions of the wise utterings of Greek philosophers, such as 'Know Thyself' and 'Nothing in Excess'. The chasm from which the priestess inhaled the intoxicating vapours has not been found; all that is known is that it was somewhere within the temple.

Above the temple is the well-preserved 4th-century-BC **theatre**, which was restored by the Romans. From the top row of seats there are magnificent views. Plays were performed here during the Pythian Festival, which, like the Olympic Games, was held every four years. From the theatre another path leads up to the **stadium**, the best preserved in all of Greece.

From the Sanctuary of Apollo, walk towards Arahova along the paved path which runs parallel to the main road and you will come to the **Castalian spring** on the left,

EXCURSIONS

where pilgrims had to cleanse themselves before consulting the oracle. Opposite is the **Sanctuary of Athena** (free admission), where Athena Pronaia was worshipped. This is the site of the 4th-century-BC **tholos**, the most striking of Delphi's monuments. It was a graceful circular structure comprising 20 columns on a three-stepped podium – three of its columns have been re-erected. The purpose of the tholos is unknown.

Delphi Archaeological Museum
Ⓦ www.culture.gr ⊙ 7.30am-6.45pm Tues-Sun Apr-Oct, noon-6.15pm Mon Apr-Oct, 8.30am-2.45pm daily Nov-Mar Ⓢ adult/student 1200/600 dr

Ancient Delphi managed to amass a considerable treasure-trove, and this is reflected in its magnificent museum collection. Most labels are in Greek and French only, with the exception of some of the major exhibits. The museum is on the right of the main road as you walk towards modern Delphi.

On the landing is a copy of the **omphalos**, a sculpted cone which once stood at what was considered the centre of the world – the spot where the eagles released by Zeus met. In the second room along from here are two 6th-century **kore figures**. To the right of this room are displayed parts of the frieze from the **Siphnian treasury**, which depicts the battle between the gods and the giants, and the gods watching the fight over the corpse of Patroclus during the Trojan War.

In the rooms to the left are fragments of metopes from the **Athenian treasury** depicting the Labours of Hercules, the exploits of Theseus and the Battle of the Amazons. Farther on you can't miss the large **Acanthus Column**, with three women dancing around it. In the end room is the celebrated life-size **Bronze Charioteer**, which commemorates a victory in the Pythian Games of 478 or 474 BC.

PLACES TO STAY & EAT
There are more than 30 hotels to choose from, so finding a room is not normally a problem. Reservations are recommended at weekends, especially in winter. High season in Delphi is from 20 December to 5 January, otherwise low season prices apply.

Hotel Tholos
Apollonos 31 ☎ 82 268 fax 83 268 Ⓢ singles 11,000/8000 dr; doubles 16,000/11,000 dr; triples 20,000/16,000 dr Ⓒ none
The cheery Hotel Tholos is a good budget choice, run by a helpful woman from New Zealand and her husband. All the rooms have private bathrooms.

Hotel Parnassos
Frederikis 32 ☎ 82 321 fax 82 621 Ⓢ singles 15,000/10,000 dr; doubles 22,000/15,000 dr; triples 26,000/18,000 dr Ⓒ MC, V
The Parnassos is a another place with an Antipodean connection. The owners are a friendly Greek-Australian couple. It's a stylish place, recently refurbished. All rooms come with private bathrooms.

Taverna Vakhos (Greek taverna)
Apollonos 31 ☎ 83 186 ⊙ 8am-midnight daily Ⓢ breakfast 800-1400 dr; starters 500-1200 dr; mains 900-2000 dr Ⓒ none
The Taverna Vakhos turns out tasty food at reasonable prices, and offers an unparalleled view of the valley below.

GETTING THERE & AWAY
There are six buses a day to/from terminal B in Athens (three hours, 3300 dr).

Saronic Gulf Islands

The five Saronic Gulf Islands are the closest group to Athens. The closest, Salamis, is little more than a suburb of the sprawling capital. Aegina is also close enough to Athens for people to commute to work. Along with Poros, the next island south, it is a popular package-holiday destination. Hydra, once famous as the rendezvous of artists, writers and beautiful people, manages to retain an air of superiority and grandeur. Spetses, the most southerly island in the group, receives an inordinate number of British package tourists.

Accommodation on the islands can be nigh on impossible to find between mid-June and mid-September, and weekends are busy all year round. If you plan to go at these times, it's a good idea to book ahead.

The islands offer very few places for budget travellers to stay – no camp sites and only a couple of cheap hotels. There is good accommodation available if you are happy

EXCURSIONS

to pay 12,000 dr or more for a double. Midweek visitors can get some good deals.

The Saronic Gulf Islands are named after King Saron of Argos, a keen hunter who drowned while pursuing a deer that had swum into the gulf to escape.

AEGINA

Αίγινα

☎ 0297 • postcode 180 01 • pop 11,000

EXCURSIONS

Unassuming Aegina (eh-yee-nah) was once a major player in the Hellenic world, thanks largely to its strategic position at the mouth of the Saronic Gulf. It began to emerge as a commercial centre in about 1000 BC. By the 7th century BC, it was the premier maritime power in the region.

Athens, uneasy about Aegina's maritime prowess, attacked the island in 459 BC. Defeated, Aegina was forced to pull down its city walls and surrender its fleet. It did not recover.

The island's other brief moment in the spotlight came during 1827 to 1829, when it was declared the temporary capital of partly liberated Greece. The first coins of the modern Greek nation were minted here.

Aegina has since slipped into a more humble role as Greece's premier producer of pistachio nuts. The writer Nikos Kazantzakis was fond of the island and wrote *Zorba the Greek* while living in Livadi, just north of Aegina Town.

Aegina was named after the daughter of the river god, Asopus. According to mythology, Aegina was abducted by Zeus and taken to the island. Her son by Zeus, Aeacus, was the grandfather of Achilles, of Trojan War fame.

AEGINA TOWN

Aegina Town, on the west coast, is the island's capital and main port. The town is a charming and bustling, if slightly ramshackle, place; its harbour is lined with colourful caïques.

Temple of Apollo & Museum
🕘 8.30am-3pm Tues-Sun $ 500 dr

'Temple' is a bit of a misnomer for the one Doric column which stands at this site. The column is all that is left of the 5th-century Temple of Apollo which once stood on the hill of Koloni. The hill was the site of the ancient acropolis, and there are remains of a Helladic (early) settlement. The site also has a museum.

PLACES TO STAY

Hotel Plaza – Ulrika & Christina
Kazatzaki 4 ☎ 25 600 fax 28 404 $ singles 7000/5000 dr; doubles 12,000/8000 dr; triples 14,000/10,000 dr; air-con 2000 dr; breakfast 1200 dr [C] none

The Plaza Hotel, on the waterfront, is the best place to head for. In recent years it has expanded and is now jointly operated with the Ulrika and Christina Hotels, both located 100m from the Plaza. The Plaza Hotel acts as the reception for all three. All have good rooms overlooking the sea.

Hotel Artemis
Kanari 20 ☎ 25 195, 28 466 fax 28 779 [e] pipinis@otenet.gr $ singles 10,000/8000 dr; doubles 14,000/10,000 dr; triples 16,000/12,000 dr; breakfast 1500 dr [C] none

Hotel Artemis has a wide range of rooms all with bathroom, balcony and air-conditioning, and offers discounts to midweek visitors.

PLACES TO EAT

The harbourfront is lined with countless cafes and restaurants – good for soaking up the atmosphere, but not particularly good value. Locals prefer to head for the cluster of small *ouzeria* and restaurants around the fish markets at the southern end of the harbour.

Restaurant I Agora (Greek)
Pan Irioti 47 ☎ 23 910 🕘 7am-late daily $ starters 400-2000 dr; mains 600-2000 dr [C] none

This tiny restaurant is a good place to start. Here you'll find the local speciality, barbequed octopus (1000 dr), as well as fresh calamari (1300 dr) and sardines (900 dr).

GETTING THERE & AWAY

Ferry

In summer there are at least 10 ferries daily from Aegina Town to Piraeus (1½ hours, 1400 dr). There are at least three boats daily to Poros (1½ hours 1100 dr) via Methana (40 minutes, 1000 dr), two daily to Hydra (two hours, 1600 dr), and one to Spetses (three hours, 2400 dr). The ferry companies have ticket offices at the quay, where you will find a full list of the day's sailings.

Hydrofoil

Hydrofoils operate almost hourly from 7am to 8pm between Aegina Town and the Great Harbour in Piraeus (35 minutes, 2700 dr). Services south are restricted to two daily to Poros (40 minutes, 2400 dr) via Methana (20 minutes, 1900 dr). Tickets are sold at the quay in Aegina Town.

POROS

Πόρος

☎ 0298 • postcode 180 20 • pop 4000

The island of Poros is little more than a stones throw from the mainland. The slender passage of water that separates it from the Peloponnesian town of Galatas is only 360m wide at its narrowest point.

Poros was once two islands, Kalavria and Sferia. These days they are connected by a narrow isthmus, cut by a canal for small boats and rejoined by a road bridge. The vast majority of the population lives on the small volcanic island of Sferia, which is more than half covered by the town of Poros. Sferia hangs like an appendix from the southern coast of Kalavria, a large, well-forested island that has all the package hotels.

POROS TOWN

Poros Town is the island's main settlement. While not wildly exciting, it is a pretty place of white houses with terracotta-tiled roofs and there are wonderful views over the mountains of Argolis. It is a popular weekend destination for Athenians as well as for package tourists and cruise ships.

PLACES TO STAY & EAT

Poros has very little cheap accommodation, but a couple of excellent restaurants.

Vila Tryfon
☎ 22 215, 25 854 Ⓢ doubles 14,000/10,000 dr Ⓒ none
The charming Vila Tryfon is the place to come for a room with a view. All rooms have bathroom and kitchen facilities as well as great views over to Kalavria. To get there, turn left from the ferry dock and take the first right up the steps 20m past the Agricultural Bank of Greece. Turn left at the top of the stairs on Aikaterinis Hatzopoulou

Karra, and you will see the place signposted up the steps to the right after 150m.

Hotel Seven Brothers
☎ 23 412 fax 23 413 ⓔ 7brothers@hol.gr
Ⓢ singles 13,000/10,000 dr; doubles 16,000/13,000 dr; triples extra 3000 dr for the bed
Ⓒ none
This smart C-class hotel has large comfortable rooms all with own shower, air-con, TV and mini bar.

Taverna Platanos (Traditional Greek)
☎ 25 409, 24 429 ◷ 7pm-late daily except closed Nov & Dec Ⓢ starters 500-1200 dr; mains 1400-1600 dr Ⓒ A, MC, V
Taverna Platanos is a popular choice with the locals. Owner Tassos is a butcher by day and the restaurant specialises in spit-roast meats. You'll find specialities like *kokoretsi* (offal) and *gouronopoulo* (suckling pig), both for 1400 dr.

GETTING THERE & AWAY
Ferry

There are up to eight ferries daily to Piraeus (three hours, 2100 dr), via Methana and Aegina (1½ hours, 1200 dr), two daily to Hydra (one hour, 1000 dr), and one to Spetses (two hours, 1600 dr). Ticket agencies are opposite the ferry dock.

Hydrofoil

Services from Poros and Piraeus are evenly split between the Great Harbour and Zea Marina, with up to five daily to each. Two travel daily via Methana and Aegina (40 minutes, 2400 dr). There are also seven hydrofoils south to Hydra (30 minutes, 2000 dr) and five to Spetses (one hour, 3300 dr) and Port Heli. The Flying Dolphin agency is on Plateia Iroön, and has a timetable of departures outside.

HYDRA

Ύδρα

☎ 0298 • postcode 180 40 • pop 3000

Hydra (ee-drah) is the Saronic Gulf island with most style. The gracious stone, white and pastel mansions of Hydra Town are stacked up the rocky hillside that surround the fine natural harbour. Filmmakers were the first foreigners to be seduced by Hydra's beauty. They began arriving in the 1950s when the island was used as a location for the film *Boy on a Dolphin*, among others.

EXCURSIONS

The artists and writers moved in next, followed by the celebrities, and nowadays it seems the whole world is welcome ashore.

Hydra has no motorised transport except for sanitation and construction vehicles. Donkeys (hundreds of them) are the only means of transport.

HYDRA TOWN

Most of the action in Hydra Town is concentrated around the waterfront cafes and shops, leaving the upper reaches of the narrow, stepped streets virtually deserted and a joy to explore.

Historical Archives Museum of Hydra
🕐 10am-5pm Tues-Sun $ 500 dr
The museum houses a collection of naval oddments, with an emphasis on the island's role in the War of Independence.

Byzantine Museum
🕐 10am-5pm Tues-Sun $ 500 dr
The museum houses a collection of icons and assorted religious paraphernalia. The entrance is through the archway beneath the clock tower on the waterfront.

PLACES TO STAY

Pension Theresia
Tombazi ☎ 53 984 fax 53 983 $ singles 10,000/6000 dr; doubles 15,000/10,000 dr; triples 17,000/12,000 dr [C] none
It's hard to miss Theresia, who meets all the ferries that come in daily at the waterfront. Rooms are spacious and clean, though the beds and pillows are a little on the lumpy side.

Hotel Angelica
☎ 53 202/64 fax 53 698 [e] angelicahotel@hotmail.com $ singles 15,000/13,000 dr; doubles 24,000/21,000 dr [C] A, MC, V
Housed in a large 17th-century dwelling this family-run hotel is a charming place to spend the night. All rooms have bathroom, air-con and open onto large vine-covered balconies.

Hotel Miranda
☎ 52 230 fax 53 510 [e] mirhydra@hol.gr $ singles 20,000 dr; doubles 25,000 dr; triples 35,000 dr [C] none
Originally owned by a wealthy Hydriot sea captain, the house has been beautifully renovated and converted into a very smart hotel. All rooms have air-con, mini bar and TV.

PLACES TO EAT

Hydra has dozens of tavernas and restaurants. Unlike the hotels, there are plenty of cheap places around especially if you are prepared to head away from the waterfront.

Taverna Lulu (Traditional Greek)
Miaouli ☎ 52 018 🕐 11am-late daily $ starters 400-1400 dr; mains 1500-2300 dr [C] MC, V
Taverna Lulu offers well-priced set menus based on fish or meat dishes ranging from 3500 dr to 4500 dr – all naturally begin with an obligatory shot of ouzo.

Douskos Restaurant (Traditional Greek)
Spilios J Charamis ☎ 52 886, 53 010 🕐 5.30pm-late daily $ starters 600-2000 dr; mains 1600-2500 dr [C] MC, V
Tucked away in a small square off Tombazi, Douskos Restaurant is a delightful spot with seating beneath an aromatic sea of bougainvillea and grape vines.

GETTING THERE & AWAY

Ferry

There are two ferries daily to Piraeus (3½ hours, 2300 dr), sailing via Poros (1000 dr), Methana (1500 dr) and Aegina (1600 dr). There's also a daily boat to Spetses (one hour, 1200 dr). Departure times are listed on the board at the ferry dock.

Hydrofoil

The Flying Dolphins run up to nine services daily to Piraeus (4600 dr). Direct services take 1¼ hours, but most go via Poros (30 minutes, 2000 dr) and take 1½ hours. There are also frequent services to Spetses (30 minutes, 2300 dr), some of which call at Ermioni, adding 20 minutes to the trip. Many of the services to Spetses continue to Port Heli (50 minutes, 2500 dr).

SPETSES

Σπέτσες

☎ 0298 • postcode 180 50 • pop 3700

Pine-covered Spetses, the most distant of the group from Piraeus, has long been a favourite with British holiday makers.

The island was known in antiquity as Pityoussa (meaning pine-covered), but the original forest disappeared long ago. The pine-covered hills that greet visitors today are a legacy of the far-sighted and wealthy philanthropist Sotirios Anargyrios.

Anargyrios was born on Spetses in 1848 and emigrated to the USA, returning in

1914 as an exceedingly rich man. He bought two-thirds of the then largely barren island and planted the Aleppo pines that stand today.

He also financed the island's road system and commissioned many of the town's grand buildings.

SPETSES TOWN

Spetses Town sprawls along almost half the north-east coast of the island, reflecting the way in which the focal point of the settlement has changed over the years.

There's evidence of an early Hellenic settlement near the old harbour, about 1.5km east of the modern commercial centre and port of Dapia.

Roman and Byzantine remains have been unearthed in the area behind **Moni Agios Nickolas**, halfway between the two settlements.

PLACES TO STAY

Villa Marina

☎ 72 646/60 $ singles 12,000/8000 dr; doubles 17,000/13,000 dr [C] none

The friendly Villa Marina is a popular place to stay. All rooms have refrigerators and there is a well-equipped communal kitchen downstairs. From the ferry stop walk left 200m, then turn right off Plateia Agis beyond the row of restaurants.

GETTING THERE AND AWAY

Ferry

There is one ferry daily to Piraeus (4¼ hours, 3200 dr), via Hydra (1200 dr), Poros (1600 dr) and Aegina (2400 dr). You'll find departure times on the waterfront outside Alasia Travel (☎ 74 098), which sells tickets.

Hydrofoils

There are up to nine Flying Dolphins daily to Piraeus (6400 dr). Most services travel via Hydra (30 minutes, 2300 dr) and Poros (70 minutes, 3300 dr) and take up to 2½ hours.

Language

The Greek language is probably the oldest European language, with an oral tradition of 4000 years and a written tradition of approximately 3000 years. Its evolution over the four millennia was characterised by its strength during the golden age of Athens and the Democracy (mid-5th century BC); its use as a lingua franca throughout the Middle Eastern world, spread by Alexander the Great and his successors as far as India during the Hellenistic period (330 BC to AD 100); its adaptation as the language of the new religion, Christianity; its use as the official language of the Eastern Roman Empire; and its eventual proclamation as the language of the Byzantine Empire (380–1453).

Greek maintained its status and prestige during the rise of the European Renaissance and was employed as the linguistic perspective for all contemporary sciences and terminologies during the period of Enlightenment. Today, Greek constitutes a large part of the vocabulary of any Indo-European language, and much of the lexicon of any scientific repertoire.

The modern Greek language is a southern Greek dialect which is now used by most Greek speakers both in Greece and abroad. It is the result of an intralinguistic influence and synthesis of the ancient vocabulary combined with words from Greek regional dialects, namely Cretan, Cypriot and Macedonian.

Those wishing to delve a little deeper into the language should get a copy of Lonely Planet's *Greek phrasebook*.

PRONUNCIATION

All Greek words of two or more syllables have an acute accent which indicates where the stress falls. For instance, άγαλμα (statue) is pronounced *aghalma*, and αγάπη (love) is pronounced *aghapi*. In the following transliterations, bold lettering indicates word stress. Note also that **dh** is pronounced as 'th' in 'then', and **gh** is a softer, slightly guttural version of 'g'.

GREETINGS & CIVILITIES

Hello.
| *ya**sas*** | Γειά σας. |
| *ya**su*** | Γειά σου. (informal) |

Goodbye.
| *an**dio*** | Αντίο. |

Good morning.
| *kali**mera*** | Καλημέρα. |

Good afternoon.
| *here**te*** | Χαίρετε. |

Good evening.
| *kalis**pera*** | Καλησπέρα. |

Good night.
| *kali**nihta*** | Καληνύχτα. |

Please.
| *paraka**lo*** | Παρακαλώ. |

Thank you.
| *ef**haristo*** | Ευχαριστώ. |

Yes.
| *ne* | Ναι. |

No.
| ***ohi*** | Οχι. |

Sorry. (excuse me, forgive me)
| *sigh**nomi*** | Συγγνώμη. |

How are you?
| *ti ka**nete?*** | Τι κάνετε; |
| *ti ka**nis?*** | Τι κάνεις; (informal) |

I'm well, thanks.
| *ka**la** ef**haristo*** | Καλά ευχαριστώ. |

ESSENTIALS

Do you speak English?
| *mi**late** anglika?* | Μιλάτε Αγγλικά; |

I understand.
| *kata**laveno*** | Καταλαβαίνω. |

I don't understand.
| *dhen kata**laveno*** | Δεν καταλαβαίνω. |

Where is ...?
| *pou ine ...?* | Πού είναι ...; |

How much?
| *po**so** kani?* | Πόσο κάνει; |

When?
| *pote?* | Πότε; |

The Greek Alphabet & Pronunciation

Greek	Pronunciation Guide		Example		
Α α	a	as in 'father'	αγάπη	*agha*pi	love
Β β	v	as in 'vine'	βήμα	*vi*ma	step
Γ γ	gh	like a rough 'g'	γάτα	*gha*ta	cat
	y	as in 'yes'	για	*ya*	for
Δ δ	dh	as in 'there'	δέμα	*dhe*ma	parcel
Ε ε	e	as in 'egg'	ένας	*e*nas	one (m)
Ζ ζ	z	as in 'zoo'	ζώο	*zo*o	animal
Η η	i	as in 'feet'	ήταν	*it*an	was
Θ θ	th	as in 'throw'	θέμα	*the*ma	theme
Ι ι	i	as in 'feet'	ίδιος	*i*dhyos	same
Κ κ	k	as in 'kite'	καλά	*ka*la	well
Λ λ	l	as in 'leg'	λάθος	*la*thos	mistake
Μ μ	m	as in 'man'	μαμά	*ma*ma	mother
Ν ν	n	as in 'net'	νερό	*ne*ro	water
Ξ ξ	x	as in 'ox'	ξύδι	*ksi*dhi	vinegar
Ο ο	o	as in 'hot'	όλα	*o*la	all
Π π	p	as in 'pup'	πάω	*pa*o	I go
Ρ ρ	r	as in 'road'	ρέμα	*re*ma	stream
		a slightly trilled 'r'	ρόδα	*ro*dha	tyre
Σ σ, ς	s	as in 'sand'	σημάδι	*sima*dhi	mark
Τ τ	t	as in 'tap'	τόπι	*to*pi	ball
Υ υ	i	as in 'feet'	ύστερα	*is*tera	after
Φ φ	f	as in 'find'	φύλλο	*fi*lo	leaf
Χ χ	h	as the 'ch' in Scottish *loch*, or like a rough 'h'	χάνω	*ha*no	I lose
			χέρι	*he*ri	hand
Ψ ψ	ps	as in 'lapse'	ψωμί	*psomi*	bread
Ω ω	o	as in 'hot'	ώρα	*o*ra	time

Combinations of Letters

The combinations of letters shown here are pronounced as follows:

Greek	Pronunciation Guide		Example		
ει	i	as in 'feet'	είδα	*i*dha	I·saw
οι	i	as in 'feet'	οικόπεδο	*iko*pedho	land
αι	e	as in 'bet'	αίμα	*e*ma	blood
ου	u	as in 'mood'	πού	*pou*	who/what
μπ	b	as in 'beer'	μπάλα	*ba*la	ball
	mb	as in 'amber'	κάμπος	*kam*bos	forest
ντ	d	as in 'dot'	ντουλάπα	*doula*pa	wardrobe
	nd	as in 'bend'	πέντε	*pen*de	five
γκ	g	as in 'God'	γκάζι	*ga*zi	gas
γγ	ng	as in 'angle'	αγγελία	*angeli*a	classified
γξ	ks	as in 'minks'	σφιγξ	*sfinks*	sphynx
τζ	dz	as in 'hands'	τζάκι	*dza*ki	fireplace

The pairs of vowels shown above are pronounced separately if the first has an acute accent, or the second a dieresis, as in the examples below:

γαϊδουράκι	*gaidhoura*ki	little donkey
Κάιρο	*ka*iro	Cairo

Some Greek consonant sounds have no English equivalent. The υ of the groups αυ, ευ and ηυ is generally pronounced 'v'. The Greek question mark is represented with the English equivalent of a semicolon ';'.

SMALL TALK

What's your name?
pos sas lene? Πώς σας λένε;
My name is ...
me lene ... Με λένε ...
Where are you from?
apo pou iste? Από πού είστε;

I'm from ...
ime apo ... Είμαι από ...
America
tin ameriki την Αμερική
Australia
tin afstralia την Αυστραλία
England
tin anglia την Αγγλία
Ireland
tin irlandhia την Ιρλανδία
New Zealand
ti nea zilandhia τη Νέα Ζηλανδία
Scotland
ti skotia τη Σκωτία

How old are you?
poson hronon Πόσων χρονών
iste? είστε;
I'm ... years old.
ime ... hronon Είμαι ... χρονών.

GETTING AROUND

What time does
the ... leave/arrive?
ti ora fevyi/ Τι ώρα φεύγει/
ftani to ...? φτάνει το ...;

boat *karavi* καράβι
bus *astiko* αστικό
plane *aeroplano* αεροπλάνο

I'd like ...
tha ithela ... Θα ήθελα ...
a return ticket
isitirio me εισιτήριο με
epistrofi επιστροφή
two tickets
dhio isitiria δυο εισιτήρια
a student's fare
fititiko isitirio φοιτητικό εισιτήριο
first class
proti thesi πρώτη θέση

Signs

ΕΙΣΟΔΟΣ	Entry
ΕΞΟΔΟΣ	Exit
ΩΘΗΣΑΤΕ	Push
ΣΥΡΑΤΕ	Pull
ΓΥΝΑΙΚΩΝ	Women (toilets)
ΑΝΔΡΩΝ	Men (toilets)
ΝΟΣΟΚΟΜΕΙΟ	Hospital
ΑΣΤΥΝΟΜΙΑ	Police
ΑΠΑΓΟΡΕΥΕΤΑΙ	Prohibited
ΕΙΣΙΤΗΡΙΑ	Tickets

economy
touristiki thesi τουριστική θέση

timetable
dhromologio δρομολόγιο
taxi
taxi ταξί

Where can I hire a car?
pou boro na nikyaso ena aftokinito?
Πού μπορώ να νοικιάσω ένα
αυτοκίνητο;

DIRECTIONS

How do I get to ...?
pos tha pao sto/ Πώς θα πάω στο/
sti ...? στη ...;
Where is ...?
pou ine ...? Πού είναι...;
Is it near?
ine konda? Είναι κοντά;
Is it far?
ine makria? Είναι μακριά;

straight ahead *efthia* ευθεία
left *aristera* αριστερά
right *dexia* δεξιά
behind *piso* πίσω
far *makria* μακριά
near *konda* κοντά
opposite *apenandi* απέναντι

Can you show me on the map?
borite na mou to dhixete sto harti?
Μπορείτε να μου το δείξετε
στο χάρτη;

AROUND TOWN

I'm looking for (the) ...
 psahno ya ...
 Ψάχνω για ...

bank	*trapeza*	τράπεζα
beach	*paralia*	παραλία
castle	*kastro*	κάστρο
church	*ekklisia*	εκκλησία
... embassy	*tin ... presvia*	την ... πρεσβεία
market	*aghora*	αγορά
museum	*musio*	μουσείο
police	*astynomia*	αστυνομία
post office	*tahydhromio*	ταχυδρομείο
ruins	*arhea*	αρχαία

I want to exchange some money.
 thelo na exaryiroso lefta
 Θέλω να εξαργυρώσω λεφτά.

ACCOMMODATION

Where is ...?
 pou ine ...? Πού είναι ...;
I'd like ...
 thelo ena ... Θέλω ένα ...

a cheap hotel
 ftino xenodohio φτηνό ξενοδοχείο
a clean room
 katharo καθαρό δωμάτιο
 dhomatio
a good hotel
 kalo xenodohio καλό ξενοδοχείο
a camp site
 kamping κάμπιγκ

single	*mono*	μονό
double	*dhiplo*	διπλό
room	*dhomatio*	δωμάτιο
with bathroom	*me banio*	με μπάνιο
key	*klidhi*	κλειδί

How much is it ...?
 poso kani ...? Πόσο κάνει ...;
per night
 ti vradhya τη βραδυά
for ... nights
 ya ... vradhyez για ... βραδυές

Emergencies

Help!
 voithya! Βοήθεια!
Police!
 astynomia! Αστυνομία!
There's been an accident!
 eyine atihima Εγινε ατύχημα!
Call a doctor!
 fonaxte ena yatro! Φωνάξτε ένα ιατρό!
Call an ambulance!
 tilefoniste ya asthenoforo! Τηλεφωνήστε για ασθενοφόρο!
I'm ill.
 ime arostos (m) Είμαι άρρωστος
 ime arosti (f) Είμαι άρρωστη
I'm lost.
 eho hathi Εχω χαθεί
Thief!
 klefti! Κλέφτη!
Go away!
 fiye! Φύγε!
I've been raped!
 me viase kapyos Με βίασε κάποιος!
I've been robbed!
 meklepse kapyos Μ'έκλεψε κάποιος!
Where are the toilets?
 pou ine i toualetez? Πού είναι οι τουαλέτες;

Is breakfast included?
 symberilamvani ke pro-ino? Συμπεριλαμβάνει και πρωϊνό;
May I see it?
 boro na to dho? Μπορώ να το δω;
Where is the bathroom?
 pou ine to banio? Πού είναι το μπάνιο;
It's expensive.
 ine akrivo Είναι ακριβό.
I'm leaving today.
 fevgho simera Φεύγω σήμερα.

FOOD & DRINKS

breakfast	*pro-ino*	πρωϊνό
lunch	*mesimvrino*	μεσημβρινό
dinner	*vradhyno*	βραδυνό
beef	*vodhino*	βοδινό
bread	*psomi*	ψωμί
beer	*byra*	μπύρα
cheese	*tyri*	τυρί
chicken	*kotopoulo*	κοτόπουλο
Greek coffee	*ellinikos kafes*	ελληνικός καφές
iced coffee	*frappe*	φραππέ
lamb	*arni*	αρνί
milk	*ghala*	γάλα
(mineral)	*(metalliko)*	(μεταλλικό)
water	*nero*	νερό
tea	*tsai*	τσάι
wine	*krasi*	κρασί

I'm a vegetarian.
   ime hortofaghos   Είμαι χορτοφάγος.

SHOPPING

How much is it?
   poso kani?
   Πόσο κάνει;
I'm just looking.
   aplos kitazo
   Απλώς κοιτάζω.
I'd like to buy ...
   thelo n'aghoraso ...
   Θέλω ν΄αγοράσω ...
Do you accept credit cards?
   pernete pistotikez kartez?
   Παίρνετε πιστωτικές κάρτες;
Could you lower the price?
   borite na mou kanete mya kaliteri timi?
   Μπορείτε να μου κάνετε μια καλύτερη τιμή;

TIME & DATES

What time is it?
   ti ora ine?   Τι ώρα είναι;

It's ...	*ine ...*	είναι ...
1 o'clock	*mia i ora*	μία η ώρα
2 o'clock	*dhio i ora*	δύο η ώρα
7.30	*efta ke misi*	εφτά και μισή
am	*to pro-i*	το πρωί
pm	*to apoyevma*	το απόγευμα
today	*simera*	σήμερα

tonight	*apopse*	απόψε
now	*tora*	τώρα
yesterday	*hthes*	χθες
tomorrow	*avrio*	αύριο

Sunday	*kyriaki*	Κυριακή
Monday	*dheftera*	Δευτέρα
Tuesday	*triti*	Τρίτη
Wednesday	*tetarti*	Τετάρτη
Thursday	*pempti*	Πέμπτη
Friday	*paraskevi*	Παρασκευή
Saturday	*savato*	Σάββατο

January	*ianouarios*	Ιανουάριος
February	*fevrouarios*	Φεβρουάριος
March	*martios*	Μάρτιος
April	*aprilios*	Απρίλιος
May	*maïos*	Μάιος
June	*iounios*	Ιούνιος
July	*ioulios*	Ιούλιος
August	*avghoustos*	Αύγουστος
September	*septemvrios*	Σεπτέμβριος
October	*oktovrios*	Οκτώβριος
November	*noemvrios*	Νοέμβριος
December	*dhekemvrios*	Δεκέμβριος

HEALTH

I need a doctor.
   hriazome yatro   Χρειάζομαι ιατρό.
Can you take me to hospital?
   borite na me pate sto nosokomio? Μπορείτε να με πάτε στο νοσοκομείο;
I want something for ...
   thelo kati ya ... Θέλω κάτι για ...
diarrhoea
   dhiaria   διάρροια
insect bites
   tsimbimata apo endoma τσιμπήματα από έντομα
travel sickness
   naftia taxidhiou ναυτία ταξιδιού

aspirin
   aspirini   ασπιρίνη
condoms
   profylaktika (kapotez) προφυλακτικά (καπότες)
contact lenses
   faki epafis φακοί επαφής
medical insurance
   yatriki asfalya ιατρική ασφάλεια

NUMBERS

0	*midhen*	μηδέν	20	*ikosi*	είκοσι
1	*enas*	ένας (m)	30	*trianda*	τριάντα
	mia	μία (f)	40	*saranda*	σαράντα
	ena	ένα (n)	50	*peninda*	πενήντα
2	*dhio*	δύο	60	*exinda*	εξήντα
3	*tris*	τρεις (m & f)	70	*evdhominda*	εβδομήντα
	tria	τρία (n)	80	*oghdhonda*	ογδόντα
4	*teseris*	τέσσερεις (m & f)	90	*eneninda*	ενενήντα
	tesera	τέσσερα (n)	100	*ekato*	εκατό
5	*pende*	πέντε	1000	*hilii*	χίλιοι (m)
6	*exi*	έξη		*hiliez*	χίλιες (f)
7	*epta*	επτά		*hilia*	χίλια (n)
8	*ohto*	οχτώ			
9	*enea*	εννέα			
10	*dheka*	δέκα			

one million
    ena ekatomyrio   ένα εκατομμύριο

Glossary

acropolis – highest point of an ancient city

AEK – Athens football club

agia (f), agios (m) – saint

agora – commercial area of an ancient city; shopping precinct in modern Greece

amphora – large two-handled vase in which wine or oil was kept

Archaic period – (800–480 BC) period in which the city-states emerged from the 'dark age' and traded their way to wealth and power

architrave – part of the *entablature* which rests on the columns of a temple

Asia Minor – the Aegean littoral of Turkey centred around İzmir but also including İstanbul; formerly populated by Greeks

basilica – early Christian church

bouzouki – stringed lute-like instrument associated with rembetika music

buttress – support built against the outside of a wall

Byzantine Empire – characterised by the merging of Hellenistic culture and Christianity and named after Byzantium, the city on the Bosphorus which became the capital of the Roman Empire in 324 AD; the Byzantine Empire dissolved after the fall of Constantinople to the Turks in 1453

caïque – small, sturdy fishing boat often used to carry passengers

capital – top of a column

cella – room in a temple where the cult statue stood

choregos – wealthy citizen who financed choral and dramatic performances

city-states – states comprising a sovereign city and its dependencies; the city-states of Athens and Sparta were famous rivals

classical Greece – period in which the city-states reached the height of their wealth and power after the defeat of the Persians in the 5th century BC

Corinthian – order of Greek architecture recognisable by columns with bell-shaped *capitals* with sculpted elaborate ornaments based on acanthus leaves

cornice – the upper part of the *entablature*, extending beyond the frieze

crypt – lowest part of a church, often a burial chamber

dark age – (1200-800 BC) period in which Greece was under *Dorian*

dimarhio – town hall

domatio (s), domatia (pl) – room; a cheap accommodation option available in most tourist areas

Dorians – Hellenic warriors who invaded Greece around 1200 BC, demolishing the city-states and destroying the Mycenaean civilisation; heralded Greece's 'dark age', when the artistic and cultural advancements of the Mycenaeans and Minoans were abandoned; the Dorians later developed into land-holding aristocrats which encouraged the resurgence of independent city-states led by wealthy aristocrats

Doric – order of Greek architecture characterised by a column which has no base, a *fluted* shaft and a relatively plain capital, when compared with the flourishes evident on *Ionic* and *Corinthian* capitals

ELPA – Elliniki Leshi Periigiseon & Aftokinitou; Greek motoring and touring club

ELTA – Ellinika Tahydromia; Greek post office

entablature – part of a temple between the tops of the columns and the roof

EOT – Ellinikos Organismos Tourismou; national tourism organisation which has offices in most major towns

estiatorio – restaurant serving ready-made food as well as a la carte dishes

ET – Elliniki Tileorasi; state television company

evzones – famous border guards from the northern Greek village of Evzoni; they also guard the Parliament building

frappé – iced coffee

frieze – part of the *entablature* which is above the *architrave*
frontistiria – intensive coaching colleges

galaktopoleio (s), galaktopoleia (pl) – a shop which sells dairy products
Geometric period – (1200-800 BC) period characterised by pottery decorated with geometric designs; sometimes referred to as Greece's `dark age'
gymnasio – high school

Hellas, Ellas or Ellada – the Greek name for Greece
Hellenistic period – prosperous, influential period of Greek civilisation ushered in by Alexander the Great's empire-building and lasting until the Roman sacking of Corinth in 146 BC
hora – main town (usually on an island)

iconostasis – altar screen embellished with icons
Ionic – order of Greek architecture characterised by a column with truncated flutes and capitals with ornaments resembling scrolls

kafeneio (s), kafeneia (pl) – traditional (male-only) coffee house
kafeteria – upmarket *kafeneio*, mainly for younger people
KKE – Kommounistiko Komma Elladas; Greek communist party
klepht – independence fighter
kore – female statue of the Archaic period; see *kouros*
kouros – male statue of the Archaic period, characterised by a stiff body posture and enigmatic smile
KTEL – Kino Tamio Ispraxeon Leoforion; national bus cooperative; runs all long-distance bus services

libation – in ancient Greece, wine or food which was offered to the gods
lykeio – senior high school

meltemi – north-easterly wind which blows during the summer

metope – the sculpted section of a *Doric* frieze
meze (s), mezedes (pl) – appetiser
Middle Age – see *Archaic* period
moni – monastery or convent
Mycenaean civilisation – (1900-1100 BC) first great civilisation of the Greek mainland, characterised by powerful independent city-states ruled by kings

narthex – porch of a church
nave – aisle of a church
Nea Dimokratia – New Democracy; conservative political party
necropolis – literally `city of the dead'; ancient cemetery
nefos – cloud; usually used to refer to pollution in Athens
nomos – prefectures into which the regions and island groups of Greece are divided
nymphaeum – in ancient Greece, building containing a fountain and often dedicated to nymphs

OA – Olympiaki Aeroporia or Olympic Airways; Greece's national airline and major domestic air carrier
odeion – ancient Greek indoor theatre
odos – street
OSE – Organismos Sidirodromon Ellados; Greek railways organisation
OTE – Organismos Tilepikinonion Ellados; Greece's major telecommunications carrier
oud – a bulbous, stringed instrument with a sharply raked-back head
ouzeri (s), ouzeria (pl) – place which serves *ouzo* and light snacks
ouzo – a distilled spirit made from grapes and flavoured with aniseed

Panagia – Mother of God; name frequently used for churches
Pantokrator – painting or mosaic of Christ in the centre of the dome of a Byzantine church
paralia – waterfront
PASOK – Panellinio Sosialistiko Komma; Greek socialist party
pediment – triangular section (often filled with sculpture) above the columns, found

at the front and back of a classical Greek temple

periptero (s), periptera (pl) – street kiosk

peristyle – columns surrounding a building (usually a temple) or courtyard

plateia – square

Politiki Anixi – Political Spring; centrist political party

PRO-PO – Prognostiko Podosferou; Greek football pools

propylon (s), propylaia (pl) – main entrance to an ancient city or sanctuary; a propylon had one gateway and a propylaia more than one

psarotaverna – taverna specialising in seafood

psistaria – restaurant serving grilled food

rembetika – blues songs commonly associated with the underworld of the 1920s

retsina – resinated white wine

sacristy – room attached to a church where sacred vessels etc are kept

sandouri – hammered dulcimer from Asia Minor

spilia – cave

stele (s), stelae (pl) – grave stone which stands upright

stoa – long colonnaded building, usually in an *agora*; used as a meeting place and shelter in ancient Greece

tanbura – family of instruments characterised by a long neck, including the bouzouki, the saz, the tandura and the bulgari.

taverna – traditional restaurant which serves food and wine

tholos – Mycenaean tomb shaped like a beehive

triglyph – sections of a *Doric frieze* between the *metopes*

tsipouro – distilled spirit made from grapes

vaulted – having an arched roof, normally of brick or stone

volute – spiral decoration on *Ionic* capitals

zaharoplasteio (s), zaharoplasteia (pl) – patisserie; shop selling cakes, chocolates, sweets and, sometimes, alcoholic drinks

LONELY PLANET

You already know that Lonely Planet produces more than this one guidebook, but you might not be aware of the other products we have on this region. Here is a selection of titles that you may want to check out as well:

Crete Condensed
ISBN 1 86450 042 5
US$9.95 • UK£5.99

Europe phrasebook
ISBN 1 86450 224 X
US$8.99 • UK£4.99

Greek phrasebook
ISBN 0 86442 683 6
US$7.99 • UK£4.50

Read this First: Europe
ISBN 1 86450 136 7
US$14.99 • UK£8.99

Greece
ISBN 0 86442 682 8
US$19.95 • UK£12.99

Greek Islands
ISBN 1 86450 109 X
US$17.95 • UK£11.99

The Olive Grove
ISBN 0 86442 459 0
US$12.95 • UK£6.99

Corfu & the Ionians
ISBN 1 86450 073 5
US$14.95 • UK£8.99

Crete
ISBN 1 86450 074 3
US$15.95 • UK£9.99

Europe on a shoestring
ISBN 1 86450 150 2
US$24.99 • UK£14.99

Mediterranean Europe
ISBN 1 86450 154 5
US$27.99 • UK£15.99

Western Europe
ISBN 1 86450 163 4
US$27.99 • UK£15.99

Available wherever books are sold

LONELY PLANET

Guides by Region

onely Planet is known worldwide for publishing practical, reliable and no-nonsense travel information in our guides and on our Web site. The Lonely Planet list covers just about every accessible part of the world. Currently there are 16 series: Travel guides, Shoestring guides, Condensed guides, Phrasebooks, Read This First, Healthy Travel, Walking guides, Cycling guides, Watching Wildlife guides, Pisces Diving & Snorkeling guides, City Maps, Road Atlases, Out to Eat, World Food, Journeys travel literature and Pictorials.

AFRICA Africa on a shoestring • Cairo • Cairo City Map • Cape Town • Cape Town City Map • East Africa • Egypt • Egyptian Arabic phrasebook • Ethiopia, Eritrea & Djibouti • Ethiopian Amharic phrasebook • The Gambia & Senegal • Healthy Travel Africa • Kenya • Malawi • Morocco • Moroccan Arabic phrasebook • Mozambique • Read This First: Africa • South Africa, Lesotho & Swaziland • Southern Africa • Southern Africa Road Atlas • Swahili phrasebook • Tanzania, Zanzibar & Pemba • Trekking in East Africa • Tunisia • Watching Wildlife East Africa • Watching Wildlife Southern Africa • West Africa • World Food Morocco • Zimbabwe, Botswana & Namibia
Travel Literature: Mali Blues: Traveling to an African Beat • The Rainbird: A Central African Journey • Songs to an African Sunset: A Zimbabwean Story

AUSTRALIA & THE PACIFIC Auckland • Australia • Australian phrasebook • Australia Road Atlas • Cycling Australia • Cycling New Zealand • Fiji • Fijian phrasebook • Healthy Travel Australia, NZ & the Pacific • Islands of Australia's Great Barrier Reef • Melbourne • Melbourne City Map • Micronesia • New Caledonia • New South Wales • New Zealand • Northern Territory • Outback Australia • Out to Eat – Melbourne • Out to Eat – Sydney • Papua New Guinea • Pidgin phrasebook • Queensland • Rarotonga & the Cook Islands • Samoa • Solomon Islands • South Australia • South Pacific • South Pacific phrasebook • Sydney • Sydney City Map • Sydney Condensed • Tahiti & French Polynesia • Tasmania • Tonga • Tramping in New Zealand • Vanuatu • Victoria • Walking in Australia • Watching Wildlife Australia • Western Australia
Travel Literature: Islands in the Clouds: Travels in the Highlands of New Guinea • Kiwi Tracks: A New Zealand Journey • Sean & David's Long Drive

CENTRAL AMERICA & THE CARIBBEAN Bahamas, Turks & Caicos • Baja California • Belize, Guatemala & Yucatán • Bermuda • Central America on a shoestring • Costa Rica • Costa Rica Spanish phrasebook • Cuba • Dominican Republic & Haiti • Eastern Caribbean • Guatemala • Havana • Healthy Travel Central & South America • Jamaica • Mexico • Mexico City • Panama • Puerto Rico • Read This First: Central & South America • World Food Mexico • Yucatán
Travel Literature: Green Dreams: Travels in Central America

EUROPE Amsterdam • Amsterdam City Map • Amsterdam Condensed • Andalucía • Austria • Baltic States phrasebook • Barcelona • Barcelona City Map • Belgium & Luxembourg • Berlin • Berlin City Map • Britain • British phrasebook • Brussels, Bruges & Antwerp • Brussels City Map • Budapest • Budapest City Map • Canary Islands • Central Europe • Central Europe phrasebook • Copenhagen • Corfu & the Ionians • Corsica • Crete • Crete Condensed • Croatia • Cycling Britain • Cycling France • Cyprus • Czech & Slovak Republics • Denmark • Dublin • Dublin City Map • Eastern Europe • Eastern Europe phrasebook • Edinburgh • England • Estonia, Latvia & Lithuania • Europe on a shoestring • Europe phrasebook • Finland • Florence • France • Frankfurt Condensed • French phrasebook • Georgia, Armenia & Azerbaijan • Germany • German phrasebook • Greece • Greek Islands • Greek phrasebook • Hungary • Iceland, Greenland & the Faroe Islands • Ireland • Italian phrasebook • Italy • Krakow • Lisbon • The Loire • London • London City Map • London Condensed • Madrid • Malta • Mediterranean Europe • Mediterranean Europe phrasebook • Moscow • Munich • Netherlands • Normandy • Norway • Out to Eat – London • Out to Eat – Paris • Paris • Paris City Map • Paris Condensed • Poland • Polish phrasebook • Portugal • Portuguese phrasebook • Prague • Prague City Map • Provence & the Côte d'Azur • Read This First: Europe • Rhodes & the Dodecanese • Romania & Moldova • Rome • Rome City Map • Russia, Ukraine & Belarus • Russian phrasebook • Scandinavian & Baltic Europe • Scandinavian phrasebook • Scotland • Sicily • Slovenia • South-West France • Spain • Spanish phrasebook • St Petersburg • St Petersburg City Map • Sweden • Switzerland • Tuscany • Ukrainian phrasebook • Venice • Vienna • Walking in Britain • Walking in France • Walking in Ireland • Walking in Italy • Walking in Spain • Walking in Switzerland • Western Europe • World Food France • World Food Ireland • World Food Italy • World Food Spain
Travel Literature: After Yugoslavia • Love and War in the Apennines • The Olive Grove: Travels in Greece • On the Shores of the Mediterranean • Round Ireland in Low Gear • A Small Place in Italy

LONELY PLANET

Mail Order

Lonely Planet products are distributed worldwide. They are also available by mail order from Lonely Planet, so if you have difficulty finding a title please write to us. North and South American residents should write to 150 Linden St, Oakland, CA 94607, USA; European and African residents should write to 10a Spring Place, London NW5 3BH, UK; and residents of other countries to Locked Bag 1, Footscray, Victoria 3011, Australia.

INDIAN SUBCONTINENT & THE INDIAN OCEAN Bangladesh • Bengali phrasebook • Bhutan • Delhi • Goa • Healthy Travel Asia & India • Hindi & Urdu phrasebook • India • Indian Himalaya • Karakoram Highway • Kerala • Madagascar • Maldives • Mauritius, Réunion & Seychelles • Mumbai (Bombay) • Nepal • Nepali phrasebook • Pakistan • Rajasthan • Read This First: Asia & India • South India • Sri Lanka • Sri Lanka phrasebook • Tibet • Tibetan phrasebook • Trekking in the Indian Himalaya • Trekking in the Karakoram & Hindukush • Trekking in the Nepal Himalaya
Travel Literature: The Age of Kali: Indian Travels and Encounters • Hello Goodnight: A Life of Goa • In Rajasthan • Maverick in Madagascar • A Season in Heaven: True Tales from the Road to Kathmandu • Shopping for Buddhas • A Short Walk in the Hindu Kush • Slowly Down the Ganges

MIDDLE EAST & CENTRAL ASIA Bahrain, Kuwait & Qatar • Central Asia • Central Asia phrasebook • Dubai • Farsi (Persian) phrasebook • Hebrew phrasebook • Iran • Israel & the Palestinian Territories • Istanbul • Istanbul City Map • Istanbul to Cairo • Istanbul to Kathmandu • Jerusalem • Jerusalem City Map • Jordan • Lebanon • Middle East • Oman & the United Arab Emirates • Syria • Turkey • Turkish phrasebook • World Food Turkey • Yemen
Travel Literature: Black on Black: Iran Revisited • The Gates of Damascus • Kingdom of the Film Stars: Journey into Jordan

NORTH AMERICA Alaska • Boston • Boston City Map • Boston Condensed • British Columbia • California & Nevada • California Condensed • Canada • Chicago • Chicago City Map • Florida • Great Lakes • Hawaii • Hiking in Alaska • Hiking in the USA • Las Vegas • Los Angeles • Los Angeles City Map • Louisiana & the Deep South • Miami • Miami City Map • Montreal • New England • New Orleans • New York City • New York City City Map • New York City Condensed • New York, New Jersey & Pennsylvania • Oahu • Out to Eat – San Francisco • Pacific Northwest • Rocky Mountains • San Francisco • San Francisco City Map • Seattle • Southwest • Texas • Toronto • USA • USA phrasebook • Vancouver • Virginia & the Capital Region • Washington, DC • Washington, DC City Map • World Food New Orleans
Travel Literature: Caught Inside: A Surfer's Year on the California Coast • Drive Thru America

NORTH-EAST ASIA Beijing • Beijing City Map • Cantonese phrasebook • China • Hiking in Japan • Hong Kong • Hong Kong City Map • Hong Kong Condensed • Hong Kong, Macau & Guangzhou • Japan • Japanese phrasebook • Korea • Korean phrasebook • Kyoto • Mandarin phrasebook • Mongolia • Mongolian phrasebook • Seoul • Shanghai • South-West China • Taiwan • Tokyo • World Food Hong Kong
Travel Literature: In Xanadu: A Quest • Lost Japan

SOUTH AMERICA Argentina, Uruguay & Paraguay • Bolivia • Brazil • Brazilian phrasebook • Buenos Aires • Chile & Easter Island • Colombia • Ecuador & the Galapagos Islands • Healthy Travel Central & South America • Latin American Spanish phrasebook • Peru • Quechua phrasebook • Read This First: Central & South America • Rio de Janeiro • Rio de Janeiro City Map • Santiago de Chile • South America on a shoestring • Trekking in the Patagonian Andes • Venezuela
Travel Literature: Full Circle: A South American Journey

SOUTH-EAST ASIA Bali & Lombok • Bangkok • Bangkok City Map • Burmese phrasebook • Cambodia • Hanoi • Healthy Travel Asia & India • Hill Tribes phrasebook • Ho Chi Minh City • Indonesia • Indonesian phrasebook • Indonesia's Eastern Islands • Java • Lao phrasebook • Laos • Malay phrasebook • Malaysia, Singapore & Brunei • Myanmar (Burma) • Philippines • Pilipino (Tagalog) phrasebook • Read This First: Asia & India • Singapore • Singapore City Map • South-East Asia on a shoestring • South-East Asia phrasebook • Thailand • Thailand's Islands & Beaches • Thailand, Vietnam, Laos & Cambodia Road Atlas • Thai phrasebook • Vietnam • Vietnamese phrasebook • World Food Thailand • World Food Vietnam

ALSO AVAILABLE: Antarctica • The Arctic • The Blue Man: Tales of Travel, Love and Coffee • Brief Encounters: Stories of Love, Sex & Travel • Chasing Rickshaws • The Last Grain Race • Lonely Planet ... On the Edge: Adventurous Escapades from Around the World • Lonely Planet Unpacked • Not the Only Planet: Science Fiction Travel Stories • Sacred India • Travel Photography: A Guide to Taking Better Pictures • Travel with Children

Index

Text

Places to Stay

Bold indicates maps.

Places to Eat

Boxed Text

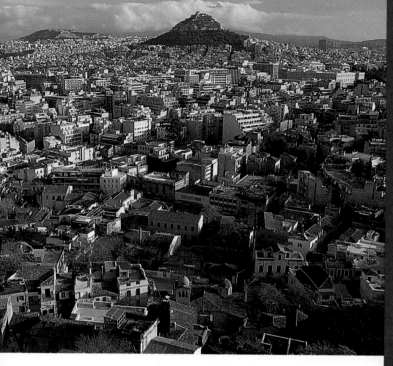

Athens Map Section

MAP A ATHENS METRO SYSTEM

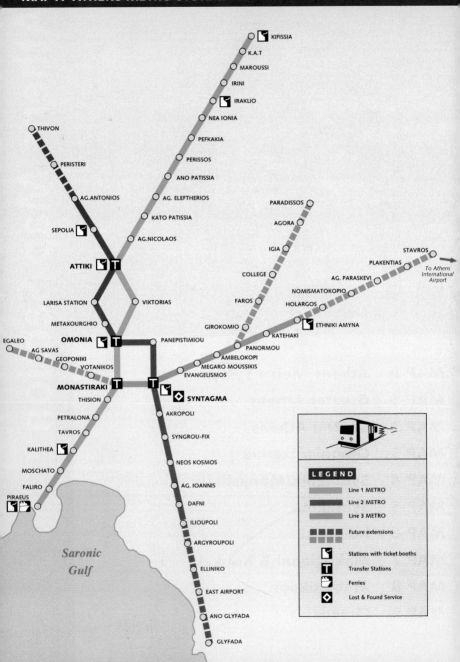

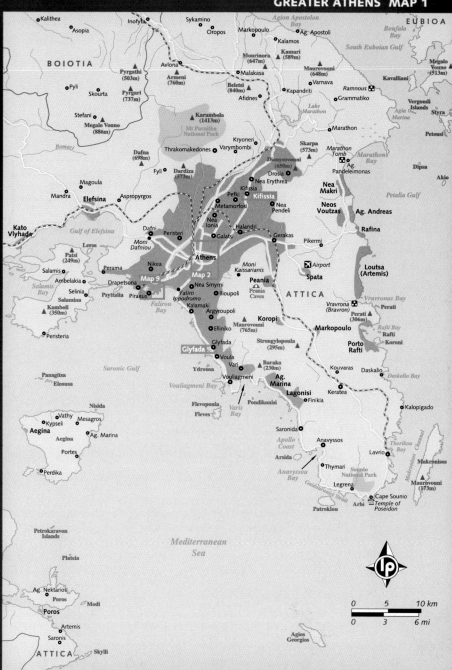

EUBOIA

Agion Apostolon Bay

Boufalo Bay

South Euboian Gulf

Kalithea

Asopia

Inofyta

Sykamino

Oropos

Markopoulo

Ag. Apostoli

Kalamos

BOIOTIA

Pyli

Skourta

Pyrgathi
(503m)

Armeni
(760m)

Pyrgari
(737m)

Avlona

Malakasa

Mourinora
(647m)

Kamari
(589m)

Maurovouni
(648m)

Megalo Vouno
(513m)

Kavalliani

Beletsi
(840m)

Afidnes

Kapandriti

Varnava

Ramnous

Vergondi Islands

Styra

Stefani

Megalo Vouno
(886m)

Karambola
(1413m)

Mt Parnitha
National Park

Kryoneri

Varymbombi

Skarpa
(573m)

Marathon
Tomb

Ag.
Pandeleimonas

Agia Marina

Marathon Bay

Petousi

Akio

Dipsa

Magoula

Mandra

Elefsina

Aspropyrgos

Dafna
(698m)

Thrakomakedones

Dardiza
(573m)

Fyli

Dionysovouni
(650m)

Drosia

Nea Erythrea

Kifissia

Pefki

Nea
Makri

Petalia Gulf

Kato
Vlyhada

Gulf of Elefsina

Leros

Dafni

Peristeri

Moni
Dafniou

Metamorfos

Nea
Ionia

Galatsi

Kifissia

Nea
Pendeli

Neos
Voutzas

Ag. Andreas

Patsi
(249m)

Perama

Nikea

Athens

Halandri

Gerakas

Pikermi

Rafina

Salamis

Ambelakia

Drapetsona

Map 9

Nea Smyrni

Moni
Kaissarianis

Airport

Spata

Loutsa
(Artemis)

Salamina
Bay

Selinia

Salamina

Psyttalia

Piraeus

Map 2

Peania

Peania
Caves

ATTICA

Vravronas Bay

Perati

Kamboli
(350m)

Faliro
Ippodromo

Ilioupoli

Faliron
Bay

Kalamaki

Argyroupoli

Koropi

Maurovouni
(765m)

Vravrona
(Bravron)

Perati
(306m)

Rafti Bay

Rafti

Koroni

Peristeria

Elliniko

Markopoulo

Porto
Rafti

Glyfada

Glyfada

Strongylopoula
(295m)

Daskalio

Daskalio Bay

Kalopigado

Saronic Gulf

Panagitsa
Eleousa

Ydrousa

Voula

Vari

Barako
(230m)

Kouvaras

Keratea

Vouliagmeni

Ag.
Marina

Thorikou Bay

Makronisos

Flevopoula
Fleves

Vouliagmeni Bay

Varis
Bay

Pondikonisi

Lagonisi

Finikia

Nisida

Vathy

Kypseli

Mesagros

Aegina

Ag. Marina

Portes

Aegina

Saronida

Anavyssos

Apollo
Coast

Arsida

Thymari

Lavrio

Maurovouni
(173m)

Perdika

Anavyssou
Bay

Sounio
National Park

Legrena

Gaidharonisi Straits

Cape Sounio

Temple of
Poseidon

Petrokaravon
Islands

Patroklou

Arhi

Mediterranean
Sea

Platia

Ag. Nektarios
Poros

Modi

Poros

Artemis

Saronis

ATTICA

Skylli

Agios
Georgios

0   5   10 km

0   3   6 mi

MAP 2 CENTRAL ATHENS

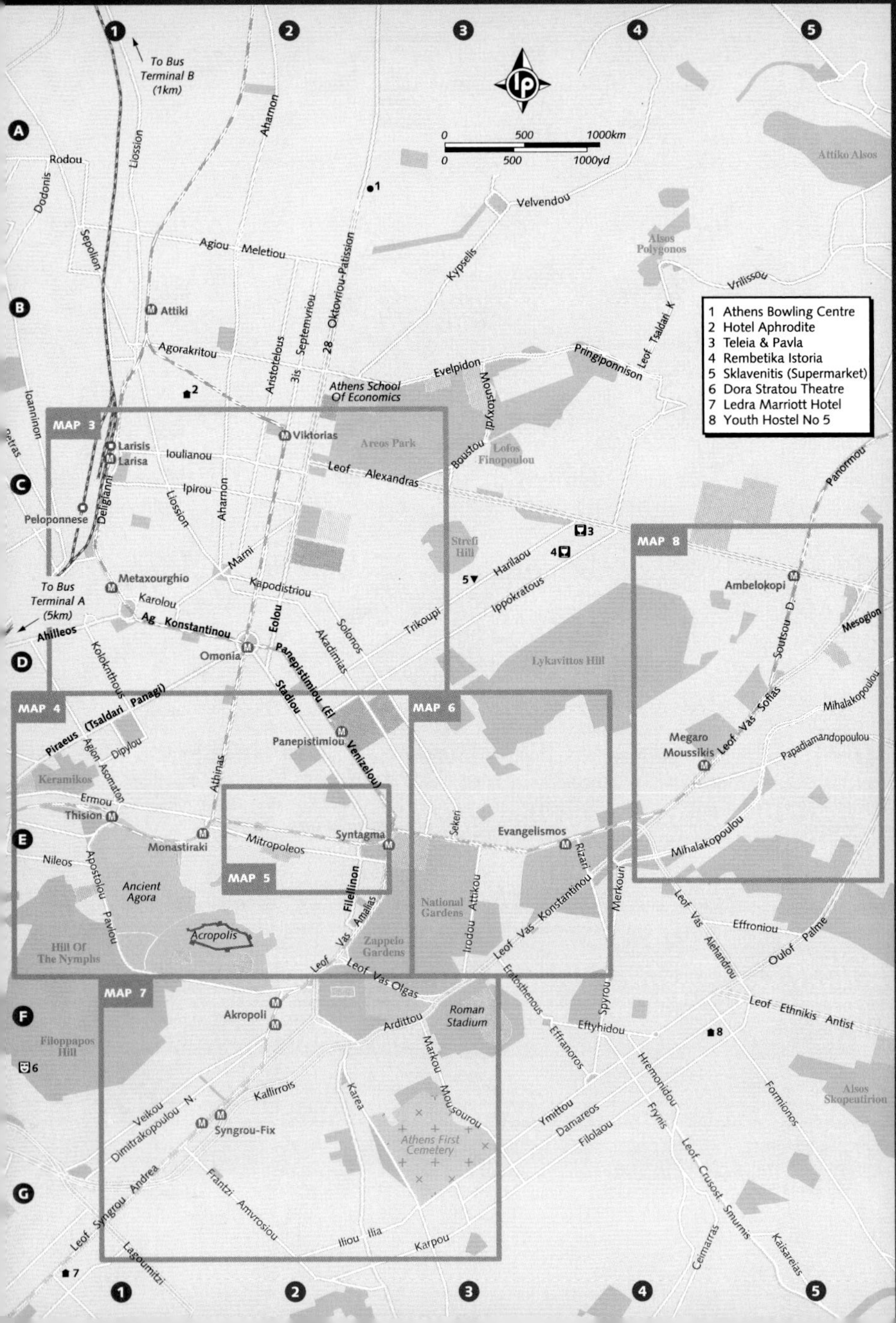

1 Athens Bowling Centre
2 Hotel Aphrodite
3 Teleia & Pavla
4 Rembetika Istoria
5 Sklavenitis (Supermarket)
6 Dora Stratou Theatre
7 Ledra Marriott Hotel
8 Youth Hostel No 5

To Bus Terminal B (1km)

To Bus Terminal A (5km)

Rodou
Dodonis
Sepolion
Llosion
Ioanninou
Ahamon
Agiou Meletiou
Attiki
Agorakritou
Aristotelous
3is Septemvriou
28 Oktovriou-Patission
Athens School Of Economics
Velvendou
Kypselis
Alsos Polygonos
Vrilissou
Attiko Alsos
Leof Taklari K
Pringiponnison
Evelpidon
Moustoxydi
Boutou
Lofos Finopoulou
Areos Park
Viktorias
Leof. Alexandras
MAP 3
Larisis
Larisa
Ioulianou
Ipirou
Ilission
Aharnon
Peloponnese
Metaxourghio
Marni
Kapodistriou
Strefi Hill
Harilaou
Ippokratous
MAP 8
Panormou
Ambelokopi
Mesogion
Soutsou D
Leof Vas Sofias
Mihalakopoulou
Papadiamandopoulou
Karolou
Ahilleos
Kolokthrous
Ag Konstantinou
Folou
Akadimias
Solonos
Trikoupi
Omonia
Panepistimiou (El Venizelou)
Stadiou
Lykavittos Hill
Megaro Moussikis
Mihalakopoulou
MAP 4
Piraeus (Tsaldari Panagi)
Agion Asomaton
Dipylou
Keramikos
Ermou
Thision
Athinas
Panepistimiou Venizelou
Nileos
Apostolou Pavlou
Monastiraki
Mitropoleos
Syntagma
Seleri
MAP 6
Evangelismos
Rizari
Merkouri
Leof Vas Aeliandrou
Effroniou
Oulof Palme
MAP 5
Ancient Agora
Hill Of The Nymphs
Acropolis
Filellinon
Leof. Vas Amalias
National Gardens
Iroou Attikou
Leof Vas Konstantinou
Eratosthenous
Spyrou
Leof Ethnikis Antist
Zappeio Gardens
Leof. Vas Olgas
MAP 7
Filoppapos Hill
Akropoli
Ardittou
Roman Stadium
Markou Mousourou
Eftyhidou
Eftranoros
Hremonidou
Frynis
Formionos
Alsos Skopeutirion
Veikou
Dimitrakopoulou N.
Kallirrois
Karea
Syngrou-Fix
Athens First Cemetery
Ymittou
Damareos
Filolaou
Leof Crusot Smurns
Ceinarras
Keisareias
Leof Syngrou
Andrea
Frantzi Amvrosiou
Iliou Ilia
Karpou
Lagoumitzi

Greek flag flies over Acropolis

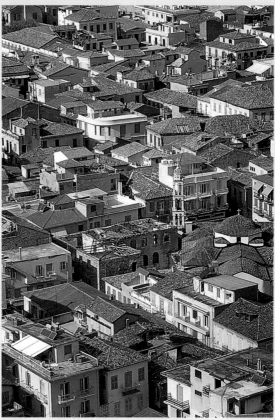
Rooftops of Nafplio from Palamidi Fortress

Temple of Olympian Zeus

The hustle and bustle of Athens' new metro system, Syntagma

Bags, bags and more bags

MAP 3 OMONIA & EXARHIA

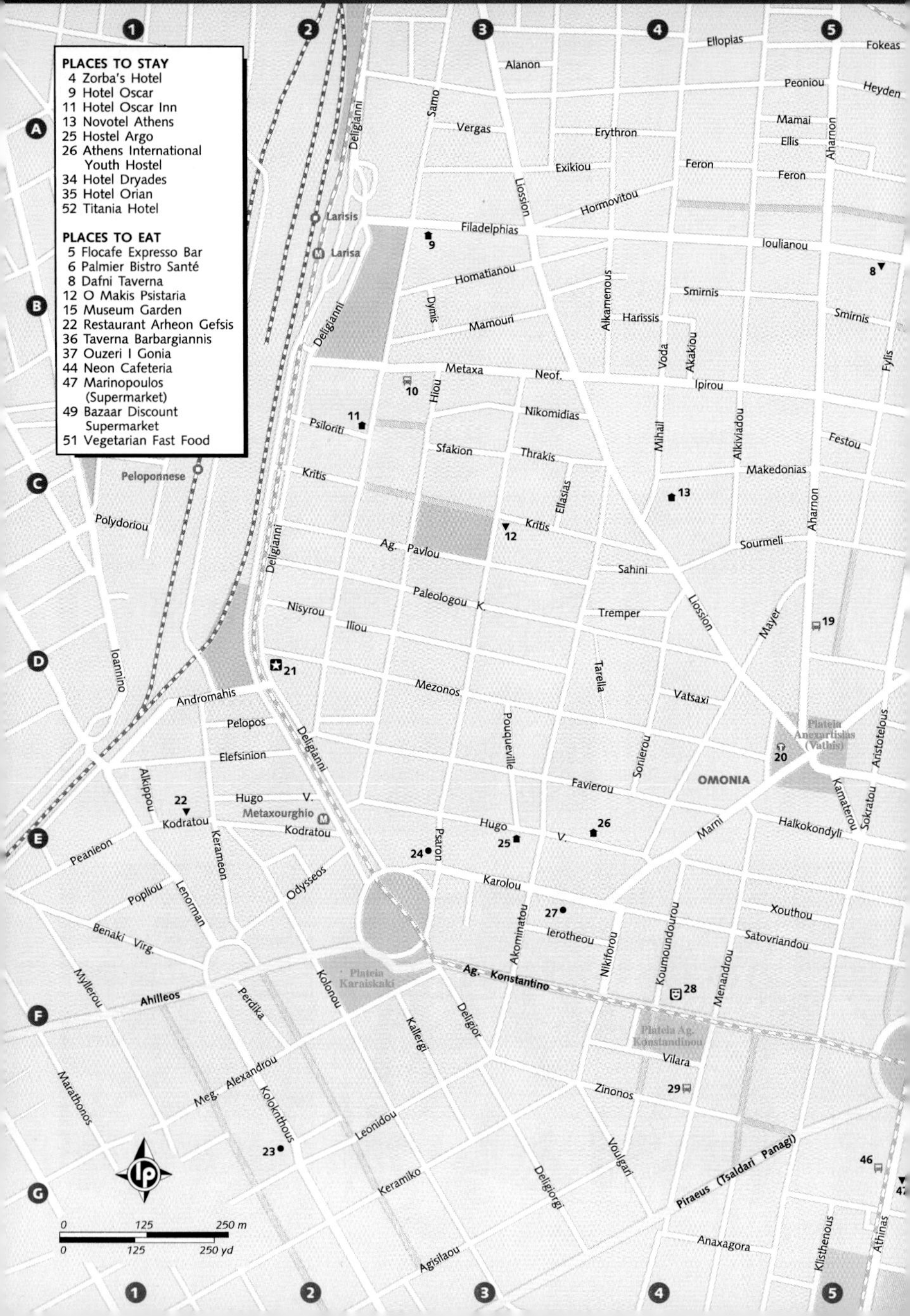

① **②** **③** **④** **⑤**

Ellopias
Fokeas
Alanon
Peoniou
Heyden
Samo
Mamaï
Vergas
Erythron
Ellis
Aharnon
Deligianni
Exikiou
Feron
Feron
Liossion
Hormovitou
Ioulianou
Larisis
Filadelphias
9
8
Larisa
Homatianou
Smirnis
Dymis
Mamouri
Harissis
Smirnis
Metaxa
Neof.
Voda
Fylis
Deligianni
10
Hiou
Akakiou
Alkamenous
Nikomidias
Ipirou
Festou
Psiloriti
11
Sfakion
Thrakis
Mihail
Makedonias
Kritis
Eliasias
Alkiviadou
Peloponnese
Kritis
13
Polydoriou
Ag. Pavlou
12
Sahini
Sourmeli
Aharnon
Paleologou K.
Tremper
Nisyrou
Iliou
Liossion
Mayer
19
Ioannino
Mezonos
Tarella
Vatsaxi
21
Andromahis
Pouqueville
Sonierou
Pelopos
Plateia
Anexartisias
(Vathis)
Elefsinion
Favierou
OMONIA
20
Alkipou
22
Hugo   V.
Metaxourghio
Hugo
26
Marni
Halkokondyli
Kodratou
Keranteon
Kodratou
V.
Peanleon
25
Xouthou
Popliou
Lenorman
Odysseos
24
Paxon
Karolou
Satovriandou
Benaki Virg.
27
Ierotheou
Nikiforou
Koumoundourou
Menandrou
Myllerou
Plateia
Karaiskaki
Ag.   Konstantino
28
Ahilleos
Perdika
Deligior
Plateia Ag.
Konstantinou
Marathonos
Meg. Alexandrou
Kolokithous
Kallergi
Vilara
Zinonos
29
46
23
Leonidou
Deligeorgi
Voulgari
Klisthenous
Keramiko
Piraeus (Tsaldari Panagi)
Athinas
Agsilaou
Anaxagora

0   125   250 m
0   125   250 yd

OTHER
1 Mavromateon Bus Terminal (Marathon & Rafina)
2 Athens School of Economics
3 OTE main office
7 Mavromateon Bus Terminal (Southern Attica)
10 Trolley Stop for Train
14 Museum Internet Café
16 USIT-ETHOS Travel
17 Flocafe
18 Rodon Club
19 Buses to Mt Parnitha
20 Public Toilets
21 Traffic Police
23 Sun Laundry
24 Laundry Self Service
27 OSE Office
28 National Theatre
29 Bus No 051 to Bus Terminal A
30 First-aid Advice
31 Astor Internet Cafe

32 Athens Polytehnio
33 National Archaeological Museum
38 Karvouras
39 AN Club
40 Fairytale
41 The Web Café
42 Bus A7 to Kifissia; 224 to Moni Kaissarianis
43 Minion Department Store
45 Brazita Coffee
46 Bus No 049 to Piraeus
48 Athens' Central Post Office
50 Metropolis Music Shop
53 Ideal (Cinema)
54 Bits & Bytes Internet Café
55 Olympia Theatre
56 Xenoglosso Vivlopoleio
57 Road Editions
58 Cafe4U
59 Pandora Music Shop
60 French Institute

MAP 4 SYNTAGMA & MONASTIRAKI

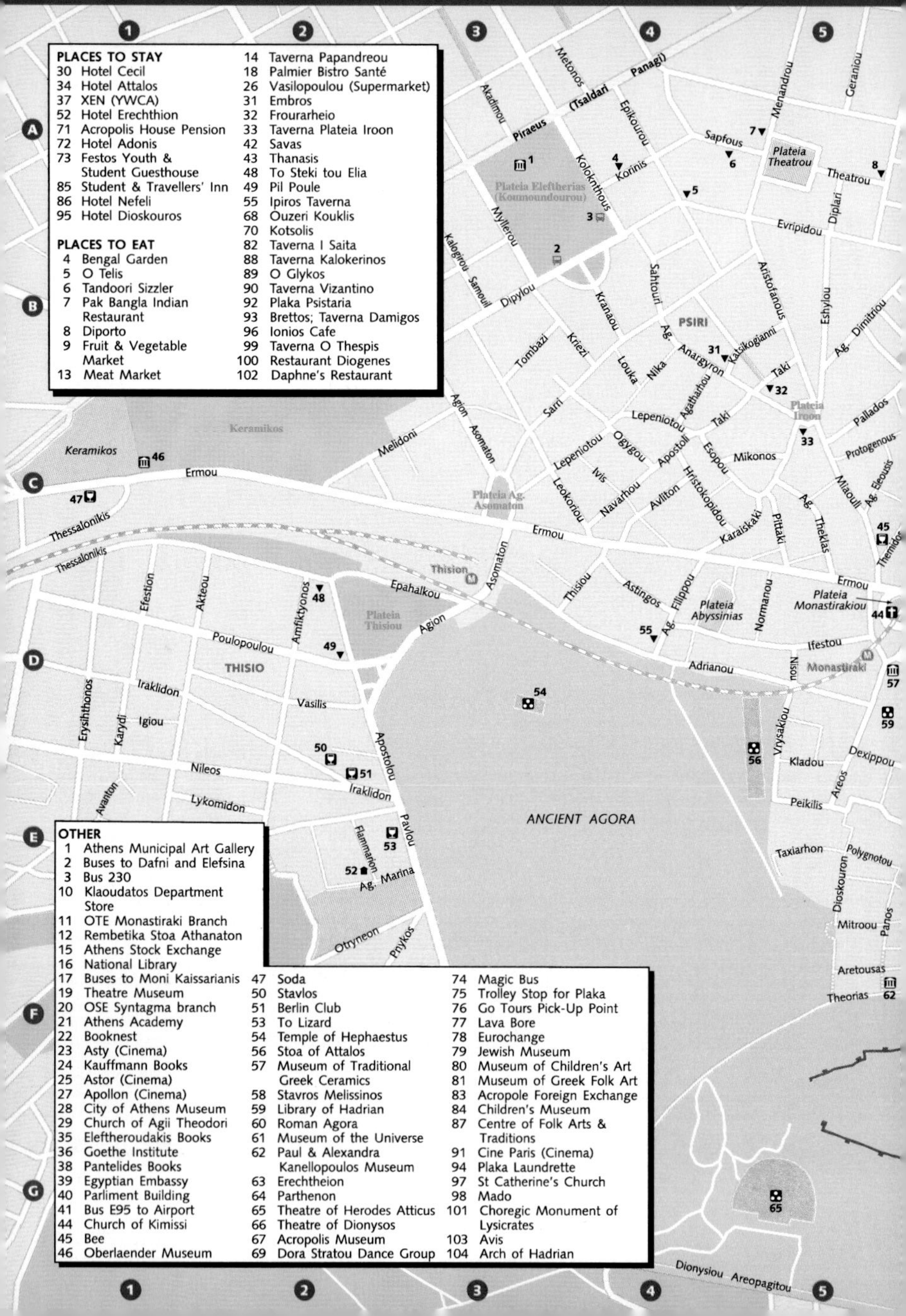

Panagi
Metonos
Piraeus (Tsaldari)
Keramikos
Ermou
Thessalonikis
Thessalonikis
THISIO
Iraklidon
Igiou
Nileos
Lykomidon
ANCIENT AGORA
PSIRI
Plateia Iroon
Plateia Monastirakiou
Monastiraki
Ifestou
Adrianou
Kladou
Dexippou
Peikilis
Taxiarhon
Mitroou
Aretousas
Theorias
Dionysiou Areopagitou

MAP 5

A
B
C
D
E
F
G

6 **7** **8** **9** **10**

Iktinou
Dimarhio
Kratinou
Klisthenous
Arsak
Akadimias
Asklipiou
Kapldnon
11
Athinas
Streit
10
Pesmazoglou
Panepistimiou (El. Venizelou)
Ippokratous
Akadimias
16
Fereou
17
18
Armodiou
12
Sofokleous
15
Stadiou
Riga
Athens University
Massalias
Solonos
Aristogeitonos
13
Eolou
Panepistimiou
M
19
14
Aristidou
Koral
23
Akadimias
21
30
Polykliltou
Dragatsaniou
Plateia Klafthmonos
22
Sina
20
Visaonaos
Kalamda
Vlahava
Praxitelous
24
Omirou
36
Plateia Karamanou
Hrysospiliotissis
Ag. Markou
29
25
Edouardou Lo
Athinas
Kalit
Miltiadou
Papparigopoulou
28
26
Amerikis
Vyssis
Nikou
Leoharous
SYNTAGMA
27
Lada Hr.
35
38 37
Vereou
Avramiotou
Vasilis
Klitiou
Romvis
Karytsi
Plateia Kolokotroni
Ag.
Katofi
Skouze
Kalamiotou
Evangelistrias
Leka
Kolokotroni
Krezotou
Irinis
Athinaidos
Voulis
39
Eolou
MONASTIRAKI
Kte
Thiseos
Periklous
Karagiorgi
Voukourestiou
42
Dionisas
Servias
Leof. Vas. Sofias
43
Plateia Dimopratiriou
Kria
Foklonos
Karnalou
Aeolan
Stadiou
58
Mitropoleos
Petraki
Petraki
Syntagma
M
Parliament Building
Pandrosou
Plateia Mitropoleos
Ipatas
Patrsou
Pendelis
Plateia Syntagmatos
40
Plateia Agoras
Karnikareas
Mnisikleous
Adrianou
Apollonos
Nikis
Othonos
41
Pelopida
ANAFIOTIKA
Diogenous
Thoukdidou
Ipitou
Skouleni
Xenofondo
60
Filotheis
PLAKA
Navarhou
Apostoli
Souri
Filellinon
Lyssiou
Kyrristou
Thrasyvoulou
MAP 5
holou
Flessa
70
Iperidou
71
72
Lmahou
Plateia Kallou Manou
76
National Gardens
61
Eratokritou
Sholiou
Tripodon
Kekropos
86
Satoris
80
73
79
74
75
Pratinou
69
Hill
88
87
Plateia Satoris
81
77
78
63
68
89
84
85
82
83
Rangavi
91
90
Plateia Filomousou
Acropolis
92
Fabriki
94
Dedalou
Periandrou
Zappeio Gardens
64
67
99
98
93
Afroditis
Herefontos
96
Thalou
95
Goura
pittaou
100
101
Shelley
Adrianou
97
Galanou
103
66
Vakhou
Vyronos
Lysikratous
Fnyhlou
Eshinou
104
Leof. Vas. Olgas

0   125   250 m
0   125   250 yd

6 **7** **8** **9** **10**

MAP 5 SYNTAGMA

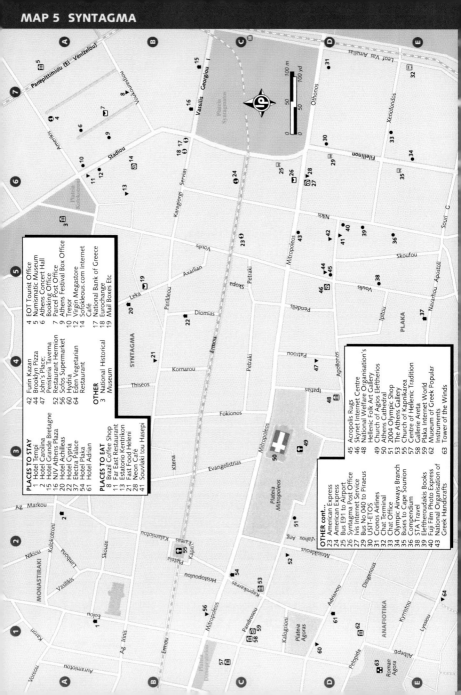

PLACES TO STAY
1 Hotel Tempi
15 Hotel Carolina
16 Hotel Grande Bretagne
20 NJV Athens Plaza
22 Hotel Achilleas
37 Hotel Cypria
54 Electra Palace
61 Hotel Plaka
   Hotel Adrian

PLACES TO EAT
8 Brazil Coffee Shop
11 Far East Restaurant
13 Estatorio Kentrikon
21 Fast Food Heleni
28 Neon Café
41 Souvlaki tou Hasepi

42 Furin Kazan
44 Brooklyn Pizza
47 John's Place;
   Peristeria Taverna
56 Restaurant Hermion
60 Sofos Supermarket
60 Hydra
64 Eden Vegetarian
   Restaurant

OTHER
3 National Historical
   Museum

4 EOT Tourist Office
5 Numismatic Museum
6 Athens Concert Hall
7 Booking Office
9 Parcel Post Office
9 Athens Festival Box Office
10 Tresor
12 Virgin Megastore
14 Sofokleous.com Internet
   Café
17 National Bank of Greece
18 Eurochange
19 Mail Boxes Etc

OTHER cont...
23 American Express
24 American Express
25 Bus E91 to Airport
26 Syntagma Post Office
27 Ivis Internet Service
29 Bus N040 to Piraeus
30 USIT-ETOS
31 Cronos Airlines
32 Chat Terminal
33 Chat Office
34 Olympic Airways Branch
35 Buses to Cape Sounion
36 Compendium
38 STA Travel
39 Eleftheroudakis Books
40 Fuji Film Photo Express
43 National Organisation of
   Greek Handicrafts

45 Acropolis Rugs
46 Skynet Internet Centre
48 National Welfare Organisation's
   Hellenic Folk Art Gallery
49 Church of Agios Eleftherios
50 Athens Cathedral
51 2004 Olympic Shop
53 The Athens Gallery
55 Church of Kapnikarea
57 Centre of Hellenic Tradition
58 Gallerie Areta
59 Plaka Internet World
62 Museum of Greek Popular
   Instruments
63 Tower of the Winds

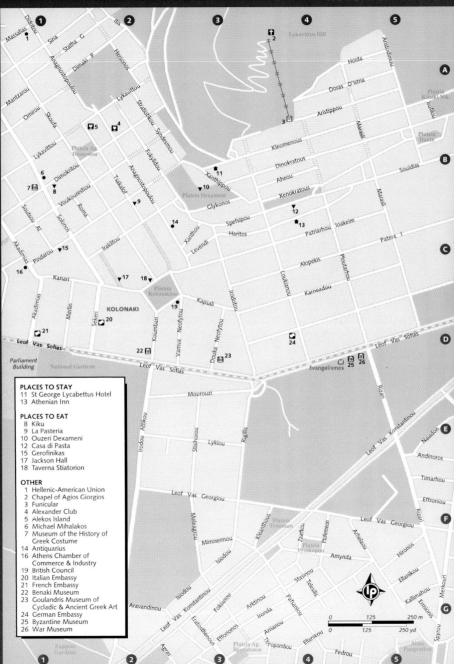

MAP 7 MAKRIGIANNI & KOUKAKI

Dionysiou Areopagitou

Erethiou

Weisster

Kallisperi

Rovertou

Galli

Kalyatdon

Mitseon

Dionysiou Areopagitou

Akropoli

MAKRIGIANNI

Diakou

Poirinou

Fratti

Promáhou

Kavalloti

Kavalloti

Zitrou

Hatzihristou

Mitromara

Akropoli

Lembesi

Plateia
Tsokri

Anguilara

Ratzieri

Thiramenous

Fenaretis

Sofroniskou

Parthenonos

Petmeza

Strateon

Karvaldi

Propyleon

Tsami Karatasi

Drakou

Veikou

Strattgou

Falirou

Andrea

Negri

Nakou

Koryzi

Th

Filoppapos Hill

Liakou

Botsari

Markou

Gioni

Dimitrakopoulou

N

Falirou

Leof

Syngrou

Kondouli

Dimitrakopoulou

Kallirrois

Plateia Ag.
Pandeleimonos

Mouson

Karatza

Dikeou

Dikeou

Lazeon

Aiginou

Plateia
Gargarettas

Diladhos

Andrea

Kallirrois

Panetoliou

Dinathou

Ambati

Oitof

Goufie

Zaharitsa

Botsari Noti

Sismani

Plateia
Kynosargous

Filopappou

Galinou

KOUKAKI

Dyovounioti

Beles

Ayali

Botsari Tousa

Androutsou

Od

Falirou

Vyzandiou

Syngrou-
Fix

Syngrou-Fix

Irakleous

Andimahidou

Theohritou

Akimou

Sehiou

D

Inglesi

Fotomar

Tymfistou

Klada

Theodorou

Veikou

Zini

Zan

N

Aglavrou

Meindani

Dimitrakopoulou

Olymbiou

Moreas

Falirou

Leof. Syngrou Andrea

Kallirrois

Kallirrois

Vrytou

Kalkon

Botsari

Lahouri

Markou

Argendi

Andsthenous

Kallirrois

Mysonos

Roikou

Sikelias

Kallirrois

Ahilokou

Tharypou

Zini

Kazantzi

Ipponikou

Theodorou

Lysimahias

Vresthenis

Theodortou

Mykoniou

Hatzimihali

Sostratou

Lassani

Volierou

Strogonof

Kasomouli

Koromila

Pissa

Efstr.

Mandrokleous

Leof. Syngrou Andrea

Aftokrat Nikolaou

Dymon

Decarte

Dourm

Kaklamanou

Mauer

Aminokleous

Kleovoulou

Ipponaktos

Frantzi Amvrosiou

Kapetan Varda

Prokhis

Filinou

Lagoumitzi

Stingos

Smith. Fr. Stanhope

Satkoudiou M.

Kritiou

Ipzgzi

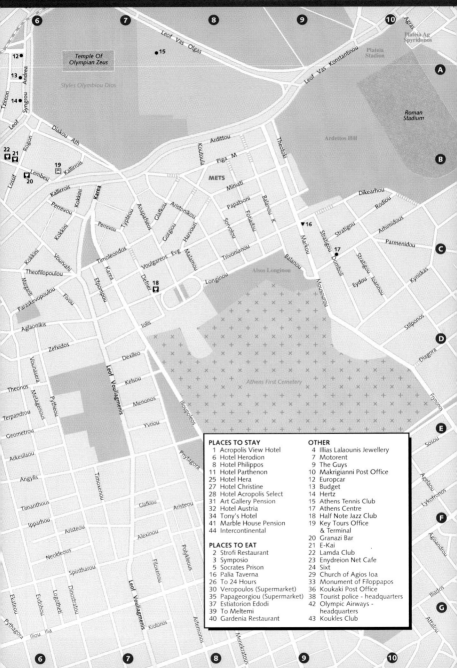

Temple Of Olympian Zeus

Styles Olympiou Dios

Roman Stadium

Ardettos Hill

METS

Alsos Longinou

Athens First Cemetery

Plateia Ag Spyridonos

Plateia Stadion

PLACES TO STAY
1 Acropolis View Hotel
6 Hotel Herodion
8 Hotel Philippos
11 Hotel Parthenon
25 Hotel Hera
27 Hotel Christine
28 Hotel Acropolis Select
31 Art Gallery Pension
32 Hotel Austria
34 Tony's Hotel
41 Marble House Pension
44 Intercontinental

PLACES TO EAT
2 Strofi Restaurant
3 Symposio
5 Socrates Prison
16 Palia Taverna
26 To 24 Hours
30 Veropoulos (Supermarket)
35 Papageorgiou (Supermarket)
37 Estiatorion Edodi
39 To Meltemi
40 Gardenia Restaurant

OTHER
4 Illias Lalaounis Jewellery
7 Motorent
9 The Guys
10 Makrigianni Post Office
12 Europcar
13 Budget
14 Hertz
15 Athens Tennis Club
17 Athens Centre
18 Half Note Jazz Club
19 Key Tours Office
& Terminal
20 Granazi Bar
21 E-Kai
22 Lamda Club
23 Enydreion Net Cafe
24 Sixt
29 Church of Agios Ioa
33 Monument of Filoppapos
36 Koukaki Post Office
38 Tourist police - headquarters
42 Olympic Airways -
headquarters
43 Koukles Club

MAP 8 AMBELOKPI

Leof Alexandras

Trihonidos
Areteou
Orestiados
Koroni
Megalou
Vatheos
Xyniados
Kouzi
Milcon
Efpatorias
Prousou
Ambelakion
Amaliados
Vatopediou

Boukouvala
Katsoni Lambrou
Kohar
Panathinaikou
Leof Alexandras

Armatolon
Ke Klefton
Kosma Etolou
Nikotara
Tsoha An
Mih
Filimonos
Aldou Manoutou
Athanasiadi

Argyroupoleos
Gerodimou Stathi
Livni
Palingenesias
Daskalogianni
Mela
Venizelou Elenas
Oroloya
Synis
Kotyeou
Timoleontos
Plateia Venizelou Elenas
Vournazou
Hi

Pilanis
Gerostathi
Skopetea L
Dtoyleou
Timoleontos
Soutsou
Hatzikosta
Pasteur
AMBELOKOPI

Athineon Efivon
Dimoharous
Dinokratous
Gelonos
Kokkali P
Evzonon
Matedomon
Kerasoundos
Lampsakou
Evrou
Kartali
Xenias
Nestou
Alexandroupoleos

Anapiron
Souidias
Monis Petraki
Polemou
Evzonon
Evzonon
Sofias
Semitelou
Lourou K
Mihalakopoulou
Sevastias
Papadiamandopoulou

Gennadiou
Iasiou
Ravine
Ypsilandou
Iridanou
Dimitressa
Alkmanos
Meandrou
Laodikas
Alkeou

Plateia Megalis Tou Genous Sholi
Veniti K
Sisini
Alyos
Potamianou II
Andriou
Semelis

Mihalakopoulou
Niriidon
Alkimahou
Astydamantias
Nind on
Alexandrou
Thetidos
Dioharous
Orminiou
Dragoumi I
Dioharous
Neofronos

Plateia Madritis

Eleftherias Park

Megaro Moussikis

ILISSIA

Plateia Vrazilias

PLACES TO STAY & EAT
4 Veropoulos Supermarket
6 Hotel Andromeda
7 Hotel Alexandros
11 Hotel Riva
14 Golden Age Hotel
17 Hilton
18 Holiday Inn

OTHER
1 Mistagogia
2 Panathinaikos Stadium
3 Athens Central Police Station
5 Australian Embassy
8 Athens Tower (ELPA)
9 Eleftheroudakis Books
10 Mike's Irish Bar
12 US Embassy
13 Megaron Moussikis
15 Canadian Embassy
16 National Art Gallery

Mesogion

Plateia Evangelismos Sholi

Plateia Ag Dimitriou

AMBELOKOPI

Plateia Mavili

Mihatakopoulou

0   150   300 m
0   150   300 yd

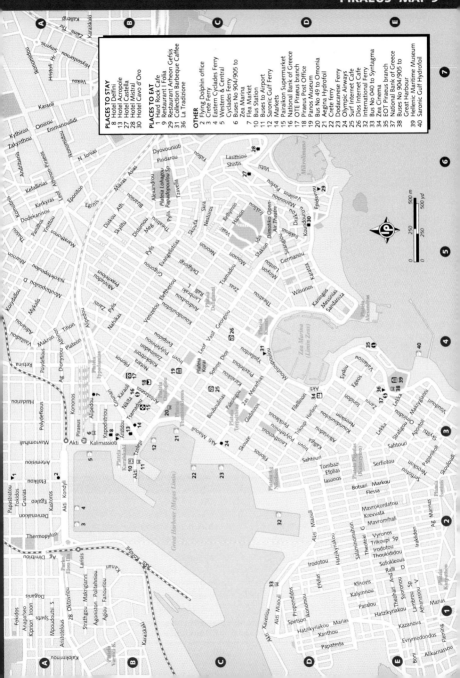

PLACES TO STAY
8 Hotel Delfini
13 Hotel Acropole
27 Hotel Castella
28 Hotel Mistral
30 Hotel Cavo d'Oro

PLACES TO EAT
1 Hard Rock Cafe
9 Restaurant I Folia
29 Restaurant Arheon Gefsis
31 Collection Barbeque Caffee
36 La Tradizione

OTHER
1 Flying Dolphin office
3 Crete Ferry
4 Eastern Cyclades Ferry
5 Western & Central
  Cyclades Ferry
6 Buses No 904/905 to
  Zea Marina
7 Flea Market
10 Bus Station
11 Buses to Airport
12 Saronic Gulf Ferry
14 Markets
15 Parraikon Supermarket
16 National Bank of Greece
17 OTE Piraeus branch
18 Piraeus Post Office
19 Panos Museum
20 Bus No 49 to Omonia
21 Aegina Hydrofoil
22 Crete ferry
23 Dodacanese Ferry
24 Olympic Airways
25 Surf Internet Cafe
26 Dios Internet Cafe
32 International Ferry
33 Bus No 040 to Syntagma
34 Zea Cinema
35 EOT Piraeus branch
37 National Bank of Greece
38 Buses No 904/905 to
  Great Harbour
39 Hellenic Maritime Museum
40 Saronic Gulf Hydrofoil

MAP LEGEND

CITY ROUTES

Freeway .... Freeway
Highway .... Primary Road
Road ...... Secondary Road
Street .... Street
Lane .... Lane
.... On/Off Ramp

.... Unsealed Road
.... One Way Street
.... Pedestrian Street
.... Stepped Street
.... Tunnel
.... Footbridge

REGIONAL ROUTES

.....Tollway, Freeway
.... Primary Road
...... Secondary Road
.... Minor Road

BOUNDARIES

—·—·—·............. International
—··—··—··................... State
— — — —.............. Disputed
━━━━........ Fortified Wall

HYDROGRAPHY

.... River, Creek
.... Canal
.... Lake

..Dry Lake; Salt Lake
.... Spring; Rapids
.... Waterfalls

TRANSPORT ROUTES & STATIONS

·····O·······················Train
————·. Underground Train
·—·—M·—·—·............ Metro
—————·.................Tramway
+—+—+—+·.. Cable Car, Chairlift

————···..................... Ferry
— — — —...........Walking Trail
·········.......... Walking Tour
...............................Path
.... Pier or Jetty

AREA FEATURES

.. Archaeological Site
.... Building

.... Campus
.... Cemetery

.... Market
.... Park, Gardens

.... Plaza
.... Swamp

POPULATION SYMBOLS

◌ **CAPITAL** .... National Capital
◉ **CAPITAL** .... State Capital

● CITY .... City
● **Town** ....Town

● Village ....Village
.... Urban Area

MAP SYMBOLS

▪ .... Place to Stay

▼ ....Place to Eat

● .... Point of Interest

Airport
Bank
Bus Stop
Bus Terminal
Cave
Church
Cinema

Embassy
Hospital
Internet Cafe
Lookout
Monument
Mountain
Museum

Music Venue
National Park
Parking
Police Station
Post Office
Pub or Bar
Ruins

Shopping Centre
Swimming Pool
Telephone
Temple
Theatre
Tourist Information
Zoo

Note: not all symbols displayed above appear in this book

LONELY PLANET OFFICES

Australia
Locked Bag 1, Footscray, Victoria 3011
☎ 03 8379 8000 fax 03 8379 8111
email: talk2us@lonelyplanet.com.au

USA
150 Linden St, Oakland, CA 94607
☎ 510 893 8555 TOLL FREE: 800 275 8555
fax 510 893 8572
email: info@lonelyplanet.com

UK
10a Spring Place, London NW5 3BH
☎ 020 7428 4800 fax 020 7428 4828
email: go@lonelyplanet.co.uk

France
1 rue du Dahomey, 75011 Paris
☎ 01 55 25 33 00 fax 01 55 25 33 01
email: bip@lonelyplanet.fr
www.lonelyplanet.fr

World Wide Web: www.lonelyplanet.com *or* AOL keyword: lp
Lonely Planet Images: lpi@lonelyplanet.com.au